Y0-BSQ-521

STUDIES
IN
ACTS

STUDIES
IN
ACTS

The Church in the House

by
William Arnot

KREGEL PUBLICATIONS
Grand Rapids, Michigan 49501

Studies In Acts by William Arnot
Copyright © 1978 by Kregel Publications
a division of Kregel, Inc. All rights reserved.

Library of Congress Cataloging in Publication Data

Arnot, William, 1808-1875.
    Studies in Acts: the Church in the House.

    Reprint of the 1883 ed. published by R. Carter, New York,
under title: The Church in the House.
    1. Bible. N.T. Acts—Criticism, interpretation, etc. 2. Church
history — Primitive and early church, ca. 30-600. I. Title: The
church in the house.
BS2625.A7   1978   226'.6'07   78-59141
ISBN 0-8254-2120-9

Printed in the United States of America

CONTENTS

vi / Contents

PUBLISHER'S PREFACE

Like the sun-glistened dew which anoints and freshens earth's vegetation is the invigorating insights gained by the reader and student from *Studies In Acts*. Each brief chapter is filled with distilled truth that can be expounded into practical living, positive preaching, and perceptive teaching. Arnot discerningly cuts through the theological debates and vocabulary to open to the reader the elemental essense and explanation of what the Book of Acts is really all about.

It is as though Arnot joins Luke, Peter, John, Paul, and the others and shares their experiences as they behold the Holy Spirit correctly establishing the New Testament church. Then, suddenly, the reader receives the benefit of viewing God's church from a 19th century perspective. Arnot compares the valiant and victorious Scottish Covenanters with the vigilant and valued Stephen. His characterizations and commentary of Philip and Paul are classic. It is with great profit and rejoicing that they are herein published again.

In no way do you sense a sectarian slant, a localized look, or a pseudo scholasticism in this valued devotional commentary. Arnot's comments are as relevant and refreshing as a warm meal. He has well prepared and presented the essential teaching without becoming side-tracked in doctrinal debate. The work is thoroughly seasoned with motivational interest that will send the earnest serious student searching and researching the depths of eternal truth springs.

This volume will be a special help to students seeking answers and explanations. Sunday School teachers, along with Pastors, will find it a valued aid to supplement their Bible. *Studies In Acts* does not in any way refute but it clearly supports the view that the Bible is God's inspired revelation to mankind and the church is the body of Christ on earth.

Families will find this book to be one of the finest study guides to the Book of Acts for family devotions. Whether used by a couple or a large family it may be used with insight, information, and inspiration. May this excellent volume be used anew by the Holy Spirit to bless all who read... teaching those things which concern the Lord Jesus Christ, with all confidence... Acts 28:31 is our prayer.

THE PUBLISHERS

STUDIES
IN
ACTS

STUDIES IN ACTS

The Gospel and the Acts
(Acts 1:1)

"The former treatise have I made, O Theophilus, of all that Jesus began both to do and teach."

IN determining the relation which subsists between the evangelic histories and the Book of the Acts, it is not enough to observe that while the Gospels contain the history of the Master's own ministry, this book records the labors of the apostles. Both alike narrate the work of the Lord: the Gospels, what he did in person when he was here; the Acts, what he did by the ministry of his chosen witnesses after he had ascended.

This distinction is marked in the first verse. Luke intimates that in the former treatise he had recorded "all that Jesus *began* both to do and teach"; implying that the history which he is now about to compose will be occupied with what Jesus *continued* both to do and teach after he had sat down at the right hand of the Father. The distinction is not that the former treatise dealt with what Jesus did, and the latter with what was done by the apostles; the distinction is, that the former treatise told what Jesus did in the first place, and the latter what Jesus did in the second. The first part of Christ's work has already in the Gospels been recorded; and now in another treatise the second part, or the continuation, of his work will be told. His ministry, death, resurrection, and ascension constituted only the beginning or foundation of the Redeemer's work. But after the foundation has been laid a lofty temple must be reared upon it; and the builder of this temple is Christ the Lord. When he ascended from the Mount of Olives, a way was opened from earth to heaven; but a multitude whom no man can number must be led by it into glory: and none can lead them but himself, the Captain of their salvation, the Bishop of their souls.

This book, then, is the continuation of "the life of Jesus" by the evangelist Luke. Nor did the Lord's work on earth cease at the date when this history closes. Hitherto the Son worketh, and will work till the end. He shall not cease from his work until the kingdoms of this world shall have all become his own. The working of Christ upon the earth does not cease when the inspired history of it ceases. The track of the Redeemer's way is marked on this inspired chart only a stage or two into the desert, and there it breaks abruptly off; but the way of the Lord does not stop where this track of it comes to an end. In a map of the city; you may see the road that leads to another city laid down for a little way beyond the wall, and then broken off abruptly in a field. The first stage is traced on the map to show that there is a road, and in what direction it goes; but the road does not terminate in that field a few yards beyond the city walls: the road leads all the way to the capital, and passengers throng it from end to end, from day to day. It is thus that the Book of the Acts marks our Lord's goings after his resurrection only a stage or two forward as a specimen to show us the character of his rule; but his goings continue with his people still, and will continue until the last of the ransomed shall enter rest.

This latter treatise does not begin precisely where the former treatise ends. By design, and not by accident, the two overlap each other. The resurrection and ascension of Christ constitute the last portion of the Gospel, and the first portion of the Acts. The same facts appear at the close of one book and at the outset of another.

Thus, when a bridge of two arches spans a deep river, both arches lean on one pillar that rises in the middle of the flood. In the midst of the gulf that separated God and man, and in the midst too of the tide of time, stood Jesus: on him the old dispensation rests, and on him the new.

In the beginning God created the heavens and the earth. From the solid shore of a past eternity sprang the covenant of grace; but it bent over and bent down seeking support in the middle of the ages. It cannot go over from eternity to eternity at a single span. But here and among men there was nothing which could bear our side of the covenant, corresponding to God's side of it, leaning on eternal righteousness before time began. There was nothing here but a fathomless deep of sin and misery. Man's extremity was God's opportunity. Through this flood went the person and work of Christ, and became a foundation, in humanity, equal to and corresponding with the eternal righteousness which supported the arch at the other side. God with us stands up in the sea of humanity, as a pier in midstream. Divine justice found a resting-place on him. This is my beloved Son, in whom I am well pleased. Thus the purpose of mercy, like the bow of promise, spanned the space from eternity down to the fulness of time, when the Son of God took our nature, and wrought out a righteousness for us and in our stead. There stands the arch now, resting on the Father's eternal purpose on the one side, and on the Son's atoning death on the other. In the end of the Gospel history we found the first hemisphere of the Divine dispensation, terminating in Christ crucified and ascended. That part of the redemption was finished when Messiah died. Now, at the beginning of the Acts, we find the second arch springing where the first was finished. This second part begins, as the first part ended, with the death, resurrection, and ascension of the Lord. Resting there, it rises into the heavens, and stretches away into the future. We lose sight of it, as we often lose sight of the rainbow, in mid-heavens; but we know assuredly that it will traverse all the intervening space, and lean secure on the continent of a coming eternity. From shore to shore the way of mercy reaches across the bottomless gulf of fallen humanity, the last side of the first circle and the first side of the second resting both on the representative Man, our Brother and Substitute, the second Adam, the Lord from heaven.

Between the birth of Christ in Bethlehem and his ascension from the Mount of Olives intervened a period of nearly thirty-four years. This space which, according to the measurements of time is considerable, becomes a point when it is viewed from eternity; as vast worlds seem shining sparks when they lie deep in the infinitude. The life of Jesus in the world was the point of contact between the finite and the Infinite —the meeting-place between God and man. At that point God touched us, and we were not consumed; we touched him, and yet lived.

When the Infinite and Eternal would make himself known to us, he needs must fix on a point in space—a moment in time. Somewhere on the surface of this inhabited world, and at some period in the course of the ages, the meeting must take place. In Judæa, and about eighteen hundred and seventy years ago, the Word—who was with God, and was God—became flesh, and dwelt among us.

Although, according to our mode of reckoning, the contact extended over a portion of space and a period of time, it will seem only a point, when angels look down on it, or saints look back. With the ascension from the Mount of Olives, Christ's personal ministry on earth was closed. Here the eclipse went off, and the Sun of Righteousness shone forth again in the sight of the unfallen, free from the obscuration, partial and temporary, which he had undergone.

When an eclipse comes on the sun, a strange gloom is spread over all the heavens, and the sun seems to have been robbed of his glory; but when you have waited a while, and marked the changing phases of the phenomenon, you observe that the sun is shaking off the cold shadow of our satellite that seemed to cover his disc. The last remnant of the darkness disappears, and the light of day emerges in all his former glory.

One can well imagine that to angelic spirits, who imperfectly understood his attributes and his plans, the incarnation of the Son might seem like a solar eclipse. Some cold, dark, earthly orb comes in contact with their Lord, and his glory is to their view for the time obscured. Throughout those thirty-three years the angels may have been occupied inquiring in

curious wonder what had caused the unwonted dimness of their day; and they may have experienced a
glad relief when the obscuration passed off, and He
whom they worship resumed his throne.

We, on our part, are permitted to draw near also
and behold the great sight. The parting scene is de-
picted in this history. The Son of God had grasped a
fallen world that he might save it, and now he lets
that world go again—no, he is not really letting it go;
for he has taken hold of our nature and has borne it
with him to his throne. He still holds fast this world;
ever tight is the line of love that binds him to all his
own. Keen and sensitive, as the nerves that unite
head and members, are those lines through which his
love thrills down into his people, and their hope goes
up to fasten on the anchor, sure and steadfast, within
the veil.

Final Instructions
(Acts 1:2-7)

" *Until the day in which he was taken up, after that he through the
Holy Ghost had given commandments unto the apostles whom he had chos-
en: to whom also he showed himself alive after his passion by many infallible proofs, being seen of them forty days, and speaking of the things pertaining to the kingdom of God: and, being assembled together with them,
commanded them that they should not depart from Jerusalem, but wait for
the promise of the Father, which, saith he, ye have heard of me. For John
truly baptized with water; but ye shall be baptized with the Holy Ghost not
many days hence. When they therefore were come together, they asked of
him, saying, Lord, wilt thou at this time restore again the kingdom to Israel? And he said unto them, It is not for you to know the times or the
seasons, which the Father hath put in his own power.*"

IN this his second statement of the event, the inspired
historian has been directed to express very precisely
the kind of evidence by which the resurrection of Jesus
was proved to the original witnesses, and through them
to us. "To whom he showed himself alive after his
passion, by many infallible proofs; being seen of them
forty days, and speaking of the things pertaining to
the kingdom of God." As the faith of the whole Church
depends absolutely on the resurrection of our Redeemer, it pleased God to give ample evidence of the fact.

But he gave no other evidence than that which appeals to the senses of men. There is no other possible way of proving a fact than by the evidences of the senses. Even our Maker cannot give us other and better evidence of a fact, unless he should first change radically our nature. The evidence of Christ's resurrection is complete. Faith is satisfied, and reason too. But observe how this bears on the Romish dogma of transubstantiation. The pillar on which that house stands is the assumption and assertion of the priests that the senses may deceive, and cannot implicitly be trusted. Themselves being witnesses, if this assertion falls, their whole doctrine falls with it. But the self-same assumption that sustains transubstantiation, would leave the resurrection of Christ unproved and incapable of proof. Either the evidence of the senses is valid proof of a fact, or it is not. If it is, transubstantiation is false; if it is not, the resurrection of Christ is not proved. The very same evidence in kind and degree which proves that Christ has risen, proves also that the bread and wine, after priestly consecration, remain bread and wine, and are not changed into the very body and blood of Christ. Thus the Roman apostasy cannot sustain its fundamental superstition, without at the same time and by the same means destroying the proof that the Redeemer has risen. Antichrist! But, alas! such superstition goeth not out by reasoning, however clear. Those who drink the wine of Rome's abominations, would not throw aside their falsehood, although one rose from the dead to tell them it was false. No Protestant should make light of Popery, as if it were out of date and effete. It is a power of darkness; but it is a power. It sees its own way and knows its own mind better than the statesmen who, without believing it, fawn upon it and flatter it, apparently from sheer fear of being counted illiberal in religion. The signs of the times bode trouble. Perhaps the present generation of Protestants may need to learn again the meaning of their own name. It is not flattering to the intellectual pride of the age, if the age had eyes to see it, that one of its great movements is towards a system which is at once an irrational superstition and an unmitigated tyranny.

The last question which the disciples addressed to their Master immediately before he ascended out of their sight—" Wilt thou at this time restore again the kingdom to Israel ? "—has been perhaps too hastily represented as evidence of their great ignorance and great earthliness, up to the period of the Pentecost, notwithstanding their privilege of constant intercourse with the Lord. The question, I apprehend, sprang from a true spiritual desire, and from a sound though defective knowledge regarding Messiah's kingdom.

When you look up to the sky on a clear night, and fix your eye on two stars shining near each other with equal brightness, they seem to your sense equally distant from the earth. But if one is a planet of our system, and the other a fixed star, the difference between their distances is very great—not indeed beyond the power of figures to express, but beyond the power of imagination clearly to conceive. The distance of the planet from the earth is only a small fraction of the distance of the star. Into the spiritual firmament these men of Galilee looked under the instruction of the Lord, but as yet they looked as children. They saw objects distinctly; but they could not judge correctly of relative distances and magnitudes. The two objects were clearly set before them in the writings of the prophets and the words of Jesus,—these two, their own baptism with the Holy Ghost as with fire, and the restoration of the kingdom to Israel—the union of all nations under David's sceptre in the New Jerusalem. The Master had now given them the distance of one of these objects: it was at hand—" Ye shall be baptized with the Holy Ghost not many days hence." In the same prophecy of the Old Testament they had read of that baptism, and of the universal submission of the nations to the throne of David. They saw the two stars in the same direction, and they thought that they were in the same plane. Now they had obtained express intimation regarding one of these twin promises, that its fulfilment was at hand. It was natural that they should expect that the same bright particular star, which they had been accustomed to see shining side by side with it in the pure expanse, would approach also at the same time. Hence their question,

"Lord, wilt thou at this time restore again the kingdom to Israel?"

Their conceptions, I think, were by this time much more elevated than they were at the beginning of their course. Their idea of the kingdom was now truer than when the sons of Zebedee sought by early application to secure places near the throne; and yet it may also be freely owned that their thoughts fell far short, not only of the reality, but even of the views which themselves a few days afterwards obtained.

The baptism by the Holy Spirit will come immediately. Its time is known and declared; but the gathering of the nations under the sceptre of David's Son, although fixed in the heavens and shining brightly thence, is still far away. Times and seasons, ages and epochs, intervene. By these, in indefinite measure and unexpressed number, its approach is indicated. The time of the end lies hid in the Father's counsel. A wide expanse, by man immeasurable, lies between the baptism by fire of the first apostles for their ministry, and the cry, "The kingdoms of this world have become the kingdoms of our Lord and of his Christ." The business of these men is to strike in upon the work, and leave the issue to God. When shall the kingdom of Christ be complete? Answer: What is that to thee? follow thou me. These ages and epochs are not only hidden in the Father's purpose, they are also held in the Father's hand. He doeth according to his will in the armies of heaven and among the inhabitants of the earth. He will not fail in his purpose; he will not miss his mark.

While it is right and proper for Christians in this age of the world to observe the signs of the times, and endeavor to gird up their loins and watch for the coming of the Lord, it is an evidence of shallowness, and cause of much evil speaking, when at every political event, supposed to be very great because very near the observer, they give forth a new calculation to fix the date when the dispensation will come to a close. Unbelievers are indeed ready to scoff at the simplest and purest profession of faith in God; but disciples should beware lest they give adversaries occasion to repeat their sneers. The prophecies of Scripture reveal the coming event, and keep it before us like a star in the firmament; but they do not inform us how near it is. The Master, when the disciples asked him, besides refusing to give them the day and the date of his own final victory, told them why he withheld the information. He withheld it for their sakes. His language is not, I shall not tell you the times and seasons; but, It is not for you that I should. We could not go so steadily in harness for present labor, if there were not blinders before our eyes, to conceal the plan of Providence and the goings of God in the world. It would not be for us, but against us, if we were able to count on our fingers, from a prophetical text or two, how many years the world will last. Such knowledge would puff up, and therefore it is not given; it would lead us to talk and speculate, instead of doing with our might what our hand finds to do. It is not enough that we submit to leave the ages and epochs in the Father's hand, because we cannot wrench them out of it: we should be glad and grateful that he spares us such sights into the future as we should not be able to bear. It is the part of a dear child to read eagerly all that the Father reveals, and to trust implicitly wherever the Father indicates a design to conceal. "Blessed are those servants whom the Lord, when he cometh, shall find"—not prying or predicting, but —"watching."

Witnesses

(Acts 1:8)

" But ye shall receive power, after that the Holy Ghost is come upon you: and ye shall be witnesses unto me both in Jerusalem, and in all Judæa, and in Samaria, and unto the uttermost part of the earth."

THE chosen band, diminished now by the fall of Judas, are clustering affectionately yet reverently round the risen Lord, as they ascend together the slope of Olivet, looking their last look upon their Master, and eagerly drinking in his last words. They knew, for he had told them, that his departure was expedient; but in their hearts they felt it sad. With a presentiment that the separation was at hand, they united all in one final question, "Lord, wilt thou at this time restore again the kingdom to Israel?" In these circumstances a desire to pry into the future was natural; but in the estimate of the Master it was unwise. Accordingly, he firmly checks their disposition to speculate about the date of the Millennium; but he does not leave them dangling idle for want of an object, when the object which they endeavored to grasp was placed conclusively beyond their reach. In removing the speculative inquiry from their mental vision, he placed a great practical work in their hands. This is the Lord's method, and it manifests a Divine wisdom. As often as any of his disciples evinced an inclination to follow a curious speculation regarding other persons, he diverted the stream of their energies into some channel of practical duty for themselves. The normal example of this method is the reply to Peter's inquisitiveness regarding the rumored immortality of John: *Question*—"And what shall this man do?" *Answer*—"What is that to thee? Follow thou me." Away from other people and other times the word of the Lord always called the disciples, and fixed them down to what concerned themselves and the present.

It is of great importance to observe that the Lord did not cut short their speculation into the secrets of the Divine purpose, and stop there: he gathered up the broken ends of their energy, and fastened them to an immediate work. If the planets should at any time stand still in their course, they would be drawn into the central fire and consumed. It is necessary to their well-being that they should be flung with all their force on a path of activity. Disciples of Christ, both in ancient and modern times, lie under a similar necessity. Unless they are thrown out in a course of vigorous action, they will be drawn into an orbit so narrow that action will be no longer possible.

The specific office to which the disciples are called is to be witnesses unto Christ; and yet for that office they were and are unfit, except in as far as the Lord imparts the power through the communication of the Holy Spirit. "Ye shall receive power after that the Holy Ghost is come upon you: and ye shall be witnesses unto me." The power of witness-bearing depends on the Spirit, and the Spirit is the gift of Christ. Although those men were themselves saved, they were not fit to work any deliverance in the earth by their own wisdom or strength. Their demand for fire from heaven might have consumed their adversaries, but could not have converted them. On this method it would have been long ere they had filled God's guest-chamber by a multitude gathered from the highways and hedges of the world. Wanting the Spirit, even the apostles were inclined to persecute; and, wanting the Spirit, the self-styled successors of the apostles have persecuted in all subsequent times.

The Spirit is like the air. The Lord breathed on his disciples, and said, "Receive ye the Holy Ghost." We could not live our present natural life without air. The sun in the heavens would not warm us if the atmosphere were not wrapped round the globe. The air is near, and the sun is distant. It is the sun's heat that sustains life; but the sun's heat could not be communicated to plants and animals without the intervention of the atmosphere. The earth is as completely dependent on air for its supply of water as for its supply of heat. The air obtains a supply from the ocean, and pours it on the dry land. Thus disciples in every age obtain grace from the Lord through the ministry of the Spirit.

But the specific function which a disciple is fitted, through the ministry of the Spirit, to discharge, is to be a witness unto Christ. Whom Christ saves from the world, he employs in the world. The captives taken from the enemy in this warfare are one by one incorporated into the army of the great King, and sent into the field to fight against their former master. Conspicuous and instructive, in this aspect, is the experience of Paul. When the Lord overcame and took captive that emissary of the Wicked One, the victory was the seed of other victories. The subdued enemy became a good and great soldier of Jesus Christ. The captive, when smitten to the ground, and seized and disarmed, was not sent to prison; was not, except for a very short time, sent even to the rear, but ordered to the front, where the battle between Christ's kingdom and the god of this world was raging.

To every true Christian these two things may be said: first, you have need of Christ; and second, Christ has need of you. He saves you; you serve him. The simple fact that a Christian is on earth and not in heaven, is proof that there is something for him here to do; and if he is not doing it, the neglect shows either that he is not yet a Christian indeed, or that he is a Christian who grieves Christ. A broken limb hurts him who owns it more than if it were completely severed from his body. Thus the Lord is hurt by those who, being his members, do not witness for him.

The specific reason why the saved are left in the world awhile is, that they may be witnesses to their Lord. In heaven he does not need such witnessing. There, seeing is believing. The Lamb is the light of heaven, and there is no need of lesser lights to show his glory; but in this dark world Christ's countenance shines through the spirit and life of his people. Here he has need of such witnesses.

He needs vessels to bear his name about among men; and for this purpose he chooses earthen vessels, that the power may be known to be his own. He does not send angels to proclaim his message; he does not employ the thunder to proclaim his name, or the lightning to write his character in the sky. The life of his own disciples is the epistle in which he desires to be read. The evidence with which he will convince the world is the walk of the people whom he has bought with his blood and renewed by his Spirit.

It is an honorable but difficult function. The task of a witness is often very arduous. The real strain comes in cross-examination. Every witness first emits his testimony, and is thereafter cross-examined on both its substance and its details. The evidence that a Christian gives directly, and in the first instance, consists in the whole course of his profession. He worships, he prays, he sits with fellow-disciples at the table of the Lord. By all this he testifies, and is well understood to testify, that when he was lost with the world in sin, Christ the Son of God by dying saved him. A great multitude in this land emit readily this evidence in chief; and in this department the majority acquit themselves well. With such a body of consistent testimony for Christianity—a body flowing ever on with the momentum of a river, one might expect that all the obstructions of unbelief would soon be broken down and swept away. Why, when there is so great a cloud of witnesses, is the heart of the world not won ? Much is due to the hardness of that same world that receives the testimony; but something is due also to the fickleness of the disciples who give it. The evidence in chief is easily given, and is, on the whole, given well; but the cross-examination—alas, many of the witnesses break down there!

Either or both of two persons may, according to circumstances, conduct the cross-examination—the judge or the adversary. It is ordinarily done by the adversary, but the judge permits the adversary to cross-examine, and occasionally puts a question himself. The life of a disciple is one long stance in the witness-box, under cross-examination by a severe adversary, who goes as far on every side as the law allows him. You are set down in the market-place—wherever the buying and selling is conducted. You have lately worshipped in the house of prayer, and devoutly commemorated the death of the Lord. Those who meet you in the market know this. What then ? They may be themselves unreconciled, unrenewed; they are probably not easy—not satisfied with themselves—in neglecting the salvation of God. The presence of Christians fresh from their solemnities renews their misgivings regarding their own position. It is not needful to repeat in the market-place the same testimony that was given at the communion table. A Christian, when he enters the market-place, should do business there— should not forthwith begin to preach, but to buy and sell, and get gain. It is the cross-examination that takes place on this sphere. It is not now, What do you believe ? but, Is your life, both in great things and in small, consistent with the profession which you have made ? The cross-examiner generally begins on some distant and apparently indifferent theme; but the questions are so linked to the main subject that if, in answering them, anything escapes from the witness which clashes with his original evidence, his good confession is thereby undermined and destroyed. Over-reaching in trade, unfairness in a bargain, unkindness to dependents, untruth and evil-speaking, expose the Christian profession to scorn, and shear it of its power. The adversary goeth about, especially at unsuspected turns of the Christian life-course, seeking whom he may devour.

The sphere of the witness-bearing, hitherto confined to Israel, is about to be enlarged. In the first instance, the twelve were not fit for a wider missionary field. They were called in, and were not yet ready to be sent out—that is, to be apostles. They must undergo a preparatory training at the feet of Jesus, and at length be baptized with the Holy Ghost. Then the embargo will be taken off: when they have served their apprenticeship in a home-mission under the Master's own eye, they will be intrusted with a commission to the ends of the earth. As soon as they have obtained the crowning qualification in the gift of the Spirit, he will loose them and let them go. Forth, then, from Jerusalem the word of God will run through Judæa and Samaria, nor halt in its progress till it strike the ends of the earth.

In that age it spread fast and far; but it was soon afterwards arrested. For many ages it made little progress. The Church became corrupt at its centre, and its extremities were paralyzed; the root lost its own life, and therefore the branches could not spread to overshadow the land. More has been done during the present century to spread the word of the kingdom, than for many ages before. For the immediate past the Christian community should thank God; and for the future, though the horizon which bounds the view seems greatly troubled, they should, notwithstanding, take courage.

Whatever of comfort or reproof lay in that word for the earliest disciples, belongs also to ourselves. The clause in their commission, "beginning at Jerusalem," applies in its spirit to our mission-work. The charity that will convert the world, is a charity that begins at home—begins at home, but does not end there. If it do not begin at home, it will not convert the world. If it essay to reach the heathen by leaping over many ranks of unslain enemies to Christ in our own hearts, and many ranks of unreproved blasphemers of his name on our own streets, it will never reach its distant mark among the heathen, or it will reach the mark with a force already spent, lacking power to penetrate the armor in which idolatry is encased.

The Gospel in a true disciple is like a fire: it burns; it causes vivid joy; but it will not permit indolence. It must be out: but, like light and heat, it cannot reach the distant circumference without passing through the intermediate space, and kindling all that it touches on its way. The Colonies, the Continent of Africa, the peoples of India, and the Chinese, are the legitimate objects of missionary enterprise; but we cannot succeed in melting these icy regions at a distance, if our own home remain frozen like the poles. The laws of nature forbid it. Unless our love be of such a kind as greatly to disturb a godless neighborhood at home, it will not set on fire a distant continent. We cannot overleap the vice and misery and irreligion of our own city, and pitch our missionaries with power by ship into India.

Besides the more hidden spiritual law, there is an obvious material fact that will in these circumstances prevent success. While a great mass of our home community remain unchristian, specimens of our population, cast up in foreign lands like drift-wood on the ocean shores, will counteract effectually the efforts of the missionaries. When settlers or seamen from this country, partakers of our name and our civilization, partakers too of our Christian profession, appear among the heathen, and act as the heathen do, the way of the Gospel is obstructed; the work stands still, or goes backward. A ship heaves in sight in a bay on the coast of Africa, where Christian missionaries have long labored among the rude natives. The ship hoists British colors, and the men speak our language, and claim kindred with the missionaries. When they open the hatches of their ship, it is found that the cargo consists of rum for barter with the natives. It is found on trial that, besides the mischief which rum is fitted in its own nature to inflict on an uncivilized tribe, the article is so grossly adulterated that it produces a wide-spread sickness, and endangers life: The discovered cheat reacts, in the minds of simple savages, against the missionaries and their message.

It would be a great mistake to abstain from foreign work till the home field be completely brought under culture: this counsel is sometimes given to missionaries by men who are not Christians at all. We must not fall into that trap. Some at home harden their hearts against the Gospel, and some abroad are predisposed to receive it. We must hasten to go out to the uttermost parts of the earth with our message; but we must let the men who are beside us feel the glow of our zeal as it passes by. The command of the Lord is still the rule for his people,—Beginning at Jerusalem, but not ending till we reach the uttermost part of the earth.

These words, constituting the disciples his witnesses in the world, were his last words; for when he had spoken them he was taken up. This command, therefore, every Christian should regard with especial veneration and tenderness. At his departure he left his Church in the world,—left it a legacy to the world, that it might in all times be a living epistle of himself. Promoted to such an honor, and charged with such a function, what manner of persons ought we to be?

The Ascension
(Luke 24:50-52)

" And he led them out as far as to Bethany, and he lifted up his hands, and blessed them. And it came to pass, while he blessed them, he was parted from them, and carried up into heaven. And they worshipped him, and returned to Jerusalem with great joy."

THE Gospel according to Luke and the Acts of the Apostles are the two books of one continuous history, by the same author. The first book contains the personal ministry of our Lord; and the second gives sketches of the great mission work conducted by the apostles, under the ministry of the Spirit, after their Head had withdrawn from their view. The ascension of the Lord Jesus is the point of contact between the two books; and, as is natural in such cases, they overlap each other a little there. From the end of the Gospel we gather some features of the ascension which are not repeated in the Acts. There we learn in succession how the ascending Lord regarded his disciples, and how the disciples regarded the ascending Lord.

I. How the Lord regarded his disciples when he was in the act of leaving them.

Look unto Jesus at the moment of his departure. If we acquaint ourselves with him as he goes away, we shall be prepared to welcome him when he returns. As he has gone, so will he come again; with this difference, that at his second coming every eye shall see him.

1. The place: "He led them out as far as to Bethany." It was the village on the further side of Olivet, where Lazarus and his sisters dwelt. The heart of the man Christ Jesus was not indifferent to the associations connected with the spot. There he had often rested when he was weary. There he had proclaimed and proved himself the Resurrection and the Life. Perhaps it was at Bethany that the eleven could best bear to let him go out of their sight. "He that believeth on me, though he were dead, yet shall he live." There human love clothed itself with omnipotence, and recalled a brother from the grave. If the disciples, in their weakness, could anywhere endure to look the last time in this world on their Lord, it was on the spot where their friend Lazarus was loosed and let go. Places have power on human hearts. He who knows our frame acknowledges this principle, and uses it. Some spots of this dull Earth are consecrated by bright, blessed memories, which, when occasionally revived, refresh a weary soul. Do not be superstitiously subject to places; but, on the other hand, beware of despising them; for though they cannot save, they may serve. "All things are yours."

2. The parting act: "He lifted up his hands, and blessed them." Those hands were never lifted up to smite; those lips blessed, and cursed not. Let those who bear his name strive to follow his steps. Let our hands, our lips, be like his. Jesus is the revelation of God—is God revealed. Not by his words only, but

also by his life, he showed us the Father. Off that blessed life we may read while we run the legend,— "God is love."

Bear in mind that Christ is God's visit to the world. From first to last that visit was love. His appearing was gentle as a summer's dawn. He was born a babe, wrapped in swaddling clothes, and laid in a manger. Such was the step by which a holy God approached our world when it rebelled against him. Angels sang the advent as peace on earth and good-will to men. The key-note struck at his birth was maintained throughout his history; and you catch its cadence in his dying agony, when he prayed, "Father, forgive them." In the moment of his ascension you recognize still the Lamb of God: "He lifted up his hands, and blessed them."

In the last glimpse we get of Jesus, as he leaves the world, he appears lifting up his hands to bless. He disappears in the act of giving; Mary, on the contrary, disappears from our view in the act of receiving. He, at his departure, as becomes the Saviour of sinners, gives to the needy out of his own fulness; she at her departure, as becomes a sinner saved, is opening her mouth wide, that she may receive from her Redeemer's grace. He lifts up his hands to bless; she bends her knees to pray (Acts i. 14). Even so; for there is but one Mediator between God and man.

3. His departure. He went to heaven as he came to earth—for his people's good. "It is expedient for you that I go away." We need an advocate with the Father; and we have one, Jesus Christ the righteous. We need an anchor of the soul while we are exposed on the stormy sea; and we have one, for our Forerunner has, on our account, gone before us within the veil.

But though he went out of their sight, he did not go far from them. He has left the promise, "Lo, I am with you alway." Leaning on his arm, they look for his appearing.

II. How the disciples regarded their ascending Lord.

1. "They worshipped him." This is a great word. This is a great step in the path of those who followed Christ, and the print of it is full of meaning for us to-

day. It is worship: it is the homage of a human heart, which is due to God alone. "See thou do it not," is the angel's stern command, as soon as a man proposes by mistake to offer worship to any created being.

Man is made for worshipping. This is shown by the two facts: that he has been made, and that he has been made so great. The beasts that perish have, like him, been formed by the Creator's hand; but they have not the faculties necessary for recognizing their Maker. We, as much as they, are the work of God's hand, but, unlike them, we possess intelligence to observe and own the hand that made us. By the double fact that we are high enough to know God, and not high enough to be God, we are constrained to worship. Man is constitutionally a religious being. In his heart there lies a capacity for worship, and a tendency to exercise it. But while there is something allied to an instinct within us prompting to worship, a darkened mind and a defiled conscience continually turn the stream aside from its proper channel and pollute all its volume. It is human to worship; but no human being since the Fall, when left to himself, worships aright.

Error, which apart from Revelation and the ministry of the Spirit is universal, parts practically into two, and flows in diverging channels. Worship is directed either to the true God, and in that case is dead; or to an idol, and in that case it can afford to have a species of life. Man finds it easy to offer ardent worship to a creature, but impossible, without the intervention of a Mediator, to give real worship to the living God. Hence idolatry is frequently earnest; while the worship of Jehovah, apart from the knowledge of him in Christ, is a form.

The gulf was bridged for man by the incarnation of the Son of God. Here men worship a Man, and yet there is no idolatry. In Emmanuel a human heart may dissolve in Divine homage to a brother of our own flesh and blood, and yet not be defiled by spiritual unchasteness. Here man worships a Man, and yet preserves purity of spirit. Only in Christ can he find an object whom he can worship without fear, and yet worship without sin. God has bowed his heavens and come down. He has taken hold of our nature: we, when we feel his touch, awake and worship—worship him that touched us, and yet worship only God.

2. "They returned to Jerusalem." This was a great point gained. The master did not miscalculate the strength of the love to himself which he had kindled in the breasts of those poor men. It was difficult for them to take the first step. It required the ministry of angels to tear them from the spot. "Ye men of Galilee, why stand ye gazing up into heaven?" (Acts i. 11.) Ah, ye angels that excel in strength, something that ye know not of rivets these men to the spot. These ministering spirits asking the disciples why they stood gazing after the risen Lord, are like persons who never knew a mother's joys or sorrows expressing surprise to see a mother melting away with grief when her babe is dead. He took not on him the nature of angels; but in the own nature of these Galileans the Lord of Glory had kept them company, and won their hearts and redeemed their souls. Therefore they stood and gazed toward heaven at the spot where he ascended.

Their spiritual life hitherto had depended on the presence of the Lord, as an infant's life depends directly on its mother. They were children, and at that moment children weaned. The branches seemed broken from the tree, and they thought they must droop and die. But he who made them new creatures had so constituted their spiritual life that it could survive the weaning and grow stronger thereby. "Greater things than these shall ye do, because I go to my Father." His departure was necessary for their development into the stature of perfect men.

They were not disobedient to the heavenly vision. They did not, on the one hand, continue gazing from the mountain up to heaven, in a fervent but unpractical devotion; neither, on the other hand, did they return to Galilee to their farms and their fishings. They did not demand the return of their Lord, neither did they desert his cause when they were deprived of his presence. They returned to Jerusalem. This simple act, in their circumstances, proved two things: first, their firm conviction that the promised Spirit would come; and second, their settled determination to accept the task of converting the world. They came into the city to wait for the Spirit; but they waited for the Spirit in order that they might go forth in his power to win the nations to Christ.

There was much in this act. When those poor and afflicted men went back to the city where their Master's blood had been shed, it was at the risk of spilling also their own. If they had not been sustained by a superhuman courage, Jerusalem would have been the last place to which they should have turned their steps. It was the power of their unseen Lord that nerved their hearts, as they made their way down the western slopes of the mountain and entered Jerusalem as the followers of Jesus the crucified Nazarene.

3. They returned with great joy. What have we here? Great joy! How comes this? As well might you expect a flame to burst from yonder altar after the piled wood has been soaked and the ditch round its base filled with water. But a fire from heaven, at Elijah's cry, made the dripping fuel burn; and light from the love of God kindled these men's hearts and made their faces shine in spite of the sea of troubles that surrounded them.

They had witnessed the rage of the Jews against their Master, and they had been distinctly warned that a similar persecution would overtake those who should dare to witness to his name and cause. In Jerusalem no comfort awaited them. Among its multitudes they had no friends except a few timid men, who dared not face the danger; and a few faithful women, who were weeping themselves away in some obscure hiding-places. Jerusalem contained the Roman governor and his soldiers; the Sanhedrim and the mob; the multitude that heaved and stormed like the sea, until its cruel appetite was appeased by the blood of Jesus. O Jerusalem, Jerusalem, thou that killest the prophets, and stonest them that are sent unto thee, there was nothing in thee to make these men of Galilee glad when they returned from Bethany without their Lord.

They are not permitted to enter rest with their Lord, but they are sent to work for him; and this made them glad. They worshipped him; and now they go from worship down to work: from the work they will, in due time, return again to worship. Thus, between these two, the pendulum of their life will vibrate, until its last hour strike; and then the laborer, at a bound, will enter his eternal rest.

Thus, a Christian who lives up to his privilege leads a sort of charmed life. Nothing can come wrong. To depart is to be *with* Christ; to remain is to work *for* Christ: and both are joyful.

Waiting and Praying
(Acts 1:9-14)

" And when he had spoken these things, while they beheld, he was taken up; and a cloud received him out of their sight. And while they looked steadfastly toward heaven as he went up, behold, two men stood by them in white apparel; which also said, Ye men of Galilee, why stand ye gazing up into heaven? this same Jesus, which is taken up from you into heaven, shall so come in like manner as ye have seen him go into heaven. Then returned they toward Jerusalem from the mount called Olivet, which is from Jerusalem a sabbath day's journey. And when they were come in, they went up into an upper room, where abode both Peter, and James, and John, and Andrew, Philip, and Thomas, Bartholomew, and Matthew, James the son of Alphæus, and Simon Zelotes, and Judas the brother of James. These all continued with one accord in prayer and supplication, with the women, and Mary the mother of Jesus, and with his brethren."

"AND when he had spoken these things." These words! They were the last and yet not the last. The last in the ministry of his visible presence; but he will continue to teach them still. His word liveth and abideth for ever. He will make good his promise, "Lo, I am with you alway."

We linger on the last words: "It is not for you to know the times or the seasons." Himself knows them, and, knowing them, knows that it was not expedient to impart these deep things of God to men. But in the act of intimating that the date of the event must remain concealed, he clearly declares that the event itself is sure,—the establishment of the kingdom in Israel—the universal reign of the Son of David. The event is sure, and the date also is fixed; but the knowledge of the date cannot be revealed. For their sakes it is concealed; for manifestly the absolute declaration of the date would thwart and hinder the establishment of the kingdom. It would have closed the lips of suppliants, and paralyzed the hands of those who should be fellow-workers with God.

When the Lord declines to declare the date of the expected consummation, he gives them another thing instead. He gives them what he counts better. Something which they asked *was not for them*, and therefore it was withheld; something which they did not ask *was for them*, and therefore it was bestowed. It is thus that we treat our children day by day.

He never gives his disciples a blank refusal. When he declines one thing, he bestows a better. That which he bestowed in this case was the combined promise and command of the eighth verse: "It is not for you to know the times or the seasons; but ye shall receive power after that the Holy Ghost is come upon you, and ye shall be witnesses unto me," etc. Instead of permitting them to occupy their minds with an unknown future, he sends them into present work. Instead of telling them when the kingdom will come, he assigns to them the work of bringing in the kingdom. It is by their witnessing that the nations will be made subject to Christ. "The God of peace shall bruise Satan under your feet shortly;" but you must arise and contend; you must cast down the old serpent, and stamp upon his prostrate folds.

"And while they looked steadfastly toward heaven as he went up, behold, two men stood by them." Whoever the messengers may have been, the message which they bear is clear: "This same Jesus, which is taken up from you into heaven, shall so come in like manner as ye have seen him go into heaven." The interval must be occupied, not in pensive, fond upward gazing, but in hearty, earnest work. He will come again; but times and seasons which man cannot number will intervene. These are times of witnessing for all the disciples of Christ. They must receive the Spirit; they must be witnesses for Christ; they must begin at Jerusalem; they must reach the ends of the earth. After that shall the end be. The time seems long; and yet it is approaching quickly. That fixed star seems fixed indeed to our eyes; there it has stood in the deep of heaven, and glittered down on the upturned eyes of longing disciples these eighteen hundred years—the bright promise of his coming; but though it seems to stand still, it is moving; it is approaching. Be of good cheer, disciples, your Redemption is nearer than when those Galileans first left their nets to follow Jesus. The fixed star is not fixed—it is rushing through space to its goal, although its movements cannot be detected by our instruments. The kingdom is coming, although it is beyond the power of our calculus to predict the time of its arrival. Its sudden appearing will surprise and gladden the waiting Simeons and Annas of that day.

This Earth is a small body; it is like a grain of sand on the shore of Immensity—a Bethlehem-ephratah among the worlds which constitute God's universe: yet the Earth is, and ever will be, the most valued of all his works, because into it has come and from it has ascended the Divine Redeemer, in whom all things shall yet be gathered into one. Here he passed through his humiliation, and here will his glory be displayed.

When the disciples reached the city, they betook themselves to a large upper room—some hall, either hired for the purpose or gratuitously placed at their disposal by some believer, such as Joseph of Arimathea, who owned property and loved the Lord. From the beginning the Lord needed men of property, and from the beginning he provided them. To the poor the Gospel was preached; but at the same time the love of Christ constrained some of the rich to minister unto him of their substance whatever material means were necessary for the work.

As they enter the upper room the names of all the Eleven are taken down and transmitted by the record to the latest generation. Peter is restored, and his backsliding healed; Thomas is confirmed, and believes, although he no longer sees. We have here what in modern phraseology would be termed the minutes and sederunt of the first missionary meeting. With the apostles other believers, men and women, assembled, until the company in the upper room numbered about a hundred and twenty.

Here is the first assembly of the Christian Church

after the ascension of the Lord. This is the well's eye near the summit of the mountain, and the tiny rill that trickled over its brim that day has grown into a mighty river now. Down through the generations the stream has flowed without ceasing; and at this day, although many things impede its progress, the Christian Church is the greatest power in the world. How great the numbers that go up to the house of God to worship in the name of the one Mediator! From a very small mustard seed a mighty tree has grown.

In that upper room were all the elements that go to constitute "the Church." The first assembly was the germ of all that followed. United worship is a Divine ordinance. Not only is it in accordance with the revealed will of God, it is manifestly suited to the need and the capacity of men. It is true that the spiritual life depends primarily on the individual; but it is also true that for spiritual growth and health we are instrumentally dependent on association with fellow-Christians.

Our soul's state is much affected, either for good or evil, by the company of our kind. A human being has a separate personal identity, and also social relations with his neighbors. Some of our actions are solitary, and terminate on ourselves, such as breathing, thinking; others are necessarily social, and presuppose society, such as speaking, hearing, loving. If a man were entirely separated from his kind, he would no longer be what he is—would soon cease to be. Half of his faculties would lie dormant for want of exercise; and lying long dormant, they would die; and the death of one half of his faculties would soon take the life out of all the rest.

Thus necessary is society for man. God has not neglected this feature of the human constitution in the structure of his covenant and the organization of the Church. Our individual relation to God is the first thing: Simon, son of Jonas, lovest thou me?—*thou me*. But when this first commandment of the Gospel has been enforced, the second, which is like unto it, is not neglected. None can save his brother: every one must enter into relation with God for himself; but every man both gets and gives in intercourse with society. Every disciple helps or hinders his fellow-disciple. In all earnest times they that fear the Lord speak often one to another; and the Lord hearkens and hears when any company, great or small, agree to seek him together.

There was perseverance in the prayer of the primitive Church—"they continued." There was unity in those early prayer-meetings—they prayed "with one accord." The prayers were not soon broken off, and were not hindered by disagreements among the suppliants. They ascended straight to heaven in a pillar of pure incense, and descended soon in showers of blessing—a great refreshing from the presence of the Lord.

The Spirit at Pentecost
(Acts 2:1-4)

> " And when the day of Pentecost was fully come, they were all with one accord in one place. And suddenly there came a sound from heaven as of a rushing mighty wind, and it filled all the house where they were sitting. And there appeared unto them cloven tongues like as of fire, and it sat upon each of them. And they were all filled with the Holy Ghost, and began to speak with other tongues, as the Spirit gave them utterance."

THE only event recorded in the interval of ten days between the ascension of Christ and the mission of the Holy Spirit is the election of an apostle in the room of Judas, which occupies the latter half of the first chapter. The disciples waited at Jerusalem for the promise, and the promise was in due time fulfilled—"When the day of Pentecost was fully come, they were all with one accord in one place." They waited for the Spirit as those who wait for the morning; as eager for its coming, and as sure that it will come at the set time. Although they were sure of the event, they did not relax in the use of the means to procure it. Persevering prayer and oneness of heart, were the forces by which they drew the blessing down.

At the feast of the Passover, the lamb was slain; at the feast of Pentecost, the law was given. Coincident with the slaying of the lamb was the death of Christ; coincident with the giving of the law was the descent of the Spirit. The long-continued, oft-repeated prophecy was at length fulfilled. Passovers and Pentecosts may now cease. Like the seed cast into the ground, they perish in the act of producing. As the sacrifice of Christ was the substantial fruit from the typical promise of the Passover, so the descent of the Spirit was the real and effective giving of the law to men. On the first Pentecost the law was written on tables of stone; on the last Pentecost came the Spirit, whose office it is to write that law on the living tables of the heart.

"Suddenly there came a sound from heaven, as of a rushing mighty wind." Not a rushing mighty wind, but a sound that seemed like it. It pleased the Lord to manifest the descent of the Spirit by signs that appeal to the senses, that by the mouth of two witnesses the fact might be confirmed;—the sense of hearing, this sound; the sense of sight, the tongues of fire. The fire was like cloven tongues—that is, it was distributed so that a tongue touched each, licking his head like a flame. The tongue was not of fire, but "like as of fire;" there was the brightness, but not the burning. The tongues indicated speech, and the fire promised that the words spoken to spread the Gospel would be burning words.

At an earlier period the Pharisees, tempting him, asked a sign from heaven. He refused; he would not give a sign to satisfy the curiosity of unbelievers. But when his own disciples are sad, he gives them, without being asked for it, a sign from heaven to cheer them; to prove that he is there, and that all power is in his hands. When Joseph sent the royal chariots from Egypt to bring his famishing father into a land of plenty, the sight of the vehicles—with perhaps the royal arms emblazoned on their sides, according to the fashion of Egyptian art—restored Jacob's fainting heart, convincing him that his son was alive, and possessed of kingly power (Gen. xlv. 26–28). In some such manner this sign from heaven was fitted to confirm in the trembling hearts of those primitive disciples the struggling conviction of their faith, that Jesus their elder brother lived, and reigned, and remembered them with all his wonted love.

"And they were all filled with the Holy Ghost."

Hitherto communications of the Spirit had been made in smaller measure, as foretastes of the promised blessing. Man, by the Fall, lost communion with God. He became flesh, not only in the sense of being human, but in the sense of being destitute of the Spirit, without God in the world.

Through the covenant by which Christ undertook redemption, glimpses of the Spirit were vouchsafed in the earlier times, so that the world was not left in complete darkness. The Spirit of God did strive with man in the evil days both before and after the Flood; but it was only when the Word became flesh and dwelt among us that the Spirit in fulness returned to the earth. In the second Adam the Spirit dwelt without measure. He had no sin, and when he became flesh the Spirit was restored to humanity. When he ascended up on high he retained a connection with his disciples on earth through their faith; and by that thread the Divine Spirit thrilled down from the Head into the members.

"They were filled with the Holy Ghost." The vessels were prepared and gathered together. The long-cherished expectations and the long-continued prayers were all brought to a point when the day of Pentecost was fully come. To that point drawn, the Spirit came, and all the vessels were filled to overflowing.

Then was the disaster of the Fall remedied. Firstfruits the Church had previously obtained, but now came the full harvest.

The Tongues of Fire
Acts 2:4)

" *And they were all filled with the Holy Ghost, and began to speak with other tongues, as the Spirit gave them utterance.*"—ACTS II. 4.

"THEY began to speak with other tongues;" that is, in other languages than their own; especially in the languages of the various nationalities enumerated below.

This is not a miraculous gift bestowed on the missionaries, and to be used in their ministry so as to supersede the use of ordinary means. There is no trace of such a gift in the Scriptures of a later date; and no trace of it in the subsequent history of the Church. It would have been unlike the way of the Lord—against the analogy of Providence. It was a sign graciously given on that day to confirm the faith of the disciples at the crisis of their need; not a convenience to render exertion unnecessary. In like manner, the Lord, in a crisis of his personal ministry, fed a famishing multitude with a few loaves. This was done for a sign, that they might believe. But he did not interfere with the ordinary course of Providence; he did not free men from the necessity of tilling and sowing the ground.

" As the Spirit gave them utterance." Their hearts were filled with the great things of the kingdom, and they labored to pour them forth as glory to God. The Spirit given to them infused the thoughts, and framed the thoughts into words; so that the emotions and sentiments that filled the hearts of these Galilean fishermen were poured out in the tongues of Greece and Rome, of Persia and Africa. Thus the men, whether of the stock of Israel or proselytes from the Gentiles, who had from various countries come up to Jerusalem to worship at the feast, heard in their own languages the wonderful works of God—heard and believed—believed and carried to their homes, and in their homes repeated; so that the Gospel spread in the first age farther and faster through the world than in the ordinary course of even apostolic ministry. These foreign worshippers at Jerusalem received " bread to the eater;" and having lived on the word themselves, they carried it with them to their homes, as "seed to the sower:" and thence sprang a harvest, that waved like Lebanon, in Europe, in Africa, and in the East, during the lifetime of the Eleven.

The utterance given by the Spirit to the missionaries was aptly symbolized by the tongues of fire. As water in baptism signifies the spiritual cleansing, so the fire, resting on the apostles' heads, promised the living conquering energy with which they should preach the gospel and spread the kingdom. The speech that published the glad tidings should be a tongue of fire. He who speaks the gospel coldly has not himself felt its power. When the preacher's heart is kindled, his words will burn. Enthusiasm, instead of being a blemish in a Christian, is his normal condition. "Fervent in spirit, serving the Lord;" these two have been joined together by the Word of God, and they should never be put asunder in the practice of men.

The gift of tongues—the "utterance" imparted by the Spirit—was a direct means of establishing Christ's kingdom, in that it supplied the apostles at the beginning of their work with a certificate of their call and their competence. It was evidence to all who heard that they were Divinely commissioned to make known the way of life. But besides its use as a sign to certify the calling of the preachers, it was in its own nature fitted, more than any other sign, directly to promote the cause. It both proved the doctrine true, and spread it far. The expression of the doctrine by Galilean preachers, in a language that foreigners understood, both induced the hearers to believe and enabled them to carry home what they had heard for the benefit of their own countrymen. Any other sign from heaven might have been equally effective to convince the onlookers that the apostles had a Divine commission to make known God's will; but no other sign would have suited so well as an instrument to spread the Word of life rapidly among the nations—to sow the seed in the first spring over the wide field of the world.

A question has been raised as to the precise import of the expression, "dwelling at Jerusalem," whether it means Jews born and bred in foreign countries, who in old age returned to lay their bones in the sacred city, or Jews and proselytes whose homes were in the various countries enumerated, and who were sojourning temporarily at Jerusalem, that they might worship at the feasts. There may have been specimens of both kinds; but the spirit of the narrative seems to imply that the majority belonged to the latter class, and the Ethiopian eunuch is an example. Having come so far, it is probable that he remained a considerable time in the city; and that he, and such as he, although only visitors, might correctly be represented as "dwelling at Jerusalem."

The Lord lives and rules now and in this land, as really as then in Judæa. He is the same yesterday and to-day and for ever. When a young person goes for a time to reside in town or country at a distance from home, and there hears the wonderful works of God—the work of redemption by the death of Christ—let him think, God has brought me to this place in order to speak this word to me; he means that I should receive it, and live; that, living by faith on his Son, I should return to my own home and tell what great things the Lord hath done for me.

The Seed of the Word is Spread
(Acts 2:5-11)

"*And there were dwelling at Jerusalem Jews, devout men, out of every nation under heaven. Now when this was noised abroad, the multitude came together, and were confounded, because that every man heard them speak in his own language. And they were all amazed and marvelled, saying one to another, Behold are not all these which speak Galileans? And how hear we every man in our own tongue, wherein we were born? Parthians, and Medes, and Elamites, and the dwellers in Mesopotamia, and in Judæa, and Cappadocia, in Pontus, and Asia, Phrygia, and Pamphylia, in Egypt, and in the parts of Libya about Cyrene, and strangers of Rome, Jews and proselytes, Cretes and Arabians, we do hear them speak in our tongues the wonderful works of God.*"—ACTS II. 5-11.

IN the cotton factories of Lancashire you may see a huge piece of machinery, fifty feet in length, and containing hundreds of spindles, moving slowly, steadily, across the floor from one side of the room to another; and then, without the touch of a human hand, turning and moving as steadily and slowly back to the place from which it started. It is a great triumph of mechanical skill to insert within the machine a power by which, after it has moved a long way forward, it shall stop, and move as far backward.

I think I see a similar contrivance in the Mosaic institutes. They were calculated and fitted to retain the word of God at Jerusalem till a certain time, and then to send the word forth from Jerusalem. The very same provision that confined the ordinances to Israel until Christ came, became the means of spreading them over the world at the appointed time—when the day of Pentecost was fully come.

All the people must come to one place with their sacrifices. Year by year they made a pilgrimage to Jerusalem at the Passover and the other appointed feasts. Even after some of the people had settled in foreign lands they still obeyed this law. The Ethiopian treasurer travelled a thousand miles for this purpose, and many others from east and west and south and north met him there. This institution seemed intended and fitted to confine all worship of the true God to one place for ever. It seemed to forbid the spread of true religion over the world, and yet it became the means of carrying the gospel forth from Jerusalem, and making it known to the nations.

This law and practice brought devout Jews and proselytes from many lands to Jerusalem at the Pentecost after the resurrection of Christ. Being on the spot when the Spirit was poured out, they heard each in his own tongue the gospel of grace, and carried the glad tidings home. Thus Christ was preached in many distant countries very soon after his own ministry was closed. That word which the strangers heard at Jerusalem they carried home as seed, and from that seed an early harvest sprung.

In a still, hot, sultry day of autumn, as you walk through the fields, your attention is arrested by a tiny sound of brief intervals, as if it were an explosion in miniature. You stand still and listen. Now and then you hear a sharp shot, and a few seconds thereafter a shower of tiny balls falling on the ground or on the leaves of the larger plants. It is the bursting of seed-pods in the sun. The casket that contains the seed of some plants is composed of four or five long narrow staves, joined together like cooper work, but without the hoops. The staves are glued together at the edges, and the vessel thus constructed is sufficiently strong to retain and protect the seed till it is ripe. But if the seeds were retained in the vessel after they are ripe, the purposes of Nature would be thwarted. Accordingly at this stage there is a turning-point, and the action of the machinery is reversed. The very same qualities in the seed-vessels that hold fast the seed while it is green, jerk it to a distance and sow it broadcast after it is ripe. When the pods are dried in the sun the glutinous cement holds fast, the staves of the little barrel are bent, and when at last the bursting force overcomes the adhesion, they open with a spring that flings the seed to a distance, as if from a sower's hand.

Thus the same mechanism that secures the confinement of the seed to one spot while it is green, provides that it shall be scattered to a distance when it is ripe; so that, next year, a larger space shall be covered by its growth. By this contrivance in Nature, although no human hand were near, a whole field would soon be sown by seed from a single plant.

Thus the law in Israel that confined the sacrifices to one spot, and so brought Jews and proselytes from all the surrounding countries to Jerusalem at the Pentecost, threw the seed of the Word as by a spring out from Jerusalem into all the neighboring nations. These Parthians, and Medes, and Elamites, and dwellers in Mesopotamia, were the seed-vessels, charged with precious seed at Jerusalem, and then thrown back on the several countries whence they had come. In this way the gospel was in a single season brought to regions which otherwise it might not have reached in the course of a century.

We know, in point of fact, from ancient history that the Christian Church sprang up in many widely separated regions during the lifetime of the apostles, or very soon after their death. This fact finds its explanation in the gathering at Pentecost, and the gift of tongues. Take, for example, those nations that are first mentioned in the list, and lie eastward from Palestine, in the heart of Asia. The Parthians and Medes and Elamites were contiguous and allied peoples. Elam corresponds to Persia, and the two others were closely related to that ancient and celebrated kingdom. The Persians maintained an empire independent of Rome for several centuries after the commencement of the Christian era. In ancient times the Persians were fireworshippers; and that portion of the race who, under the name of Parsees, are still found in Western India, adhere to the religion of their fathers. The sun is their chief god, but they worship fire wherever it occurs. Perhaps these Persians had emigrated eastward before their country was overrun by Mahomet.

We may be assured that the proselytes from Persia would experience peculiar emotions when they saw the tongues of fire, and heard the gospel in their own language from the lips of Galileans. Here is fire that really sheds light on the darkness, and kindles life where death had reigned before.

A Christian Church existed in Persia in the earliest centuries of our era. In the year 333 it endured a violent persecution, in many respects similar to that which has raged against the Christians of Madagascar at various periods in the present generation. At one time the principal bishop, with a hundred ministers of inferior rank, were put to death. The bishop, Simeon, when brought into the king's presence for trial, refused to prostrate himself, as he had formerly done without scruple; giving as his reason that the act might have been misunderstood when he was called to witness regarding his religion and his God. Ordered to worship the sun, he refused, saying that the sun was even less worthy of worship than the king, as it was not a living creature at all. He was sent back to prison for a day, that he might have time to reflect. Next day the prisoners were all brought out for execution. The bishop and two companions were kept to the last, in the hope that the sight of so many executions would soften them, and induce them to deny Christ. He remained firm. One of his friends having manifested symptoms of fear, an officer of the king's household, named Phusek, a Christian, said to him, "Fear not; shut your eyes but a moment, and you will open them on the light of Christ." When this was reported to the king, he upbraided his servant Phusek; but that Christian witness replied that he would gladly give away all the honors the king had bestowed, in exchange for the crown of martyrdom. His tongue was thereupon torn out, and he died in torture.

In this persecution the common Christian people were for the most part permitted to escape, while the chiefs were sought out and put to death. It lasted, with greater or less violence, for a period of forty years.

Nothing could show more clearly than these sad events the great extent to which Christianity had spread in those early ages. A great harvest sprang in many lands from the seed that the worshippers found at Jerusalem—a great flame of spiritual life was kindled in the far East by those fiery tongues of the Pentecost revival.

Missions
(Acts 2:12)

" And they were all amazed, and were in doubt, saying one to another, What meaneth this ? "

WHEN the noise was heard, the multitude came together, and were confounded: they were poured together, and lost all distinct thought and judgment. In this state of confusion and amazement, some mocked the speakers, attributing their language to drunkenness; others, grave and solemnized, but uncertain, uttered to each other the question, "What meaneth this ?"

We have already endeavored to reach the meaning of the fact for that generation; but it will be profitable also to inquire what it means for our own. After the first ages, there came a period of feebleness and decay. The Church was extinguished in some countries, and corrupted in others. The vine that grew on the mountains of Judah, and threw its branches westward to the Mediterranean, and eastward to the Euphrates, was on all sides assailed and cut down. In the East it was destroyed; and in the West, although the branches remained in their place, they lost their life-sap, and withered.

After a long period of midnight, the Reformation dawned. God granted a revival to the slumbering nations of Europe. Jesus seemed to stand, as once he stood at the grave of Lazarus, and call the dead to life. The dry bones of the valley started up, an exceeding great army of living men.

It would have been well if the men of the Reformation, when they shook off the yoke of Rome, had betaken themselves to this text, and considered the question, "What meaneth this?" They missed one half of its meaning. They caught the Pentecost revival in as far as it meant the getting of spiritual life for themselves; but they missed it, in great measure, in as far as it meant the publishing of the glad tidings in all lands. They secured the Spirit, descending as *fire* to kindle love to Christ, in their own hearts; but they did not, in any large measure, receive the Spirit as *tongues of fire*, to spread the light through the dark places of the earth. They gladly accepted the privileges of sons; but they did not with sufficient energy exert themselves as servants. They became Christians, but not missionaries. Their circumstances, indeed, as compared to ours, were adverse. They were involved in controversies, and crushed by persecuting wars.

In our times a great reviving has again visited the Church of Christ. Disciples have in the present century again learned to know the meaning of the sign from heaven. We have enjoyed comparative peace, and we have at command much greater resources. More in the way of talent has been given to us, and, therefore, from us more in the way of work will be required. The Church of this century has accepted this sign both as a baptism of fire for spiritual life in itself, and as a tongue of fire to tell in burning words the Redeemer's love in heathen lands.

"What meaneth this" for the present generation of believers? It meaneth pre-eminently MISSIONS. The best paraphrase of the passage was given in the words of the Lord Jesus, when he said, "Go ye into all the world, and preach the gospel unto every creature."

One of the chief external hindrances to the spread of the gospel is the confusion of tongues. A strange language, which the missionary meets when he crosses a sea or a mountain-range, is like a wall that stops his progress, saying, "Hitherto shalt thou come, but no further." The men of Galilee, at the Pentecost, were enabled to surmount that difficulty by a miracle of Divine power. They might have sung with David, "By my God assisting me, I overleap a wall." The unlearned Jews opened their lips to speak of Christ, and the strangers from various countries instantly heard, each in his own language, the wonderful works of God. A missionary of our day might pine for such a privilege. If a Christian starting from Britain or America, and arriving in China, had nothing more to do than open his lips and preach the Word as if he were at home, the work would be easy. Yes, it would be easy; and, also, it would be easy to live, if, by a word of blessing uttered over it, a little bread should grow into rations for five thousand men. But this is not, in either sphere, the way of the Lord. It would not be difficult to prove that the miracle, which, occurring once, served a great and good purpose, would, if it became the ordinary rule, destroy all. Enough, that the will of the Lord is, that we should till and sow in order to obtain bread; that we should patiently learn strange tongues, in order that we may make known through them the redemption of Christ.

We have greater things than these men of the Pentecost enjoyed. We are better off than they. Greater numbers are converted every year by ordinary natural speech than ever were converted by the extraordinary gift of tongues. In the Great Exhibition at London, as far back as 1851, the Bible was shown in one hundred and fifty languages. Behold, a greater privilege than the gift of tongues, a greater than the Pentecost miracle, is here ! This acquisition is permanent. The way once opened to one hundred and fifty different tribes remains open. These canals once, by much labor, excavated, remain to convey the living water to a thirsty land from generation to generation. The miracle of Pentecost did not last long: the flickering light of those fiery tongues was soon extinguished. The extraordinary gift was not itself a permanent substance, but a shadow that pointed to something better, and then passed away. These polyglot Bibles of the London Exhibition were the fulfilment of the Pentecostal prophecy. The sign from heaven only pointed out the direction in which our efforts should be made, and then withdrew.

This sign then, for us, manifestly meaneth, that we should break forth on every side, and burst through or overleap the barrier of strange tongues, and all other barriers that stand in the way, and never rest until the kingdoms of this world shall have become the kingdoms of our Lord and of his Christ.

Our own tongue has, in the sovereign providence of God, been more highly favored than any other; and from them to whom much is given much shall be required. This language is nowhere now desecrated by a state law to prohibit any human being from reading the Word of God. In this language there are more Bibles than in any other; and this is the language that is spreading faster and farther than any other over the world. The two nations that speak it, Great Britain and the United States, are the greatest maritime powers; and together they hold sway over a fourth part of the earth, and a sixth part of men. Not only are these two nations already so far advanced, but they are advancing at a much greater ratio than other nations. God is giving the earth to those people who give his Word to mankind without restraint and without limit. That tongue which most freely circulates the Bible bids fair to become the paramount language of the human race. "Them that honor me, I will honor." Let the two nations which use in common this mother tongue be faithful to the Head and loving to each other and their destiny, even in the near future, may be grander than any prophet has yet been able to conceive.

This in regard to the tongue; but what of the fire? Would that it were already kindled by the Holy Spirit in the secret of believing hearts, wrapping first the Church and then the world in its flame.

An Apostle Preaches
(Acts 2:14)

" But Peter, standing up with the eleven, lifted up his voice and said unto them, Ye men of Judæa, and all ye that dwell at Jerusalem, be this known unto you, and hearken to my words."

IN the life of the Lord himself, it was after the Spirit had descended upon him at his baptism that he broke forth into a positive, aggressive ministry. In this respect the Church, which is his body, follows the same rule. Before the mission of the Spirit at Pentecost the disciples remained at Jerusalem, and remained silent there. Upward to God there was much sighing and crying in the interval, but no word going outward to men. It was a time to receive, not a time to give: they waited for one great receiving, which should enable them to give out all their life afterward.

There were, first, prayer with one accord; next, the gracious answer in the gift of the Spirit; and then the positive ministry began. Now the apostles have received power; and now they will become witnesses of Christ. Beginning at Jerusalem, they will not cease from their labors until all ends of the earth shall see the salvation of God.

The multitude who had gathered round the disciples, and had heard the wonderful works of God, were now divided into two portions,—the overawed inquirers, and the light-hearted mockers. Thus far and no farther can signs and wonders go. The work of conversion, in its completeness, is due to another power. Although the earthquake and the storm may prove effectual to shake the heedless out of their lethargy, the still small voice must come after these signs ere a human soul can be reached with renewing grace. The miracles of Pentecost avail to divide the multitude only into two classes; some were solemnized and amazed; others in the vanity of their hearts attempted to laugh down the whole matter as a drunken freak. But when the Word is preached with the power of the Spirit—the Word of God that goes like a sword through the joints and marrow—it will be found that the two classes grow into three. Besides the mockers, and the solemnized inquirers, the believers will emerge—those who receive the word with gladness and live by faith.

Having now received the power, the apostles will immediately exercise it. They will seize the opportunity of being witnesses for Christ. Peter, as usual, is spokesman. Prince, that is, "foremost," of the apostles, he certainly is, in the sense that he is always ready to spring to his feet and to speak for himself and his brethren.

Peter stood up. Possibly there were some private consultations between him and those who happened to be nearest as to who should first speak, and what line of argument the speaker should adopt. I could even conceive that John stood next the spokesman, and helped him with the quotations from Scripture as he went along. It would appear also (verse 14) that the whole college of apostles stood up while Peter spoke, that they might adopt his words as the testimony of all. He lifted up his voice, perhaps in a very loud tone, in order to reach the outskirts of the vast congregation.

Here the preaching of a completed redemption began. This is the first sermon. Since that time the preaching of Christ has exercised a great power on the world; and it must continue until, like the sun, the light of the Gospel shall compass the earth.

In this first specimen of preaching peculiar honor is given to the Scriptures of the Old Testament. The preacher plants his foot on the Prophets and the Psalms as on a sure and everlasting foundation. All is grounded on the inspired Word. Further, this earliest example of a sermon is in the main a narrative. The apostles considered themselves to be the witnesses of a fact to the world. They depended neither upon argument nor rhetoric: they told a story, and looked to God for the power. At a subsequent period, even in apostolic times, it became necessary to intermingle doctrinal discussion with the narrative of facts; but at the outset it was testimony merely, and it continued to be testimony mainly to the last.

Even now the essence of preaching is the statement of a fact. When the Evangelist Luke at the commencement of his second book takes a retrospective view of his earlier work, he calls it a record of "all that Jesus began both to *do* and *teach*." The doing goes before the teaching, and lies under it to sustain, as the foundation sustains the superstructure. The teaching is secondary, and subordinate to the acting: the teaching is of use only in as far as it explains and applies the action. It is what Jesus did that saves; and preaching is valuable only in as far as it explains and enforces his saving work.

Another feature of Peter's sermon is that it presents Christ as the fulfilment of Scripture. The disciple had learned this from his Master. When Jesus had read the text from Isaiah in the synagogue at Nazareth (Luke iv. 16–22) he closed the book and gave it again to the attendant; and, presenting himself to the audience, he said, "This day is this Scripture fulfilled in your ears." It is only when we read them in the light of Christ risen that the Prophets and the Psalms can be understood. It is when the sun rises and shines on them that all the gems scattered over the ground and partly embedded in the earth begin to sparkle like stars in the sky.

Towards the close of his discourse, Peter exhibits great skill and boldness in pressing home his doctrine to the hearts of his hearers. This is an outstanding characteristic of apostolic preaching: we must adopt this method if we would see the kingdom coming in our own day. If we draw weapons from the Lord's great armory, and suspend them in the air, that spectators may see and admire their sheen and sharpness, and if we then cease, our labor is vain. These weapons are made for wounding; and he handles them uselessly and faithlessly who does not bring their points to bear on the enemies of the King that lurk in human hearts.

In this case the preaching was successful: the sword went home. "They were pricked in their hearts," and the wounded sought the Healer. The apostles led the convicted to Christ. The words of Peter generated a great thirst in many souls; the thirsty were led, on the instant, to the water of life. They gladly received his word, and the same day were added unto them about three thousand souls.

Rightly Dividing the Word of Truth
(Acts 2:37-40)

" Now when they heard this, they were pricked in their heart, and said unto Peter and to the rest of the apostles, Men and brethren, what shall we do ? Then Peter said unto them, Repent, and be baptized every one of you in the name of Jesus Christ for the remission of sins, and ye shall receive the gift of the Holy Ghost. For the promise is unto you, and to your children, and to all that are afar off, even as many as the Lord our God shall call. And with many other words did he testify and exhort, saying, Save yourselves from this untoward generation."

IN order to understand how they received the Word " Gladly," we must remember that they had been " pricked in their hearts." They had been wounded; and now the healing is grateful. The Word had wounded; and now the Word heals. A little religion is a painful thing; but more religion takes the pain away. The Word is both a hammer to break the rock in pieces, and a balm to heal the broken heart. Its first effect is to convince a sinner that he is lost; its next, to make the lost rejoice in his Saviour.

It is of first-rate importance to keep these two functions of the Word distinct, and to keep the right one foremost. To preach a healing gospel where there is no wound on the conscience, is like pressing draughts of cold water on those who experience no thirst. I know of nothing sweeter than water to the thirsty; but I know of nothing more insipid than water to those who are already satisfied.

The apostles after Pentecost were skilful preachers —they rightly divided the word of truth. If you examine Peter's discourse, as far as it is recorded here, you will find that its specific and consistent aim is, in the first place, to produce in the audience a conviction of their own guilt. The immediate purpose for which he appeals to Scripture is to bring home to those Jews who stood before him the guilt of crucifying the Son of God. It was not with gladness that they received that word: it was with grief, shame, remorse.

It was when the preacher saw that his first word had taken effect, that he delivered the second. He has succeeded in wounding; and at the cry of the suffering patient, he comes forward now to heal. The old stem has been cut off, and the tree is bleeding; he will turn now the knife that is in his hand, and with its other side insert the new graft, that there may be a tree of righteousness, the planting of the Lord.

You pour from your phial some burning drops upon a sore: their first effect is to increase the pain; but knowing the sovereign power of the remedy, you continue to pour it on the ailing place, sparing not for the patient's crying. At length the continued application of that which caused the pain, takes all the pain away. When the Word of God wounds a soul, continue to ply that soul with the Word, until the sword that wounded becomes the balm that heals. Then, in this second stage, the hearer will receive the Word gladly.

Indeed, he who receives the Word will receive it gladly; for those who do not receive it gladly, will not long continue to receive it at all. These believers were immediately baptized. Of many interesting questions connected with this baptism, which might in proper time and place be profitably discussed, I shall here touch only one. It is clear from the narrative that regeneration was not the result of baptism, but baptism the result of regeneration. It was when they had received the Word with gladness, that they were baptized. The order of events is precisely that which the Master had enjoined (Matt. xxviii. 19, 20): "Go ye therefore, and—

1. "Teach [make disciples of] all nations,

2. "Baptizing them in the name of the Father, and of the Son, and of the Holy Ghost;

3. "Teaching them to observe all things whatsoever I have commanded you."

In this case, Peter and his companions, in striving to build up the Church, strove lawfully. They first laid themselves out to make disciples of the people. Then, when they perceived by the successive pain and gladness produced by the preaching that the multitude had become disciples, they baptized them; and lastly, it is clear, from the concluding verses of this chapter, that these newly-accepted members of the Church were successfully taught to observe all the commandments of the Lord, for their subsequent life abounded in faith and charity.

But a dash of sadness is thrown into the midst of this happy scene; for "fear came upon every soul." But this points to the outer circle—to those that as yet believed not. The conversions—many, sudden, and complete—shone like a light in the darkness. The on-lookers were startled. When they saw so many entering into life, they were smitten with a sudden fear lest themselves should be left without and perish.

From the apostle's view-point, however, this fear which they observed in their neighbors was a hopeful symptom. The example of believers had begun to tell. It is a good sign, when those who have hitherto lived without God in the world begin to be uneasy. Especially is it a good sign when the sight of multitudes pressing through the strait gate into the kingdom, stirs in those who are still without, a dread of being left behind. When one or more are raised up from the miry pit, and get their feet set on a rock, and a new song on their lips, many shall see it and fear, and shall trust in the Lord (Ps. xl.) The Christian community, in the freshness of a first faith, was suddenly thrown into society; and society was perturbed and put about by the new and unwonted presence. If a new planet should be projected into our system, it would make the old worlds stagger in their paths. Bodies in contact reciprocally affect each other, especially in respect of temperature. Pour hot water into a cold vessel; the water contributes to heat the vessel, but the vessel also contributes to cool the water. If a constant and strong stream of hot water is supplied, it will bring up the vessel to its own temperature.

A process like this goes on continually between the Church and the world. Fervent disciples, especially in a time of first love, affect with somewhat of their own warmth the society into which they are poured; but society, on the other hand, clasping round the converts, affects them with its own coldness. The world, being the larger body, will soon cool, will soon freeze these few disciples' hearts, unless they contrive to maintain constant contact with the Head, and continually draw from his fulness.

A word here to those who live without Christ in the

world. My friends, I confess that the Church in contact with you is more or less cold in spirit. Its faith and love are not lively. The visible Church in contact with society is not so bright and burning as to arrest and compel your regard. The disciples are not so manifestly like heaven as to send a thrill of terror through you, lest you should fail to join their company. If you remain careless, I confess that we are much to blame. You have cause to blame Christians. But if you stumble over their coldness—stumble so as to fall—what comfort will it afford you that you could blame the Church for its lukewarmness? To blame them, even when they are blameworthy, will not save you when you are lost.

Lately in this city the father of a family had occasion to look over some workmen who were engaged in building a house for him. After the work was far advanced, he found one of the men lighting his pipe among the dry, light, inflammable shavings which were strewn about in all directions. Addressing the workman, the owner said, "If my house is burned by these sparks, the blame will rest on you." Pausing and thinking over what he had said, he added with a sigh, "The blame will be yours, but the loss will be mine; for you cannot repay." The thought sank into the proprietor's heart; he saw the risk was too great: he went away and *insured the house.*

Oh, my brother, go and do likewise. Yourselves—not the house, but the immortal inhabitant—yourselves are in instant danger of being lost. Let it be confessed there is not such ardent faith in the Church as to awaken a slumberer—the Church deserves blame; but the *loss is yours.* Go and insure. Your soul's life is too much exposed; hide it in a place of safety; hide it "with Christ in God."

Christian Festivity
(Acts 2:46)

" And they, continuing daily with one accord in the temple, and break-ing bread from house to house, did eat their meat with gladness and single-ness of heart."

WHEN you ascend from the centuries that succeeded the apostles' days, into the upper stratum of history, in which the apostles themselves were actors, you seem to emerge from a stifled, airless cave, where all manner of fungous growths luxuriate, into the open field where fresh breezes play, and sunbeams glitter, and dew-besprinkled flowers shed their varied perfume on the air. In the Acts of the Apostles you find not only a purer religion, but more of common-sense and manliness, than in the history of the Fathers.

We fall into a great mistake if, while we seek in the Scriptures and by prayer for direction in matters of faith, and the larger turning points of life, we leave smaller affairs, such as our feasts, our company, and recreations, to the arbitrament of chance, or the ex-ample of the world. "In *everything* by prayer and supplication, with thanksgiving, let your requests be made known unto God." "Whether therefore ye eat, or drink, or whatsoever ye do, do all to the glory of God." It is an unspeakable privilege to be permitted to run into our Redeemer's presence with the minor anxieties of life, as well as with the great concerns of eternity. In this very thing lies the distinctive pecu-liarity of a child's position, as distinguished from that of a stranger. Only on the great things may the stranger approach the king; but in everything the ap-peal of a child is welcome to the Father. "Casting *all your care* on him; for he careth for you."

Avoiding for the present the question regarding the dispensation of the Lord's Supper, and the relation which it bore in primitive times to the common meals of the disciples, we shall endeavor to concentrate at-tention on the common meals themselves, and the manner in which Christians then enjoyed them. "They

did eat their meat with gladness and singleness of heart."
But a preliminary to this gladness in eating their own
food, was a liberal contribution for the comfort of poorer
brethren, according to the narrative immediately preceding. Not indeed by a community of goods, for it
was optional with each proprietor whether he should
retain his property, and even when it was sold, the
proceeds were distributed by himself according to his
own judgment of the claimant's need,—not by a community of goods, but by a great and general generosity, the believers in Christ who possessed substance
had satisfied the poor with bread. This is a necessary
ingredient in the gladness with which a Christian enjoys the plenty that may have fallen to his lot. The
Master reminded us, "The poor ye have always with
you;" and he meant that the grace of liberality should
not die out of our lives for want of exercise. But, supposing this duty accomplished, or rather this privilege
enjoyed,—the larger of the two blessings, that of giving to our brethren who are in need, the question
remains, What is it to eat our common meals with
gladness of heart, and how may that pleasure be fully
and habitually obtained?

Although the Lord's Supper was more frequently
administered, and in more close proximity to family
meals than would be possible or suitable now that the
Christian community has grown so great, it is evident
that here in the latter clause it is not the religious ordinance, but the common meal that is signalized as
having been simple and joyful. Here the footsteps of
the flock have been marked in history for us: by this
way they went, when they met together to eat their
daily bread.

Some may think this is a matter on which examples and instructions from the Christian Scriptures are
not required: some may suppose that eating and drinking is the concern of man as such, and provided for in
the laws of nature. But the Scriptures do claim the
control of this matter, and lay down rules for its conduct. We need Divine guidance even on this natural
process. Even here we lack wisdom, and should ask
it of the Father, who giveth to all men liberally.

Providing, preparing, and partaking of food, is a

very important work in the life of man. A very large proportion of our time and energy is necessarily devoted to it. The three allied questions, What shall we eat, and what shall we drink, and wherewithal shall we be clothed? are legitimate questions for humankind: they are not evil in themselves; they become evil only in their excess, and when they usurp the place of greater interests. It concerns us much to do in a right way and a right spirit those necessary acts which occupy a large proportion of our time and energy.

They did eat. These ancient Christians were not hermits. They did not deny themselves their necessary food, or the company of their kind. In particular, they enjoyed their food more by enjoying it together. They acknowledged and fell in with that instinct of nature, which craves cheerful company and conversation at table. They did not denounce and desert convivial meetings. The sight of a friend's face and the sound of his voice while we eat, are good gifts of God as well as the bread that sustains us, and should be received with thanksgiving. It is neither the aim nor the effect of true religion to thwart the affections and instincts of nature. Grace comes not to destroy these appetites, but to fulfil: it comes not to forbid their use, but to purify them from the abuses that sin has introduced. A convivial meeting is an object of dread, particularly to Christian parents in our land and day; but it is not in itself evil; in as far as it retains its etymological meaning, eating together, behold, it is very good. It is good in its origin, and it may be good again, when the various abominations that the god of this world has associated with it shall have been brushed away. In convivial meetings the earliest Christians did eat their meat with gladness and singleness of heart, before luxury corrupted them; and in convivial meetings Christians might yet enjoy the cheerful society in eating and drinking, which conduces to health as well as to happiness, if all intemperance, and frivolity, and licentiousness, were banished from the board.

One good reason for eating our bread with gladness is that we have bread to eat. An additional cause of joy may be found in the fact that a self-acting machinery has been set up in the constitution of our nature, which reminds us when nourishment is needed, and compels us to take it at the proper time. If this had been left dependent on our memory and faithfulness, it would have been grievously neglected. It is not necessary that we should painfully remember the necessity of sustenance for our bodies, and live in fear lest life should through neglect be lost. A watcher has been placed within our own being like the ambassador of another sovereign within our own capital, whose business it is to see the needful food administered at the needful time. That sentinel is faithful, and powerful: he never sleeps: and he lacks not compulsitor of pain to enforce his commands if we should be slow to obey. Hunger seems the twin brother of conscience; the one watching for the health of the body, the other for the well-being of the soul: both are gifts of God, and both invested with authority over us, for our own good.

These grounds for gladness in eating our daily bread are common to all: but there are other reasons which belong to Christians as such. Those who have obtained peace with God through Christ the Mediator, have not less, but more enjoyment in their food than other men. Instead of merely gathering their sustenance from the ground like cattle, they enjoy communion with the Father of their spirits every time they eat. To give thanks and ask the blessing by one voice at the social meal, constitutes the framework through which that communion in spirit seeks expression. It is the living gratitude in Christian hearts that has thrown out these seemly expressions; but the presence of the form does not necessarily prove that the substance continues to dwell within it. These articulate formulas of peity are like the shells which mollusks throw out: but the shell, when once it has been produced by the energy of life, may remain, symmetrical and beautiful, after the living creature has wasted all away. Do not despise the external forms; but see that there be life within them. Let there be filial confidence in a giving God while you enjoy your food, and that emotion trembling in the heart will find or frame fit channels through which it may flow.

Singleness of heart accompanied the gladness; and in point of fact, wanting that companion, the gladness itself would soon disappear. "A double-minded man is unstable in all his ways;" and even in the matter of eating and drinking in the company of his friends, the shreds of pleasure that come and go, never consolidate into a substantial joy. In very many cases, the simplicity is destroyed and the true gladness consequently lost, by a huge, burdensome, irrational luxury. The cares of the meal are sometimes as heavy as the management of a small estate. They distract and oppress the entertainer. Instead of singleness, doubleness of a very troublesome type is the occupant of his heart. One half of his mental vision squints aside to calculate the estimation in which the elaborate festival is held by the guests. Simplicity may be marred too by the cost of the entertainment in relation to the resources of the entertainer. With a few of the wealthiest citizens the shoe may perhaps never pinch at this spot; but with a great number of their imitators it becomes a real burden. Some approach to simplicity in the cost of entertainments might both replenish the coffers of charitable institutions, and facilitate the settlement of tradesmen's bills. In relation to these matters our age and nation greatly need the old Apostolic injunction, "Add to your faith courage." In very many cases it is courage that is needed—courage to be singular, and strength to stem the stream. But where may we expect to find the virtue that can dare to stand alone amongst men, unless in those who already have faith in God through the Lord Jesus Christ? A Christian, who may obtain the breath of the Spirit in his sail, should not helplessly glide down with the stream.

Immoderately late hours do much to mar both the simplicity and the heart-gladness of social meals. That very lateness, I confess, constitutes an essential element in the kind of merriment which a vitiated appetite demands: but it is fatal to the calm, deep joyfulness which corresponds with our position as disciples of Christ, or even as the intelligent creatures of God. To turn night into day, and day into night, is not simplicity, and cannot promote real gladness. It is like the transactions within the walls of a lunatic asylum, where the opinion might prevail, that people should lie in bed while the sun shines, and be active with gaslight during the night. What would you think of the gardener who should cover your green-house with thick matting till noon, and make up for the deficiency of light by burning lamps beside the flowers at midnight? You would dismiss the man as drunk or incapable. We should discharge Fashion from the management of our life, as we would discharge an inebriate from the care of our flowers or our horses. Treat yourselves as you treat your gardens. "Behold the lilies of the field, how they grow." Young men and young women would be more like the lilies in freshness and beauty if they followed nature more closely: and they would gain as much in strength of mind, as in comeliness of person.

I have not yet alluded to that which in our country and our day constitutes by far the greatest danger in connection with festivity,—the free use, often running over into the vile abuse, of highly concentrated intoxicants. There is ground for joy and thankfulness in the comparative freedom from excess which generally characterizes the entertainments of the more cultivated classes in the present day. A portion also of the humbler classes have emancipated themselves completely from the bondage of intemperance: but very large numbers, ranging from the lowest to the highest as to social position, are miserably enslaved. The numbers of this class, alas, are continually recruited from the ranks of the rising generation, through the influence of social customs, and the dangerous power of the stimulants in ordinary use. Efforts, zealous and protracted, to restrict the traffic on the one hand, and to persuade to personal abstinence on the other, have shown as yet only very limited results. An accumulation of sin and shame, of poverty and crime, proceeding from the intemperate use of stimulants, lies on the nation and the Church most appalling in the aggregate, and heart-rending in the contemplation of its multiform details.

Here is a subject eminently worthy of a Christian's regard, especially at festive seasons, and in connection with social joyful assemblages. After all the efforts that benevolent men and public institutions have been able to put forth, an evil of fearful magnitude remains, —a work of incalculable difficulty still demands the help of all who fear God and regard man. How shall the disciples of Christ most effectually bring each his own influence to bear against this devastating vice? I shall not presume to supply an answer. The wisdom that shall answer this question seems not yet to have come to the Church: the Church must learn to feel deeply the lack of wisdom adequate to the crisis, and to ask the supply from God. But in the meantime, failing an answer, I should count the cause half won, if each brother and sister of the Christian family were led, in godly simplicity and without passion or prejudice, to entertain the question. Questions are sometimes most precious and practically effective, although the answer cannot yet be given. When Christians shall individually and collectively cease to regulate generally their lives, and particularly their entertainments, by the mere mandate of the world's fashion, issuing like a Delphic oracle, without a reason from an unknown God, and begin to mold their actions, great and small, by a glad, free, deliberate purpose, in a matrix constituted of the twin motives which bind heaven and earth together,—serving the Lord that bought us, and saving our brother lost; then shall the lowest point have been reached and passed,—then shall Society, like the earth after Christmas, creep gradually out of its winter darkness, and creep forward to its perfect day. These two— my Redeemer's servant, and my brother's keeper—are the hedges on the right and left of a believer's path, between which, if they are kept up, he may walk through the wilderness, without fear of wandering from the way.

It is a happy thing to have a purpose,—a purpose that is pure and lovely,—that you can present to your own conscience and to God, that you can prosecute in secret without meanness, or avow in public, if need be, without shame, running through your life and bringing all into harmony. And, so far from being inappropriate if applied to the lesser and lighter enterprises of life, it is precisely in these that it contributes most to safety and satisfaction. Graver matters have a certain weight in themselves that contributes to their solidity; the lighter leaves of life need more a sustaining thread running through the whole. I call on Christians in festive seasons, and in festive companies, not to submit to the restraints of duty, but rather to enjoy freely their privilege. It is not required, it is not permitted, that you should leave Christ at the door when you enter the Guest Chamber. If you leave him without when you go in to the feast, you need not expect to find him within, your Intercessor, when you enter your closet and shut the door, and pray to the Father in secret. Those who trust in Christ for the greatest things, have the right to lean on him for the least. Accept the food as the Father's gift; accept the feast as an act of his bounty; accept the company of your kind, knit to your heart either by the bonds of nature or the bonds of grace; accept that gladness of heart which the Maker of men has connected with a social meal. It is a needful and a useful part of Christian witness-bearing in these days to exhibit meekly, but legibly, on our conduct generally, that, while the world and the things of the world are not permitted to become our masters, we are not prohibited from using them as servants; and in particular, that the "gladness," which food eaten in congenial company imparts to a human heart, so far from being the exclusive property of the profane and careless, cannot possibly be in its integrity enjoyed by them, precisely because of their profanity and carelessness, but belongs, by the Father's gift and the children's unsuspecting appropriation, to the whole family of God.

At Once Godly and Popular
(Acts 2:47)

"Praising God, and having favor with all the people. And the Lord added to the church daily such as should be saved."

"PRAISING God:" behold the natural history of the regeneration. Those who are bought with a price are constrained to glorify God. "In everything by prayer and supplication *with thanksgiving* let your requests be made known unto God." The thanksgiving is a constituent element of prayer. If the prescription is made up without this ingredient, it is ineffectual: mere prescription however will never produce true thanksgiving: the gratitude which comes only through prompting is not gratitude. The real emotion is spontaneous, and could not be restrained. As soon as Israel get through the Red Sea, they cluster on the cliffs and make the desert ring with their jubilant psalm, "Sing unto the Lord; for he hath triumphed gloriously." Who can forbid a song, when persons or peoples are redeemed by the blood of Christ, and satisfied with bread from a heavenly Father's hand, that their pent-up emotions may get vent? This is the kind of thanksgiving that breaks forth from loving hearts on earth and reaches the throne of heaven,—the thanks, not that you draw out, but that you could not keep in.

"Having favor with all the people." In the first stage of their progress immediately after Pentecost, the Christian converts were not persecuted. The people looked on, admiring, applauding. They saw a beauty in holiness, when holiness in those revival days had the dew of its youth upon it, and were betrayed for the moment into an admiration of a goodness which themselves had not attained. This phenomenon is eminently worthy of observation. On the surface lies a difficulty; but from beneath a precious lesson may be drawn. In the matter of favor or enmity shown by the world, two opposite experiences alternate in the history of the Church. Providential administration does not proceed uniformly on one method; the way of the Lord, rather, is to balance two opposites, so as to make them work together for good. When hope and holiness adorn the character of disciples, the world outside sometimes admire and applaud, sometimes revile and persecute. It is not possible to construct a general rule by which it could be determined beforehand in any given case whether the world will favor or frown on a company of true disciples. If there be a law that determines the sequences of these alternate courses, it lies beyond our reach. We might, indeed, conclude on general principles that neither the one nor the other would be permitted uniformly to prevail. If true godliness should always and in all places obtain the favor of the world, counterfeits would spring up in such strength and abundance as would suffice absolutely to smother and destroy the truth; and, on the other hand, if godliness should always, and in all places, bring down the world's enmity, the spark of Divine truth in humanity might be quenched, and the gates of hell at last prevail to blot out Christ's name from the earth. The Head on high holds the balance in his own hands. He permits as much of the wrath of man to break forth as suffices to praise himself by purging his Church of its hypocrisy, and then he restrains the remainder thereof.

Although we could not, in the first instance, have invented this method, we are able to perceive, when we see it exemplified in history, that it is the best. When a spark is imbedded in the flax and it begins to smoke, a blast permitted to burst upon it would blow it out; therefore, the blast is by Divine command restrained. But after the fire has fairly caught, the blast will spread the flame, and, therefore, it is permitted to blow. The Lord will not permit the smoking flax to be quenched by a premature severity. He commands a calm till the fire take hold, and then permits a tempest to make the fire spread. In those first days after the Pentecost, the Christians were not persecuted. Many were added to the Church, and the faith of the members was confirmed. When the spark had made some advancement in a calm, the storm that afterwards arose, did not blow it out, but blew it in. Both these principles may be seen alternately operating in society at the present day. In some cases godliness wins favor; in others it stirs enmity. All is in the Lord's hand; disciples may well pray with Agur that in this matter he would give them neither poverty nor riches:—neither too much of the world's favor, nor too little, lest grace should be choked under the weight of its embrace, or withered by the scorching of its anger.

If the rule were absolute, The more likeness to Christ, the more favor from the world, the faith of the Church, like corn sown in land too fat, would grow rank, cleave to the earth and bear nothing but chaff. If on the other hand the rule were absolute, The more likeness to Christ, the more persecution from the world, the faith of the Church, like corn sown on a mountain-top, would wither long before the harvest.

We cannot in any case tell beforehand whether a true exhibition of the Christian character will conciliate kindness or provoke enmity; as we cannot tell to-day whether the wind to-morrow will blow from the East or the West: but both the winds of heaven and the hearts of men are under law to God although we cannot detect the law or predict the result.

" And the Lord added to the Church daily such as should be saved." Here again we have a thing with two sides: all real things have two sides. The Lord added them; and yet they added themselves. The Good Shepherd carried the stray sheep home on his shoulders; and yet the prodigal walked home on his own feet. The sheep and the prodigal in these twin parables certainly do not point to different persons, but to two sides of the same person. On one side, the upper, it is the Lord's doing: on the other side, the lower, it is the man's. In this verse we read the historic fact, " The Lord added them:" and in the context we hear the Divine command, " Save yourselves." At one place the saved are " whosoever shall call on the name of the Lord:" at another they are, "as many as the Lord our God shall call."

When I know myself to be like a withered leaf on the stream that flows to a sea of perdition, it is sweet to think that help is laid on One that is mighty, and to hope that when I am utterly helpless the Lord adds me to his Body, the Church,—to himself, the Church's Head. My comfort in temptation springs not from consciousness of my own strength to hold by him, but from knowledge of his strength to hold me. But woe to the man, who with no liking for the presence of the Lord or the company of his people—no willingness to crucify the flesh, and press through the narrow gate, dares to comfort himself in his coldness and worldliness with the thought, It is not in my power to make myself better, I must wait till the Lord put forth his strength. Nay, brother: the Lord is ready now to do it, if you were willing that it should be done.

" Daily:" every day some. There is no blank in the birth registers of God's family. The Lamb's Book of Life has a page for every day of time, and names in every page. I suppose some of the pages are more crowded than others. At that first Pentecost, as at many seasons since, they came as doves to their windows, a great cloud coming at one time. At other periods they seem rather one here and one there, like the gleaning of grapes after the vintage.

The Romish calendar is crowded with saints. They cannot find room in the circle of the seasons, for all whom the pope delighted to honor. But there are more real saints written in heaven than false ones in Romish heraldry. Daily, ever since men were multiplied on the earth, have the saved streamed through the strait gate into life, and now a multitude whom no man can number inhabit the mansions of the Father's house.

He added the saved to the Church: added them in the act of saving, saved in the act of adding. He does not add a withered branch to the vine; but in the act of inserting it, makes the withered branch live. When pure water is drawn from the salt sea, it is added to the clouds in heaven. In being drawn from the salt sea, these fresh drops are added to the white clouds of the sky. It is thus that the Lord adds the saved to the Church, winning them from a sea of wickedness, and leaving their bitterness behind.

" Daily " some are added: every day some; but only while it is day this process goes on. The night cometh wherein no man can work,—not even the Son of Man, Son of God. He is now about his Father's business: he is finishing the work given him to do. He works, works, works, in wrenching lost men from the devil, the world, and the flesh, and inserting them as living members of his own body for eternal life. " To-day, if ye will hear his voice, harden not your hearts," for the day is wearing away, the day of grace. The night cometh, cometh;—how stealthily it is creeping on,—the night wherein not even this Great Worker can work any more. In the last, that great day of the feast, Jesus stood and cried, " If any man thirst, let him come unto me and drink."

The Use of Miracles
(Acts 3:12,13)

" And when Peter saw it, he answered unto the people, Ye men of Israel, why marvel ye at this ? or why look ye so earnestly on us, as though by our own power or holiness we had made this man to walk ? The God of Abraham, and of Isaac, and of Jacob, the God of our fathers, hath glorified his Son Jesus; whom ye delivered up, and denied him in the presence of Pilate, when he was determined to let him go."

THE healing of the lame beggar at the gate Beautiful, as narrated in verses 1–11, needs no comment. There the picture stands, full bodied as in the stereoscope. Our business, like Peter's, lies mainly, not with the fact, but with the use to which the fact was applied in the progress of Christ's kingdom.

These Galileans were not alone. The words of the Lord, "Lo, I am with you," were still sounding in their ears. The Master puts forth the power, and they yield themselves as his instruments. This is the footing on which the work proceeds. Here, in the ministry of the apostles, as also in his own, the Lord employs power to cleave a path for grace. When the mountains close in and block the way, a miracle will rend them, that the Word may burst the barriers and spread through the land.

Those who refuse to believe in anything supernatural do not gain much at this point. They only shift the difficulty from one spot to another. The fact remains patent to the whole world and undeniable, that in the hands of these Jewish missionaries the religion of Christ, with its self-denying doctrines, made way against the culture of Greece and the might of Rome,—made way until it obtained supremacy. This fact, if it is not based on miracles, is itself a miracle greater than all.

The effect of this cure upon the public was a great and general amazement. Now was Peter's opportunity; and he improved it with promptitude and skill. The Master in calling him had promised to make him a fisher of men; and here the tact and energy of the fisher appear. He knew the favorable juncture. When Peter plied his trade on the lake of Galilee, he did not think it enough that he spread his net and drew it, in the approved fashion, so many times every day. His business was, not to spread his net in an unexceptionable manner—in the very manner that all the ablest fishermen in those parts had uniformly followed—his business was to catch fish; and toward that end he bent all the energy, not only of his stalwart arm, but also of his inventive mind. Peter would fish as his forefathers had fished, if their method seemed to him best; but he would fish as nobody had ever fished before, if he saw that by a new method he could obtain greater success.

So, now that he has become a preacher of the gospel, Peter is not content with delivering, at the proper time, an evangelical sermon. He does not think of the sermon or the preacher. He thinks of men in their need, and of God's grace in their offer now. He rushes in, and strikes home to win souls. He waits and watches till he sees the multitude moved and susceptible. As soon as he perceives some movement on the gathered waters, he follows quickly the angel's steps, lest his opportunity should slip away.

The commotion took the form of a reverential regard directed upon the apostles personally. The wonder that the people had witnessed drew their eyes to the immediate instruments. At that moment the apostles, taught by the Spirit, recognized accurately and promptly the precise place and use of mighty works in their ministry. Such works could not convert the people, but such works then held an important place among the means of conversion. The miracles broke up the hard ground, and these faithful watchers were ready to run in and cast the living seed into the open furrow. From this timely sowing a great harvest sprang.

Peter, as usual, is spokesman. I think the modest and meditative John would not take a prominent public place when Peter was present. Whatever he may have contributed by private suggestion, he left public work to his more forward and more fiery colleague.

Mark how skilfully the speaker begins. It is no longer the affectionate blunder, "Far be this from thee, Lord;" it is no longer the cowardly falsehood, "I know not the man." He has now obtained both wisdom and strength. By this time the Holy Ghost had come upon him, and he had "received power" to be a witness of Christ. He has courage to confess his Master now, and skill to arrange his argument aright.

In presence of the healed cripple the people were overawed; and their veneration, after quivering awhile uncertain, like a ship's compass in a broken sea, began to settle down steadily upon Peter and John as the authors of the miracle and the objects of praise. Observing the current flowing in a devotion which would soon have developed itself into idolatry, Peter ran in, and seized it, and bent it aside from the servants that it might flow full upon the Lord. "And when Peter saw it, he answered and said unto the people, Ye men of Israel, why marvel ye at this? or why look ye so earnestly on us, as though by our own power or holiness we had made this man to walk? The God of Abraham, and of Isaac, and of Jacob, the God of our fathers, hath glorified his Son JESUS," etc. The servants, when they saw worship springing up in human hearts, hastily retired, and presented Jesus alone to receive it.

It is eminently instructive to compare and contrast with this the conduct of the Lord himself in similar circumstances. When he had read the prophecy in the synagogue at Nazareth (Luke iv. 16–22), and all eyes were turned in eager expectation toward him, he did not intercept the stream, or divert it into another channel. He accepted it in full. He closed the book and removed it; then he presented himself to the people as the fulfilment of the prophecy, and the expected Messiah. The absolute contrast between his method and that of the apostles in such a case is peculiarly valuable, as showing incidentally the Divinity of Christ.

In the meantime, Peter's fidelity affords a fine lesson both to preachers and hearers of the gospel in all times. Through the ministers, if possible, as earthen vessels, let the word of life come; but let the ministers present, and the people receive, only the Lord himself as the bread of life.

It is said that when Leonardo da Vinci had finished his celebrated picture of the Last Supper, which still stands on the wall of a convent in the city of Milan, he introduced a friend to inspect the work privately, and give his judgment regarding it. "Exquisite!" exclaimed his friend; "that wine-cup seems to stand out from the table as solid glittering silver." Thereupon the artist quietly took a brush and blotted out the cup, saying: "I meant that the figure of Christ should first and mainly attract the observer's eye, and whatever diverts attention from him must be blotted out." Here is a devotion which, in a more enlightened age, we should do well to imitate.

It is an aim of the ministry to get listless people aroused and interested. It is a great point gained when a multitude are gathered together round the preachers in Solomon's porch, greatly wondering at the word or the work of the Lord. But woe to the preacher who lacks the wisdom or the will to lead the aroused and interested listeners at such a crisis direct to Christ.

Wounding to Heal
(Acts 3:14-26)

"*But ye denied the Holy One and the Just, and desired a murderer to be granted unto you; and killed the Prince of life, whom God hath raised from the dead; whereof we are witnesses,*" etc.

WHEN Peter observed that his audience was becoming tender, he hastened forward to them with the Word; but it is not in the first instance a word of comfort that he administers. His first effort is to wound. He brings a sharp accusation; he heaps coals of fire on their heads, when he sees these heads already beginning to droop. Not that the apostle takes pleasure in putting his countrymen to grief. He is glowing all over with love to these men of Israel, bone of his bone and flesh of his flesh. Seeing them already quivering he deals another blow, in the hope that thereby he may break altogether the already yielding heart; for as soon as the cry, "What must we do?" shall burst from broken hearts, the healing balm is ready. God "hath glorified his Son Jesus; whom ye delivered up, and denied him in the presence of Pilate, when he was determined to let him go." Pilate, the Roman, from a natural sense of justice, desired to save the innocent; but ye, the Israel to whom he came, denied him, and compelled the governor to put him to death. Never was a sharper sword pointed at naked breasts; and never did a mightier thrust send the weapon home to the marrow: "Ye killed the Prince of life." But it is the Physician and not the enemy who is piercing here. He wounds in order that the distressed may seek the Healer. At verse 17th he changes his voice. He withdraws the weapon as soon as its work is done. As soon as the preacher sees that the dividing Word has taken effect, he begins to give consolation. I think it was Whitefield who, when his audience of coal-miners was so large that he could not read in the distant faces the emotions of their hearts, perceived by certain white streaks, like African tattoo, made by coursing tears on sable cheeks, that the Word had cut into the conscience. This was for him the turning-point. The strokes for wounding may now safely cease, and the healing work begin.

Changing his voice, Peter the preacher begins to insinuate a tender consolation. He will present the truth on another side. He had said, "Ye killed the Prince of life:" but now he informs them that it is of God that Christ should suffer the just for the unjust.

There are two opposite ways in which the blood of Jesus may be upon men: "His blood be upon us, and upon our children!" exclaimed the Jewish leaders, when they had hemmed Pilate in, and extorted from him the sentence of death. Ah! that was not the blood of sprinkling for the pardon of sin. It was the blood of Christ upon them, but it did not cleanse. It was the blood of the curse, not the blood of blessing. At first, and for a specific purpose, Peter speaks of the blood of Christ in that evil sense. He takes it and pours it on the murderers' heads, a scorching flood. But when the work of conviction is done, he addresses himself to the work of saving; he takes that same blood in his other hand, and pours it out for blessing. The blood of Christ, although shed by them, is presented now as the blood shed for them—is presented now not as their sin, but as their redemption from sin.

It was a great transition; and it was suddenly made. But the same transition all the new-born make; and most of them make it quickly. It is like a leap from Christ crucified by you, into Christ crucified for you. From trampling under-foot the blood of the covenant, they pass over to take shelter, like the Hebrews in Egypt, under the besprinkled lintel, safe from the angel of death, and ready to march out free towards the promised land.

"Now, brethren, I wot that through ignorance ye did it": and so he opens up to the convicted a door of hope. The drift of the discourse changes to tenderness. So, when the frost has congealed the ground into rock, the sun and rain beating on it make it broken and contrite ground—a fitting soil for the seed of the kingdom.

Then in verse 18th the preacher carefully engrafts his gospel upon the Scriptures of the Old Testament: "But those things, which God before had showed by the mouth of all his prophets, that Christ should suffer, he hath so fulfilled." The New Testament grows upon the Old, like branches in the root and stem. If you undermine Moses, Christ, as far as you are concerned, will fall. Chaos will return. Darkness will again be on the face of the deep, and no Spirit of God will move upon the waters.

Those who eat out, by acid drops of criticism, the authority of the Old Testament, intending to hold fast by Christ and his gospel, are victims of a delusion. These blessed flowers and fruits cannot grow on a dead root.

When I was young, I took pleasure in ornamenting the front of my father's cottage with flowers. One particular effort was eminently successful, and attracted the notice of every visitor. By budding, I inserted several fine kinds of roses on one common root. For two or three years the flowers of various hues, flourishing simultaneously on one stem, became a spectacle to the rural neighborhood. But, alas! the original stem, not chosen as suitable for the purpose, but adopted as it happened to be there, was not a hardy species.

There came a night of severe frost. The plant that sustained my beautiful branches died, and all my beautiful branches died with it. Alas! for men in whose hearts the Divine authority of Moses and the prophets is withered by the frost of a hard, cold, earthly philosophy. Faith cannot grow upon Kant and Hegel, when God has departed from Moses and the Psalms!

That is not the first of Christ when the Babe is born in Bethlehem. Before the foundation of the world he took his people's place in the eternal counsel. As soon as men needed a Saviour he appeared for salvation in the promise spoken at the gate of Eden. Christ interpenetrates the Scriptures of the Old Testament through and through. The Plant of Renown that appeared in man's sight in the fulness of time, has a root that goes down to the beginning. If you cut away the word which holy men of old spake as they were moved by the Holy Ghost, you cut through that root, and your own hope withers in your breast.

The First Persecution
(Acts 4:1-4)

" And as they spake unto the people, the priests, and the captain of the temple, and the Sadducees, came upon them, being grieved that they taught the people, and preached through Jesus the resurrection from the dead. And they laid hands on them, and put them in hold unto the next day: for it was now eventide. Howbeit many of them which heard the word believed; and the number of the men was about five thousand."

THE persecution has begun. Peter's discourse was rudely interrupted. The preacher was speaking very winsome words (iii. 26) when his mouth was closed. He was making Jesus—that new name—sound sweetly in the people's ears. He was making offer of redemption to Israel in the clearest words and in the most tender spirit; but, "as they spake unto the people, the priests, and the captain of the temple, and the Sadducees, came upon them." So it has happened from the beginning hitherto: persecutors are blind. In all lands and all generations they endeavor to extinguish the light, because they love the darkness.

The first persecution of Christ's disciples exhibits, in its main characteristics, the type of all that have followed. A corrupt and cruel priesthood, in possession of office, gave the word, and led the way; and they were never at a loss to find some "captain of the temple"—some person who nominally held a civil office, but might be employed as a willing tool.

Whether the high priest at that time was personally a Sadducee is not certainly known; but it is evident, both here and in verse 17th, that the sect of the Sadducees supported the officials with all their influence. These men of the short creed were at that period either in or out of office. If they were in power, they wielded the machinery of the hierarchy to suppress the preaching; if they were not in power, so zealous were they in the work, that they entered into alliance with their rivals to make it quick and sure. Those who were at daggers drawn against each other, combined to put this doctrine and its preachers down. Herod and Pilate become friends in order that Christ may be again crucified in his members. Those who believe very little may become persecutors as well as those who believe very much. Sadducees and Pharisees combined against the gospel of Christ.

We obtain here a clear glimpse of the work which these apostles were engaged in when they were thus interrupted: "They taught the people, and preached through Jesus the rusurrection of the dead." The infant Church was charged with grand lessons, and she did not keep them secret. From the first the apostles made it their business to publish all they knew. The resurrection of the body, although not first revealed, was illustrated and confirmed by the gospel. After the Lord had risen, it became so much clearer and surer that it seemed to be a new revelation.

This doctrine they taught "in Jesus." Accustomed as we are now to assume the resurrection without reasoning, we cannot well conceive how great the fact of Christ's resurrection seemed when it was thrown upon the world. After the darkness that had covered the nations, and the comparative dimness of the light that shone in the Old Testament record, it seemed in this respect a new world for humankind when Jesus first raised Lazarus and then himself from the grave. When the apostles desired to teach the doctrine, they presented the fact.

These new teachers addressed their lessons to "the people." The gospel, wherever it is preserved pure, exhibits a broad and hearty sympathy with the mass of the community. This was given by its author as a mark of his mission: "to the poor the gospel is preached." It does not overlook "the people;" it does not oppress or hoodwink them; it does not keep them in ignorance in order to make them docile to authority: it teaches them. It appeals to their understanding while it wins their hearts. "The common people heard Him gladly;" and well they might then, well they may now. "If the Son make you free, ye shall be free indeed:" there is no other security for popular liberty. Wherever the Word of God is concealed, the people are oppressed.

The gospel is not an eclectic, aristocratic system. There is no respect of persons with God. His word addresses itself to the common people, to enlighten, emancipate, and purify them; but it never flatters their prejudices, or palliates their sins.

The apostles elevated the poor man by teaching him, in Jesus, his own immortality. They might well get the ears of the multitude when they had such a tale to tell. This doctrine raises the poor from the dust, and sets them among princes. These preachers were truly levellers; but they "levelled up." They made all equal, not by materially bringing down the high, but by spiritually elevating the lowest to the place and name of God's dear children.

It grieved this heterogeneous band of Pharisees and Sadducees to observe that these grand lessons were taught to the multitude. It is sad in any case to be in such a state of mind as to grieve over a neighbor's good. But there was a measure of conscientiousness in these primitive persecutors. They thought they were doing God service. It is this vein of truth and reality running through it that has imparted to persecution its perseverance and its power. The most fearful crimes are perpetrated at the instigation of conscience, when it is dark and depraved. Conscience is not a safe guide for man if it be not enlightened and purified by the Word and Spirit of God. Not conscience, but the Scriptures spiritually understood and conscientiously applied, are the rule of human life.

"They laid hands on them, and put them in hold." Probably the act of arrestment was performed by "the captain of the temple," on a hint from the high priest. Like their successors of Rome, they found it convenient to have a pliant magistrate at hand as their executor. The apostles did not on this occasion dispute the authority under which they suffered. These priests possessed jurisdiction, but they did not judge righteous judgment. They imprisoned the apostles in the meantime, and adjourned the case.

"Howbeit, many of them which heard the word believed." Man proposes, but God disposes. The more that the adversaries attempted to extinguish the light, the more brightly it blazed. "The number of the men was about five thousand." Probably at this time two thousand were added to the three thousand who were formerly admitted into the Church. The specific term "men" in this case may be used in the looser sense of persons; or it may be that no women were present.

Already the Christians were a large family. The corn of wheat had fallen into the ground and died, therefore it is not now left alone. A great harvest has quickly sprung. Christ exalted, sees here of the travail of his soul and is satisfied. The stream of the new-born has begun to pour into the house of many mansions. The stream has flowed from that day to this, without intermission, as waters that fail not, and yet there is room. There is joy in heaven, not in the angels, but in their presence—that is, in Him whom they all adore —over "one sinner that repenteth;" and therefore a flood of five thousand joys that day filled the Redeemer's heart on high. The Shepherd who misses one sheep that strays will not fail to mark each prodigal that returns. Each entrant adds another articulate delight to him who bought them with his blood. The joy set before him—the joy made up of the aggregate of all the saved, as the ocean is composed of water-drops— was very great; and for the sake of it he endured the cross and despised the shame.

These revival seasons, when they come in thousands, like doves to their windows, will be happy eras, marked as harvest-homes in heaven. The gate is open: many are pressing in. Come: whosoever will, let him come. There is pleasant company by the way, and an abundant entrance at the close. Reader, when He maketh up his many jewels, will you and I be there? "Now is the accepted time: now is the day of salvation."

Add to Your Faith, Courage
(Acts 4:7-13)

" And when they had set them in the midst, they asked, By what power, or by what name, have ye done this? Then Peter, filled with the Holy Ghost, said unto them, Ye rulers of the people, and elders of Israel, if we this day be examined of the good deed done to the impotent man, by what means he is made whole; be it known unto you all, and to all the people of Israel, that by the name of Jesus Christ of Nazareth, whom ye crucified, whom God raised from the dead, even by him doth this man stand here before you whole. This is the stone which was set at nought of you builders, which is become the head of the corner. Neither is there salvation in any other, for there is none other name under heaven given among men, whereby we must be saved. Now when they saw the boldness of Peter and John, and perceived that they were unlearned and ignorant men, they marvelled; and they took knowledge of them, that they had been with Jesus."

THE key-note of the last stanza is still sounding in our ears: the number of the men—saved men—was about five thousand. These more crowded parts in the way of life are memorable in earth and heaven. The expanse of time when it is over will, in the Saviour's eye, be like the expanse of heaven now in ours: the milky way, everywhere bright, exhibits at some places a glory that excelleth, where revolving worlds, like dust of gold, are more thickly strewn upon the blue. That day when the first stroke of persecution fell on the first preachers will be a bright day in the annals of the kingdom. The page allotted to it in the sealed book will be deeply laden. In the family register it is the birthday of many sons.

" On the morrow " the court sat, and the panels were called to the bar. The Sanhedrim seems at that time to have been packed by the relatives and partisans of the high priest. The accused had nothing to expect from their judges; but they trusted in God, and possessed their souls in patience. Referring to the cure of the cripple, the court demanded of the apostle in what kind of power and in what kind of name they had effected that miracle of healing. The Jewish leaders, during the life and ministry of Jesus, in order to explain his miracles, broached the theory that by aid of the devil he cast the devils out. It is probably an idea of this kind that suggests the question of the court.

A third time Peter speaks, and a third time bears witness for Christ with great fulness and boldness. These successive witness-bearings of Peter are all framed on one model, all strike the same note. In every one there is—1st, A Scriptural argument, more or less full, identifying Jesus with the Messiah of the prophets; 2nd, A plain, piercing charge, laying the guilt of crucifying Christ to the door of his audience and judges; and, 3rd, A tender and pressing offer of mercy, through the blood of Christ, to his murderers.

Like his three confessions, Peter's three denials also were all conceived in the same strain. With circumstantial differences, they were substantially the same: "I know not the man; I know him not; I know not what thou sayest."

How like each other, too, were the Lord's three questions addressed to Peter in order to complete his restoration? Thrice the question pierced the repenting disciple's ear, "Simon, son of Jonas, lovest thou me?" and thrice the answer echoed from the repenting disciple's burning heart, "Lord, thou knowest that I love thee." By the same spirit this apostle, strong now by faith, emits the threefold confession of his Lord.

These were not the only occasions on which Peter bore testimony to Christ in the beginning of the gospel. Both he and his fellow-laborers did much that has not been recorded; but I think it is of the Lord that at the outset of his public ministry three successive confessions of Peter's faith have been recorded in full. He had fallen more than any of the faithful eleven; and correspondingly fuller evidence is given that he had not fallen away—that through the intercession of the Lord his backsliding had been completely healed.

After this period, although Peter appears as a performer of miracles, an exhorter of believing Jews, and a messenger to a Gentile family, he does not come forward again in this history as a public preacher. He gives place first to Stephen, next to Philip, and ultimately to Paul and his missionary associates.

The most remarkable feature in the three successive examples of Peter's preaching is the indictment, charged directly home upon the consciences of his hearers, that they were the crucifiers of Christ (Acts ii. 23; iii. 14, 15; iv. 10). He found that this sharp method was successful the first time, and therefore repeated it. It was thus that Nelson's victories were won. When the enemy's ships were extended in a line before him, he formed his into a column, pierced their line with its point, and fought them from the other side. Finding this method successful, he always followed it.

The boldness of Peter as a witness here is amply accounted for by the intimation that he was "full of the Holy Ghost." The Master had fulfilled his promise, and the servant was thereby enabled to execute his task. Cause and effect are as clearly connected in this experience as in the processes of Nature. Wanting the Spirit, Peter was not able to bear witness for the Lord in the presence of a serving-maid; with the Spirit, Peter held his judges fascinated by the glance of his eye, while he pierced them with his word. This apostle experienced the truth of Paul's paradox on both its sides: "When I am weak, then am I strong;" and when I am strong, then I am weak.

Peter interprets the prophecy about the Stone rejected by the builders as Jesus had interpreted it in his hearing (Matt. xxi.). He applied it directly to the Messiah whom the Jewish priests had slain; and added, "Neither is there salvation in any other." There has been at various periods much foolish disputation on the question whether there be any salvation beyond the pale of the Pope's Church. Away with all these profane babblings! It is not out of this Church or out of that; it is, Out of Christ there is no salvation. This is the only limit that God has set: it is blasphemous as well as foolish to suggest any other.

Behold the arraigned and accused man! He ar-

raigns and accuses his judges—convicts his judges.
Nay, more, he stands at their bar and offers them
mercy; he proclaims to them the free pardon of their
sin through the blood of Jesus whom they crucified;
he warns them with tenderness and calmness which
must have struck terror into their hearts, that unless they
accept mercy by this channel, no mercy will ever reach
them. This Name, this manifestation of God, is given
among men. It comes from heaven to earth. It comes
to save, not to destroy; but it will not save those who
reject it. By this Name we must be saved, or perish.

The judges were amazed at the boldness of Peter
and John. But as they wondered, some one recognized the two men as having been seen in company
with Jesus; and this accounted for their courage. Companionship with Jesus makes a hero, the enemy being
judge. But is there any need or room for heroism in
our plain, prosaic days? Persecution for conscience'
sake has, indeed, in its grosser forms long ceased in
our country. We have no opportunity of displaying
precisely that form of courage which the Sanhedrim
observed in Peter and John. But heroism is needed
yet in the world. A Christian needs the boldness
which is attained only through companionship with
Jesus.

Many fall miserably in life's battle for lack of courage—fall before ignoble foes. It were less discredit to
show the white feather in presence of the prison and
the scaffold; but our youth strike their colors to meaner terrors. And yet, let me do justice to men of my
own generation. The adversaries are, indeed, softer
individually, but they are mightier in the mass. The
sword, indeed, does not penetrate the flesh; the fire
does not wrap itself round the living body; but the
world's course, like a river composed of many soft
drops, rolls downward in a vast volume, and carries
even strong swimmers away. When acts are weighed
in the balance of the upper sanctuary, it may possibly
appear that as much boldness is needed to stand in
our day, and withstand, all our days, the constantly-
sucking stream of vanity and earthliness, as it required
at the beginning of the gospel to be faithful unto death
against principalities and powers. But the conclusion

of the whole matter is, that near the Lord—consciously enjoying his favor and leaning on his love—near the Lord we shall be able to resist the greatest of our enemies; far from him, we shall fall before the least.

Every Creature After its Kind
(Acts 4:23)

" And being let go, they went to their own company, and reported all that the chief priests and elders had said unto them."

A SECRET, mysterious, reciprocal attraction drew Peter and John together, although the two men were by no means similar in character. They were companions in their visit to the empty sepulchre, and companions in the dangerous duty of preaching Christ in Jerusalem immediately after the Pentecost. Perhaps the difference, or even the contrast between them in natural disposition, rendered them more suitable to each other for mutual help. As a man's strength and a woman's gentleness bind two into one in married life, the robust impetuous Peter clung to the calm, self-possessed tenderness of John; and John, in his weakness, was fain to lean on Peter's strength.

This noble pair of brothers, when their own love was warm, and the hatred of their enemies sharp, stood side by side in the courts of the temple and in the streets of the city, charging home upon the Jewish rulers and people with the terrible indictment, " Ye have crucified the Lord;" ready, whenever the sword of the Spirit should pierce the conscience of the hearers, to run in and apply for healing the blood of atonement.

Grieved that these two witnesses should teach the people, through the risen Jesus, the resurrection of the dead, the Sanhedrim had arrested Peter and John at the close of their day's labor, and shut them in prison for the night.

How the two prisoners spent the night we are not informed. Perhaps they sang praises, like Paul and Silas at a later date; or perhaps they were not yet so far advanced. It may be they could not do more than secretly cast their burden on the Lord, without being able as yet to glory in tribulation.

Next day the Council called the prisoners and examined them. Having heard from Peter more of plain truth than was pleasant to their taste, they ordered the panels to be removed from the bar, and consulted privately regarding the case.

The aim of the judges was not to arrive at the truth, but to crush the witnesses. There was not much debate, and their resolution was quickly taken. They recalled the prisoners, and straitly threatened them that they should speak thenceforth to no man in the name of Jesus. Lame and impotent conclusion! They omitted the main element from their calculation. They knew not the fire that the love of Christ had kindled in the hearts of those two men.

Suppose that some savages have seen a cannon charged and discharged. Suppose that when they saw it charged a second time, dreading the consequences, they should gather stones and clay, and therewith ram the cannon full to the muzzle, by way of shutting in the shot, and securing the safety of the neighborhood. They know not the power of gunpowder when it is touched by a spark. This is the sort of blunder into which the Sanhedrim fell. They thought they could stifle the testimony of the apostles by ramming a threat of punishment down their throats. They knew not the power of faith in Christ, when it is kindled by a spark from heaven.

Peter and John did not deceive their judges. With beautiful simplicity and sublime courage they answered, "Whether it be right in the sight of God to hearken unto you more than unto God, judge ye." These Jewish rulers have committed a blunder. They have summoned the sea into their presence, and proclaimed to it, Hitherto shalt thou come, but no further!

"We cannot but speak the things which we have seen and heard." It is by no means a universal rule that every man is bound to proclaim all that he has seen and heard. Many things that we see and hear it is both our inclination and our duty to conceal. It is the peculiar nature of the message which these men have received that lays an obligation on them to make it known. The condition on which any one receives mercy in the covenant is that he should hasten to publish the glad tidings abroad. When a polished gem receives a sunbeam on its surface, it is under a natural necessity of spreading out the light in all directions; and so a human soul that receives the light of life from the face of Jesus is under law to let that light shine before men: "Freely ye have received, freely give."

After another interdict against preaching Christ, the prisoners were dismissed from the bar. It is intimated that the Court would willingly have adopted a severer measure, but were restrained by a fear of the people. This is an illustrious specimen of special providence. When God has given out his decree, "Touch not mine anointed, and do my prophets no harm," he has suitable instruments always at hand to execute his will. The people, as such, would be a broken reed for any persecuted witness to lean upon. At the next turn of the tide it might become necessary that a military chief should rescue an apostle from a mob that were ready to tear him limb from limb. This is the doing of the Lord. The shields of the earth are his: now with one and now with another he covers his servants' heads in the day of battle.

Accordingly, the two apostles were dismissed; "and being let go, they went to their own company." Behold a particular fact occurring under the operation of a general law. Like draws to like. When an evil deed was about to be done, the persecutors assembled and laid their heads together: when the Christian mission was about to issue from Jerusalem upon the world, the disciples of Christ congregated in an upper room for prayer. Birds of a feather flock together; and if one bird has been for a time imprisoned—separated from its companions—it is beautiful to see, when the cage is at length opened, how straight and quick is its course through the air to the place where it left its mates and expects to find them again. On this principle proceeds the pigeon-telegraph, which has been long known in the world, but never attained the magnitude of a great national institute till the necessities of the siege forced it to the front in Paris.

The instincts of animals are like the laws of inanimate matter—perfect in their kind. When one lamb is caught and kept for a time separate from the fold, it submits only to superior force. As soon as it regains liberty, it bounds across the plain, and never halts till, with beating heart and panting breath, it has pressed into the midst of the flock again.

With equal exactness in an opposite direction, the sow that was washed returns to wallow with her fellows in the mire. Thus suddenly and surely did a worldling, who had for a time been arrested by the discourses of Jesus, leap back into his element of filthy lucre. As soon as a pause in the sermon let him go, he went to his own. When the Lord had finished one of his lessons in the midst of a promiscuous audience, one of the company cried out, "Master, speak to my brother, that he divide the inheritance with me." The word of Him who spake as never man spake had fascinated even this man, and for a moment separated him from his chosen company and conversation. But the word that arrests attention does not always renew the heart. As soon as the voice of the preacher relaxed, and let go the momentarily entranced listener, he bounded back into his element. He rushed after his covetousness, as water flows down when some interrupting barrier has been removed.

An example of the opposite tendency in a renewed heart is exhibited in the experience of the possessed man whom the Lord delivered at Gadara. Satan had bound him soul and body, and separated him from all good; but when the chain was broken by the Redeemer's word, the liberated man ran to his deliverer, and sat at his feet, clothed and in his right mind. Being let go, he too went to his own—to his own Saviour and his own fellow-disciples. It is good when the spring in the heart is sound, and a Christian, by a strong instinct of the new nature, as soon as he is freed from alien entanglements, bounds back into congenial company and congenial employment.

It is sometimes remarked, that when persons who at home maintained a Christian profession, have gone abroad—gone to a distant colony where ordinances were wanting, or to a Papal country where ordinances were superstitious,—they have left their religion behind them, and abandoned themselves to godless pleasures or godless gains. In these cases, as the result proves, the religion was an external thing from the first. It was of the nature of a bondage. At home the cords of the general Christian profession of the country were sufficiently strong to keep the man away from the employments and company that he secretly loved; but when these cords were broken by the simple fact of his removal from home, he was a free man, and like other creatures, animate and inanimate, when he was let go he went unto his own. Thus worthless, in the last resource, is the Christianity which acts as a restraint to prevent a man from following his own inclinations: beyond expression precious is the faith in Jesus which takes the inclinations and changes them so that they instinctively seek the pure. This false religion of bonds is the direct contrary of the true. Christ's work is a redemption; Christ is a Redeemer. He sets the captive free. "If the Son make you free, ye shall be free indeed." This glorious grace turns upside down the world which blindly counts religion so much restraint, to which some men prudently submit, with a view to a larger return in a future life. The man who only submits to the restraints of religion, runs wild in all evil when these restraints are removed. "Create in me a clean heart, O God." "Thy people shall be willing in the day of thy power." "I will run in the way of thy commandments, when thou hast enlarged my heart."

A young man has been accustomed from childhood to the order and sobriety of a Christian household. As the lines of restraint were laid on him while he was an infant, and have never been removed throughout his youth, he is not very vividly conscious that they are only external bands that confine him within the course of a well-favored morality. The time arrives at last when he must leave his father's roof and be lost to view in a great metropolis, like a drop of rain when it falls into the lake. Now is the moment of danger to that youth; now, if ever, for him is the hour and the power of darkness. He feels himself alone as if he were in the heart of an American forest. If his religion has been only a

cord round his neck, like the bit and bridle with which
a horse is held, he is now free from his religion.   If his
religion is a thing that can let him go, he will depart to
his own: he will seek the company and occupation of
the careless, it may be of the profane.

Cords of this sort were fastened on Judas, and as
long as they remained they confined his evil practices
within very narrow limits; but when at last he was let
go, what a fearfully sudden leap he made to his own
—his own course, his own company, and his own place.

Demas was brought and kept for a time under the
mighty influence of Paul.   But the hold which even
such a natural leader took, could not always be maintained.   It gave way one day, and to the present world,
his own chosen portion, gravitated Demas, as a stone
sinks to the earth when you let it go in the air.   The love
of Paul could not hold him—Paul was not crucified for
him.   The love of God shown to men in the gift of his
Son, a bond soft and silent, but omnipotent, like that
which keeps the planets in their places, when once it
is folded round you, cannot be wrenched away.

But we may find many bright examples of the same
principle on the opposite side.   The new creature acts
after its kind, as well as the old; when the chains of
bondage are broken, the captive returns to his Father's
house.

A youth who has already gotten a new heart and
enjoys a blessed hope, has been sent as an apprentice
into a great engineering establishment, where several
hundred men are employed.   His lot is cast in a corner
of the huge workshop occupied by a group that have
grown old and bold in profanity and licentiousness.
In the first hour they discover that a saint is among
them, and with a malignity altogether devilish, they
gloat in anticipation over their prey.   The ribaldry and
blasphemy are increased: they do everything that ingenuity can suggest to rub off the youth's religion, and
make him such as one of themselves.   If his religion
had been a conventional gilding on the surface, it would
have been rubbed off in the first week; but as it was
all steel, the more roughly it was rubbed the brighter
it grew.

The first day wore on towards evening: at six o'clock

the bell, in a small tower over the gateway, was rung,
and every man threw aside his tools and hastened away.
The apprentice engineer, articled by an eternal covenant to Christ his Saviour, and thereafter indentured
to a master engine-maker, was at length let go. Let
go, he went to his own:—to the fields, the flowers, the
birds, with which he had been wont to keep company
at home; then to his food, which he enjoyed with the
fresh relish of a laborer, and the fresher relish of a child
of God constantly getting daily bread from a Father's
hand; then to the Bible, his own book, the gift of God
to him; then to his own Saviour, in faith's confiding
prayer. A whole legion of devils, or wicked men, will
not overcome this youth. The anchor of his soul is
sure and steadfast within the veil. God will shield
him at first, so that the fiery darts shall not hurt him,
and after a little put a sword in his hand—the Sword
of the Spirit, which is the Word of God; and this weapon he will wield aggressively, so as to subdue some
of these enemies, and lead them captive unto Christ.

Yet another lesson. The grave has a greedy appetite, and a firm grasp. It takes many, and keeps
what it gets. Deep in the earth, and deeper in the
sea, lie the bodies of those who have been redeemed
by the blood of Christ. A strange place for Christ's
members to be in! But there they shall not always
be. They must one day be let go; and when let go;
they will return to their own—their own Redeemer,
and their own rest.

An atom of atmospheric air may have been imprisoned
in some strong vessel at the bottom of the sea for ages.
After thousands of years, that vessel at last gives way
and breaks up. The atom of air, although it has been
long an exile, has not forgotten its home, and will not
miss its way. Whenever it is released, it rises in a
sheer straight line through the thick heavy waters—
rises a little air-bell, nor halts in its course, until,
emerging from the sea with a gentle joyful bursting
sound, it reaches its own,—the heaven, the home
which it left many ages before.

Be of good cheer, disciples of the Lord Jesus. Ye
are of more value than many atoms of air. Doth God
in nature care for the birds of the air and the flowers

of the field, and the elements of matter; and how much more shall he clothe and house you, O ye of little faith. The grave must relax its grasp. Its stubborn nature has been already tamed into obedience. The Lord has risen, and become the first-fruits of them that slept. The way by which he went stands open, and through it all his members will return to him. Earth and sea must give up their dead, and the released prisoners will unerringly find their way home. According to the power and the constancy of Nature, which is the power and constancy of God, like will draw to like at last,—the living to the living, the living saved to the Living Saviour.

The Prayer of the Primitive Church
(Acts 4:24-29)

" And when they heard that, they lifted up their voice to God with one accord, and said, Lord, thou art God, which hast made heaven, and earth, and the sea, and all that in them is: who by the mouth of thy servant David hast said, Why did the heathen rage, and the people imagine vain things ? The kings of the earth stood up, and the rulers were gathered together against the Lord, and against his Christ. For of a truth against thy holy child Jesus, whom thou hast anointed; both Herod, and Pontius Pilate, with the Gentiles, and the people of Israel, were gathered together, for to do whatsoever thy hand and thy counsel determined before to be done. And now, Lord, behold their threatenings: and grant unto thy servants, that with all boldness they may speak thy word."

PETER and John, providentially delivered from the hands of the persecutors, plunged into a meeting of their fellow-disciples, and forthwith reported all that had happened. The company as soon as they heard of the danger that had threatened, and the deliverance that had been wrought, forthwith "lifted up their voice to God" and prayed. They were neither cast down nor uplifted. They did not propose to try this method or that method of improving their circumstances. They proposed no plan. They lacked wisdom and strength, and in their need applied to God by prayer.

Prayer is not the origin of a movement. It is the result of one that preceded. You stand on the margin of a Highland lake, and hear a mysterious but distinctly articulate sound coming from the dead wall of a gray, ruined castle that stands on a miniature island not far from the shore. The sound, however, was not generated in that ruin. It could not generate a voice. The words of a living man on the shore, wafted over the still water, struck the old silent keep, and its wall gave back the echo. If that living voice had not struck the wall, the wall would have remained dumb.

Prayer—man's cry to God—is the second of a series of vibrations. The voice of prayer, on earth, is an echo awakened in ruined, dumb humanity, by God's sweet promise coming down from heaven. In general, prayer is the echo of a promise; in particular, we may discover the specific promise to which this prayer replies (Isa. xl. 26, 27).

What a sublime position these suppliants occupy! They are admitted into the Divine counsel. "The secret of the Lord is with them that fear him." They knew that all these events were foreseen, and would be overruled for good. They were able to mark in the Scriptures the precise spot they had reached in the scheme of Providence, as a shipmaster marks his latitude on his chart. In the quiet confidence of faith they realize and confess that the combination of princes and peoples —of Jews and Gentiles—to put to death the holy child Jesus, only accomplished the gracious purpose of God. These principalities and powers of the world imagined that they were quenching the kingdom of Christ in its infancy; whereas they were the unconscious instruments of laying its foundations deep, and spreading its influence through the world.

Now, in verse 29th, comes the most important of all their requests. Petitions sent to Parliament are sometimes of considerable length. There may be a narrative of facts, long and intricate; there may be the citation of precedents; there may be arguments and pleas; but it is common to pass over all these when the document is presented, and read only what is denominated "the prayer of the petition"—that is, the clause at the end which declares articulately what the petitioners want—what they wish to be done for them, or given to them. Verse 29th contains the prayer of the petition. It expresses what the petitioners desire —what they would be at, if they had their will.

It is most interesting and instructive to mark what they really crave. Not a word of vengeance upon their enemies. In the recital they have clearly described the cruel injustice of their adversaries; but they do not follow up that recital by a request for punishment. Neither do they plead for immunity from danger for themselves. There is a recital of their danger; but not a petition for safety. The request is, not that they may be shielded from persecution, but that they may have grace to be faithful under it. "Grant unto thy servants, that with all boldness they may speak thy word."

It is a beautiful example of distrust of themselves and confidence in God combined. They feared lest the danger which threatened their persons should intimidate them in their work. Their anxiety was lest their natural shrinking from suffering should tempt them to conceal the pungent parts of their testimony in order to shield themselves from persecution. They were jealous over themselves with a godly jealousy. They were conscious that nature within them shrank instinctively from pain and shame. They knew that to proclaim the whole counsel of God would gall the men who had the power of life and death in their hands. They feared, accordingly, lest they should be tempted to make the gospel more pleasant for the sake of peace.

The application of this Scriptural example to our own circumstances is attended with some difficulty; and yet it may be made with certainty and success. It is difficult to clear our way here, but not impossible.

The circumstances of our place and time seem to be so diverse from those of the first preachers, that no direct lesson from their experience can be transferred to ours. No persecutor dare raise a hand against a minister here and now, to prevent him from declaring the Gospel in all its fullness. We are free: and yet the pressure which tempts to timid unfaithfulness is only removed from one side and applied to another. The fear of man bringeth a snare; and ever since Peter said, "I know not the man," the feet of even true witnesses have, in all generations, been often entangled miserably in its toils. But snares are not all of one shape or of one material—either the bodily snares of the fowler, or the snares set for the spirit by the wiles of the wicked one. They may be of iron or of silk. They may be varied indefinitely in matter, form, and position, according to the character of the victim, and the opportunities of the ensnarer. A force that is diffused and soft, may exercise a greater pressure than one that is sharp and hard, as the atmosphere over a man's body lies heavier on him than any other burden he ever bore.

To threaten a witness for Christ with the prison or the scaffold is one way of turning him aside from faithfulness; to set before him the favor of a polished but worldly circle is another. You may, if you please, pronounce that the man who should weakly yield to these soft seducements is a far less noble specimen of humanity than those men who quailed before a scaffold, and held their peace to save their lives; although, even here, something might be said on the other side. But the distinction is of no practical importance. If the seductions of modern society do, in point of fact, deflect the compass of the witness as far aside as the ancient persecutions, the difference in the character of the instrument makes nothing in the result.

If two ships are lost at sea by the false pointing of their compasses, it will make no difference either as to the loss of property or the loss of life, that the compass of the one ship was prevented from pointing truly by a nail that fastened it to the deck, and the compass of the other ship secretly drawn aside by a mass of iron concealed in the hold. In both cases, and in both alike, the compass failed to declare the truth, and that faithlessness caused the loss of the ships. Thus an ancient minister of the gospel who held back the truth for fear of the dungeon, and a modern minister who softens and disguises the truth because a gay, worldly, critical congregation listen to the Word, must stand side by side, repenting and pleading for the pardon of their unfaithfulness. On the other hand, an ancient minister who proclaimed the whole truth with a halter round his neck, and a modern minister who, fearing God and having no other fear, declares the whole counsel of God to every class and every character, will stand together at the great account to hear the approving sentence,

"Well done, good and faithful servants: enter ye into the joy of your Lord."

The request is simple, specific, and full: "Grant unto thy servants that with all boldness they may speak thy word."

1. That they may *speak*, and not be dumb. Speech is a chief gift of God, a chief prerogative of man. Where there is a living spring, it finds or makes a channel through which it may flow; and where there is a living soul, it finds or makes an avenue of egress. A soul cannot be imprisoned in a body of flesh, as a spring cannot be imprisoned among the mountains. Either life, according to its nature, must have a means of outflow. On the other hand, where there is no spring, no channel is needed, and none is found. Among living creatures, accordingly, where there is not a soul, there is not speech; but in that one creature who was made in the image of God—into whom God breathed a living soul—there is speech, the open channel for its forthgoing. Reverence human speech. It is the mark of a being who has been made, and may be re-made, a child of God. Reverence human speech, for it is a divinely formed capacity for a divinely prescribed use. Dread false speech, proud speech, impure speech, profane speech,—for these are the bright weapons with which the King has accoutred us wielded against the King. High treason !

"That they may speak;" for why should they be silent who have tasted that the Lord is gracious ? Let them tell to all who are willing to listen what the Lord hath done for their souls. Let the compressed love which glows in renewed hearts find utterance in spoken praise. Bless the Lord, O my soul, and forget not all his benefits !

In another aspect it behoves all who hear to speak. Silence is sin, if your cry might prevent a neighbor from stumbling over a precipice. Silence is sin, if neighbors are treading the broad path that leadeth to destruction, and your word might lead their steps into the way of life. Silence is sin, if a believing brother is sliding back, while your loving reproof might become to him a healing balm. Silence is sin, if a believing brother is oppressed with doubts and fears, while your lips might pour the consolations of God into his weary heart.

The prayer points mainly to a public ministry, and yet nothing is said about sermons—nothing said even about preaching: "Grant unto thy servants that they may speak." Whether the address be long or short, whether the audience be many or few, whether the style be eloquent or stammering, the pith and marrow of the whole matter is, that one man, hoping in Christ and loving his neighbor, speaks to that neighbor about Christ's redeeming love. All preaching may be reduced to this. Out of this, as the germ, all true preaching springs. If its whole mass were by some chemical process reduced to its elements, this would be found the essential residuum remaining indestructible after all ornaments and accessories had been melted away. I suppose Philip preached pretty fully to the anxious Ethiopian in the desert; but the Spirit in the Word performs that chemical analysis which we have imagined, and retains only that ultimate and indestructible essence of the discourse, which is small in bulk and easy of transmission—Philip "*preached unto him Jesus.*"

2. The prayer of these primitive Christians is "that they may speak *thy word.*" The word of God supplies alike the authority and the material of preaching. The seed is the word: the sower need not scatter any other in his field. This alone is vital—this alone will grow.

3. Their ambition is to speak the word of God "*with boldness.*" Let no man assume too readily that he has attained this qualification of a witness. In this department, all is not gold that glitters. Beware of counterfeits in these payments, for a considerable quantity of base coin is in circulation. To rasp like a file on other people's tender points, because you have no tender points of your own, is not the boldness for which these disciples prayed. In that species of courage some of the inferior creatures greatly excel us.

An essential constituent of courage is tenderness. In feudal times, when military valor held the supreme place in universal opinion, the prevailing conception, although disfigured by some foolish and grotesque features, contained a basis of truth. Battle courage was held to be only one half of a knightly bearing; the other half consisted of a tenderness, in some cases almost feminine. Tenderness is as essential to spiritual as to secular heroism. The boldness of speech which costs the speaker nothing is neither beautiful in itself nor successful in its object. It is like a stroke on hollow wood; instead of penetrating the beam, it rebounds in the face of the operator.

Paul was a bold man, but he was not an unfeeling one. It was a bold word that he addressed to certain professors at Philippi, and he spoke it once and again—"Ye are enemies of the cross of Christ;" but he wept as he spoke. These tears did more to make a way for the reproving word into the joints and marrow of the culprits than all the sharpness of the reproof itself. Observe a mechanic boring through a bar of iron. He has a properly-formed instrument of steel. This he turns quickly round, under a strong pressure, upon the bar which he desires to perforate. But this is not enough. If only on the hard beam of iron a harder point of steel were pressed and turned, they would set each other on fire. But the skilful operator quietly drops oil on the point of contact, while he plies his task. This anointing keeps the instrument from heating, and carries it through. These tears of Paul served the same purpose for the Philippian backsliders that the mechanic's oil-drops served for the iron beam. Human tenderness baptized by the Spirit poured on the point of contact, when the sharp sword of the Word is pressed against a brother's heart, prevents the pressure from begetting a burning heat, and carries the weapon home.

To my mind there is hardly a more melancholy spectacle in this world than that of a man, orthodox in faith but coarse in the natural grain, who rattles out his censures on all and sundry who differ from himself without an effort and without a pang; looking down, meanwhile, with contempt on men of greater modesty as unfaithful to the truth. The stream of words that condemns a neighbor, without scalding the speaker's own skin as it flows, is like the clack of a windmill set up to frighten birds—as hard and as wearisome, and as powerless. The greater the boldness any man ventures to exercise, the greater tenderness he needs to attain. The boldness which those primitive confessors asked and obtained was saturated with a sanctified human tenderness; and this was the secret of their power.

4. In their eagerness for effective work, they desire to speak with *all* boldness. Even courage may be partial and one-sided. This virtue vanishes whenever it begins to show respect of persons. That is not true courage which is severe to the poor but quails before the rich. As the water of a reservoir will be completely lost unless the circle of its lip be kept whole on all sides, all the dignity and power of boldness vanishes when it fails on one point.

Perhaps the weakest point of all the circle for every man is himself. If courage is needed to speak the truth to a neighbor, it is still more needed in dealing with ourselves. A surgeon needs firmness. If he faint at the sight of blood, he has mistaken his profession. He needs a stout heart when he is called to operate on other men; but he is much more liable to flinch if he need to operate upon himself. Alas ! we lack courage to press the sword of the Spirit home to the root of the ailment when it is seated in our own souls. Strike, and spare not for the patient's crying. This old prayer is a word in season still: grant unto thy servants boldness. Nerve this arm to strike this blow.

Power to be Witnesses
(Acts 4:31-35)

" And when they had prayed, the place was shaken where they were assembled together; and they were all filled with the Holy Ghost, and they spake the word of God with boldness. And the multitude of them that believed were of one heart and of one soul: neither said any of them that ought of the things which he possessed was his own; but they had all things common. And with great power gave the apostles witness of the resurrection of the Lord Jesus: and great grace was upon them all. Neither was there any among them that lacked: for as many as were possessors of lands or houses sold them, and brought the prices of the things that were sold, and laid them down at the apostle's feet: and distribution was made unto every man according as he had need."

THESE feeble Christians in the upper room moved the Hand that moves the world. The place was shaken,

but not the people. The ground trembled, but
they had found another resting-place. God is our
refuge.

"When they had prayed, the place was shaken."
It is after, and in answer to the prayers of his people,
that the Lord arises to shake the earth. Quick and
strong vibrations have of late been felt in the political
sphere. Some mighty thrones have fallen under the
shock, especially the anomalous throne of Peter's pretended successor at Rome. The supports of the Pope's
temporal power in Austria and France were successively undermined, and the kingdom that leant on
them has accordingly fallen. Prayers have long been
ascending to the Lord of hosts for the downfall of that
great tyranny, and at last the sword that has often
been stained with the blood of saints has been wrenched
from the usurper's hand.

The shaking of the ground after the prayer of this
persecuted company was a sign that their prayer had
been heard. They had expressly acknowledged God
as the maker of heaven and earth. In answer to this
portion of their prayer, he gives them a token that almighty power is at hand for their protection. The
commotions of our day are encouraging rather than
otherwise to the disciples of Christ: "He that believeth shall not make haste." Hollow hypocrisies are
shaken down, in order that the things that cannot be
shaken may remain erect (Heb. xii. 27).

But besides this symbol of power, a more specific
answer was given to their request; for "they were all
filled with the Holy Ghost, and they spake the word
with boldness." They did not fear their enemies, but
they distrusted themselves. They dreaded not danger, but they dreaded lest danger should shake them
from their steadfastness. Now they have obtained
what they asked, and they are at ease—at ease as is
the magnet of the compass on board ship in a surging
sea—steady when all else is moving—fixed because
loose—fixed to its pole in the distant heavens, and all
its holds slackened from below. The steadiest thing
on a shaking world is a disciple whose life is hid with
Christ in God, and whose heart is loosened from its
cleaving to the dust. His weight hangs on heaven,

and the shaking of the earth under his feet does not imperil his position, or disturb his repose.

The apostles stood forth as leaders. They were endued with great power; and yet all that was required of them was to be witnesses of a fact. Their power was exerted in giving "witness of the resurrection of the Lord Jesus." Christ had specially promised them power to be his witnesses, and now that promise was fulfilled. Peter has recovered from his weakness now. It is no more "I know not the man."

The main characteristic of their witnessing was not great eloquence, or great learning, but great power. When you travel by night through a mining district, you see mighty volumes of flame throbbing fitfully from the mouth of lofty furnaces, and illuminating for miles around the nocturnal sky. This phenomenon is the ordinary accompaniment of power, but it is not the power. You must approach the bottom of the furnace, and examine whether miniature streams of white hot lava are coursing forth in prepared channels along the smoking ground. This—this is power. The heat in the heart of the furnace is melting the ore, and the metal, separated from its dross, is flowing out pure. The great flickering flame is not by itself the proof of power. In like manner there is often a blaze issuing from a really effective ministry of the gospel, which attracts the gaze of a miscellaneous multitude; but there is also sometimes such flame flung up against the clouds where there is no melting heat below. We should not despise the conspicuous and dazzling accompaniments, for they may be the sparks that naturally and necessarily rise from a melting heat; but neither should we trust in them, for they may be the pithless flash from blazing straw. God grant the great power in secret, with or without the visible demonstration.

The power seems to have been a special gift bestowed upon the apostles, but a suitable portion was imparted also to the whole company,—"great grace was upon them all." A specific example of the grace displayed by the disciples is immediately recorded—the grace of liberality and brotherly love. This is a great grace, and, like other great things, rare.

They abandoned themselves at that time to a ruling passion. They did out-of-the-way things; they were singular people. If they turned the world upside down, they had themselves first of all undergone the same change. Instead of the native and habitual greed of the old man, gravitating to self as matter gravitates to the ground, there appeared the self-sacrificing love of the new man—the man created anew in Christ Jesus for the very purpose of producing fruits like these. In this new appetite the new man takes after Christ. Every creature after his kind, and the new creature too. It is good to be singular in the world, when the singularity consists in greater conformity to the Saviour's will and way. Not singularity for its own sake—that is a contemptible thing; but the courage to obey the law of Christ, although obedience should make you singular.

The disciples now experienced the truth of the Master's prediction,—"In the world ye shall have tribulation." No promise had been given of exemption from danger. The world was not so changed that the disciples should not need defence; but they were so changed that they possessed within their own souls a complete defence against the world's assault. Their protection consisted of these two woven into one—namely, courage to bear witness of Christ, and brotherly love among themselves. Towards those who were without, unflinching courage; towards those who were within, open-handed charity. The world had cause to say two things with equal emphasis regarding them —*first*, behold how these Christians defy us; and, *second*, behold how these Christians love each other.

Alas for the Church in our day! Surely we are weak on the two points where they were strong—courage to bear witness for Christ, and fervent charity among ourselves. The atmosphere of the society in which Christians live seems to have grown thicker in these last days. It is like a frozen sea, in which all things grow hard and cold. The breath of life seems to freeze. A melting is needed—the baptism of fire.

A Son of Consolation
(Acts 4:36,37)

" And Joses, who by the apostles was surnamed Barnabas, (which is, being interpreted, The son of consolation,) a Levite, and of the country of Cyprus, having land, sold it, and brought the money, and laid it at the apostles' feet."

ANOTHER outburst of generous love occurred in the form of selling their property and distributing the proceeds. This law and its limitation were noticed in connection with an earlier example. But now, besides the general intimation, two specific examples are submitted —a true and a false. Barnabas and Ananias are photographed in the Word, that all generations may learn, by specimen as well as by description, the difference between genuine and counterfeit charity.

The name of this good man was Joses, and the name Barnabas, by which he is now universally known, was attached to him by the apostles, in order to express the character which he displayed. This name was given to indicate a nature. They called him the Son of Consolation because he was a succorer of many, and a comforter of the downcast.

He was a Levite, and yet he possessed land. This is contrary to the old economical law in Israel; but probably at that period, on account of frequent and great political changes, it was found impossible to maintain the ancient constitution in its integrity.

Barnabas is indeed a good name when you learn what it means. Alas! how rife is its opposite—the Son of Complaint—of gloom. To such a man everything appears in its darkest colors. He looks at the earth and the sky through a yellow glass. He sees no green on the earth, and in the heavens no blue. It is not so easy to remove the jaundiced glasses from the eyes of the mind as to take away the colored medium which impeded your enjoyment of the landscape. Functional derangements of the body through disease sometimes also supervene to tinge still further the atmosphere through which the spirit looks.

Barnabas, we may be well assured, did not grudge

his gifts. He was not grieved when a call for another contribution came. He was a great giver, and yet he was a cheerful giver. The Lord loved Barnabas.

I conclude that Barnabas had much comfort himself, for he had much to bestow on others. If we see streams flowing from the well's brim to refresh the neighborhood, we may be assured that the well itself is full.

The great contributions which he made did not embitter his spirit. The flow of bounty from that man's hand acted as the flow of water from the drain on the ploughed field—it sweetened and made fertile the whole breadth of his life. It is the gorging up of the water for want of outlet that makes the land sour, and leaves it barren; and it is the habit of holding in all for self that spoils the pleasure and profit of a life.

A Son of Consolation is a fine character. He who has consolation gives it; and he that gives it, has it. The more of it you have, the more you give; and the more you give to others, the more you retain for your own use. This is not one of the things that perish in the using. Like the bread in the hands of Jesus, it multiplies as it is given out. It increases by expending, and diminishes by hoarding. In the matter of comfort, or consolation, "there is that scattereth and yet increaseth; but he that withholdeth more than is meet, it tendeth to poverty."

To possess consolation is to give it, and to give it is to possess it. This circle, when it is set agoing, moves perpetually, like the sea giving out its waters to the sky, and the sky sending back the boon by the rain and the rivers to the sea again. Nor is the consoler cut short in his labors for lack of supply. As the trouble grows greater, the corresponding comfort increases. However deep the distress may be, he has a heaven above his head deeper than the abyss below, to fill it all with joy. His resources consist of "the fulness of the Godhead bodily," and in that ocean he will never touch the ground.

Barnabas was a Levite;—but why take note of his pedigree, since all are one in Christ? There is a reason. In estimating character and giving each his due, there are two opposite extremes, into one or other of which

human judgments, under the influence of various prejudice, continually tend to fall. Men err sometimes on
this side, sometimes on that: the Word of God marches
in the midst and holds the balance even. It throws out
an arm to uphold him who is ready to stumble, now on
the right side, now on the left.

The priests and their order, supported by the Pharisees, counted themselves righteous and despised others.
Speaking for their reproof and instruction, the Lord,
in the parable of the Good Samaritan, represented the
priest and the Levite as self-pleasing and unloving—
consulting their own ease, and refusing to help one who
was ready to perish. This he did in order to show them
that a sound creed and a scrupulous ritual could not
compensate for the neglect of charity. He taught them
that although they were of the family of Levi, and enrolled in the ranks of the hereditary priesthood, if they
had not charity, their privileges profited them nothing
—their profession was as sounding brass and a tinkling
cymbal.

But the Lord did not teach that all the Levites were
hard-hearted; for here, by the pen of the same historian,
Luke, the hedge is planted on the other side of the path.
There were then, and there are to-day, certain persons
and classes who entertain strong prejudices against all
ministers of religion. They seem to have persuaded
themselves, or, at least, try to persuade themselves, that
ministers as a rule are hypocrites. Accordingly, they
delight to tell or to hear stories in which ministers of
religion are represented in an odious or ridiculous light.
This result is extremely natural: we have no reason to
expect that it should be otherwise. The hypocrites, of
course, deserve to be so treated; and the true cannot
altogether escape, because their testimony really gives
discomfort to people who do not yield to it. To put
the witness in the wrong feels like putting themselves
right, as the sight of a train running backwards on a
near and parallel line of rails, beguiles you into the belief that your train is running forward.

Barnabas was a Levite—a religious teacher. The
profane of his day would have been comforted if they
had been able to quote the parable of the Samaritan to
show that the Levites were all sneaking, selfish fellows.

But the Lord comes in to protect the innocent. Barnabas was a Levite, but he was not cold and cruel. The opposite graces grew in his life, thick and fruitful like wheat in a harvest field. This passage is the counterpart of the parable—the hedge on the other side of the road.

He was of the country of Cyprus, an island in the Mediterranean. Even at that date the Jews were dispersed; yet they endeavored in their exile to maintain the distinction of tribes. In respect to his birth-place, he came out of a bad nest. Cyprus was occupied by Greeks, and latterly had been subdued by the Romans. But as it lay near the eastern shore, its people partook of the Phœnician and Oriental character. They were heathen, and more. The worship that prevailed was abominable even among heathen systems. Their religion consisted in the consecration of vice. As a Jew, Barnabas in his youth must have been carefully kept apart from these profligate rites; but still he was brought up in an atmosphere of extreme and exceptional wickedness. Can any good thing come out of Cyprus? In the Master's experience, the servants may obtain ground of hope. Nothing is too hard for the Lord. He can bring a clean thing out of an unclean. As the sun draws up pure water to the sky out of stagnant pools, cleansing it in the act of drawing it out; so the Lord by the beaming of his love can bring a bright witness to himself from amongst the most degraded population. Barnabas was of the country of Cyprus.

The Beacon - Ananias
(Acts 5:1-10)

" But a certain man named Ananias, with Sapphira his wife, sold a possession, and kept back part of the price, his wife also being privy to it, and brought a certain part, and laid it at the apostles' feet." etc.

To illustrate the remarkable development of brotherly love which appeared among the first disciples, the historian adduces two characteristic specimens. The first is the case of Barnabas, the subject of our last exposition; the second is the case of Ananias, which invites our attention now.

The two cases sprang from the same movement, and equally illustrate the same principles; yet the two cases are not like each other. They are reciprocally opposites. But this is, in most cases, the best method of throwing light on any subject; it is the ordinary way, both in the Bible and providence. Both in the sacred record and in common history examples of two opposite characters are frequently submitted, in succession or simultaneously—examples of the good that should be imitated, and of the evil that should be shunned. It is as necessary to moor a buoy over a rock or a sand-bank, as to show a light in a line with the safe entrance to the harbor. Barnabas the Levite, by his deeds of self-sacrificing love—Barnabas is a light at the pier-head, streaming outward through the night, marking for the mariner the way of life: Ananias, dying with a lie on his lips, buoys a rock where many have perished, and warns the wayfarer from the place of doom. Though the two men are not alike good, both examples are for us alike useful. The death of them that die may work for our good as much as the life of them that live. We may reap profit alike from the truth of the true, and from the lie of the false.

When the Lord would teach his disciples how to pray, he did not count it enough to exhibit the publican, standing afar off, and smiting on his breast, and crying, "God be merciful to me a sinner." He placed near that humble and true suppliant a solemn hypocrite thanking God that he was not as other men. When the Master taught his disciples the blessedness of pressing in while the door is open, he taught them also how dreadful it is to be, even by a little, too late. Of the ten virgins, five were wise, and five were foolish. The wise win souls—their own; and the foolish lose them. This dual method is adopted everywhere in Scripture to enforce moral lessons. In morals, as well as in physics, you exert greater power if you apply at the same time an attraction on the one side, and a pressure on the other. Israel of old, and Israel now, are

more effectively impelled toward righteousness, if the
curse and the blessing are proclaimed, simultaneous or
alternate, from two opposite hills.

"But a certain man." The little word "but" is the
hinge on which great issues turn. For example, "The
wicked is cast away in his iniquity; *but* the righteous
hath hope in his death." The door that swings on this
sharp pivot opens and shuts the way of life. Sometimes,
as here, it turns from light to darkness; and sometimes
from darkness to light. In this case you are conducted
from Barnabas to Ananias; you step from the bright
sunshine of a loving Christian life to the graveyard
damp of a hollow hypocrisy—a spirit of darkness caught
in the act of putting on the garment of an angel of
light.

The plan was concocted by "Ananias, with Sapphira
his wife." There is concert in evil. It is not the sudden impulse of an unguarded moment. It argues an
extreme hardness of heart when two persons, united
by the tenderest bond, plan a lie together, and engage
to support each other in carrying it out.

The persecution which the primitive Church endured
was an efficient means of purifying it. To a great extent the fire did in fact purge the dross away. For the
most part the first disciples might be counted on for
truth and sincerity. But even that terrible ordeal could
not make the society immaculate; it did not wash out
every stain; it did not turn earth into heaven.

Some chaff is found among the wheat even after the
fiercest fanning. You may not be able to explain how
the fact has happened, but you observe the fact. It
would be difficult to explain the motives which induced
this pair of hypocrites to join the company of the Christians, at a time when the profession of that faith endangered liberty and life. Nor is the easy-going explanation open to us, that as good things were going
among the Christians, they might hope to get a share;
for, as Ananias was a landed proprietor, he could not
possibly expect to be a receiver. A giver, if he joined
this society, he must obviously be.

There is a deeper, sadder cause. It is too true that
the religious emotions may be much stirred, while the
moral sense is not correspondingly quickened and puri-

fied. There may be much devotion, of a certain kind, where honesty or truth or purity is feebly rooted and liable to die out. The gospel of Christ when understood and accepted tends to purify the heart and life. This can be demonstrated both from its nature and its results. Hope produces holiness: "Every man that hath this hope in Him purifieth himself, even as He is pure" (1 John iii. 3). But these two which God hath joined, are often put asunder by men.

It is often said, and in certain quarters said with much passion, that a man who does not make a profession of religion is more trustworthy than a man who does. Some persons seem to take a delight in affirming that pious people are greatly given to cheating and lying. It is obvious that this opinion is grounded on the common fallacy of magnifying a few glaring examples into a general law. If those who count that all piety is hypocrisy, a mask worn to gain an end, would take time to calculate, they would soon discover that their theory cannot possibly be true. It destroys itself. The assumption is that rogues put on the garb of piety in order to obtain credit, and having thus obtained credit, cheat the credulous. Why do dishonest men adopt this method? Obviously because it suits their purpose. Because they seem to be religious men, people trust them. But if it were the common rule that religious men were dishonest men, they would cease to obtain credit: it would not pay a villain to assume a religious profession; and when it ceased to pay, he would cease to assume it. The averment that bad men make a profession of piety in order to cheat goes to prove that pious men, as a rule, are honest.

But while to this extent the defence of Christians against that calumny is clear and sure, I don't think it is right or safe to deny the imputation altogether. There is some truth in it. Indeed, it is the truth which any calumny contains that makes it formidable. Mere calumny, altogether false, has no force, and can do no harm. It soon dies. But falsehood which has some truth interfused lasts longer, and spreads further.

I do not refer to those conscious scoundrels who, having no sense of religion, deliberately make a profession for the purpose of gain. Besides this class, I own that you meet here and there a man who is not consciously to himself a hypocrite—a man who has been moved in a period of religious fervor, and who notwithstanding has not acquired a proper sense of the binding character of the ten commandments. In short, there is such a thing as a piety, after a sort sincere, dissociated from truth and justice and purity.

The Antinomian is not a mere dried specimen found fossil in the tomes of polemical theology; he is a living species of our own era. He is sound in his creed, and evangelical in his opinions, and perhaps zealous in propagating the faith; and yet he has a defective sense of the distinction between right and wrong, fair and foul, in the intercourse of life.

Nor should a true believer faint even before such a loathsome spectacle. Such is the condition of the soil, and such the activity of the "adversary," that tares do here and there spring up and choke the good seed. But let true disciples be of good cheer. The seed is the Word; and a Divine Sower has come forth into the world to sow it. It will prevail over the tares and thistles even here in the field; and at the end of the world a separation, complete and eternal, will be made between the wheat gathered into the garner and everything that defileth. When the door is shut, all within will be found true and pure.

After Judgment, Revival
(Acts 5:11-14)

" And great fear came upon all the church, and upon as many as heard these things. And by the hands of the apostles were many signs and wonders wrought among the people; (and they were all with one accord in Solomon's porch. And of the rest durst no man join himself to them: but the people magnified them. And believers were the more added to the Lord, multitudes both of men and women.)"

THE case of Ananias serves several important ends. For one thing, it bears a very emphatic testimony to truth. Such a testimony was needed, and therefore it is given in the record. Those who have come into personal contact with the heathen, the civilized as well as the savage, bear witness that the grand difficulty in dealing with them lies in their want of truth. Among the native populations of India you do not find a sense of truth that can be depended on. A merchant who had resided a number of years in the Western Presidency narrated to me the following case:—

One native sued another at law for the recovery of a loan. He adduced witnesses, who proved clearly and minutely that he had lent the accused a certain specific sum at a certain place and time. When the defender was called to plead, he distinctly owned that he had received the money according to the testimony of the witnesses, but called other witnesses, who proved with all clearness and fulness that on a certain day and at a certain place he had repaid it. He was absolved. An Englishman who knew the defender, and knew that he had never received the loan, asked him why he had acknowledged a debt which was not due. He replied that the debt was legally proved against him by false witnesses; that he had not witnesses to refute their evidence; but that as his adversary had, at small cost, proved the debt, he had been able as cheaply to prove repayment. He had no alternative but to meet one falsehood with another. Such is heathenism, even where it is cultivated and refined.

The judgment that fell on Ananias and Sapphira is of the nature of a miracle. A true miracle is never wrought unless when there is a worthy object to be attained. Now, falsehood in the very heart of the world was a great barrier in the way of the infant Church. The new society founded by Christ was beginning its career in a world that lacked truth. It was difficult to build even that Divine edifice without a foundation, without something in humanity of which it might take hold. Unless the Church find or generate truth, it will not overcome the world; it will sink as in a mire. At the outset a pen of iron and the point of a diamond must be employed to print truth, as on the rock for ever. A blow must be dealt against falsehood, which will vibrate down to the end of time, giving all men to know that the lie which is cherished in the bosom of the world must be cast out from the body of Christ.

From the beginning till now the Christian Church is exposed to two distinct dangers; it is liable to be assailed from without, and to be corrupted from within. It is in danger from open enemies, and from false friends. This spiritual body, like the natural, may be injured either by the stroke of an adversary or by poison mingled with its food.

In the infancy of the Church the hand of the Lord was directly stretched out for its preservation on either side. While the Church was a child the everlasting arms were thrown around it; on one side it was protected from the violence of the persecutor, and on the other from the corrupting effect of falsehood within its own bosom. In the fourth chapter we learn that the Lord interfered to keep the persecutor off; in the fifth, that he interfered to cast the leaven of hypocrisy out. Enemies shall not be permitted to crush the Church by power; falsehood shall not be permitted to poison the springs of her life.

In the beginning, when the system of the world was first set agoing, there were miracles; but miracles do not interpose to carry the system on. At the beginning of Christ's kingdom in the world miracles came to its aid; but miracles are not needed, and are not employed in its ordinary administration.

That the system of the world is, proves there was once a miracle; that the Church of Christ is, proves that it was established by a miracle. The death of Ananias and Sapphira is the arm of the Lord revealed to deliver the body of the Church in her youth from a consumption which, if not so checked, might have brought her down to an early grave, although no breath of persecution had ever blown upon her. We learn here that the work of God to cast out of the body the poison that would secretly undermine the life is as stupendous as his work to shield the Church from the power of her foes. Danger of dissolution through internal corruption is as great as the danger of destruction by external violence.

The question put to Ananias by Peter is suggestive: "Why hath Satan filled thine heart?" Satan is, and acts. Evil in man is not originally a spontaneous growth. It required, so to speak, two factors—the soil and the seed. The seed was injected by an adversary. An enemy hath done this. The revelation that sin in our race had a definite beginning and an alien author leaves room for the blessed hope which the gospel brings to light,—the hope of ultimate and final deliverance.

But though the suggestion of evil is attributed to Satan, the question is addressed to Ananias. This intimates, that he could have closed the door of his heart against it, if he would. Give not place to the devil; and wanting "place" given by yourself, he has no foothold to strike any blow. The real strength of the defence of Paris against the Germans lay in occupying beforehand all the positions in the neighborhood from which the city could have been assailed. The Parisians took care, as far as they could, not to give *place* to their adversary.

Satan *filled* the heart of Ananias; Barnabas was *filled* with the Holy Ghost. The human spirit is capacious, and it cannot remain void. It must be filled with good or evil. These two—the Spirit of holiness and the Spirit of evil—cannot dwell together in one room. They cast each other out, like night and day.

As a result of these events, great fear came upon the Church itself, and also upon the surrounding spectators.

Great fear came upon the Church. It is a healthful symptom, a needful discipline. "Lord, is it I?" "Let him that thinketh he standeth take heed lest he fall."

It is of the wicked one that these dark deeds occur, but it is of the Lord that their occurrence is recorded in the Word. It was Christ himself that said, "Remember Lot's wife." Many centuries after the fact, he directed that it should be kept in memory. These dark monuments have obtained a place in the Word that liveth and abideth for ever, that their warning may be available in all nations and all times.

Fear came also on as many as heard. As a natural consequence we learn that "of the rest durst no man join himself to them." This, however, does not intimate that subsequently there were few accessions. The opposite is immediately declared. Great multitudes were then and there added to the Lord, and enrolled in the membership of the Church. The meaning is, that those who were not of them dared not pretend to be of them. The stroke of judgment scared the hypocrites : but believers came flowing in like a stream. Believers were "the more" added; that is, the judgment upon the false professors hastened, instead of hindering, conversions. This terror of the Lord effectually persuaded men to take refuge in his mercy.

Believers were added to the Lord. It was not enough that their names were found in the communicants' roll. Your life, ye living, is hid with Christ in God. The living branch is in the vine, and also intertwined with its sister branches. All its life depends on being in the vine; although some portion of its fairness and fruitfulness may depend on its being interlaced in bonds of love with other branches.

And multitudes were added. This is the common experience still. A great number come at one time with a rush; and a period of comparative barrenness supervenes. Again there is a revival, and again a period of coldness. From the beginning, tides have flowed and ebbed in the Church as in the ocean. This phenomenon, springing in the inspired record, observed from time to time throughout the course of ecclesiastical history, and emerging in bold features within the range of our own memory, is fitted to touch our hearts and impart a solemn lesson. Has the tide risen in my time, and carried in many on its wave, and am I left without and behind ? Even when the heaving of the spiritual tide in my neighborhood has ceased, the door is not shut. We are as welcome when we come one by one as when we press in with the crowd. Now is the accepted time: whosoever will, let him come.

"Both men and women." The inspirer of the Word is the Spirit of wisdom. There was a reason for specifying that the converts were not all of one sex. This feature of the narrative throws out right and left a needful warning. The converts were not exclusively men, for the gospel owns and elevates and enfranchises woman. It is in the Word and Law of her Maker that her claim of equality is secured. It is a bright incidental glory of the gospel that it reinstates woman in her original place, as the adequate and equal companion of man—the necessary complement of his being. Women have cause to love the Lord. They owe to his Divine and discriminating wisdom not only their home in heaven when they are redeemed, but also their rightful place in the society of time.

Nor women exclusively: for when the Word comes in power it makes quick work with that lordly pride in which men wrap themselves, when they select philosophy or politics as their sphere, and leave religion to women. Under this outpouring of the Spirit these high things were brought low, and these crooked things made straight. When the apostles in their first fervor preached Jesus and the resurrection, strong men bent their heads and wept, and cried, What must we do to be saved? Good for these strong men that they yielded, ere it was too late, to the melting power of grace; for what would their strength avail in the day of the Lord?

How the Seed Grew
(Acts 5:17-26)

" Then the high priest rose up, and all they that were with him (which is the sect of the Sadducees), and were filled with indignation," etc.

ALTHOUGH the people in their zeal endeavored to place their sick under the shadow of Peter as he passed, it is not said that any were healed specifically by that method. There is, however, no ground, on the other side, to deny the possibility of such a case. It was the design of the Lord at that time to magnify the apostles in the eyes of the multitude, in order that popular favor might shield them from the hatred of the chiefs, and so preserve their lives for subsequent service. There was thus a specific use for such miracles as would tend to increase the people's veneration for the preachers of the Word.

It is not expressly said (v. 17) that the high priest, whether Caiaphas or Annas, was himself a Sadducee. It is more probable that he was a Pharisee, and that he obtained the support of his rivals in persecuting the Christians. Though the two sects were at daggers drawn between themselves, they were reconciled at once when an opportunity occurred of joining hands to crucify Christ in his members.

The central point of the apostles' testimony was the resurrection of Jesus. This stirred especially the enmity of the Sadducees. They maintained the dismal creed that there is no resurrection, neither angel nor spirit. They were more offended by witnesses of a fact, than by preachers of a doctrine. Though they had no creed themselves, they bore a willing hand in hunting down those who believed.

The spirit of the Sadducees is not contemptible for influence and numbers in our day. The broad Church, in its fully developed form, is a dangerous enemy to the true Church. The Church may be destroyed by the admission of unbelievers, as well as by the ejection of believers.

One of the phases of modern indifference is the favor with which persons of influence regard the proposal to endow indiscriminately all sects and creeds. It is the firmness of the people opposing the tendencies of politicians that has hitherto prevented the Papacy from being acknowledged and maintained by the State. It is not that political parties concur in believing that Romanism is true; they only observe that it is powerful, and they wish its power to be exerted on their side.

The angel of the Lord opened the prison doors. These preternatural interpositions were not intended to remove the witnesses beyond the reach of the persecutors; for in each case the liberated apostles remained on the spot and repeated their testimony. The design was to bring a moral power to bear on both the judges and the populace. It was an appeal to the magistrates to restrain them from persecuting; and, in case it should fail on that side, an appeal from unjust power to the sympathies of the common people. In this way it pleased their Divine Protector to execute at that time his own command,—"Touch not mine anointed; and do my prophets no harm."

The angel opened the prison, and carried to the prisoners the Master's message, that they should continue to preach the gospel; but the angel himself does not preach. You never find an angel calling on sinners to repent. There is not a gospel according to the angel. Angels are like little children, employed to carry letters to the Master's friends. They may try to peep into the contents on the way, but they cannot comprehend the meaning.

The name applied by the angel to designate the gospel of Christ is worthy of notice. He calls it "this life." Here, doubtless, the messenger's memory was faithful, for it is likely that the Lord who sent him would himself give it that designation. It was he who said, "I am the resurrection and the life." In sight of the angels a new life had sprung up in the world, different from any they had witnessed hitherto.

The message further bears that the liberated apostles should continue to speak the "*words* of this life." These are the seeds from which the new life springs; the sowers must go forth and sow them. It is as if in our sight a new and better kind of vegetation should burst from the ground, more beautiful and more fruitful than any that had hitherto been known. We should, in such a case, examine curiously, and gather carefully, and sow again those precious seeds. "The seed is the Word," and the Word is the seed—the seed of this new life that grows on the old soil. Go spread it on the field, and keep nothing back: speak "*all* the words of this life."

It is of use to remember here, that it was beside a grave that Jesus uttered the words, "I am the resurrection and the life." It is light in darkness.

And, finally, in this brief but pregnant message which the angel bore, the apostles are instructed to speak all the words of this life "to the *people*." There is no respect of persons here; no pandering to rank and power. The true enfranchisement of the common people lies in the gospel of Christ. Would that the struggling, bleeding nations could see it! If the Son make them free, they shall be free indeed.

When the civil and ecclesiastical authorities (ver. 24) ascertained the facts, "they doubted of them whereunto this would grow." Some glimmer of light has penetrated at last. They are not so confident now in the efficacy of their own prescription, "Speak no more in this name." They begin to discover that this Word, which they attempted by a short process to crush, is a thing with life in it: they suspect that it will *grow*. They were right. It had begun to grow. They feared its growth, for they felt it was their enemy. So Pharaoh had a presentiment that Israel would grow—grow too great to be kept in bondage—and commanded that the male children should be drowned. But infant Moses was drawn out of the water, and grew—grew to be the deliverer of Israel, the scourge of Egypt.

Herod had a presentiment that the Babe born in Bethlehem would "grow" till he should reach the kingdom, and dealt a cruel blow against the young child's life. But the child grew, and Herod must stand before the judgment-seat of Christ. "Be wise now therefore, O ye kings: be instructed, ye judges of the earth. Kiss the Son, lest he be angry, and ye perish."

Casting our eye backward in the light of Scripture on those successive efforts by the powers of this world to crush that living Word, which is the only seed of a new life for men, we may well "rejoice with trembling" over its wonderful preservation from age to age. He who sits King upon the floods had said, "Destroy it not, for a blessing is in it;" and therefore it was preserved.

Suppose a world full of human inhabitants with a short store of prepared food, but with no seed which might produce a continued supply—a whole world without a single grain of living seed. Suppose now that a messenger from another orb should come with a single grain of wheat. Can you conceive the care with which the gift would be cherished? Can you conceive the horror that would seize upon the multitudes if they thought the precious grain was in danger of being crushed?

The seed of the Word was cherished and preserved, not by men, for they knew not that it was their life, but by the loving and wise providence of God. The seed, sown in the ground when Jesus died, grew to dimensions that the Jewish rulers recked not of. In our day it has grown great; after our day it will grow greater. The kingdoms of this world shall become the kingdoms of our God and of his Christ.

When the magistrates received a report from their officers that the prisoners had escaped, and left the doors of the prison standing open (ver. 23), they were amazed. They knew not what to make of it. But while they hesitated, another messenger arrived (ver. 25), announcing, not that the prisoners had fled, which would have been a natural and easily comprehended course, but that they were "standing in the Temple and teaching the people."

Here is a still greater difficulty. This is not a case of ordinary escape from prison. These men do not save themselves when safety is within their reach. This step in the experience of the servants is the duplicate of one that occurred to the Master. When the band came to arrest him (John xviii. 6), he cast them to the earth by his look. He showed them that he might escape, and yet surrendered himself to their will. It was another appeal to their hearts. If they yield, it is well; but if they resist, it will harden them the more. So with the apostles here; the Lord sent his angel and set his servants free. He showed the persecutors that they had no power over these men, "except it were given them from above." But having done this, the Master left the witnesses in their enemies' hands. His will was, that his servants should neither flee nor fight; that they should preach the cross, and bear it; that they should overcome as he had overcome, by enduring.

Stolid, like the band that seized Jesus in the garden, they went to the Temple and arrested the apostles; but aware by this time of the favor with which the populace regarded them, they led the prisoners gently into the presence of the court. But not only did the officers offer no violence to the apostles in arresting them, the apostles offered no resistance to the arrest. Such was the temper and attitude of the crowd, that the officers feared a rescue if they should apply force. Peter and John were sharp enough to observe the situation. They had nothing more to do than make some show of resistance, and a disturbance would have taken place, in which they could escape.

But this was not in their way. They understood better the instructions of their Lord. Had these two men, who bore the first brunt of the persecution, adopted the method of saving themselves by favor of a riotous multitude, the Christian Church might never have obtained a footing in the world. If they had taken the sword, they would have perished by the sword. They witnessed and suffered: so, the blood of the martyrs became the seed of the Church.

Again at the Bar
(Acts 5:27-29)

" And when they had brought them, they set them before the council: and the high priest asked them, saying, Did not we straitly command you that ye should not teach in this name? and, behold, ye have filled Jerusalem with your doctrine, and intend to bring this man's blood upon us. Then Peter and the other apostles answered and said, We ought to obey God rather than men."

AGAIN the apostles are placed at the bar and examined. The accusation this time is simply that they had not complied with the former judgment. The magistrates had enjoined them not to speak any more in that Name, and now they charge the panels with contempt of court. Peter and John, however, although they had disobeyed the order of the Sanhedrim, had not broken their own *parole*, for they had given no parole in the case; on the contrary, they had declared, in the face of the tribunal, that they would continue to preach in the name of Jesus.

The judges on this occasion are thinking, not of how they may discover the truth regarding the accused, but how they may provide for their own safety. "Ye have filled Jerusalem with your doctrine, and intend to bring this man's blood upon us." It is not a question of truth and justice; these men do not seem capable of rising to such thoughts. They believed that the apostles were **working up the multitude to demand vengeance upon** the rulers for the murder of Jesus. It was a vulgar fear for their own skin that inspired these contemptible intriguers who sat on the bench of justice that day in Jerusalem.

"Ye mean to bring this man's blood upon us!" And they trembled for their own base lives in presence of the excited populace. It is a sad scene for us who can look at leisure on it, and look beyond it. How near the kingdom they seem to be!—"this man's blood upon us;" and yet they think of that blood only as vengeance; they have gotten no glimpse of its atoning power. "Who is blind, but my servant?" They who sit in Moses' seat reject the Prophet whom Moses promised.

It is interesting to observe how shy the rulers are of introducing the name of Jesus. They say "this name" and "this man," but they do not venture to pronounce his name. This stone which the builders rejected is dreadful to the rejecters. They seem already to labor under some dim conception that upon whomsoever it shall fall, it shall grind him to powder. On the other hand, in proportion as the rulers avoid that name, the apostles cleave to it. To them it is a name above every name. In all these troubles they continually presented it as a shield over their heads. That name of the Lord is a strong tower; and these righteous men, in every danger, run into it.

Another concise and sublime word, spoken by Peter and assented to by his companions—"We ought to obey God rather than men." We who have all our days been familiar with it, do not perceive its grandeur. Are not all these who speak Galileans? Whence, then, hath this man this wisdom? He speaks as he is moved by the Holy Ghost. This courage is not earth-born. "Every good and every perfect gift is from above, and cometh down from the Father of lights." The apostles had prayed specially for courage to speak God's Word: they had asked, and now they received.

How much the world owes to the word that Peter uttered before the Sanhedrim that day! It is the foundation of all the true liberty that exists in the world. On this rock—the word that the Holy Spirit spake by

Peter's lips—has the liberty of the Church been built, and the gates of Hell shall not prevail against it.

Nothing that rested on the world could resist and overcome the world. Here is a word let down from heaven, a word that liveth and abideth for ever. By leaning on this, human liberty has been able to maintain a footing on the world during the dark centuries that are past; and that liberty wherewith the Son has made his people free, is waxing apace, as the dawn advances into day. Freedom of conscience—the subjection of a human spirit to God, and its emancipation therefore from all inferior control—is deposited here in the ground as a living seed. Thence it has sprung and spread: thence it will spring and spread until all superstition and tyranny shall be swept away.

The power—the paramount value of this heaven-sent principle—has never and nowhere been more clearly illustrated than in the history of our own country. It is the action of this principle in conflict with persecuting rulers that has made our land illustrious among the nations. Especially it is this aspect of Divine truth that has imparted to Scotland its peculiar historical character. Woe to the fatherland if a degenerate race should arise who should be ashamed of the conflicts in which our liberty was won! When it becomes fashionable to laud the chivalry of Claverhouse, and cast ridicule or bestow pity on the rudeness or fanaticism of his victims, the golden age of our country is gone. The suffering unto death for liberty of conscience ennobled the men of that day, and secured liberty for their descendants. We are like sons who have inherited the wealth that their fathers won: a humble, thankful spirit becomes us. We should maintain and improve our heritage.

Critics have noticed the structure of Peter's brief defence as one of the finest specimens of pleading on record. It is a proof that the promise, "It shall be given you in that hour what ye shall speak," was amply fulfilled. It is clear and cogent; it is very short, but it is long enough. The speaker says all that is needful, and stops when he is done. In this short space he defends himself, confounds his adversaries, and commends Christ to the bystanders. The address assumes the form of a syllogism, which would not have been so remarkable in the lips of Paul, but which we are surprised to find in the unpremeditated defence of the simple and impetuous fisherman. After announcing the general principle, that wherever God claims obedience man's claim must stand in abeyance, he proceeds to show that this case comes under the rule. "The God of our fathers;" he takes care to trace all up to the God of Israel, whom the Sanhedrim acknowledged. Peter and John did not stand before the priests as aliens, guilty of subverting the Jewish faith or the Jewish commonwealth. He claims to be with themselves an Israelite, and interested as much as they in the inheritance of Israel. "The God of our fathers raised up Jesus, whom ye slew." The point of the arrow is at their breast again. He will not spare them. In one sense he is in their power; but in another they are in his. They tremble in their seats under this home-thrust. "Ye slew;" for they compelled Pilate to pronounce sentence of death. Nor does the preacher spare them the aggravation—"and hanged on a tree." They knew the curse and shame associated with the cross. "Whom ye slew, him hath God exalted." He pillories the priests as the enemies of God, the crucifiers of the Messiah.

But this bold, unsparing, personal piercing is not the dictate of anger or revenge. All that dross has been purged out of the witness by the baptism at Pentecost. The servants are about their Master's business. They are feeling for an opening into the consciences of their judges, that they may introduce the gospel. They intimate that God hath exalted Jesus to be a Prince and a Saviour; a King to rule, and a Redeemer to forgive. They offer, through this Redeemer, repentance to Israel and remission of sins. The preachers have an eye both to the magistrates and the bystanders. They cherish no enmity against the persecutors. Their rule already is, all things to all men, in order that they may save some. The judges who oppressed them, and the populace who for the time favored them, are all alike in the eyes of these witnesses. The business of the apostles is to win souls, and this precious gain is alike welcome from all quarters. To the judges on the bench; to the young advocates, such as Saul of Tarsus, who might be hanging about the precincts of the court; to the spectators; to the officers; to all alike the suffering witness proclaimed repentance and remission of sins in the name of Jesus. And who shall tell whether Saul, through Peter's word, received an arrow in his heart, which would not out by all his intemperate zeal to crucify Christ in his members, and which at last brought the furious persecutor down to the dust before the gates of Damascus. The witnesses were careful to sow beside all waters, not knowing which of their words might fail, and which might bear fruit unto life eternal.

Exalted to Give
(Acts 5:30,31)

" *The God of our fathers raised up Jesus, whom ye slew and hanged on a tree. Him hath God exalted with his right hand to be a Prince and a Saviour, for to give repentance to Israel, and forgiveness of sins.'*

THE murderer is haunted by the ghost of his victim. The haunting is real, although it may exist only in the mind of the criminal. It is of God that the shadow should follow and torment him. It is a part of the sublime machinery of Providence constructed for the punishment, and so for the prevention, of crime. It is one of the lines of defence thrown around human life by the Creator's watchful care.

All history teems with examples to show that the innocent blood which tyrants have shed rises up to avenge. Witness Herod: his courtiers imagined they would interest their master when they told him of the mighty miracles performed by Jesus. But the news only filled him with horror. The gory head of the Baptist came back; and though the murderer shut his eyes, he was compelled to see. He could only reply to his officious informants: " It is John the Baptist, whom I beheaded; he is risen from the dead." Many a time and oft the Baptist " rose " in the haunted imagination of that unjust judge. When the victim rises, the murderer undergoes a righteous retribution. He gave no mercy; and in his blind terror he expects none.

These high priests who had compassed the death of Christ were in Peter's address compelled to undergo this inevitable sentence, "Whom ye slew, God has exalted." Their victim has risen, and the murderers tremble. Woe to them if he whom they crucified is exalted! They showed him no mercy, and they expect none at his hands.

But come, ye crucifiers of Christ, come to him and be forgiven. Take the truth which fell once from your own lying lips, "This man receiveth sinners." That sneer becomes now the hope of your souls. It is because he receiveth sinners that now, when he is exalted, he will not put forth his power for vengeance. "Him hath God exalted to be a Prince and a Saviour, for to give repentance to Israel, and remission of sins." Strange and attractive word! *Exalted to give!* When these Jewish rulers, who had sworn his life away before the tribunal of the Roman governor, heard first of his resurrection, they remonstrated with the witnesses— "Ye intend to bring this man's blood upon us." The resurrection of Jesus had no other meaning to them than vengeance coming on their own heads. They reasoned, If he whom we slew is exalted, woe unto us. But it is to these very men that the apostles preach pardon. They proclaim that Jesus is exalted for the purpose of showing mercy to his murderers. He is exalted *to give;* and he gives even to them—he gives to all, and upbraideth not. Now that he is exalted, and his enemies are in his power, instead of *taking* vengeance, he *gives* remission of sins.

Fix your minds on this precious word. It belongs to us as well as to them. It is over all, like the vital air. In this end of the world, it is as cold waters to thirsty souls to hear that Christ is exalted in order that he might more largely "give." In the Seventy-second Psalm this remarkable promise concerning the Messiah is found,—"He shall come down like rain upon the mown grass: as showers that water the earth" (verse 6). It is true, as elsewhere written, that God "giveth us rain from heaven, and fruitful seasons." But a greater gift is here. It is not he shall *bestow* the rain, but he shall *be* the rain. Not he shall send down the rain, but he shall come down as the rain. This refreshing is by the presence of the Lord.

The water is exalted into the heavens in order that it may give rain upon the earth: it is exalted to give. It is drawn up, as by a resurrection; and arises pure into the heavens, that it may be in a capacity to send refreshing to the thirsty ground. In the same way, he who comes as rain on the mown grass was exalted that he might give—that he might give himself, as the living water to his own.

This exalted Giver bestows every kind of good. He is head over all things to his Church. Every good and perfect gift is from above. But the fundamental benefit—the boon without which all others would be of no avail—is the twin gift promised in the text, "repentance and forgiveness of sins."

These two go together to constitute one whole redemption. These two God hath joined, as he has joined right and left sides of a body to make one organized life. As well might the contending mothers at Solomon's judgment-seat be comforted by getting each a half of the divided child, as any sinner expect to be either safe or happy with one of these gifts if he wanted the other. These two are one; to separate is to destroy them.

Forgiveness of sin is an act of the supreme God, and repentance is an act of sinful man; and yet both are the gift of the risen Redeemer. It is not like two portions of an extended straight line; it rather resembles two halves of one great revolving ring. As it goes rapidly round, all in one solid piece, it seems sometimes as if this half were impelling that; and sometimes as if that half were impelling this. From one point of view, repentance in the man seems to draw forgiveness from God; from another point of view, forgiveness freely given by God seems to work repentance in the man. In some sense both these views are true; but the one is not a living truth apart from the other. It is the circle that revolves, not either half of it. One thing we know, that the whole circle and all its movements have been bestowed as a free gift by him who is exalted a Prince and a Saviour. It is true that repentance draws pardon from God; and it is also true that pardon from God bestowed free makes the sinner's heart melt in penitence.

It is true that Christ says, " If any man open, I will come in;" but it is also true that no one would open unless he were moved and won by the plaintive voice of the Divine Endurer, "Behold, I stand at the door and knock." It is the opening from within that lets the Saviour enter; but it is the pressure of the long-suffering Saviour without, that causes the fastenings of the closed heart to give way at length. " The kingdom of heaven suffereth violence, and the violent take it by force." We are accustomed to think of this as a description of faith's agonizing pressure at the gate of heaven's mercy; and the thought is right. But the phrase, in the light of Scripture, has another and greater meaning. Christ himself is the strong man who by force casts out the usurper, and spoils his goods and occupies his room. The kingdom of heaven is within us. And if it come not first into us, we shall never enter into it. Now this kingdom suffereth violence; the mighty One takes it by force. The force he applies is this same "forgiveness of sins." It is forgiving love, streaming from Christ exalted, and beating on the closed gate of a human heart, that drives the fastenings in at length, and floods it to its brim.

We cannot determine the precise point at which the process begins. We cannot be certain that it begins in all cases at the same point. In the circle which consists of forgiveness and repentance, I do not know the very point which the Spirit of the Lord touches in order to communicate motion. All that I know is that he gives it motion; and that when one point moves, all points move.

And this wheel is like Ezekiel's, " so high that it is dreadful." The upper part of its rim is in the heavens, while its lower edge rolls upon the earth. Forgiveness of sin is an act done by God; it is an official act of the Judge on the great white throne. Repentance is a work and a rending and a melting here on earth. It goes on within a human heart. The lower part of this circle is in the chambers of a sinner's heart here; and yet every movement of a hair's-breadth in that deep place is accompanied by a corresponding movement on high.

"There is joy in heaven, in the presence of the angels, over one sinner that repenteth." Repentance in the deep places of your soul is so connected with the fountain of grace in God, that the slightest movement here is felt there.

I dare not say that in any case there is repentance in man before there is forgiveness from God; neither can I dare to say that in any case there is forgiveness with God before there is repentance in the man. But I know that wherever may be the spot where movement begins, the whole system moves together. In proportion as my soul draws by repenting, God gives by pardoning; and in proportion as God gives by pardoning, my soul receives through repenting. When the receiving channel is clogged, the outflowing channel is left dry; when the outflowing channel is filled by a rushing flood, the clogs that choked the receiving channel are washed away, and there is a great refreshing.

There is one obvious practical lesson that should be interposed here—it is repentance that lies to our hand. It is with it that we have to do. Our business is to repent.

These two were joined in Peter's own experience. When Peter had denied his Lord, the Lord looked on Peter; that look conveyed pardon, and the repenting disciple went out and wept bitterly.

Gamaliel
(Acts 5:33-42)

" When they heard that, they were cut to the heart, and took counsel to slay them," etc.

THE word on Peter's lips was "sharper than a two-edged sword." The audience were cut to the heart. Such convictions cannot pass away without some practical result. They will either melt the heart on which they fall, or make it harder. Those who have trembled like Felix under the preached word will either submit to the gospel or resist it with increased enmity.

In the case of judges and rulers, if there is not true penitence, the enmity reveals itself in active persecution; but in private life the convictions that are resisted are for the most part kept secret. When conviction ripens into conversion and peace, the fact becomes known in the Christian brotherhood: but those piercings which are successfully resisted seldom become known beyond the breast of the convict. When he overcomes his convictions, he keeps the conflict to himself; when his convictions overcome him, his friends will hear of his surrender. I think there is many a conflict between Christ and the world which is never blazed abroad in history. When the world wins, and shuts the door in the face of Jesus, the strong man armed not only keeps his goods in peace, but keeps his victory a secret. When the lion has caught his prey, he devours it in silence.

At first the prevailing opinion in the court was that measures should be taken forthwith to secure the death of these two troublesome preachers. The Jewish rulers thought that they should carry out the policy which they had already begun, and treat the scholars as they had already treated the Master. At this juncture they were turned from their cruel purpose by the politic persuasion of one of their own number, " named Gamaliel, a doctor of the law, had in reputation among all the people." On his suggestion the accused were removed from the bar, that the court might deliberate in private on their sentence. In the private conference, Gamaliel succeeded in persuading them that it would be wiser in all the circumstances to desist, and leave the case to Providence.

In ancient times the opinion prevailed that Gamaliel interfered from secret sympathy with the Christians. There is an ecclesiastical tradition that he became a disciple. It was thought by many that he was already in secret a Christian when he exerted his influence to save the lives of Peter and John.

The prevailing opinion in modern times is different. Later critics have thought that it agrees better with all the circumstances to suppose that Gamaliel was really a Pharisaic Jew, that he had no sympathy with the disciples of Jesus, and that he continued to the end an unbeliever.

He was indeed a calmer and fairer man than any of his fellows. Besides, being a leading doctor of his sect, he had a personal and party interest in protecting the apostles at this crisis; for the real root of the charge against them was their doctrine of the resurrection. The apostles were suffering under Sadducean influence for the very doctrine which the Pharisees maintained as their distinguishing characteristic. The Sadducees were the movers at this stage of the persecution, and they moved in it because the resurrection of the body, as taught by Peter and John in connection with Jesus, went to demolish the corner-stone of their distinctive system.

As the Sadducees gave their influence against the apostles because they preached through Jesus the resurrection from the dead, it was natural that the Pharisees should draw back when they discovered that by joining in the persecution they were in effect strengthening the hand of their rivals. Gamaliel, accustomed to lead his party, seems to have discovered as the case advanced that the Pharisees had glided unawares into a false position. He found that in swelling the triumph of the Sadducees in their crusade against the witnesses of the resurrection, they were mining the ground under their own feet. Accordingly, by a cautious speech and a temporizing motion, he succeeded in extricating his party from the scrape into which they had inadvertently stumbled.

In all that lay between the Pharisees and the Christians, Gamaliel was a Pharisee and anti-Christian; but in as far as the Sadducees were compassing the death of Peter and John for asserting the resurrection of the dead, he felt that his proper place was on the side of the apostles, and against the rival sect. At a subsequent stage of the history, Paul employed the conflict between the two parties on this very point, to rend asunder the cordon which his united enemies had drawn around him; and through the opening made his escape. (Chap. xxiii. 6.)

The Lord over all is wont to cleave a path through hosts of foes, as through the sea, when he desires to set his imprisoned servants free for further usefulness. If there had been no divisions in Israel,—if the nation at that time had not been arrayed in two hostile camps against each other, the witnesses might have been crushed at the outset of their career. In this way God in providence divides, that he may conquer the strong, and so deliver the weak out of their hands.

A remarkable parallel is found in the division of Israel into two rival kingdoms after the death of Solomon, and the consequent preservation of the Pentateuch from wilful adulteration. The mutual jealousy between Samaria and Jerusalem rendered mutilation or addition impossible. In the same way the Scriptures were preserved from interpolation in the earlier Christian ages—before the invention of printing—by the mutual jealousies between the Roman Church and the various sectaries that successively arose and asserted their liberty. Between Pharisees and Sadducees there was a rent, and the apostles went out free: between Ephraim and Judah there was a rent, and the Pentateuch came through entire.

The proposal of Gamaliel, with the reasons which supported it, have been much canvassed by modern critics; but I suppose the view generally taken now is that it does not manifest great depth of wisdom in the court. The philosophy of the speech is flimsy, and its religion more than doubtful. It is probable that the Sanhedrim were by this time frightened at their own shadows,—in bodily fear lest the people should rise in insurrection, otherwise they would not have yielded so readily to the arguments which the great doctor advanced. Probably Gamaliel knew very well that his reasoning was weak; but he perceived also that it was sufficient to afford an excuse, which the court wanted, for dismissing the panels from the bar. His reasoning is substantially though not formally a dilemma. He says in effect: The cause is either of God or of men: if it is of God, ye cannot overthrow it, and therefore in that case you should let it alone; if it is of men, it will crumble to pieces, and in that case also you should let it alone.

To this notable piece of wisdom they all agreed. I suspect they desired to reach this conclusion with a view to their own safety, otherwise they would not have reached it on such grounds. Persecutors are neither consistent nor dignified. The prisoners, though unconvicted, were beaten in presence of the court, and dismissed with a command to preach no more in the name of Jesus. The court might have understood by this time that they might as well command the tide not to rise on the beach as command these men to hold their peace.

The disciples "departed from the presence of the council rejoicing:" and what was the ground of their gladness? That they were set at liberty? No; but that they were counted worthy to suffer shame for his name. What a word! And what a thought! It was new in the world. The world was incapable of comprehending the idea which inspired these martyrs. This joy of theirs was as new and strange as if a second sun had appeared in the sky. This is a joy which their Redeemer gives—a joy that no man taketh from them.

Again they grandly disobeyed the impotent orders of the Sanhedrim. Every day, in public and in private, they continued to teach and preach Jesus Christ. There is a great lesson in this last word. It is not enough to say they preached. The power lies not in the act, but in the object. They pressed Christ as a Divine Redeemer to the hearts of weary men. This is the true apostolical succession—to know nothing as a cure for men's sin but Jesus Christ and him crucified; and no sin which his blood cannot wash away. None but Christ for any; and Christ sufficient for all.

The Deacons
(Acts 6:1-6)

" And in those days, when the number of the disciples was multiplied, there arose a murmuring of the Grecians against the Hebrews, because their widows were neglected in the daily ministration," etc.

As an introduction to the narrative of the discontent that sprang up, it is intimated that "the number of the disciples was multiplied." We gather here that the bulk of the society had something to do with the troubles that arose. In a large community certain disorders are apt to occur, from which a smaller body may be comparatively free. It was necessary to institute new offices to meet new demands.

But besides the increased numbers, we must also take into account the liberal provision for the poor that had been made through the generosity of a fresh young faith. It is remarkable that both the internal disorders —the hypocrisy recorded in chapter v., and the murmurings recorded in chapter vi.—sprang directly from the open-handed charity exercised towards the poor. In that rich soil, several rank weeds suddenly sprang up, to test and exercise the wisdom and faithfulness of the infant Church. The falsehood of Ananias, and the discontent of the Hellenists, grew in different compartments of the same field. One root of bitterness grew in the givers, and another in the receivers. Both are recorded, that Christians in subsequent ages might be warned on either side.

From the beginning hitherto, the Church has been exposed to manifold dangers at the point where she comes into necessary contact with the world. How many sorrows and how many sins have sprung up with gifts—with money! Contributions are necessary: without them, even the faith of disciples would often be crippled in its action for want of instruments. But the contributions, especially in large bodies and in an artificial state of society, afford a cover in which the adversary conceals himself when he seeks to devour.

Both givers and receivers need to be watchful. No Church on earth can be free altogether from danger here. Our prayer should be, not that we should be taken out of the world, but that we should be kept from the evil. Great liberality is a beautiful fruit of faith; yet in this sweet fruit a worm may gnaw.

Hitherto the apostles had personally superintended the distribution of the gifts. It was not possible that they should take charge of every detail. The work must have been to a large extent delegated. It was natural that Jews of Palestine should in the first instance be employed. These would be best acquainted with their own countrymen; and so it might happen that the native poor were at first better provided for than the poor Jews who had been born in Greek countries and understood only the Greek tongue. How far the grievance was real, and how far sentimental, we do not know; we know only the fact that the Hellenists complained of undue partiality in favor of the Palestinians. Murmurings are dangerous to the peace and prosperity of the Christian society. As soon as the apostles heard of the complaint, they took effective measures to satisfy, and so remove it. They surveyed the case, and promptly formed their resolution. At a glance they perceived that if the same methods should be continued, they must personally attend more minutely to the details of the distribution. But this would distract their attention, and occupy their time with secondary affairs, to the manifest detriment of their chief work, the ministry of the Word.

A new order of officials must be appointed to superintend this business. The apostles, in the first instance, made up their own mind as to the kind of office that should be instituted, and the qualifications which the officials should possess; then they submitted their proposal with reasons to " the brethren." Thereupon " the whole multitude " accepted the proposal, and at once proceeded to choose fit and proper persons for this specific work. Having elected the seven deacons, they presented them to the apostles. The apostles on their part accepted the choice of the people, and ordained the deacons by prayer and the imposition of hands.

In making the proposal regarding the institution of the deacons, the apostles state briefly the grounds of their decision. These grounds are permanently true and precious. The foundation so laid will bear more than the particular weight then and there imposed. If the apostles declined to administer charitable gifts to poor disciples, lest it should interfere with their spiritual ministry, many other things, if they had lived in our days, they would have declined for the same reason. It becomes all Christian ministers to walk humbly in the apostles' footsteps, rather than to set up an exclusive claim on some transcendental ground, to be accounted their successors.

It is eminently worthy of regard, that although the specific work to which the deacons were in the first instance called was the distribution of money and other material gifts, a necessary qualification for office is, that they be "full of the Holy Ghost." Grace in large measure is announced to be a necessary requisite in one who shall handle "the outward things of the house of God." It is on this border belt, where the Church and the world meet, that corruption is apt to spring; and it is especially important that those who are called to duty in that sphere should be eminently spiritual men.

In distinguishing the specific sphere of the deacon, the apostles incidentally define their own. This definition is of great value. The duties of their office are "prayer, and the ministry of the word." Like the rest of the "acts" recorded in this book, and in strong contrast with the flimsy and fantastic ideas of the sub-apostolic age, the definition exhibits both the clearest logic and the broadest common sense. The work consists of two parts; and these two are arranged in their natural order. By prayer they *get* from God, and through the ministry of the Word they *give* to men. Like Paul, they are "vessels;" the vessels must first be filled, and then they bear about and spread the blessed Name that fills them. We find no priesthood and no ritualism here. These two constitute the apostolic ministry as understood and explained by the apostles. They knew their own mind better than monks of the Middle Ages. It is in the Scriptures that you breathe the free fresh air of heaven; when you descend into the arena of the fathers, real mountains and mist-clouds are so intermingled that you cannot distinguish with certainty between them.

Prayer and preaching, alternate or simultaneous, are the right and left side of a living ministry. The preaching work may be laboriously and conscientiously performed without comfort and without success if the other side be from any cause paralyzed. I watched once with interest the operations of a brick-maker in a field of clay. There was great agility in his movements. He wrought by piece, and the more he turned out the higher was his pay. His body moved like a machine. His task for the time was simply to raise a quantity of clay from a lower to a higher level, by means of a spade. He threw up one spadeful, and then he dipped his tool in a pail of water that stood by. After every spadeful of clay there was a dip in the water. The operation of dipping the spade occupied almost, if not altogether, as much time as the raising of the clay. My first thought was, if he should dispense with these apparently useless baptisms, he might perform almost double the amount of work. My second thought was wiser; on reflection I saw that if he had attempted to continue the work without the alternate washings, the clay would have stuck to the tool, and his progress would have been altogether arrested. Right well did the skilful workman know that to plunge his instrument in water every time it was used furthered and did not hinder his work. Indeed, it was this that made his work possible.

I said to myself, Go thou and do likewise. The ministry of the Word, as the world goes, is like the effort of the workman to lift the clay; prayer is the baptism which makes progress quick—makes progress possible.

Troubles Bearing Blessed Fruits
(Acts 6:7-15)

" And the word of God increased; and the number of the disciples multiplied in Jerusalem greatly; and a great company of the priests were obedient to the faith. And Stephen, full of faith and power, did great wonders and miracles among the people," etc.

THESE wise and prompt measures were immediately followed by blessed results. The murmuring was silenced. The irritating leaven of discontent was cast out of the Church. This was done, not by a high-handed authority, exerted to silence the murmurers, but by acknowledging the existence of the grievance, and instantly devising the means of redressing it. Justice was administered at once; there was no vexatious delay. The boon was bestowed gracefully, and left no sting. There was no taunt. The redress was complete as well as prompt; for there is reason to believe that all, or nearly all, the deacons appointed belonged to the section that complained. All the seven have Greek names. This does not necessarily imply that they were all Hellenists, for many Palestinian Jews bore Greek names. Andrew and Philip, in the college of the twelve, bear names that are purely Greek, and yet they were natives of Palestine. These two, although really Hebrews, may have had some family connection with Greeks. Besides their names, there is the interesting circumstance, that when some Greek strangers at Jerusalem (John xii.) desired to obtain an interview with Jesus, it was to these two disciples that they applied for an introduction. It is probable that most of the elected deacons were Hellenists; for it was in order to satisfy that section of the Christians that the appointment was made.

There is great wisdom in this straightforward and frank mode of dealing. It takes all the bitterness away, and sweetens the breath of the society. Best of all, it removes the hindrance, and promotes the spread of the Word. Divisions impede the progress of the kingdom; but divisions wisely, generously, promptly healed, not only restore matters to their former condition, but carry the common cause further forward. When a broken bone is healed, the limb is stronger than it was before. Thus it often happens in Christian communities, that where faith and love are in exercise, incidental difficulties become the occasion of edification and progress, according to the promise that God will make all things work together for good to his own. The troubles, in regard to the distribution of charity, that threatened the peace of the Church, became the occasion of displaying truth and love and fairness in the character of the leaders, and so a new impulse was communicated to the common work. "The word of God increased, and the number of the disciples multiplied in Jerusalem greatly."

Of the seven men Stephen comes first to the front, and stands out the chief. After him Philip is distinguished in the apostolic history. These two men, of one spirit, were led by different paths, and employed in different kinds of service. Stephen suffered early, and Philip preached long. The Lord had need of both as his witnesses. Stephen by his faithfulness unto death, and Philip by his faithfulness in life, served the Lord in their generation; and now they rejoice together.

Without explanation and without comment the narrative proceeds to intimate that these men, chosen and ordained for the specific duty of distributing the Church's charity, proceeded forthwith to preach, and to preach with power and success, the gospel of the kingdom. Stephen was full of the Holy Ghost and of faith; we need not therefore be surprised that he could not limit himself to the serving of tables. The very qualities which recommended him for that office, carried him beyond it. He burst through the borders of his own special department. He volunteered apostle's work in addition to the work of a deacon which had been prescribed to him. No one interposed to restrict his efforts within the narrower sphere. I take the facts as I find them. I love them as they are. There is great freedom and elasticity along with order in the organization of the Church as it appears in the New Testament. A free development belongs to the nature of the gospel. Wherever the love of Christ is kindled within the heart, it will burn its own way out. It will keep the higher law of the Lord; but it bursts through all human official regulations. In a quickened time the lower offices instinctively rise to the higher work: in a dead time the reverse process may be observed—the higher offices, and those who hold them, gravitate down to the sphere of the lower, and beyond it. At such seasons those who claim the apostolate practically desert prayer and the ministry of the Word, and strive for mastery in the various ambitions of the world. In our day the stream has often manifested a tendency to overflow its banks. Those who hold only private station in the Church have, through strong spiritual instincts, glided ere they were well aware into the heart of the ministerial work—into prayer and the ministry of the Word. Irregularities may be expected to appear at such a time. Let these be watched and corrected with all the wisdom and faithfulness available to the Church: but beware of mere suppression. I would rather undergo much toil and trouble in looking after the embankments and guiding the course of the stream, than be relieved of labor by seeing the waters fall like a tropical torrent, and leave the land a desert.

Stephen's great power provoked a great opposition. There is a list of the adversaries, but not of the subjects in debate. We know, however, what the contention was. These Jewish teachers, even the most devout, held to the dead letter of the law, overlaid as it was by the endless superstitions of the Talmud. The preaching of Stephen made short work with their childish ritualism. It tore up their phylacteries, and interrupted their long prayers. It grasped the Pharisee fast by his conscience, and threw his stately figure prone on the ground beside the repenting publican, announcing, with authority and not as the scribes, except ye repent ye shall perish. This preacher did not go about the bush. He told them that all their sacrifices and all their washings would not serve as a substitute for faith and holiness. All this, they thought, was a bold assault on Moses and the law.

Saul's name has not been pronounced yet; but here we begin to feel the firmness of his hand. Saul was there, acting in some formally subordinate but really dominate capacity. The business is not conducted as it was at the last meeting of the court, when, under the temporizing initiative of Gamaliel, the persecutors allowed the victims to slip through their hands.

Here from the first the reins seem to be held in an inexorable grasp. The witnesses are ready: they have conned their tasks; their precognitions have been taken. The prisoner is placed on his defence with a foregone conclusion that he shall not escape.

The martyr has a distinct presentiment that this will be his last witness-bearing. The sheen on his countenance betokens the triumph in his soul. It has generally been considered to be a supernatural glory. I am not disposed to dispute this theory; for it would be in accord with other examples, and with the purpose of God to give unbelievers yet another testimony. But I rather like to think of it as a natural brightness—as the direct and non-miraculous effect of great inward peace coinciding with great outward trouble. All God's children attain in measure to the serenity of countenance which corresponds to internal faith and hope; but in some cases this effect is produced to such an extent as to excite the admiration of observers. I think it probable that it was Stephen's victorious faith, and blessed hope, fanned by the fierce persecution into greater force, that glistened that day on his face, and almost persuaded some of his persecutors. At eventide there shall be light. In the near prospect of glory, he was so elevated above the world, that the dawn of an eternal day reached him before the time, and a halo of that light crowned the victim for the sacrifice.

Stephen's Testimony
(Acts 7)

"Then said the high priest, Are these things so? And he said, Men, brethren, and fathers, hearken;" etc.

" MARK the perfect man, and behold the upright." That object is worthy of regard anywhere; but here it is placed in a position peculiarly fitted to display its grandeur. Everything about the faith of Christians is interesting; but the trial of their faith especially is found unto praise, and honor, and glory, at the appearing of Jesus Christ (1 Pet. i. 7). The flame may live throughout the day, if the supply of oil be constant; but it is by night that the flame is seen. So, though a disciple's faith may survive through a period of prosperity, as a secret bond between him and his Saviour, it is not observed by other men until the night of adversity settles down. "Mark the perfect man, and behold the upright;" but choose the time for marking him. The beauty of his course is generally best seen towards its close: "The end of that man is peace." The sufferings which enemies have inflicted become the darkness which reveals his light.

Stephen stands before the Sanhedrim, not to be tried, but to be condemned. When he distributed alms to the poor widows, I suppose his face was pleasant to look upon—as that of a loving, benevolent man; but when he stands before his murderers, in the immediate prospect of martyrdom, it is like the face of an angel. The sun is more beautiful at his setting than at his meridian; and if dark clouds cluster on the horizon round him, they serve to receive and reflect his light, and so to increase the loveliness of the departing moment.

The specific charge preferred against Stephen is, that he spoke blasphemous words against the Temple and the Law. The presiding judge, conducting himself in the first instance with at least external propriety, intimates to the accused that he is put on his trial, and invites him to plead: "Then said the high priest, Are these things so?" Not wanting in courtesy, the accused begins with a general salutation of respect.

A question of much interest has been raised regarding the sources whence Luke, the historian, obtained a report of this address. Besides the Church in Jerusalem, where a record of all the circumstances may have been kept, the narrator had a competent reporter at hand in the person of the apostle Paul. Saul of Tarsus was present at this trial: and every word of the martyr's defence was graven on his capacious memory, as

with a pen of iron and the point of a diamond.   After
he became a preacher of the faith, which at that time
he persecuted, he would still recall the same facts,
though invested with a new meaning.   Doubtless the
beloved physician took the opportunity of the enforced
leisure of a long sea voyage to learn authentically from
Paul's lips all the particulars of this extraordinary
history.

It is in the spirit of a devout believer that Stephen
traces the course of Hebrew history.   He touches tenderly, and with devout reverence, all the great events
in God's dealing with Israel.   His speech, in this aspect,
must have gone far to refute the accusations that were
brought against him.   This is not a reviler of the Temple and the Law.   This is not a renegade Jew who
abjures the authority of Moses.   It was not by his historical discourse that Stephen offended his judges; it
was rather by his unsparing application of the Word
to their consciences.   His elegant apologetic essay
would have pleased his judges, as the story of the
ewe lamb pleased the guilty king; it was his concluding onslaught, "Thou art the man," that enraged the
persecutors, and sealed the doom of the intrepid
witness.

Whether he had reached the point whence he could
most effectually launch his premeditated bolt, or whether
he was interrupted by some commotion in the audience,
we cannot with certainty determine; but at the 51st
verse the discourse takes a sudden turn.   From an abstract disquisition on the Divine plan, as shown in the
Old Testament history, he changes in a moment to a
bold, personal denunciation of his judges: " Ye stiff-
necked and uncircumcised in heart and ears, ye do
always resist the Holy Ghost: as your fathers did, so
do ye."   This sudden charge must have produced a
great excitement in the court.   Hitherto, there is good
reason to believe they had listened with rapt attention.
The sketch of their own history, given by the accused,
must have been grateful to their ears.   Perhaps they
may have begun to think, " This man doeth nothing
worthy of death or of bonds."   He had honored Abraham and Moses and David.   He had spoken reverently
of God, and acknowledged Israel as the chosen people.

As far as he had yet gone, they would have found it hard to convict him of blasphemy. Stephen, I suppose, had a well-defined plan in his mind. He desired to win their attention, and soften their hearts. When at last he saw the gates open and the watchmen off their guard, he made a sudden rush, in the hope of taking the city by assault, and leading its defenders captive—captive to Christ.

The preacher's plan was in the first instance successful. The word in Stephen's lips proved quick and powerful. The sword ran into their joints and marrow. The immediate object is gained: there is conviction. The judges are "cut to the heart." This is one step of progress, but it is not the end. For those who seek to win souls, as well as for those who try to make a fortune, there is many a slip between the cup and the lip. Conviction goes before conversion; but conversion does not always follow conviction. When such a home-thrust takes effect on the conscience, a great anger is generated. That anger burns like fire, and it must have some object to consume. It will either burn inward to consume your own sins, or outward to persecute the preacher who exposed them. In such a case there must be a victim. You will wreak your vengeance either on your sins or on your reprovers. Such a word as Stephen preached to his judges will be a savor of life or a savor of death. It makes the hearer better or worse.

In this case the anger which the word generated went the wrong way; instead of going inward to crucify their own lusts, it went outward to take the life of the faithful reprover: "They gnashed on him with their teeth."

As the fury of the persecutors increased, so did the ecstasy of the martyr. The blast of their wrath against him, like the wind against a kite, carried him higher toward heaven: "But he, being full of the Holy Ghost, looked up steadfastly into heaven, and saw the glory of God, and Jesus." These two sights lie close together. Stephen, I suppose, saw them blended into one, and could not separate them. If the glory of God should appear without Jesus, the Spirit would fail before him, and the souls that he has made. In the Apocalyptic vision of the blessed state, it is said that "the Lamb is the light thereof."

It is noticed with interest by all the commentators from the earliest times, that Jesus was *standing* on the right hand of God when the first martyr obtained a supernatural foresight of his exalted Redeemer. He was not sitting, as in peace and ease; but standing up, as one who felt the pain that his member on the earth endured. This attitude of the Lord in heaven already foreshadows his own subsequent word: "Saul, Saul, why persecutest thou me?" The preparation for stoning Stephen stirred the heart of his Lord. He stood up in anticipation as well as in sympathy. He was preparing to receive with suitable welcome the first witness who should, after himself, ascend in a fiery chariot.

Stephen's ecstatic exclamation was the signal for an uproar in the court. What had up to this point seemed, externally at least, an orderly trial, degenerated now into a fanatical disturbance. The peace and triumph of the martyrs has always fanned the persecutors into a fiercer flame. The murderers have never been able to bear the dying testimony of the victims. In an age comparatively recent, they beat the drums to drown the last words of the Scottish Covenanters. "Argyle's sleep," on the night before his execution, made the blood run cold in his enemies' veins.

While the rude executioners were doing their work under the eye of a zealous young Pharisee, lately appointed the chief agent of the inquisitors, Stephen himself is occupied too. He is praying. Finding himself in the valley of the shadow of death, he addresses Jesus, present to faith, as David long ago had done: "I will not fear, for thou art with me."

Stephen's Death
(Acts 7:60)

"And he kneeled down, and cried with a loud voice, Lord, lay not this sin to their charge. And when he had said this, he fell asleep."

I THINK the young man Saul was an attentive listener, both to the martyr's sermon and the prayer that followed it. I think that he obtained the germs of his systematic theology that day. Sometimes in our Divinity halls a young man receives instruction in the great things of the covenant as he learns languages and mathematics, without having for the time any specific use for his acquisition. The truth is stored in an unrenewed heart, and lies there dormant until the quickening Spirit come. The seed of the Word has been dropped into frozen furrows; and when the melting comes it is there ready to spring. Thus the word from Stephen's lips dropped into Saul's memory. I like to entertain the conception that in Stephen's speech Paul found the idea of the Epistle to the Hebrews.

Another stage of the martyrdom: "He kneeled down." The stones were overcoming—overwhelming him. He is fainting from loss of blood. Stephen will not remain on his feet till he fall. While he has strength left he will bow down to pray; and he prays aloud for his enemies: "Lord, lay not this sin to their charge." A secret sigh might have reached the throne as well; but the loud voice made known, both to friends and to foes, the latest exercise of the martyr's spirit. The expression of that prayer may be the means of winning souls, and therefore it is articulately expressed. That prayer may have remained like a barb in the conscience of some of his murderers, which would not let them go until it led them to the blood of the covenant.

"When he had said this, he fell asleep." All things are yours, when you are Christ's, and death among them. This dreaded name is an article in the inventory of a Christian's possessions. When death becomes the property of a disciple, it is baptized and gets a new name. It has many different Christian names. For Paul, it was a departing to be with Christ; for Stephen, it was to fall asleep. When the earthly house of this tabernacle is dissolved, we have a building of God, an house not made with hands. A relative of my own lately gave a new name to this messenger, which I had not heard before, and which I rather like. Leaving her own home, to pay a visit of some weeks in the neighboring city, she said to a friend, with reference to the possibility of not returning, "I am like a passenger, with my ticket in my hand, waiting at the station till the train come up." According to her secret anticipation the train did come up, ere the visit was over, and she was carried gently away.

Sleep is a very impressive and appropriate Christian name for death. If we were not made indifferent by familiarity with it, natural sleep would seem a very solemn and mysterious experience. We might well be familiar with death, for we have a symbol and rehearsal of it every night. We might be familiar with the resurrection, for we have a symbol and rehearsal of it every morning. If faith were lively, we might lie down every night as an infant lies down to sleep in a mother's arms: we might be comforted in the morning when we awaked by remembering that this same Jesus stands yet at the right hand of the throne, girt for mighty work, as our protector, and alert to receive all his own, when life is over, into the joy of the Lord.

It is remarkable, that of all the Christian names of death, this one should be employed here. It might seem an appropriate epithet, when an aged Christian, on his chair or his bed, after a gradual decay of strength, with a gentle smile on a wan countenance, speaks this moment of his hope in Christ, and the next moment glides away. When death in such circumstances is called a sleep, the analogy is easily apprehended, and at once accepted as true. But a cruel death by stoning, amid the yells and curses of infuriated executioners, stripped like gladiators for their bloody work— death in such a tumult called a sleep! Yes; and there is a design in the choice of the name. God sits King on these floods. Jesus stands up and speaks again to the sea; and at his word there is a great calm. At sight of him "standing" over the waves, the weary voyager is instantly at the land where he desired to be. Sweeter to the martyr would be the glory of Emmanuel's land when he touched its shore, because of the storm through which he had passed.

The executioners, engaged and paid, and held in readiness, to do the work quickly, lest the sentence, lacking the due authority, might be recalled, "laid down their clothes at a young man's feet, whose name was Saul." Such is the first introduction of this man to the readers of the Bible. The Apostle of the Gentiles steps upon the stage, the acknowledged head of a ruffian band, in the very act of shedding the first martyr's blood. What hath God wrought! How unsearchable are his judgments, and his ways past finding out!

"When he had said this, he fell asleep; but Saul was consenting unto his death." We should not overlook the connection and the contrast, which the division of the chapters here rather tends to obscure. These two men met for one day, and then went on their several paths;—the one, right on to the joy of the Lord; the other, to the work of wasting the Church. The intimation at the beginning of chapter viii. means that Saul approved of the policy adopted in taking Stephen off. It would be an error to impute to him any inhuman cruelty. Saul was never a man of low tastes and brutal passions. From early years he was a man of most acute intellect, earnest opinions, and lofty aims. At this time his belief was that Stephen's doctrines were subversive of the true religion; and that the best way of checking a heresy was to put the heretics to death. These principles did not die out with the conversion of Saul. They survived, and deluged Europe with blood down to a very recent period. It is only now, in our own generation, that religious toleration has been established. The position of Saul at the death of Stephen was due, not to natural cruelty, but to a perverted judgment. He thought he did God service by slaying the disciples of Christ. His own description is clear and true: "I verily thought I ought to do many things contrary to the name of Jesus of Nazareth; which thing I also did."

He held the opinion that it was just and right to take Stephen off, as a subverter of the law.

I have often tried to conceive the scene at the next meeting of these two men, when Saul also became a martyr, and joined the general assembly and church of the first-born. When they met in the presence of the Lord, there would be no upbraiding on the one side, and no shame on the other. Saul's guilt was indeed very great. The young Pharisee who conducted the case against Stephen with skill and vigor, and plunged into another as soon as the dark deed was done—that young Pharisee was a chief sinner; but the blood of Jesus Christ, God's Son, cleansed him from all sin. Stephen would be so much occupied remembering his own guilt, and praising the grace that had blotted it out, that he would have no time and no inclination to cast up the sins of other men. We have not the means of determining whether Stephen or Saul owed most to the Lord. By looking on the surface of the sea we cannot tell what place is deepest; but we know that all places, alike the deepest and the shallowest, are filled, and all present one level surface to the sky. In like manner, as far as we can perceive, all the forgiven are alike. It is only He who bore their sins who can distinguish the aggravations of every case. Certain it is that the first martyr and the man who kept the clothes of the executioners at his death are now at peace. They are one in Christ.

The Persecution of the Christians
The Increase of the Church
(Acts 8:1-4)

" And Saul was consenting unto his death. And at that time there was a great persecution against the church which was at Jerusalem; and they were all scattered abroad throughout the regions of Judæa and Samaria, except the apostles. And devout men carried Stephen to his burial, and made great lamentation over him. As for Saul, he made havoc of the church, entering into every house, and haling men and women committed them to prison. Therefore they that were scattered abroad went everywhere preaching the word."

ON that day a great persecution sprang up. The translators have taken the definite term in a general sense —" at that time—" which it may sometimes bear; but there seems no necessity here for avoiding the more specific meaning. It is natural that when the flood of rage had been permitted once to break out, it should flow on and cover all the neighborhood. It broke out like a flame, and instantly seized and licked up all that could be converted into fuel. The leaders of such a movement found it their interest that the passions of the multitude, once excited, should have no time to cool. The tiger has tasted blood, and now the creature thirsts fiercely for another victim. On that day a great persecution broke out.

The favor of the people had gained for the Christians a brief breathing-time, and they had occupied it well. In the interval several thousands had become obedient to the faith. Of these a large proportion were priests, who might be expected to be of special service afterwards to the cause. When they had learned that the Scriptures testify of Christ, they would be better fitted by their previous training than disciples of another class for the work of convincing gainsayers and edifying the Church.

But the popular favor soon failed the Christians. That protection seems to have sprung up as quickly as Jonah's gourd, and withered as soon. Already the defenceless heads of the witnesses were exposed to the full fury of the persecution. They were scattered abroad, – –the assemblies broken up, and the individual disciples compelled to flee. They betook themselves to the country around Jerusalem, and some penetrated northward into Samaria. Thus, although their steps were directed by events beyond their control, they were exactly fulfilling the Master's commission, — first in Jerusalem, next in Judæa, then in Samaria, and thence to the uttermost parts of the earth. The six surviving deacons, and other prominent members of the Church, sought refuge in flight; but the apostles remained still in Jerusalem.

As for Saul, he pursued his vocation. "He made havoc of the Church;" but he was employed as an instrument in promoting the Divine plan. The havoc made by Saul scattered the Christians; the scattered Christians were like sparks, kindling a great flame wherever they fell: "They that were scattered abroad went everywhere preaching the word."

At this point the historian, according to his custom, abandons the method of general description, and exhibits, by way of example, the details of a particular case. The portion of Christian history selected in this section is the ministry of Philip the deacon. Two specimens of his preaching are given in this chapter; and I think these two have been chosen as a sign for all places and all times. The gospel first reaches Samaria, and then the ends of the earth. The first example of Philip's ministry is among the nearest neighbors of the Jews; and the next is addressed to an Ethiopian, representative of the distant Gentiles. The first is a ministry in a city to a multitude; the next is a ministry in a desert to a single man. These two are types of all. And in both, the preacher's theme was one:—when he went to a city of Samaria, "he preached Christ unto them:" when he met the Ethiopian in the desert, he "preached unto him Jesus."

In the gallery of missionary portraits which this book displays, although some are larger, none are more distinctly traced than that of the evangelist Philip. The sketches given of his life and labors are very short, but very clear. He comes suddenly upon the stage, marches quickly across it, and disappears on the other side when his part is played. Very little time is allowed to examine him, and yet we do not forget him when he is gone. All his movements are remarkable for directness and precision; there is no ambiguous haze hanging over the horizon of his life. This is not the man who at first possesses ten talents; but this is the man who lays out his five with such a will, that they soon become ten in his hands. His movements remind you of Ezekiel's wheels. Like them, he goes straight forward, without turning to the right hand or to the left—whether in going forward or in coming back—whether on his way from the city to the wilderness, or on his way from the wilderness to the city. Like them, too, he moves with the Spirit, and by the Spirit: he goes not unbidden, and goes not alone. Where the Spirit leads, he follows.

Philip was driven into Samaria by the violence of the persecution at Jerusalem. This is the way by which the gospel was propagated in those days. The blood of the martyrs was the seed of the Church. In this matter the plan of Providence has been to a great extent changed in our time. It is not by the persecution of Christians in one place that Christianity is carried into another now. In the cognate kingdom of nature vegetation is spread, not always and everywhere by one and the same agency. A part of the work is done by the wind bearing the winged seeds over mountains and moors, a part by birds carrying heavier fruits for objects of their own, and a part by the progressive outspread of the roots under the ground. There is a similar diversity in the methods employed by the Omniscient Husbandman to scatter the seed of the Word over the world. Missionaries are now for the most part *sent* out, not *driven* out. This method, though more gentle, is not less effectual. It is the spontaneousness of the scattering that constitutes its glory. "Thy people shall be willing in the day of thy power." On the part of the Church, it is eminently a reasonable service; and yet men are drawn into it by the loving-kindness of the Lord.

Two methods are in operation among civilized nations for filling up their armies: one is a forced conscription from the inhabitants, the other a voluntary enlistment.

Both methods have in practice made good soldiers; but in its nature the voluntary service is the nobler of the two, and in its operation the sweeter. In this manner the missionary army of the present day is recruited. It is not that the disciples of Christ preach to the heathen because they are driven from home; it is that they go from home that they may preach to the heathen.

Nor is there any room for self-complacency on our part, when the two periods and the two processes are compared. It is not that we adopt the gentler method because our love is stronger: I rather think the Lord spares us the sterner method because our faith is weaker. If we were persecuted as the early Christians were, I fear, instead of imparting our religion to our neighbors, we should let go our own. Let us appreciate our privileges and thank the Giver. Let us not be high-minded, but fear.

Further: seeing we enjoy abundant peace, we ought to be abundant in our mission labor. The early Christians did much mission work because they were persecuted; we ought to do more because we are not. Peace has multiplied our resources; if our efforts were proportioned to our resources, we might occupy a continent as easily as the hundred and twenty from the upper room occupied Samaria and Galilee. Our lives and our strength are not consumed by the fires of persecution; we should therefore devote more energy and effort to the service of the Lord.

Philip Preaching in a Samaritan City
(Acts 8:5)

" Then Philip went down to the city of Samaria, and preached Christ unto them."

PHILIP (1.) went down to a city of Samaria; and (2.) preached Christ unto them.

I. *Went down to a city of Samaria.*

1. *Went down;* that is, from Jerusalem. The place physically was high; and so the form of expression for going away from Jerusalem naturally came to be, "Going down." Jerusalem was the centre. There were both the thrones and the altars of the house of David. Thither the tribes went up to worship; thence the law flowed out, and thence the gospel.

If there is one grand supereminent and central mountain in a country, to it the clouds of heaven come, around it they congregate. From that mountain, in turn, the water flows in every direction to refresh the land. Such, spiritually, was Jerusalem to the world.

The clouds gathered grand and multitudinous around it on the Pentecost that immediately followed the death and resurrection of the Lord. Under the influence of the rushing mighty wind they were precipitated on its summit, and flowed in vast volumes back to all the surrounding nations, bearing the gospel of grace to people of every tribe and tongue. Out of the temple that day flowed waters that at first rose to the ankles, and then to the knees, and then to the loins, and afterwards became waters to swim in—a great flowing river coursing through a desert world; and wherever it flowed changing the desert into a fruitful field.

Christ's name and work is that central mountain now. The Spirit without measure is poured out on him. The Jerusalem that now is, is the Church of Christ in the world. Around it all heavenly influences congregate; on it they drop down; and from it then flow forth. Hence missions to heathen and Jews. If you ask, Why do Christians engage in mission work? the answer is, They cannot help it. Why do the rivers flow down the mountain sides upon the parched plains when once the clouds have discharged their burdens on the mountain's summit? They must flow down, by the law of their being. So Christians must flow: love in the hearts of the redeemed swells, and would rend them, unless they opened to give it vent. From Jerusalem, throughout all Judæa and Samaria, and unto the uttermost parts of the earth,—behold the law of the kingdom, the kingdom established in Christian hearts.

2. *To a city.*—In congregated masses of humanity, the evil is great when they are evil, the good great when they are good. The efforts of the first Christians were directed not exclusively, but chiefly, to the great cities. The spiritual warfare in this respect follows the analogy of the temporal: when the strongholds are won, the surrounding territory is more easily occupied.

Cities seem destined to play a greater part in modern than they played in ancient times. As yet no symptom appears of any natural law that shall check their increase. The corruption of such vast heaps of corruptible matter is enough to make the stoutest heart falter. In presence of modern cities and their phases of corruption we may well lose heart. "This is the victory that overcometh the world, even your faith." Lord, increase our faith; for the sight or the thought of London makes our hearts flow down like water.

3. *A city of Samaria.*—It was near; it was needy. Long before, the native Jewish inhabitants had been carried away, and a colony of heathens planted in their stead. These added the worship of Jehovah to their variegated creed. They were a mixed people, with a patchwork religion. In later times they had in a great measure conformed externally to Jewish modes of worship, but conducted it on their own soil. They made a merit of having a common worship with the Jews, and eagerly claimed a common descent.

Samaria is near us to-day; if we are willing to go down to it, we need not lack a mission field. We have not far to look down to Samaria; and she has not far to look up to us.   If she see us like herself,—if she see us as covetous, as vain, as godless,—she will get comfort from us; and such peacemakers are not blessed. (See Ezek. xvi. 54.)   If we give the profane and careless multitudes any ground for counting that we are no better than themselves, we heal their wounds slightly, and say Peace, peace, when there is no peace.   But if we go down to them with reproof on our lips—with reproof silent but mighty in our lives,—we shall, indeed, make them sorry at first, but out of that godly sorrow the joy of the Lord will in due time spring.

II. *He preached Christ unto them.*—When Philip had reached his proper mission field, he forthwith began his proper mission work.

1. *He preached.*—Take it literally; for in that aspect it conveys a true, an appropriate lesson.   The first and chief work of a missionary is to preach.   The missionary is a herald, sent from the great King to a rebel country, bearing his terms of reconciliation.   The first business of the herald is to proclaim his message.   Indeed, the word which we translate *preach*, has been borrowed from that ancient office of a herald.   Teaching and printing become in certain circumstances important auxiliaries; but they defeat their own end, if they occupy the foreground, or usurp the centre.

Nor must we shut our eyes to the reproof which the term conveys to ourselves.   Arguments and disquisitions, however just in themselves, and however important in respect of their themes, cannot serve as substitutes for preaching.   To preach is to proclaim— to proclaim, as a herald from the great King, the terms on which the rebels will be received into favor.   This is the real bone and marrow of preaching.

2. *Preached Christ.*—To this the teaching of the Bible constantly comes round.   The true minister preaches, not law, not morality, not doctrine—preaches not philosophy, not religion, but Christ—not the Scriptures, not the true doctrine, but Christ.   Proclaims, offers, presses Christ upon men.

3. *Preached Christ* UNTO THEM.—He brings the matter home to themselves,—brings it home to each heart.   To preach that Christ came into the world to

save sinners, is right, but it is not enough. I think I see many near the kingdom, and yet falling short of it on this side: We are all sinners, and we all need Christ as our Saviour. I think I see souls slipping through the opening there and sinking. I fear, through that opening many may be lost. Why so pertinacious in taking a whole armful of other people into your confession? I fear it is sometimes the same instinct that said, "What have we to do with thee, thou Jesus? art thou come to torment us?" What if a soul grasp a great multitude of others along with itself, when it comes near Christ, precisely in order that it may escape personal contact with him! Let others go for a time; change your method; instead of speaking about Christ as a Saviour of all, speak to him, that he may save you. Lord, I am lost, but I cling to thee. Christ to you; you to Christ.

Let the sunbeams passing through ordinary glass be spread over your naked hand; you may hold it under these bright rays for an hour, and experience no inconvenience. If you should shut your eyes, or look another way, you would scarcely know that the sunbeams were streaming on your hand at all. But now let the rays pass through a convex glass, and so be concentrated in one point upon your flesh. That one point will shine with great brightness; and what is more, that one bright point will burn. It will go to the quick, and compel you to withdraw.

Precisely the same diversities occur in preaching and hearing the gospel. It may be the same truth in two cases, as it was the same sunlight; and yet in the one it may be so spread out, in giving it or receiving it, that it exerts no power—that it falls on indulged sins, and shines on them, without ever making the sinner wince. The glorious gospel, the very truth of God, may be so diffused in the preaching or the hearing, or both, that it shall fall like sunbeams on a field and burn no blade. The same gospel when given on a point, or received into the conscience on a point, may run into the marrow like a sword, and compel the pierced soul to cry out, "What must I do to be saved?"

Fruit - Joy
(Acts 8:6-8)

" And the people with one accord gave heed unto those things which Philip spake, hearing and seeing the miracles which he did. For unclean spirits, crying with loud voice, came out of many that were possessed with them: and many taken with palsies, and that were lame, were healed. And there was great joy in that city."

1. THEY listened to the messenger. There was great earnestness and great unanimity. They did not rise up against the messenger to drive him away; neither did they remain unmoved, leaving him to spend his strength in vain. They came to him zealously, and they came all.

It is a great advantage to every one when an awakening becomes general. Solitary Christians, with no congenial company within their reach, are like solitary trees near the sea-coast: the cold winds keep down their growth or kill them. But in a thick wood all contribute to shelter each. The spiritual life may be best maintained where there is much spiritual life all around.

So quickly and so generally did a harvest spring up to Philip's hand in this city, as soon as he appeared on the spot, that we are compelled to believe that a sower had previously cast precious seed into the field. The Master himself had with his own hand sown the field on which his servant was now gathering a plentiful harvest. We remember how, at the call of the Samaritan woman, great numbers from the town of Sychar came out and heard the word from the Lord himself. This word was not in vain. One soweth, and another reapeth.

2. The people both heard his doctrines and saw his mighty works. Unclean spirits were cast out, and the diseased were healed.

Miracles, in the ordinary sense of that term, ceased with the first or second generation of Christians. We have now the same doctrines preached, and the same results in spiritual conversion, but not the supernatural cures. The miracles constituted the credentials of the first preachers. But perhaps to some minds the cessation of miracles may present as great a difficulty as the miracles themselves. If the missionaries of Christianity performed miracles once, why do they not perform miracles still ?

If this question is not articulately answered, the questioner at least is silenced by one of the clearest and surest of all analogies. It is certain and easily demonstrable that some great energy was put forth by the Creator at the beginning of the present order of nature which is not continued now. To set the world agoing at first, powers were necessary that are not necessary and are not put forth to keep it going after its course has begun; the forces of nature now acting are sufficient to account for the motion of the heavenly bodies, but not to account for how they began to move. The present organic laws are sufficient to account for the continuance of the species, but not to account for its commencement. According to the ordinary laws or sequences of nature every creature produces its kind; but we know of no law that could produce a creature where there was no such creature previously in existence.

Thus a power must have been put forth to begin the present cosmos, which has ceased, and never operates now. Why then should it be thought a thing impossible that God should exert a power to establish the gospel at first, which is not needed and is not exerted to keep it going ? This is what the Scriptures declare. The declaration is in most perfect accord with what we know of God's method in the material department of his kingdom. The constant process of generation is as wise and wonderful as the miracle of creation. So, although the miracles that introduced Christianity are not now presented to us, it does not follow that they were greater works than those that occur now in conversion by the ministry of the Spirit. The greater and the better work is that which continues to this day. The unclean spirits are cast out, the aliens are reconciled, the guilty forgiven, and the corrupt renewed. " Greater works than these," said the Lord to his followers—" greater works than these shall ye do, becau.e I go to my Father." The converting and sanctifying work that his disciples, by the ministry of the Spirit, were honored to do after his ascension, were, in his esteem, greater works than those miracles—such as the feeding of five thousand, and stilling the storm—which he had exhibited in the exercise of his Divine power over the elements of nature.

3. There was great joy in that city.—Hear this, ye butterfly flutterers, that flit from flower to flower, satiate with each sweet as soon as you alight on it, and hastening unhappy to another, trying every flower all day, and at night bringing no honey home;—hear this, all ye who study hard to keep religion at arm's-length, lest it should cast a gloom over your heart or your home; —hear this: When an earnest missionary—a man who risked his life for Christ's name—preached in a city, and when the people came out in crowds and hung upon the lips of the strange revivalist, the citizens, instead of growing gloomy, became very glad. This is a phenomenon worthy of your study.

But beware lest you mistake its meaning. The instinct which prompts the vain and worldly to shut the door and keep earnest religion outside, lest it should mar their happiness, is a true instinct. Every creature after its kind. Every creature's instinct is true for its own preservation. The apprehension that Christ's entrance into the vain or vicious heart would be the death of its joy is a just apprehension. The devils believe this, and tremble at its truth. "What have we to do with thee, thou Jesus?" To open your whole heart for a whole Christ,—to take into your bosom the Christ who was crucified for sin, does indeed torment the old man; and the old man, a strong man armed, keeps his goods in peace as long as he can. The old man will not be spared at Christ's coming; he will be crucified. When he is put off a new nature is put on, and the new nature has new joys. There was great joy in that city when Christ was preached to the citizens. This, however, is the ultimate result, not the first effect of such preaching. "This child is set for the *fall* and the *rising* again of many in Israel." These Samaritans, when we get a glimpse of them, are bearing home their sheaves with rejoicing; but the seed-time was moist with their tears. The pleasures of sin have been rent off, and the patient cried at the rending; but the joy of the Lord has now come.

In the world of a man's own heart and life he lived without God; lived and laughed because God was not there; trembled sometimes in the midst of his mirth with an instinctive dread lest God should burst into his world and quench its mirth in wrath. But at length the Stranger who long knocked outside has come in. At his presence the former joys fled; but with his presence come new joys—the peace of God that passeth all understanding.

Some people at some times—and I mention this outward and visible thing at present mainly for the light which it throws as an analogy on another that is secret and unseen—are found willing to convert the sweet still rest of night into a scene of crowded, noisy, toilsome revelry. They light up the darkness into a kind of artificial brilliance, and deck themselves into a kind of conventional beauty; and they toil like navvies in a close, crowded, suffocating room. When the sun arises on this scene its hollowness is detected, and its false brilliancy put to shame. How dull the flicker of the lamps is now ! how yellow the flush that glowed on the heated cheek ! how tawdry and dusty the light flowing robes ! They are all fain to get out of sight.

But yonder are two youths on the mountain-top, there in time to greet the sun's rising. They drink in the golden glory that precedes and accompanies his appearing in the east; and then, in his mild morning light, they search among the grass for the flowers, that bend their necks to anticipate his coming, and open their bosoms to take in his light.

Suppose now that one of those night revellers should get a glimpse of these two as he is skulking home, and should say, " These are dull fellows, that shut their cold hearts against all pleasure." It is sheer ignorance and impudence. Those youths take in more joy—more natural human delight—in an hour of their morning walk, than the souls of that whole company have capacity to contain.

In like manner, in the secret of a soul, they make a great mistake who think that to abandon the crackling thorns of ungodly mirth is to plunge into spiritual gloom. They who through Christ have been reconciled to God, and walk in the light of his countenance, have indeed allowed one kind of happiness to be chased away; but it is like changing the flickering of the night lamp for the risen sun, and the breath of the dancing hall when the night is far spent for the morning breeze on the mountain.

There was joy in that city. Christ offered to a city or a soul, and kept out, seems like a cloud of wrath hanging in the heavens over it—a terror; but Christ freely offered, and believingly accepted, by a city or a soul, becomes a joy which life could not give, and death cannot destroy.

Sent to the Desert
(Acts 8:26)

"And the angel of the Lord spake unto Philip, saying, Arise, and go toward the south, unto the way that goeth down from Jerusalem unto Gaza, which is desert."

AFTER the episode regarding Simon the Sorcerer, and the mission of Peter and John from the Church at Jerusalem to visit the converts in Samaria, the narrative of Philip's ministry is resumed. He is sent now, not to a populous city, but to a desert; not to a crowd of Samaritans, but to a solitary Ethiopian. A message, which he recognized as from the Lord, reached Philip to the effect that he should "arise, and go toward the south, unto the way that goeth down from Jerusalem unto Gaza, which is desert."

Both "way" and "Gaza" being feminine, it is not certainly indicated whether it is the road or the city that is described as a desert. It so happened that Gaza was standing at the period when Philip preached, but was demolished at the period when Luke composed his treatise. Some understand accordingly, that the words "this is desert" are the historian's note on the condition of the town when he was writing. Others take the words as part of the angel's message, intimating that the path lay through a wilderness. Though both come to the same in the end, the second seems the more natural construction. The road leads through an uninhabited country. There were more ways than one from Jerusalem to Gaza. One led by Hebron southward, and the other took a westerly direction:.

"He arose and went:" he was not disobedient to the heavenly vision. If, like Jonah, he had looked for excuses, he would have found them in abundance. He was well employed in a populous district. He had a wide door—a multitude of listeners when he preached —a multitude of inquirers when he was done. Many believed. The fields were white: and the laborer was getting his bosom filled with sheaves. Had he been called from one Samaritan town to another as large and as needy, he might have perceived the reasonableness of the call. But the demand is that he should leave the city and go to a desert. It is a trial of faith analogous to Abraham's. It required a simple, unquestioning trust, while all the appearances were adverse.

Whether he took the path by Hebron or that which lies more westward, Philip at length passed out of the inhabited regions, and penetrated into the inhospitable tract which stretches southward to Egypt and the Red Sea. Here he threads his way over broken stones and shifting sands, doing his best to keep the track that former travellers have made.

Afloat on the sand-sea, the evangelist is like one of those master-mariners who, at their sovereign's command, set sail with sealed orders not to be opened till they reach a certain indicated spot of the ocean. Philip as yet did not know why he was sent to this place, or what he was expected to do there; but he counted that his orders would open when he reached the spot. The orders, accordingly, all open, like the prison-doors for Peter, of their own accord, and the whole plan is revealed: "Behold, a man of Ethiopia, a eunuch of great authority under Candace queen of the Ethiopians, who had the charge of all her treasure, and had come to Jerusalem for to worship, was returning, and sitting in his chariot read Esaias the prophet."

These two men meet in the desert: the one, a sinner uneasy seeking a Saviour; the other, a called and qualified minister of Christ. The one is a thirsting soul; the other is a "chosen vessel" charged with the water of life. The one offers, the other receives Christ. They part again: Philip to pursue his ministry; the Ethiopian rejoicing in the Lord. They met and parted in a day, perhaps in an hour. At the beginning of that interview the Ethiopian was timidly asking, "What must I do to be saved?" At the close of it he resumed his journey, a Christian in the full assurance of hope. They approached from different directions, on converging lines, until they met on a point like the apex of the letter $>$; but having met, they soon separated again, like the crossing lines of the letter $\times$, and probably never saw each other more in the body.

The two lines on which they approached rose like rivers in far distant hills, and flowed on until they met at a point in the desert between Jerusalem and the border of Egypt.

Trace the course of the Ethiopian treasurer. Late in the preceding, or early in the same year, while the mild winter of that region kept mornings and evenings cool, a commotion might have been observed in the principal street of the Abyssinian metropolis at the departure of a caravan for the north. It is the grand vizier of the queen, starting on a religious pilgrimage. The bystanders do not exactly know the reason of the journey, but one has heard a neighbor tell that the chief treasurer had been much taken up of late with stories told by travelling Jewish merchants, of a mighty prophet who had arisen in Judæa. The treasurer, it was rumored, was going all the way to Jerusalem to worship the God of Israel, and seek the Messiah who was at that time expected to come.

We lose sight of the Ethiopian grandee, alike on his toilsome journey by the bank of the Nile, and through the wilderness; we never get a glimpse of him among the crowds, native and foreign, who congregate in Jerusalem to worship at the feast. Where he was and how employed during the events which signalized that Passover, we cannot tell; but we know that, after waiting long and inquiring much, he called his servants and ordered his waggon, and started on his journey homeward, while the longing of his soul that had brought him so far remained still unsatisfied. He was thirsty; he came to the place where the springs were opened; and yet he went away still athirst. There has not been such a revival meeting since on earth as that one which took place in Jerusalem while the Ethiopian was there; and yet he came away sorrowful. On that day of Pentecost the Holy Spirit was poured on many, but not on him; at least so he thought and felt. After he has come so far, it is sad to see him returning without his errand. Yet it is written in the Scriptures, "Seek, and ye shall find." Can the promise—can the Promiser be true? Yes; and this is a conspicuous example of his faithfulness. This Ethiopian, secretly taught of the Spirit, did not limit God to times and places. As he left Ethiopia and went to Jerusalem seeking, so he left Jerusalem and returned to Ethiopia still seeking. He departed from the temple; but he still communed with God. When the period of public worship had passed, he persevered in private searching the Scriptures.

Mark the man well: he has not abandoned the search. The whole meaning of that sable chief, as he bends in silence over the parchment, seems to be, "I will not let thee go, except thou bless me." It is true he has not obtained what he sought at Jerusalem, so as to be satisfied when he departs; but he has learned something at Jerusalem which is of use to him now. Although his want is not supplied, he knows better now what his want is. As the thirsty blindly gropes for water, he comes near the place where a fountain has been opened. An instinct is astir within him, as true as that which guides an infant to its mother's breast. He is feeling for the sufferings of Christ. Before he saw Philip, or obtained any help, the place of the Scripture which he read was this: "He was led as a lamb to the slaughter." All things are now ready. This man will be born there. In that desert place Ethiopia is stretching out her hands to God, and will not be left to stretch them out in vain.

A Man of Ethiopia
(Acts 8:27,28)

"And he arose and went: and, behold, a man of Ethiopia, a eunuch of great authority under Candace queen of the Ethiopians, who had the charge of all her treasure, and had come to Jerusalem for to worship, was returning, and sitting in his chariot read Esaias the prophet."

PAUSE a little here and contemplate that interesting stranger, while Philip opens to him the word of life. He is a man of Ethiopia. In the main, it is the country which is now called Abyssinia. It lies on the eastern edge of the African continent, north of the equator, and bounded on the east by the southern portion of the Red Sea. It is a land of mountains and rivers. Its climate is warm and its soil fertile. It is of great extent. In those days it was a powerful kingdom; and if its people were civilized, it might become powerful again. Some of the streams which constitute the Nile rise in Abyssinia.

The inhabitants are very black. Although we cannot be certain of the nationality of the queen's treasurer, yet, in the absence of any information to the contrary, we must assume that he was a man of Ethiopia by birth as well as by allegiance. In that carriage Philip sits beside a colored man, and leads him into the kingdom of God. The Word is not, Blessed are the fair in skin, but, Blessed are the pure in heart. The Ethiopian's color cannot be changed, but his character may. He may become a new creature in Christ. If he is born again, he will see the kingdom, and enter it too. It does not go by good looks. There is no respect of persons with God. A few days in the grave will make white and black people all alike; and the Ethiopian, if he has been renewed, will be very beautiful in God's sight when he rises from the grave. Angels will gaze in wonder on his gracefulness, as he enters the gates of the New Jerusalem.

This inquirer occupied a very high place in his own country. He was like Joseph under Pharaoh. Inasmuch as the sovereign was a woman, the first lord of her treasury would probably enjoy more power than Joseph possessed under an intelligent and active king. Irresponsible power is not favorable to spiritual humility; but, in this case, grace triumphed over all obstacles. Although the man had much of this world's treasure, it did not satisfy his soul. He did not say, " Soul, thou hast much goods laid up for many years; take thine ease, eat, drink, and be merry." He possessed in abundance all that the world could give, and yet he was wretched. In some way, to us unknown, he had found out his sins, but had not yet discovered the way of pardon. His conscience told him of his guilt, but could not reveal a Redeemer. So the great man, to whom everybody paid court in the capital, went about bent under a load of grief, and inwardly sighing, Oh, wretched man that I am !

Some one—perhaps a little maid who had been taken prisoner in war—observing the sadness of the treasurer, intimated that he might obtain a cure at Jerusalem, where they worshipped the one living and true God. Having heard that there was a place on earth where God makes himself known, he could not rest till he found it. Judging from the length of his journey, the eagerness of his search, and the period of his return, we think it probable that he was in Jerusalem when Jesus was crucified. We have no account of how he spent his time in the city; but it is certain he would frequent the temple at the hour of prayer, and listen to those men of learning who explained the Scriptures in public, and kept alive the hope of a Messiah. It is possible he may have followed the crowd as it streamed along the Via Dolorosa early in the morning towards Calvary, and seen at a distance the elevated cross and the Man of sorrows. This sable stranger, we may be assured, did not mock, or join the cry, Crucify him. He would rather stand by in silent tears.

As yet, however, the Ethiopian did not know Christ. Never man spake like this man; never man lived, never man died, like this man; but still the stranger did not know that here was opened a fountain for sin and for uncleanness. He was very thirsty, and his lip was near the fountain of living water; yet he continued thirsty still.

He must have been present at the Pentecost revival, and heard in his own tongue the wonderful works of God, spoken by Galilean fishermen. From the public assemblies he retired to the secret study of the Scriptures, and from the Scriptures again to the public meetings for prayer; but all the while he was only a seeker—he had not found peace of conscience, pardon of sin, peace with God.

At last the time arrived when he must leave Jerusalem; and, alas! he must go empty away. He had not found what he came to seek. Having a carriage and servants at his disposal, he would doubtless carry water and other provisions, so that he would incur no danger of want in passing through the desert. But the water that he carried in a skin could not satisfy the soul of the Ethiopian prince. After he drank of that water he thirsted again. He was sitting in his carriage alone one day, with an awning over his head to defend it from the sun. A large parchment lay outspread on his knee. He was searching there for the water of life as eagerly as he would have searched near a group of palm-trees for a spring, if he had found himself alone and destitute in the desert. Some instinct in his soul, stimulated and directed by what he had seen and heard at Jerusalem, told him that near this spot the water of life would certainly be found. "He was led as a lamb to the slaughter." He pauses there. He cannot go past that spot. I think I see a great tear gather in the dark eye of the noble African, and dropping on the book. "Led as a lamb to the slaughter!" This reminds him of the wonderful man whom they had nailed to the cross on Calvary. He muses alternately on the verse which he has read and the scene which he witnessed. His heart is throbbing, and his eyes are swimming. "Of whom speaketh the prophet this? of himself, or of some *other* MAN?" Does the word point to that *other man* who died on the accursed tree? Those looks and tones were more like heaven than earth. When he was reviled, he reviled not again. When the thief at his side cried, "Lord, remember me," he answered. God-like, "To-day shalt thou be with me in paradise." That other man! Of whom speaketh the prophet this?

At that moment "the anxious inquirer" lifted up his head, and descried a solitary traveller marching on foot at some distance over the burning sand; for you can discern an object at a distance when the ground is level, and destitute of vegetation. When they meet, the inquirer's question is ready; it had already been brooding silently in his own breast; and now, when he finds a teacher, the demand comes out articulate and intense, Of whom speaketh the prophet this? of himself, or of some other man?

Deliverance is near. The Lord is not slack concerning his promise. "Seek, and ye shall find." The Ethiopian was in downright earnest: when he could not obtain pardon and peace in Abyssinia, he travelled to Jerusalem, and when he failed there he started on his journey homeward again; but he continued seeking. He never let go; the line between his soul and the Saviour whom he sought was at no time permitted to slacken. He had leaned on it, and kept it tight. At night, when he fell asleep, he fell asleep in the act of drawing, as if he would by violence draw a pardon down, and when he awoke his spirit was still in the same attitude: I will not let thee go except thou bless me.

The Lord in heaven is well pleased with this pertinacity and perseverance. He opens his hand wide, and satisfies this longing soul.

The Meeting

(Acts 8:29)

" Then the Spirit said unto Philip, Go near, and join thyself to this chariot."

MARRIAGES, they say, are made in heaven: that is, the steps of two, both being God's dear children, are so directed by an overruling Providence, that after each has passed over many windings, the two paths converge, and the two lives meet and melt into one like two rivers, flowing thenceforth one broader, deeper, stronger stream. Marriages are made in heaven; and two or three other things besides marriages are made there. Meetings that are of shorter duration, and partnerships that are less intimate, come under the same rule. God, who gives law to the ocean, does not neglect a dew-drop. The hairs of your head are all numbered. Our meetings and partings are under law to God. It is not in man that walketh to direct his steps.

The meeting of Philip and the Ethiopian prince in the desert near Gaza is recorded with great precision in Scripture. On that meeting much depended; from that meeting great things sprang. What hath the Lord wrought ! And how wonderfully he hath wrought it ! If his purposes in creation require the meeting of two circling worlds at some period in the evolutions of time, he will so arrange that the two shall approach and touch each other at the very point of space and time which he has designed. The same might and the same wisdom have been at work to arrange a meeting wherever and whenever one earthen vessel charged bears Christ, and another earthen vessel empty receives Christ at a brother's hand. We must not suppose that this meeting between the evangelist and the Ethiopian was arranged by the Lord, and that he leaves our meetings to the chapter of accidents. This case is recorded as a specimen of the Lord's way. This prophecy is not of private interpretation; not a letter, but a type for throwing off millions. It is not that the Redeemer and Ruler of the world made these trysts in ancient times, and ceased to make them afterwards. He ceased to reveal and record them, after he had given characteristic specimens; but he has not ceased to make them and keep them.

These meetings have been frequent in our own land of late years. Many messengers run to and fro, each bent on fulfilling his own commission, each bent on getting a soul for his hire. How thickly the royal couriers pass and repass. If our eyes were opened, the whole mountain would seem full of chariots of fire and horses of fire. See that ye walk circumspectly, not as fools, redeeming the time; for ye know neither the day nor the hour when the messenger sent by God to meet you on your path may heave in sight, and offer you the friendship of the King. The place whereon you now stand may be holy ground to you—the birthplace for a better life. On the right hand or the left, in the house of prayer, in the public street, in the lonely path, the messenger may appear, charged to win a soul to Christ.

Brother or sister still unconverted, if a message of love is out from the King to you, it would be sad to miss the bearer in the busy throng of life. Would you not grieve if he should go by? Then fear not: those who desire to meet him will not miss him. That vacuum in a longing heart would draw the messenger and the message to your bosom although they were at the utmost end of the earth. Though the place was desert and the path but dimly traced, and the time not told at all, Philip and the Ethiopian met, with all the exactitude of the tides and seasons.

See on a map—for the actual landscape is too wide to be comprehended in one view—the track of two converging rivers, from their several sources on separate mountain ranges to the point of confluence in the intervening valley. There are many windings in their courses. At some parts, indeed, they flow right away from each other, and sometimes back toward their springs; but in spite of all these partial and temporary divergencies, on the whole the two streams come slowly but surely to a common meeting-place. So spring far apart two human lives, and so these distant lives flow into one. God, who made the mountains and the valleys, and bade the rivers run among them, brought these lives into being, and brought them into one. He brought them together: and that for a purpose of his own. Stand in awe of the meetings and partings of life. Reverence the friendships which you form and the farewells which you pronounce. When one is a disciple of Christ, and the other is still of the world, the Master meant by the meeting that grace should find its way from the vessel that has been filled into the vessel that still remains empty. Vessel filled, freely you have received, freely give. Vessel empty, although all good comes from Christ the Head, much good comes through Christians the members. The one should strive to be, and the other to get, a blessing.

These meetings, long prepared and wisely arranged in providence, are sometimes lost through obstinate unbelief. What a meeting that was in Herod's judgment hall at Cæsarea between Paul and Felix! How far up the lines of preparation for it ran; and how skilfully they were held in the hands of the Omniscient until the missionary of the cross and the Roman ruler met at last! The Roman listened, and the missionary began: Now, Felix, now is your time; now or never. But he hardened his heart and turned away. He cast out the arrow of conviction after it had gone more than half way through the searing of his conscience. "Go thy way for this time:" this time! fool! you will never get another. He thought he was only politely putting off the Christian; but, in reality, he was rudely rejecting Christ. To lose such a meeting may be to lose your soul.

That Ethiopian, on the contrary, being thirsty, welcomed the cold water. He received the kingdom of God as a little child; and the kingdom became all his own. He believed to the saving of his soul, and went on his way rejoicing. If any place in this world can remain consecrated more than another in the memory of the saints, that spot in the desert near Gaza is a sacred spot to one of the saved multitude who stand round the throne in white clothing, for there he was born to the inheritance which he possesses now.

Philip ran to meet him. Hitherto he had walked, and that, perhaps, slowly. So when two objects afloat attract each other by hidden magnets, their mutual motion towards a meeting is slow at first and scarcely perceptible; but when they have approached near, the movement quickens, and they traverse the rest of the space at a rush.

The evangelist, on approaching the chariot, heard its occupant reading. The student, though alone, must have been reading aloud. It is a mark of simplicity and earnestness. Like Jacob in a similar solitude, this man wrestled with the angel of the covenant. The kingdom of heaven suffereth violence, and the King loves to feel the violent pressing with all his might at the gate.

The reading aloud also gave Philip a natural and easy opportunity of introducing himself: "Understandest thou what thou readest?" A very suggestive question, by the way, and very suitable in our own times. To read the Scriptures is a duty and a privilege, but it is only a means to an end. If the ground do not take in the seed, the seed left on the surface is soon carried away.

The Seed Sown and the Harvest Reaped
(Acts 8:30-39)

"And Philip ran thither to him, and heard him read the prophet Esaias, and said, Understandest thou what thou readest?" etc.

SOMETIMES a sermon is reported and published word for word in full. At other times the report gives, in a more or less condensed form, the substance of the discourse. We possess a report of Philip's discourse delivered that day in the desert to a solitary listener, but it is in an abbreviated form. It is the briefest report of a sermon that I ever saw; and yet it is the most complete. It is a wonderful example of much in little. "He preached unto him Jesus." One precious word expresses the doctrine which the evangelist taught: that word is "Jesus." The matter of the sermon lies all in that one blessed name. But even that is not enough. The saving doctrine contained in this name was pressed on the heart and conscience of the hearer. It was not only Jesus; but Jesus unto him, then and there.

It is perhaps at this latter point that most of our preaching fails. In evangelical Churches there is a full declaration of the gospel. There is much sound exposition. All that is implied in the name Jesus, is exhibited skilfully and faithfully before the multitude. But the ministry often halts for want of courage to press Jesus upon the conscience of every man. The outspread sun-rays make all the ground bright; but the concentration of the rays on a spot makes that spot burn. Under the skilful preaching of Philip, the Ethiopian felt that Christ Jesus was then offered and pressed upon him the same as if there had not been another man in the world, the same as if the Son of God had come for the single purpose of redeeming him from sin, and leading him into holy rest.

While preaching depends effectually on the demonstration of the Spirit, it depends subordinately and instrumentally on the pointed application of the gospel method to the heart of the listener as if he were the only listener, and as if the Lord from heaven stood before him demanding an immediate answer. This home preaching took instant effect. The Ethiopian understood the message, and accepted Christ. He believed, was baptized, and went on his way rejoicing.

"He went on his way." He must tread the desert, although he is now a son of God and an heir of glory. He is not instantly carried home. He pursues his journey under the hot sun, and upon the hot sand. When Christ prayed for his disciples, he said, "I pray not that thou shouldest take them out of the world, but that thou shouldest keep them from the evil." The winter is as cold and the summer as warm to Christ's disciples as to other men. They pass through fire and water; but the Father brings them to a wealthy place at last.

The Ethiopian began that journey before he had found and accepted the Saviour; and now that he is in Christ a new creature, he does not stop or turn aside. He will complete the journey: when he reaches home he will do homage to his sovereign, enter his office, examine his books, give audience to his subordinates, and generally attend to all the duties of his high office in the kingdom.

Here is a useful lesson for Christians of all ranks and in all times. If your business was lawful and honest before, you need not desert it when you become a Christian. A child at school, a servant in the house, a clerk in the counting-room, a laborer in the field, a mechanic in the workshop, a seaman before the mast, a merchant in the exchange, need not desert his calling when he enters a new life of faith.

Some people indeed must abandon their calling when they come to Christ. If the business has been sinful and injurious, the man will not remain in it an hour after he has become a new creature. Those fortune-tellers who haunted the precincts of the temple at Ephesus gave up their trade as soon as they believed. They came to the apostles to confess their wickedness and to burn their books. They gave up their trade and their stock in trade because, as soon as their minds were enlightened, they perceived that they were involved in an occupation which offended God and injured men. This becomes a test of truth in men, and an instrument of glory to God. Many a mischievous business has been abandoned and many an unjust gain abjured, when the eyes of an evil-doer's understanding have been enlightened and his heart made new.

But this Ethiopian gentleman would probably do more good by going home and conducting his business, than if he had abandoned his office and followed Philip northward. The Lord has need of witnesses everywhere, in schools and workshops, in families, in evening parties, in halls of judgment and legislation, in the army, and in ships at sea. Everywhere the earth is corrupt and needs salt. Every true Christian is a grain of salt; and for the world's good the salt must be distributed, so as to be in contact with evil at every point. It behoves every disciple to have always his savor in him, for he does not know how soon and how often the Lord may have need of him as a witness to truth.

He went on his way *rejoicing*. Reader, did any one ever whisper in your ear that though religion may be safe to die with, it is sad and melancholy to live in? Meet the enemy with the Master's own reproof: " Get thee behind me, Satan, for thou savorest not the things which be of God, but the things which be of men." It is not a sorrowful thing even for this world to know that the next is all your own. It is not a sad thing for any part of your pilgrimage over time to be assured that a place is prepared for you at the journey's end—

a place in the mansions of the Father's house, purchased, prepared by him who loved you. It is not fitted to damp your joy in youth to have a hope each time you lie down to sleep that if you should not awake in this life you would awake in heaven. This Abyssinian prince did not wait till his dying day for the beginning of his gladness in Christ—he began to rejoice the moment he believed; and it is the nature of that light to shine more and more unto the perfect day.

Observe, as a closing lesson, what power a thirsting soul exerts, not over earth, but over heaven. An empty human heart, longing for the living water, can command all the fulness of the Godhead for its supply. There could not be rest in heaven while the eyes of that dignified negro were filled with tears and straining upward in the desert of Gaza. It is said of Jesus once in his personal ministry that "he must needs go through Samaria." What power laid that necessity on the Son of God? Ah! the power was unseen by men, but felt by men's Redeemer. A poor sinful woman at Sychar was thirsty, and he must cast himself in her way. So here, Heaven could not be still while the Ethiopian suffers from an unquenched soul-thirst on earth.

The drawing power of that longing soul was great beyond all calculation. It not only drew Philip away from his successful ministry in the cities; it drew forgiving love from its fountain in the eternal God.

In certain sandy tracts, both of Africa and America, where no rain ever falls, travellers sometimes fall in with a living plant. The sand is dry in which it is rooted, but it is not a dry root; it is a succulent herb. Its leaves are thick and full of sap. When they are cut, a stream of water flows from their veins to refresh the traveller.

How comes this? So far from being left in want, that lowly herb in the Sahara has all the waters of the Atlantic at its disposal. Although chained to the spot, and apparently doomed to die of thirst, it can draw a supply at will from earth and sea. A multitude of microscopic mouths open on the surface of every leaf. These, as they open and shut like the lips of a panting animal, suck the air that leans on their surface—suck from the air what moisture it contains. The air, divested of a portion of its moisture, draws from the distant ocean to fill the void. Thus the little lonely plant in the heart of the continent, growing in a rainless waste, by the mere silent, passive power of emptiness, draws its supply from the world's great reservoir without stint. The mighty deep is compelled to part with its plenty, in order to supply the wants of the solitary, feeble herb.

Be of good cheer, disciples of the Lord Jesus, ye are of more value in his esteem than many succulent plants of the African desert. Blessed are they that thirst, for they shall be satisfied. Seek, and ye shall find. When I am weak, then am I strong. In the emptiness of a soul, feeling its want, and longing for supply, resides a power which will draw the water of life from the throne of God and of the Lamb.

Saul

(Acts 9:1-3)

" And Saul, yet breathing out threatenings and slaughter against the disciples of the Lord, went unto the high priest, and desired of him letters to Damascus to the synagogues, that if he found any of this way, whether they were men or women, he might bring them bound unto Jerusalem," etc.

EVERY one goes his own way; every creature after its kind.

The Ethiopian Treasurer, having obtained all he desired—having gained more than a whole world in that desert place, "went on his way rejoicing." Philip, having finished one work, instantly betakes himself to another. He does not become a hanger-on in the palace of his powerful convert. From Ashdod, the first town he reached on his return, all the way to Cæsarea, his home, he preached the gospel in every city. A faithful servant, not hiding but exercising his talent, he was not content with the successful accomplishment of his errand to the desert place, but took advantage of his return journey to scatter the seed of the kingdom in all the towns of the south. Saul, too, on his part, acting according to his nature, is as busy as the rest. When last we saw him, he was acquiescing eagerly in the martyrdom of Stephen (viii. 1); and now, after a considerable interval, he appears again, still bent on getting new victims. Perhaps, when the Christians were either driven away from Jerusalem, or concealed there, he found his occupation gone, and determined to find a new hunting-field.

Damascus was a great city only about one hundred and forty miles distant. Many Jews resided permanently there; and probably some of the fugitives from Jerusalem had recently reached it in quest of a refuge. It is intimated in a subsequent verse (13) that believing Jews, who had left Jerusalem after Stephen's death, informed Ananias of Saul's arrival.

Damascus is the oldest city known to history still flourishing. It has a population of 250,000. Travellers describe with enthusiasm the marvellous beauty and salubrity of its site. A bright rapid river, flowing from the slopes of the eastern Lebanon range, divides into several branches in the plain. Soon after passing the city these streams are absorbed, and never reach an outfall in any sea.

"And Saul, yet breathing out threatenings." The instigator and manager of the first martyrdom has not *yet* changed; he *still* breathes out threatenings and slaughter against the disciples of Jesus, but will not do so much longer now. This part of his course is near an end; this is the last journey he will undertake as the waster of the Church. The days of his rebellion are numbered; the hour of his conversion is on the wing. He is still the persecutor; but a little while, and he will persecute no more. After this day, all his days he will be persecuted, until, like the rest of the martyrs, he is sent up in a fiery chariot to join the company of the crowned saints.

Saul demanded from the high priest a commission empowering him to require the assistance of the synagogue authorities in Damascus in prosecuting there his work of blood. From his own lips, at a subsequent stage, we learn that this demand was successful; he went to Damascus "with authority," and not as an adventurer on his own account. By connivance of the Roman governor, the Jewish ecclesiastical council were permitted within certain limits to rule their own countrymen according to their own laws; and it appears that their jurisdiction extended in some form to the persons of Jews residing in foreign cities.

The commission granted by the high priest bore "that if he found any of this way," he should bring them bound to Jerusalem. We have here a new designation of the Christian faith. It is called *the* way*, and those who believe it are said to be *of the way*. The expression in the same sense occurs in three other places of the Acts: "But divers spake evil of the way" (xix. 9); "And the same time there arose no small stir about the way" (xix. 23): "Felix, having more perfect knowledge of the way" (xxiv. 22). From a comparison of these passages in their context it may be clearly seen that "the way" was a specific designation of the Christian system.

Two questions spring here: Who gave the Christians that name? and, Why was it given? I think it is not a nickname imposed by enemies, but a significant designation adopted by themselves. It may indeed have been either voluntarily adopted by themselves, and thereafter employed by enemies as a term of reproach; or, conversely, employed by adversaries as a reproach, and ultimately accepted by themselves.

In the use of the term there may have been something of the nature of a cipher, used for purposes of concealment. It seems not improbable that the early disciples, remembering the words of the Lord Jesus, how he said, "I am the way, the truth, and the life," might adopt, as their distinguishing title, the first constituent of that blessed trinity. The word would be very precious in those troubled times. Christ was their way to the Father; faith in him was their way to pardon and peace. "The way" in those times was their path across the wilderness, and their entrance into rest.

---

* The meaning is partially obscured by the introduction of the pronoun "this" in the English version. In the margin it is given correctly—"the way."

The term "Methodist" has been similarly employed in recent British history; and it is interesting to notice, although the English terms do not reveal the circumstance, that the same Greek word is the root of both epithets.

Women were not exempt: when and where have they been exempt, when persecution for Christ's sake was raging? From the commission given to Saul, empowering him to drag women as well as men before the Jewish tribunals, down to the time when godly women were tied to stakes in the rising tide of the Solway by order of a blood-thirsty government, the persecutor has always succeeded in quenching the voice of nature in his own breast. He spares neither age nor sex. From the beginning women have followed the Saviour in his suffering, and suffered for his sake.

The authorized agent was charged to bring the prisoners to Jerusalem for trial—such trial as Stephen obtained there—such trial as the Inquisition accorded to its victims in the dark ages—such trial as the Pope and the Jesuits would give us to-day, if they had power.

"And as he journeyed, he came near Damascus: and suddenly there shined round about him a light from heaven." We are approaching the crisis now. I think this was, and was intended to be, the most striking and important individual conversion between Christ's ascension and his return to judge the world. In its results, direct and indirect, it is the largest single fruit that has yet been gathered from the tree of righteousness that the Lord by his death and resurrection planted in the world.

As we approach the turning-point—the meeting-place, we stand in awe. For Christians this spot is holy ground. Like the three disciples on the mount, we fear as we enter the cloud; for here the Redeemer is transfigured, and displays more of his glory than mortal eye may easily bear.

From a comparison of this narrative with the accounts of the same event given subsequently by Paul in his public apologies, it results that while his companions heard a voice, Saul only distinguished the articulate speech of a person; and that while they all fell to the earth at the first appearance of the light, the rest of the company soon rose to their feet again, while Saul continued prostrate to hear the word of the Lord. All the company beheld the light with which the risen Jesus that day clothed himself as with a garment; but Saul alone saw the Divine Person who wore that robe of glory. All heard a sound; but he alone felt the word as a two-edged sword penetrating his joints and marrow. Similar distinctions occur in our day. One is taken, and another left. A thousand may hear the word of the kingdom, and the kingdom come in power to only a single soul.

Here the Lord takes unto himself his mighty power and reigns. He subdues and leads captive the greatest enemy of his throne. He makes openly a show of Jewish unbelief in the person of its chosen champion, and uses the captive then as an instrument to promote his own design. The Lord had need of human energy and genius in its highest measure—of a moral power that sweeps all lighter things before it in whatever direction it may move, like a river in flood—of Hebrew lore and Greek culture blended together in one capacious mind,—of all these the Lord had need for the work of the kingdom; and sovereignly he seized the vessel which contained them all in fullest measure, that he might employ it as he employed the ancient prophet, "to root out and to pull down, and to destroy and to throw down, to build and to plant" (Jer. i. 10).

The Lord's Word - Consolation
(Acts 9:4)

" And he fell to the earth, and heard a voice saying unto him, Saul, Saul, why persecutest thou me ? "

IT was near Damascus; it was at mid-day; there was a considerable company; great publicity was given to the transaction; every circumstance is a separate witness to the truth of the narrative. But the best evidence of the fact is the mighty effect that followed. By the conversion of Paul the course of human history has been diverted; the extant result bears witness of the efficient cause.

A circumfused light appeared to all the company; to Saul alone the glorified Redeemer articulately appeared. All heard a voice; Saul alone heard him, the manifested Man, speaking to himself. The voice said to him, "Saul, Saul, why persecutest thou me?"

It is not very long since these words were spoken. A succession of nineteen men, if each should live a hundred years, would suffice to span the space; and nineteen men, with hands outspread and touching each other, would not constitute to our vision a very long row. It is less than two thousand years—in God's account, less than two days—since the Lord Jesus uttered these words to check the career of a persecutor, and shield his suffering little ones. It may not be very long ere that voice shall speak again, so that every ear shall hear it. The Lord is not slack concerning his promise.

We are now suspended between the first and second appearings of the Lord. It is but a little time since he was here—and it is but a little time till he come again. In the interval he abideth near, with his watchful eye over us, and his everlasting arms underneath. His ears are open to his people's cry, and his heart sensitive to their pains and fears. "Lo! I am with you always."

This word of the Lord Jesus is a two-edged sword. It carries comfort to those who are within, and reproof to those who are without. It is spoken *to* an adversary; but it is spoken *for* a friend. It is worthy of remark here that the first comfort given to fallen men was conveyed in a word spoken to their destroyer. It was in a rebuke addressed to the serpent that the gospel was first preached (Gen. iii. 15). After the same manner was Israel comforted in times of trial; the word spoken for them was not spoken to them: "Touch not mine anointed, and do my prophets no harm." From time to time a reproving word or a judgment-stroke was sent against Pharaoh or the King of Babylon; and this was God's way of protecting his chosen heritage. Here, too, the Head will sustain the members, by a reproof addressed to the waster of the Church.

I scarcely know a more comforting word than this in all the Bible. Nowhere else is the oneness of Christ and his people more clearly expressed. The speaker is not now the Man of Sorrows. He asserts the identity of himself and his people, after all power in heaven and in earth has been placed in his hands. He is God over all, and blessed for ever, who proclaims here to the persecutor, "Inasmuch as you have done it unto the least of these my brethren, you have done it unto me."

As you experience pain when any member of your body is hurt, Christ, the Head of the spiritual body—the Church that he has bought with his blood—cries out when an enemy's hand strikes some poor saints in Damascus. So when Satan desired to have Peter, that he might sift him as wheat, and drive him by the power of temptation, like chaff unto the fire, the Lord himself felt the strain in his own breast, and interfered to shield his frail disciple. The life that is "hid with Christ in God" is truly a charmed life. No assassin's weapon can reach it in its hiding-place. Although the powers of darkness should bind themselves under a great oath to shroud this lower world in perpetual night, they could not accomplish their purpose unless they had power to pluck the sun from the sky. So these powers of darkness could not quench the light of life in any Christian, unless they should first extinguish the Sun of righteousness.

Nor is this privilege confined to those who are eminent in the faith. Safety is secured, and therefore measured, by the power, not of the saved, but of the Saviour. A British subject is found on the territory of a powerful but barbarian king. The tyrant casts his eye on the forlorn stranger, and would fain take away his liberty or his life. But the power of the Queen overshadows him. The advisers of this savage chief show him that if he touch a hair of that stranger's head a British ship will bombard his capital, and subvert his throne. The man is safe; but his safety is not due to his own strength or skill. The feeblest woman, or the tenderest child, would in such a case be as safe as the most stalwart soldier. Safety in no sense and in no measure depends on the individual's power, but on the power of the government which recognizes him as its subject. It is on a principle somewhat similar that the safety of disciples is insured. Their resource is not, I am strong; but, I am His—and He is almighty.

Why persecutest thou me? Saul was not directing his stroke up to the heavens; he pointed not his spear to Jesus' side. Our goodness—our badness, Lord, reacheth not unto thee. How, then? "Thou persecutest me"—"of whom speaketh the prophet this? of himself or of some other man?" Of some other man, some trembling disciple cowering in the lanes of Damascus, and dreading lest Saul should stone him, as he stoned Stephen, for being a disciple of Christ. Of this man Christ speaks; but speaks of him as a part of himself—feels as we feel when a member is pierced. The principle was abundantly explained by the Lord in the course of his earthly ministry.

Let Saul venture to say, Lord, when did we search thee out in thy humble hiding-place, and drag thee before the judge, and witness against thee, and put thee to death? The King shall answer him from his throne, Inasmuch as ye have done it unto the least of these my brethren, ye have done it unto me.

Here is my safety—that he counts me his; and not only so, but has made me part of himself, so that a stroke dealt by the enemy against me runs up and pains him on his throne.

Who shall tell how many dangers have been thus averted from us, when we did not know or think of either our danger or our deliverer? I suppose some of the saints in and near Damascus had heard of the persecutor's approach, and feared him; but it is probable also that others in danger by his approach did not know that he was near. By that light-flash which prostrated Saul without the gate, these persons were protected, although they were not aware either of the danger or the deliverance.

I suppose the saved when they reach the Father's house will have occupation for their leisure in numbering up all God's mercies; and perhaps nothing will be sweeter as an ingredient of their joy than the discoveries

of one and another signal rescue that Christ achieved
for them, while they, like an infant sleeping in a burning house, were aware neither of the flame that was
already singeing their garments, nor of the strong arm
of that Brother who bore them beyond its reach.   Oh,
that will be joyful, joyful ! when from the open books
we shall read the entries of many fiery darts that flew
pointed to our breast, and all these received and quenched
on the interposed shield of almighty, unslumbering love.

The Lord's Word - Reproof
(Acts 9:4)

*" And he fell to the earth, and heard a voice saying unto him, Saul, Saul,
why persecutest thou me ? "*

THE word of the Lord to Saul carried, as we have seen,
great consolation to disciples: it bears also a terrible
reproof to the adversaries of the gospel.

Mark well here, first of all, that although Saul is an
enemy to this Jesus, this Jesus is not an enemy to Saul.
This word is not spoken to cast him out, but to melt
him down, and so win him near.   " My thoughts are
not as your thoughts."   " Though your sins be as scar-
let, they shall be as snow."   It is written of Jesus, in
the time of his humiliation, that when he was reviled,
he reviled not again.   This is true of him also in his
glory.   He draws clear, deep distinction between the
converted and the unconverted; but the distinction
does not lie in that the converted are received into
favor, while the unconverted are cast away: it lies in
this—those that are already near are cherished as dear
children, and the distant prodigals are invited to turn
and live.   He does indeed divide the world into two:
his favor compasses about his own people; but even
his enemies he does not consume with the breath of his
mouth.   Christ's word out of heaven to his enemies
is a tender entreaty that they should arise and go to
the Father.

Nor should any one that now enjoys peace in the Beloved be surprised at this Divine generosity. It is a generosity that every saved sinner has himself enjoyed. If Christ had always shown favor to his friends, and always cast his persecutors into the pit, where would you and I have been to-day? If, when we were his enemies, he melted us by his mercy and won us over to himself, we need not wonder to find that he still keeps the door open for those who are without.

The form of this address, in the first place, betrays the tenderness of Jesus before we reach its substance. There is a peculiar meaning in the two-fold repetition of the name. This formula expresses at once sharp condemnation and tender pity. When you intend a simple approval or a simple disapproval, you call the name only once. It is when you intend both to condemn and to win back that you duplicate the call. When a child is called to receive either a reward or a punishment, he is named only once; but when you intend first to reprove him for his fault, and then to invite him to favor, you name him twice. John, sounded out singly, may be the prelude either to praise or to blame; but John, John, always means both that he is doing evil, and that you mean him good. You may find examples in Scripture.

John xx. 16, "Jesus saith unto her, Mary!"—all tenderness, all approval. On the other hand, Luke x. 41, 42, "Martha, Martha," at once rebukes her cumbering care, and invites her to sit at Jesus' feet. "Jerusalem, Jerusalem," "Simon, Simon," will be found, by examination of the context, to contain a stern reproof woven in with a tender invitation. In Matt. xvi. you will find two examples of a single call both simple: the one (verse 17) simple approval, with no reproof; the other, addressed to Satan possessing Peter (verse 23), simple condemnation, with no invitation to return. It was the double call that Jesus uttered that day in the persecutor's ears; and it is the double call that he addresses to the wide world to-day. At the winding up of the world's history, when the day of grace is done, there will be no double call. The call is single then—the call either to the saved or to the lost. On this side, Ye cursed, depart; and on that side, Ye blessed, come. Saul, Saul, meant both that Saul was wicked, and Christ was merciful; both that Saul was hating Christ, and Christ was pitying Saul. This is the type of call that the risen and reigning Jesus is now addressing to the world. He names a sinner once to announce the condemnation which he deserves; he names the sinner a second time, to intimate that in the blood of the Lamb that condemnation may be taken away. The first stroke is the charge, bringing guilt home to the guilty; the second stroke is the discharge, offered without money and without price. Welcome that first word as a sharp sword to penetrate the conscience, and compel you to exclaim in agony, " Oh, wretched man that I am, who shall deliver me from the body of this death ? " for the second stroke will quickly follow, manifesting a tender, divine compassion which will cause you to sing, " I thank God, through Jesus Christ my Lord." Out of thy mouth, glorified Redeemer, issues a sharp two-edged sword. Strike me with it once, O Lord, that I may cry, What must I do to be saved ? And strike again, Lord, that the word may heal the wound which the word has made.

In Saul's case, the redoubled stroke was effectual. The persecutor's heart was very hard, and yet under the repetition it yielded. He grieved for the sin that was rebuked, and accepted the pardon that was offered.

Listen, all who are still without; who are not living in Christ, but beating by a self-pleasing will against him —listen to this double word. Worldling, worldling, why neglectest thou me ? Hypocrite, hypocrite, why woundest thou me ?

The one word is spoken to smite—the Lord is angry: Melt, stony heart, and flow down. The other word is spoken to heal and pardon: Awake, thou that sleepest, and arise from the dead, and Christ shall give thee light.

Return now to the main lesson of this text—consolation to believers. As a member depends for life and growth on its union with the living body, so a disciple depends on faith's union with the Head. Remember the words of the Lord Jesus, how he said, " I am the vine, ye are the branches." So closely is the life of a

Christian entwined round the life of Christ, that when an enemy smites the member, the Head in heaven cries out. One inference from this fact is, How safe a believer is. But another inference is, How sober a believer should be. The seal set upon him is two-fold—has an inscription on either side. If the legend on the upper side be, " The Lord knoweth them that are his," surely the legend on the under side should stand out boldly relieved, so that he may run who reads it, " Let every one that nameth the name of Christ depart from iniquity" (2 Tim. ii. 19).

The Head cries when the member is hurt by foreign violence; but, oh, the Head is still more agonized when the member suffers from internal disease ! The tainted blood of the member circulates upward to the heart. Thus the vanity, pride, envy, avarice, impurity of a disciple, hurt the heart of the Holy One. If we have hope that our life is hid with Christ in God, there is no motive so strong for putting away all that defileth: " Every man that hath this hope in him purifieth himself, even as he is pure" (1 John iii. 3).

When the viper fastened on Paul's hand he shook it off into the fire. I think he did not shake his hand slowly and softly on that occasion. I think he shook the viper off his flesh with a shudder. But he would not cast it off with nervous violence merely on account of the wound, not more than skin-deep, that it might possibly make on his hand. In such a case it is not the scratch on the skin that we think about. We are aware that the blood tainted in the member passes in a few moments to the heart. It is this that imparts an awful gravity to the case.

In like manner, when life in the Lord is enjoyed and realized, the heart of a believer shakes off sin with eager horror, because it will hurt the heart of Christ.

There is a skilfully contrived apparatus by the use of which a man can dive to the bottom of the sea; can remain there long; can walk about and search for lost treasure within the hold of a sunken ship, and bring it up with him when he rises to the surface again. The person in charge above, both sends down the breath of life to the diver while he is under the water, and draws him up out of the water when his work is done

Christians in this life are like divers busy at the bottom of the sea. They are not only in the sea—they are beneath it. Many waters overflow them, but these waters cannot quench their life; for a mysterious invisible line is stretched between them and their Redeemer in the heavens. He sends down to them the breath of life, so that though the waters overflow they cannot drown them; and when they have seen his wonders and done his work for a while in the great deep, —when they have trodden for a time this watery, slimy wilderness, and gathered treasures there for him who sent them down, he will draw them out of the waters. He will bring them into a large place.

When time is done, and the affairs of the world are wound up, he will gather unto himself all his own. None of them shall be lost, for he must be full. The command will go forth, North, give up; South, keep not back; Earth, give up thy dead; and, Sea, surrender thine! If the earth should try to close and hold fast any of his little ones, the cry would issue from the throne, the cry of this same Jesus: "Grave, grave, why holdest thou me?" On that day he will do all his pleasure; on this day, blessed are all they that are found in him.

The Enemy Surrenders
(Acts 9:5-14)

" And he said, Who art thou, Lord? And the Lord said, I am Jesus whom thou persecutest: it is hard for thee to kick against the pricks. And he trembling and astonished said, Lord, what wilt thou have me to do? And the Lord said unto him, Arise, and go into the city, and it shall be told thee what thou must do," etc.

SAUL was immediately and fully aware that he had a person to deal with. Whether, in the first moment of his terror, all that Stephen had preached of Jesus living and reigning flashed into his memory, we do not know; but it is probable that the thought of Jesus, whom Stephen saw at his dying moment, was on Saul's mind

when he put his first question, "Who art thou, Lord?"
Jesus condescends to answer him, for he knew that the
persecutor was in earnest now: "I am Jesus whom thou
persecutest." In this expression all the reproof and
consolation contained in the first word of the Lord is
repeated and is redoubled.

The proverbial expression "kick against the pricks,"
like many of the Lord's sayings, gives a whole parable
in a single sentence. Since attention has been paid to
Oriental customs, the meaning of the phrase is clearly
and easily understood. The oxen, while under the
yoke, were goaded by a long, slender, sharpened rod.
Irritated by the puncture, they sometimes kicked against
the instrument that pained them. This, of course, only
lacerated their limbs the more. The parable curtly intimates that Saul was in the grasp of irresistible power,
and that it would be wisdom simply to submit.

His next question accordingly indicates implicit submission: "Lord, what wilt thou have me to do?" He
surrenders at discretion. As yet, however, his knowledge is very dim. It has often been remarked that he
displays the character of a novice in demanding what
he should *do;* and that the Lord, through Ananias, sent
him a message more in accordance with the cross which
he was called to bear: "I will show him how great things
he must *suffer* for my name's sake."

But while, for great purposes, the risen Lord personally meets the arch-enemy in order to subdue him, he
does not in person undertake the disciple's instruction.
He hands him over to the ministry of man. A simple
Christian disciple, not otherwise known, becomes the
educator of the great apostle.

While Saul lay prostrate, probably his eyes were
shut; it was when he rose, and endeavored to look around,
that he discovered his blindness. When he opened his
eyes he saw nothing. They led him by the hand, and
brought him to Damascus.

In Damascus he remained three days and three
nights, and neither did eat nor drink. During that
time three main channels of communication with earth
were cut off; he saw not, he ate not, he drank not.
Isolated from earth, he enters into communication with
Heaven; for, "behold, he prays." The Spirit possesses

him. Hungry, thirsty, blind, he comes to God for food, drink, sight. Nothing from the world now; all from Christ. This vessel has now been emptied, and will soon be filled again. Emptied of all below, he will be filled, through the channel of prayer, from the treasures that are at God's right hand; emptied of himself, and filled with Christ. Thus, in conversion generally, by means more gentle or more violent, a soul is severed for a time from its relations to earth, that so it may have leisure and freedom to transact with God for eternity. The new birth is sometimes more and sometimes less prolonged, with more or less of agony.

At some points the experiences of Saul and the Ethiopian are parallel, and at some in contrast. These two journeys may be compared with profit. The Ethiopian a Gentile, Saul a Jew. The Gentile journeyed toward Jerusalem to seek Christ; the Jew journeyed from Jerusalem to persecute Christians. In the one case the Scripture exemplified is, "Seek, and ye shall find;" in the other, "I am found of them who sought me not." The Lord on high looked sovereignly and mercifully down on both travellers. He gave the one what he sought, and the other what he sought not. Both were blessed, and in the end both receivers lived to the Giver's praise.

I have already thrown out the suggestion that if Saul and Stephen should meet in heaven, they might with profit compare notes of their several experiences. The meeting of Saul and the Ethiopian would be equally interesting. When the secrets of all hearts shall be revealed, it will be found that the devout and humble inquirer will get no more glory than the proud and cruel blasphemer. It will be found that both were made willing by the same power. There were indeed diversities of operation; but the Worker was one. This man was won by a secret distilling of the Spirit, like dew from heaven, upon his heart; that man was subdued by a sudden stroke of omnipotence: but both alike will ascribe all to the grace of their Redeemer.

After three days of blindness and fasting—three days spent, probably, in a great conflict between conscience and the Divine law—the fastenings of a stony heart at length gave way, and the penitent melted into prayer. Now that the wound has gone deep enough, a healing ministry will be sent. Go to him, Ananias; for, " behold, he prayeth." Now that the branch is let into the vine, it is Christ in one of his members who is hungry and blind, and weeping there. The Lord in heaven changes his voice now: " Ananias, leave not Me any longer in darkness and want in the house of Judas, in the street that is called Straight."

The conflict that raged during those three days in the stricken persecutor's breast, has been in part recorded for our instruction. The self-dissection contained in Rom. vii. must have had a great deal to do with the three days of agony in Damascus.

Although certified that Saul was praying, Ananias did not immediately feel at ease in the prospect of meeting him. The lion is now ready to lie down with the kid, but the kid naturally starts back at first sight of that dreaded beast of prey.

Another new name occurs here first as applied to the disciples of Christ—Ananias calls them " thy saints." He must have known that they deserved that name, otherwise he would not have ventured to apply it to them in speaking to the Searcher of hearts.

This last name has borne a great part in history. It was at first a true designation. The name sprang up naturally from a root of fact. These men were separated from the vanity and the wickedness of the world. They had a home on high, and they did not lay up treasures on earth. They walked with God, and did not lie to men. They expected to stand at the judgment-seat of Christ, and did not overreach their neighbors in business. They had been themselves bought with a price, and owed all to forgiving love; therefore they were ready to forgive even unto seventy times seven provocations.

But in process of time the word was turned aside from its true meaning, and applied to those whom the hierarchy of Rome delighted to honor. Some very good men, and some very bad men, have obtained at different times that Divinity degree from the Pope and his council. It is now an expensive and worthless form. As a natural consequence of the misuse of the name in what was called the Church, the world outside has in modern times turned it into a term of reproach. It is very often employed as a sneer. But, although a false pretence to saintship deserves all the mockery it gets, it remains that there is such a thing as holiness (comparative) not in heaven only, but also here on earth. Through the grace of God, and by the ministry of the Spirit, a real holiness is wrought in the heart and life of Christians. It is their part to strive after more. What a noble aim is set before us! to fill up this character with substantial purity and truth, so wrenching the weapon from the scorner's hand.

The Vessel Chosen and Charged
(Acts 9:15)

" But the Lord said unto him, Go thy way: for he is a chosen vessel unto me, to bear my name before the Gentiles, and kings, and the children of Israel."

WE shall best explain and apply the text by examining its terms in succession, one by one.

1. A *vessel*.—The term signifies the implement by which any work is done, or the dish in which anything is held. It is an instrument constructed and fitted for use in any species of operation.

All the world is the field whereon God works, and it is full of the instruments which he employs. Every flower, every leaf, every tendril is a cunningly contrived instrument, designed and fitted for carrying on some delicate process in the vegetable economy. In animals, every member of the body is a tool with which the creature,—with which the great Creator—works. The eye, the ear, the tongue, the foot, and a thousand other exquisite instruments, hang at hand in the workshop, ready for the worker's use.

Each separate part of creation, again, is an instrument in God's hands for carrying his plans into effect. The internal fires of the globe are his instruments for heaving up the mountain ridges, and causing the intervening valleys to subside. The clouds are vessels employed in carrying water from its great reservoir in the ocean to every portion of the thirsty land. The rivers are waste-pipes for carrying back the soiled water that it may be purified for subsequent use. The sun is an instrument for lighting and warming a troop of revolving worlds; and the earth's huge bulk a curtain for screening off the sunlight at stated intervals, and so affording to weary workers a grateful night of rest. Chief of all the implements provided and employed on earth is man—made last, made best for his Author's service; broken, disfigured, and defiled by sin, but capable of working wondrously yet, when redeemed, and restored, and employed again.

God has not cast away the best of all his instruments because it was marred and polluted. He has conceived and executed a costly plan for redeeming and renewing it. He spared not his own Son, that he might have from this fallen family a multitude of vessels full of his love—a multitude of fitting instruments employed in his service. A soul won is the best instrument for winning souls.

2. A *chosen* vessel.—This man, who was raised from the ground by his companions and lead blind into Damascus, is the vessel whom the Lord has sovereignly chosen, and will graciously employ.

"The eyes of the Lord are in every place." "Known unto God are all his works." Compassing him about in all his ways, God felt every throb of impotent anger that was beating in the persecutor's heart. Although the vessel was marred and occupied with evil, its Maker counted it still his own. He can employ the evil as his unconscious instruments, or make them willing in the day of his power. When he had chastised backsliding Israel by the King of Babylon, he broke the rod and threw it away. In other cases he turns the king's heart as a river of water, and then accepts the willing homage of a converted man.

It was a polished and capacious vessel that the Great King wrenched from the hands of the arch-enemy near the gate of Damascus. One of the clearest intellects that ever glowed in a human frame changed hands that day. Saul was a man of rare courage. He was a good soldier of the wicked one before he owned allegiance to Christ. He did what he said. The purposes which his heart devised his hand executed. "I verily thought I ought to do many things against the name of Jesus of Nazareth, which thing I also did." The vessel was capacious, and the capacious vessel was full. All the learning of the time had been poured into it. The traditions of the Jews and the philosophy of the Greeks lay and seethed together in that roomy and restless brain. Not only was his head full of notions; his heart was fired with a resolute purpose, and his arm was nerved by a dauntless will. He was Christ's chief enemy then in the world. He breathed forth threatenings and slaughter against the members of the Church, blasphemies against its living Head. God looks down from heaven on this man, not as an adversary whose assaults are formidable, but as an instrument which may be turned to another use. As clay in the hands of the potter this man lies. The vessel may be broken in anger, or employed in labors of love, as the Maker wills. Arrested at the crisis of its course by a hand unseen, it is turned upside down, emptied of its accumulated filth, purged from all its dross, filled from heaven's pure treasures, and used to water the world with the word of life. Under God's eye and in God's hand, this man is not a formidable antagonist, but simply a vessel to be broken in judgment, or purified for use on earth and in heaven.

Saul of Tarsus, called to be an apostle, is a conspicuous example of Divine sovereignty. He did not first choose Christ, but Christ chose him. He was in the way of evil when the Lord met him with subduing, forgiving, renewing mercy. When human pride is at last silenced by the sense of redeeming love, it is sweet to feel and own that Jesus is at once the author and the finisher of our faith—"the beginning of the creation of God" within renewed human hearts on earth, and the ending thereof when the spirits of the just are made perfect in his presence. Christ is first and last—all in all. I recognize God's command to me, that I should turn and live; I recognize my duty to close with his offer; I recognize the justice of my condemnation if I refuse to comply. God bids me believe and live: I ought to obey; but if I obey and be saved like Paul, like him I shall say and sing, as the history of my redemption, When I was wandering helpless further and further towards death, the Good Shepherd followed and found me, turned me round, and bore me back to his fold.

3. A vessel *unto me*.—Two things lie in the conversion of Paul and in every conversion: the man gets an Almighty Saviour, and God gets a willing servant. The true instinct of the new creature burst forth from Paul's breast as soon as he knew his Saviour, and before he was lifted from the ground,—"Lord, what wilt thou have me to do?" The answer, sent through Ananias in Damascus, after the tumult had subsided, indicated to the convert what he should be, rather than what he should do: "He is a chosen vessel unto me." We get a glimpse here of the two tendencies, the human and the Divine. I shall do, says the disciple in the ardor of a first love; Thou shalt be, answers that wise and kind Master, who knows that the spirit in the disciple is willing, but the flesh weak. To be like Christ is the most effectual way of working for Christ. I shall *bear* the vessels of the Lord, volunteers the ransomed sinner, when he feels that he is not his own, but bought with a price; the reply to this offer requires a less positive, more passive, and yet greater thing: Thou shalt *be* the vessel of the Lord. It is a great thing that I should take up instruments, and do a work for Christ in the world; but it is a greater that Christ should take me in his hand, and work out his purposes with me. "A people near unto him," is an ancient appellation of the saved. Surely they are near him who are held as a vessel in his hand. This is our security alike for safety and usefulness. The star that is in his right hand is held up so that it cannot fall, and held out so that it shines afar. When he chooses a vessel he uses it; he neither keeps it idle nor casts it away.

The Vessel Employed
(Acts 9:15)

" But the Lord said unto him, Go thy way: for he is a chosen vessel unto me, to bear my name before the Gentiles, and kings, and the children of Israel."

4. A VESSEL to *bear my name.*—The text tells not only what he is and whose he is, but also and specifically to what uses he will be applied. He was a vessel firmly put together, and filled to overflowing, before Jesus met him in the way. At that meeting he was emptied of his miscellaneous vanities, and filled with the name of Christ. See an account of the whole process by his own pen: "If any other man thinketh that he hath whereof he might trust in the flesh, I more: circumcised the eighth day, of the stock of Israel, of the tribe of Benjamin, a Hebrew of the Hebrews; as touching the law, a Pharisee; concerning zeal, persecuting the church; touching the righteousness which is in the law, blameless. But what things were gain to me, those I counted loss for Christ. Yea doubtless, and I count all things but loss for the excellency of the knowledge of Christ Jesus my Lord: for whom I have suffered the loss of all things, and do count them but dung, that I may win Christ" (Phil. iii. 4–8).

The whole stock-in-trade of the self-righteous Pharisee is inventoried here. Himself delights to display the filthy rags, and make a show of them openly. He appropriates the shame to himself, that the glory may rise to his Lord. He recounts how these were cast out at the great change, and counted no longer gain, but loss. When these are cast out, however, he does not remain empty. No man ever yet did cast out his own self-righteousness from mere dislike of it. As the money-changers were driven from the Temple only at and by the entrance of Jesus, so the false confidences maintain their ground in a human heart until they are displaced by the presence of the Lord our Righteousness. All these carefully gathered, tenderly cherished stores, he now counts loss; but it is for Christ. He counted them precious as long as he knew none other. He never proposed to sell off all that he had, or anything that he had, until he fell in with the pearl of great price. The old adage is true in fact although defective in philosophy: Nature abhors a vacuum; and in nature, whether its material or spiritual department, a vacuum is never found. Each man is full either of his own things or of Christ's.

The name of Christ is the precious thing wherewith the vessel is charged. So full was Paul of this treasure, that he determined in his ministry to know none other. Whether the apostle be considered for the moment a vessel for bearing seed, or one for bearing water, the result is the same. It is of the things of Christ that the ministering Spirit takes and gives to the disciples, that they may drop the seed into broken hearts, or offer cold water to thirsty souls. There is none other name given under heaven among men whereby we must be saved.

5. To bear my name *before Gentiles, and kings, and the people of Israel.*—The name of Christ is the treasure which the vessel bears; to the Gentiles, and kings, and the people of Israel the vessel bears it. This bread of life, like the manna which fell in the wilderness, is given to be used, not to be hoarded. To be ever getting, ever giving, is the only way of keeping both the vessel and its treasure sweet. The more you give to others, the more you enjoy for your own use. The twelve had a fuller meal in that desert place, after they had distributed the bread among five thousand, than they would have had if they had dined alone. Christ is with his people still, to bless and multiply the portion of every cheerful giver.

Certain classes are enumerated before whom Paul should be a witness for Christ. Before, or, more literally, "in the face of" these, this vessel must bear that precious name. The form of the expression indicates that in this ministry self-denying courage is required. Perhaps the series, in this respect, constitutes a climax. It is easier to speak of Christ and his salvation to the Gentiles than to kings, and easier to speak of him to kings than to his own chosen people. Israel's enmity against the Lord's Anointed was keener than that of the surrounding nations. He came unto his own, and his own received him not; but to some, even of these, he gave power to become the sons of God. Paul himself was one of the first-fruits of the seed of Abraham, and a harvest has been gathered since. To this day, however, the nation in its main bulk remains more obstinate than the heathen in refusing to have this Man to reign over them.

In our day, too, there are various classes and characters of men who need the testimony of Jesus. Those who possess it should be prepared to bear it about in every place, and hold it forth in any company. This witness in his day was not ashamed of the gospel of Christ: would that all our Christianity were as honest and as strong! If we quail where the majority profess to be on our side, what would have become of us if our lot had been cast in the beginning of the gospel, when its disciples were obliged to confront an adverse world? May the Lord increase our faith, and increase, too, that which hangs next beneath it in Peter's golden chain of graces—the courage to confess our Saviour before friend and foe.

But, perhaps, we should not speak of more courage being required to maintain a good confession in one place, and less in another; for with God it is as easy to keep the ocean within its bed, as to balance a dew-drop on a blade of grass; and the same principle rules in the distribution of grace to disciples of Christ. Without it, the strongest is not sufficient for anything; with it, the feeblest is sufficient for all. Our martyr forefathers, who, by the peace of God ruling in their hearts, were enabled to make a good confession at the stake, would, if left to themselves, have denied their Lord under the blandishments of a godless drawing-room. To the eye of sense, the faithfulness of this generation is not tested by so severe a strain; but the difference lies mainly in the outward appearance. The human heart is still as deceitful, and the god of this world still as powerful, as in the days of old. In our own strength we cannot overcome the least temptation; through Christ that strengtheneth us we can conquer the greatest.

Not before Gentiles, and kings, and the people of

Israel, are we summoned to bear witness for Christ; but we stand daily in a place and presence where the temptation to deny him is equally strong. A Christian young man in a great workshop, a Christian young lady in a gay and fashionable family, is either carried away like chaff before the wind, or stands fast by a modern miracle of grace.

We are so many vessels, labelled on the outside with the name of Christ; what we are really charged with may not be seen at a distance or discovered in a day. Those, however, who stand near these vessels often or long, will by degrees find out what they contain. By its occasional overflowings, especially when it is unexpectedly and violently shaken, the secret will be revealed. Some are looking on who do not believe that the Spirit which fills us is the Spirit of Christ; and they lie in wait for evidence to prove their opinion true. For their own sakes let them find it false. Before them bear the name of Christ, when needful, on your lips, the Spirit of Christ in your heart, the example of Christ in your conduct.

But the word which requires that we should be witnesses unto Christ is peculiarly apt to slip from our grasp, especially when the specimen exhibited is some eminent saint. An indolent, earthly selfishness, under pretence of humility, like Satan in an angel's dress, cunningly suggests the distinction between a common ungifted man and the great apostle of the Gentiles. He was a worthy witness; but what could we do, although we did our best? If you are a sinner forgiven through the blood of Christ, in the greatest things Paul and you are equal; unequal only in the least. In the things that reach up to heaven and through eternity, there is no perceptible difference; the distinction is confined to the earth and time. You, a lost sinner, get pardon and eternal life in God's dear Son; and what does he get more? Getting as much from your Lord, you may love your Lord as much. In the economy of grace, a shallower vessel serves nearly every purpose as well as a deeper, if both are full of Christ.

In nature, the shallowest lake, provided it be full, sends up as many clouds to heaven as the deepest, for the same sunlight beams equally on both their bosoms.

This law may often be seen at work in the spiritual kingdom. "Glory to God in the highest" rises in a stream as strong and pure from a sinner saved who lays out one talent in a lowly sphere, as from a sinner saved who wields ten talents in the sight of an applauding world. Nay, more; as a lake within the tropics, though shallow, gives more incense to the sky than a polar ocean of unfathomable depth, so a Christian of few gifts, whose heart lies open fair and long to the Sun of righteousness, is a more effectual witness than a man of greater capacity who lies not so near, and looks not so constantly to Jesus.

The Lord Reigneth
(Acts 9:15)

" But the Lord said unto him, Go thy way: for he is a chosen vessel unto me, to bear my name before the Gentiles, and kings, and the children of Israel."

In the coarser work of breaking up his own way at first, God freely uses the powers of nature and the passions of wicked men; but for the nicer touches near the finishing, he employs more sensitive instruments. A work of righteousness is about to be done upon the person of a Greek jailer at Philippi. Mark the method of the omniscient Worker. A strong coarse tool he seizes first, and therewith strikes the hard material, with the view of carrying it through a certain preparatory stage; then with an instrument of more ethereal temper and keener edge, which he had previously placed within reach, he completes the process. The earthquake, which shook the foundations of the prison, rent the outer searing of the jailer's conscience, and made an open path into his soul. In such work the powers of nature could no further go. What an earthquake could not do, God did by a renewed human heart, and gentle, loving human lips. From the same chosen vessel that Ananias had visited at Damascus, the ointment was poured forth which healed the jailer's wound. "Believe in the Lord Jesus Christ, and thou shalt be saved," said Paul: the rude heathen believed and lived.

Thus God works to-day, both in secret individual conversions and in wide-spread national revivals. Bankruptcies, storms, diseases, wars, are charged to batter down the defences, and then living disciples go in by the breach to convert a kingdom or win a soul. Missionaries seldom begin the work, and providences never complete it. Each kind of instrument is best in its own place and time. Do not go forward without providential openings, lest you should spend your strength for nought; and do not neglect providential openings, lest the lost opportunity should never return.

The inanimate machinery of war, more powerful now than in any former generation, may suffice to break down the walls of the enemy's stronghold; but these engines that pioneer so powerfully cannot capture the fortress; loyal, living men must enter and take possession in their sovereign's name. This order is adopted in the Christian warfare. Wherever the strife of men or the judgment of God has made an opening, good soldiers of Jesus Christ spring in and take possession for their Lord.

Thus, when war and treaties opened China, the Christian Church leaped in. Within those mysterious barriers Christ is now, by his chosen instruments, closing in a decisive struggle with the strong man who for ages has kept his house there in peace. By the rents which the earthquake insurrection has left in the framework of Indian society, our missionaries may, perhaps, get deeper into the nation's life than heretofore. In Italy, too, after the thunder and the lightning had done their terrible work, Christians lying on the watch, were ready to enter with the still, small word. Already the Man of Sin has been compelled to slacken his grasp, and the land is free. Chosen vessels full of Christ may bear their treasure now through the broken barriers, and pour it out in Italy—pour it out in Rome, the same unchanged treasure that Paul bore long ago to the same place. A long barren night has passed over Italy, but the Word of God liveth and abideth for

ever. By the very fact of making openings, God is
beckoning for instruments to bring it in.

But the same order prevails and the same laws rule
in the minutest scale of individual life. It is not only
China, or India, or Italy, that is long closed against
Christ, and at last opened by commotions within or assaults from without. This neighbor who has lived long
without God in the world, and fenced himself all round
against the inroad of serious thoughts, has been shaken
as if by an earthquake. It may be the insolvency of a
bank, or the death of a brother; it may be the encroach-
ment of disease in his own frame, or the spiritual awakening of sinners near him: it may be any one of these,
or of other similar shakings, that makes a breach in
the defences, and leaves an opening right through into
the soul. Now is the time for those finer instruments
which Jesus loves to use. Vessels who bear Christ's
name, bear it in at that opening now. Do not stand
and say, We are not great vessels. Little vessels will
go more easily in, and little vessels, full of Christ, will
do the work there as well as great ones.

Has Christ visited you, brother, and freely taken
all your sin away ? It shows, you think, that you had
need of the Lord. Yea; but it shows also another
thing—that the Lord has need of you.

The Apostle Paul occupies a large place in the Bible,
in the Church, in history, in heaven. No mere man,
before or since, has filled so great a space in the scheme
of Providence, or left his mark so wide and deep upon
the world. The gospel is the greatest power that has
ever operated on earth, and Paul was its greatest
minister.

Considering the tendency to hero-worship, which
seems inherent in our fallen nature, there was great
danger lest he who stood so far above his fellows should
be mistaken for a god. This danger was foreseen and
averted in the election and calling of Paul. He who
conceived the plan and executed it, hath done all
things well. The worshippers of that saint will be
put to shame when the Scriptures reveal the hole of
the pit whence sovereign mercy dug their idol. The
history of Saul's conversion proclaims more clearly, more
loudly, than an angel's voice, "See thou do it not."

This most learned doctor of the schools, the Pharisee who scrupulously tithed his mint, and devoutly buckled on his broad phylacteries, was the life and soul of the infuriated gang who shed the blood of Christ's earliest martyr. The mob executioners got their signal in the glance of his cruel eye. He satiated his own sectarian pride by the murder of the good, and crowned his wickedness by offering the bloody deed as a service done to God. To make an idol of this man, when by free grace he is highly exalted and greatly used, is either impossible or inexcusable. God needed a man to signal the glad tidings so that they might be seen afar; with this view he lifted one up from the lowest place, and set him on the highest. Thus Divine mercy found free scope, and human pride was effectually excluded. Job, though free from idolatry in fact, confessed that "the moon walking in brightness" tempted him to kiss his hand in token of reverence, as if the creature were Divine. But if he had known that moon at first, a mass of impurity lying on the earth and polluting it, and seen it then by God's hand lifted up, and lighted, and balanced in the sky, he would not have experienced any tendency to worship the once filthy and still feeble thing. All the homage of his heart would have risen spontaneously to the living and true God, who made that lesser light, and hung it in the heaven for the use of men. It is thus that we are kept from unduly reverencing the Apostle Paul, although, under the Sun of righteousness, he is the largest light of our spiritual firmament; for in our sight he was, by mere mercy, lifted from the mire of guilt, and fixed the loftiest and brightest of that cloud of witnesses who receive and reflect the "Light of the world."

Saul's First Experiences as a Christian
(Acts 9:22-31)

" But Saul increased the more in strength, and confounded the Jews which dwelt at Damascus, proving that this is very Christ. And after that many days were fulfilled, the Jews took counsel to kill him," etc.

" THEN was Saul certain days with the disciples which were at Damascus." After the great change, he did not immediately go either to Jerusalem or to Tarsus, his home. He was not yet ready to begin his mission to the Gentiles. He was, as yet, a novice; and in his own experience he first learned the rule which he afterwards prescribed, to " lay hands suddenly on no man " for ordination to the public ministry of the gospel.

" Straightway," however, it is added, " he preached Christ in the synagogues" of the city where he happened to reside. As one who had received mercy, he instantly began to make it known; but this is not yet the exercise of his apostolic office. It is the witnessing of a convert, on the method practiced by David the king. I should not expect much from a missionary or a minister after he had completed his preparation and been ordained to his office, if he had not in the course of his preparation sought and found opportunities of bearing witness for Christ.

The old proverb, " Is Saul also among the prophets ? " was revived with a new meaning and greater power. " All that heard it were amazed," and well they might. No such contrast had ever occurred in the memory of the people—no such contrast has ever been presented in the history of the Church. Already the conversion of Saul began to be felt as an evidence of Christianity. In this aspect it is a great study, and has been of late years presented with great variety of learning and skill. The more that you examine the facts, the more you are shut up to the conclusion that all suppositions fail except one—that Christ appeared to Saul in the way, and turned the heart of the king like a river of water, so that the whole volume of his life thenceforth flowed in a new channel and to an opposite sea.

If Saul was not true, he must have been either *deceived* or a *deceiver;* he must have been either a fanatic believing his own error, or a deep schemer, consciously cheating his contemporaries by an elaborate tissue of falsehoods. If you suppose that he was himself deceived, what fanatic ever exhibited the calmness, constancy, wisdom, and humility of this man, through a long and extremely active life, in contact with all classes of men, with mobs and with statesmen, and profoundly influencing all? To believe that such a life had no other origin and support than the whim of an enthusiast, is intellectually harder than to believe that it sprang from his meeting with the Lord.

If, on the other hand, you suppose him a deceiver, where shall you find a motive? He renounced place, and power, and honor. He attached himself to a small, despised, and persecuted sect: he suffered the loss of all things that he might win Christ for himself, and preach him to others. This supposition is contrary to nature— contrary to universal law. The conversion, and life, and ministry of Paul constitute a strong pillar, raised by the hand of the King in the mid-stream of human life, that mightily helps to make fast a disciple's faith, when the currents of time threaten to carry it away. He hath done all things well. "Bless the Lord, O my soul, and forget not all his benefits!"

From the simplest testimony of the new-born to the fact of his regeneration, the word of the convert increased in power until it silenced all his adversaries. "Saul increased the more in strength, and confounded the Jews which dwelt at Damascus, proving that this is very Christ." But the unbelieving Jews, true to their character, raised a persecution against him. They could not, indeed, withstand this witness in argument; but they could kill him. Already he began to suffer what he had formerly inflicted. He saw clearly that this would be his experience to the end of his course, yet he never wavered. He had counted the cost.

Somewhere in the interval between his conversion and his final escape from Damascus the sojourn in Arabia probably took place (Gal. i. 17). Arabia, like

Asia, is a very indefinite term in ancient geography. It indicates sometimes a larger and sometimes a smaller district of the same region. Whether Paul retired to the desert which lay close by Damascus, or went into the region of which Petrea was the capital, or penetrated into the Sinaitic peninsula, we cannot ascertain.

Nor are we informed of his occupation there. Probably he did not go thither to preach, like Philip, even to a single seeking soul. The object more probably was retirement, with such inner exercise of spirit as might qualify him better for his subsequent work. Here he was physically as well as spiritually in the track of Moses, and in the track of a greater than Moses. There seems to be some mysterious necessity that one who is commissioned to lead a great exodus, should be trained beforehand in solitude.

The length of this sojourn in Arabia is also left uncertain. His residence in the city immediately after his conversion, the sojourn in the wilderness, and his subsequent abode in Damascus occupied three years in all. The Jewish authorities had time to recover from their consternation, and now they took courage to resume the offensive. They took counsel to kill him; but he found the means of escape, and returned to Jerusalem.

At Jerusalem, Saul sought the society of the disciples of Jesus; but they feared a plot, and kept out of his way. No wonder that they feared him. The flock had suffered by the wolf, and they could not easily believe that the creature's nature had been completely changed. Here Barnabas appears in his proper character as a son of consolation. Knowing the history of the case, he took the convert under his protection and obtained for him a welcome into the bosom of the Church. Again the convert preached with power, and again the power of his preaching excited the enmity of the Jews. When his life was a second time exposed to danger the brethren withdrew him to the sea-coast at Cæsarea, and thence sent him to Tarsus that he might be beyond the reach of his persevering persecutors.

Then had the Churches rest. At first they were troubled by Saul persecuting, and next they were troubled by Saul being persecuted; but now that the greatest enemy had been subdued, and the most obnoxious Christian sent into Asia, there was a lull in the storm, and the Christians obtained an opportunity of consolidating their infant society. They used their opportunity well; for "they were edified, and walking in the fear of the Lord and in the comfort of the Holy Ghost, were multiplied." When they obtained relief from external persecution, they became spiritually prosperous. They grew in numbers and in grace. We are accustomed to think that a time of suffering is the most likely to be a time of reviving, either in the private experience of a Christian, or the public experience of the Church. This may be true in point of fact; but it would be a great mistake to suppose that a state of suffering is in its own nature better fitted to edify the body of Christ than a state of peace. Severe trouble tends to crush the spirit; and when deliverance comes, there is liberty if there be a will to run in the way of the Lord's commandments. The time of health and prosperity is a better time for growth in grace than a time of adversity, if it were rightly improved. Nothing more distinctly marks the spirit of adoption than to cleave closely to the Lord in the height of health: it is the sign of a carnal mind to occupy itself with the earth till a time of sickness, and then begin to cry, Lord, Lord, open to us.

Nothing is said here about the profession of those primitive Christians: the only thing mentioned is their walk; and it is described by two features. They walked "in the fear of the Lord, and in the comfort of the Holy Ghost." Both sides are given. All solid things have two sides. The engine and train cannot run on one rail; a man cannot walk on one foot; two are required to balance each other. The new life must also be sustained on two that are in some sense opposite to each other. Such was the Christian experience that issued from the empty grave of Jesus; "they departed from the sepulchre with fear and great joy." Such precisely was the life of the disciples in Judæa when they obtained a breathing time after persecution. "This child is set for the fall and the rising again of many in Israel." They were bowed down, and then raised up. Their hearts were first broken, and then healed. They feared greatly before the Lord because of sin, and then the Holy Ghost comforted them by showing them the things of Christ.

We have now passed in review the first section of Saul's new life. In that man's history the law of the Lord, that there are diversities of operation, was most conspicuously exhibited. The choice and call of the twelve did not complete the Saviour's scheme for the beginning of the Gospel. For the purpose of introducing his kingdom to the Jews he adopted one method; for the purpose of spreading it among the nations he adopted another.

In this respect especially did the call of Saul differ from that of the twelve, that he was a man of learning, and they were not. The Lord had need at one time of the simplicity and even the ignorance of the apostles, that the excellency of the power might be seen to be of God; at another time he had need of all the culture that the age possessed, that Greek might meet Greek on equal terms in the conflict.

For other purposes Saul had labored in the fires at Tarsus and at Jerusalem to acquire all the learning of the schools. For purposes of his own ambition and sectarian zeal he had amassed the treasures; but as soon as he had acquired his wealth, the Mighty One met and subdued him, and employed his wealth in building up what he had intended to destroy. The Egyptians had accumulated great riches, which they intended to employ in grinding the Israel of God; but Israel went out free, and spoiled the Egyptians in the outgoing.

Thus had Saul collected his treasures, that he might use them in wasting the Church of Christ; but he and his possessions were taken and pressed into the service of the new King. Again were the treasures of Egypt rifled to enrich the sanctuary of God.

In this extraordinary way was an educated ministry in the first instance obtained; but afterwards the supply was provided by direct human means. Only once did Israel obtain a supply by spoiling Egypt; afterwards, when they were settled in Canaan, they obtained their wealth in a normal way,—by merchandise, or agriculture, or mining in the mountains. It is thus that resources wrested from the enemy enriched the ministry at the outset of the gospel; but for ordinary times we must ply ordinary methods. We have no right to expect a qualified ministry without our own far-seeing and painstaking effort. Hence the Churches, although they know that the Head sent Paul, as it were, a gift from heaven, are content to train up their ministers as Timothy was trained, first at the feet of godly parents, and then under the instruction of more experienced teachers.

Dorcas
(Acts 9:36-42)

" Now there was at Joppa a certain disciple named Tabitha, which by interpretation is called Dorcas: this woman was full of good works and almsdeeds which she did. And it came to pass in those days, that she was sick, and died: whom when they had washed, they laid her in an upper chamber," etc.

At this point Saul disappears for a time from the horizon of our history. He is left unnoticed in his native city, and Peter reappears upon the scene. In those days he seems to have found a most appropriate field for the exercise of his energy in making tours of inspection throughout all Judæa. Here is the true work of a primitive bishop. How welcome would the venerable form of the aged apostle be in each of the small Christian communities scattered through the towns and villages of the land. Lydda was a small village westward from Jerusalem, and not far from the shore of the Mediterranean. In that place Peter performed a miracle of healing. The mighty work was first and last employed in the service of the gospel. The formula employed was, "Jesus Christ maketh thee whole." These men now were full of the Holy Ghost, and so had power to be witnesses to their Lord. The result corresponded with the design: the miracle was effectual in winning souls. All that dwelt in Lydda and Saron saw the restored paralytic, "and turned to the Lord." In the neighboring sea-port of Joppa another miracle was performed, greater in itself, and more interesting in its circumstances. This work accordingly is more fully detailed. A disciple, named Dorcas, who had endeared herself by her skilful benevolence to the whole community, grew sick, and died. The sorrowing neighbors thereupon sent express to Lydda for Peter, and Peter came at their call. It pleased the Lord, through means of Peter, to restore the dead to life. The fact became known to all the citizens, and "many believed in the Lord."

The character and special work of Dorcas are full of interest and instruction for us. She was probably unmarried, for nothing is said of husband or of widowhood. She probably lived alone, for nothing is said of father or mother, sister or brother. She seems to have been one of those "honorable women," of whom not a few have arisen in every country and every age, who, having no family to care for, adopt the poor as their children, and in this form devote their time, and skill, and resources to the service of the Lord.

She was not a nun. In order to devote a life to the service of the poor, it is not necessary to renounce, by an irrevocable vow, the privileges, joys, and duties of family life. The relations and affections of nature are God's workmanship, and do not necessarily hinder any good work.

Dorcas was a disciple full of good works. One phrase indicates the well-spring, and the other indicates the refreshing stream that overflows. She was a "disciple" —behold the root ! She was "full of good works"— behold the fruit-bearing branches ! God hath joined these two; men should never and nowhere put them asunder. The one is faith, and the other good works. These two are beautiful in unity; but either wanting its mate "is dead, being alone."

People who have a smattering of religious knowledge, but have not been taught of the Spirit, fall alternately into two opposite errors in regard to the place and worth of good works in the Christian system. In the first instance the crude conception of self-righteousness springs up: Let me crowd in as many good deeds as I can, in order that I may thereby make my peace with God, and have a good case against the great day. But when this man hears the gospel, and especially the doctrine of justification by faith alone, he begins to think that in this way of salvation there is no place left for a good life—that the gospel is jealous, not zealous of good works.

When the work of the Spirit advances another step in his heart, when he is convinced of sin, and brought to the blood of Christ for pardon, this man gets a new view-point, and consequently a different view. Good works, as a justifying righteousness, he not only does not value, but loathes as filthy rags; yet, as fruit to his Redeemer's glory, he lives and labors in them all his days.

Such was the place of works both in the profession and the practice of this honorable woman. The branch was full of grapes, sweet, and ripe, and beautiful; but the branch was in the vine, and that accounts both for its beauty and its fertility.

When she was raised to life, they gave her back to the saints and widows. She was their property, and their property was restored. Such a working Christian belongs to the neighborhood, and is their richest treasure. The work of Dorcas was personal. This is the most precious kind of benevolence, both to the giver and receiver. She knew each widow whom she clothed, each child whom she fed. Possibly she had not much money to bestow; but she contributed visits of sympathy, looks of love, and works of skill. There is no coin more welcome in the treasury of the Lord.

The coats and garments made by her hands, and exhibited by the poor after her death, were monuments to her memory. Perishable monuments, you may think. Think of an inscription to commemorate a great life sewed with thread in garments for the poor !—written, not in brass or stone, but on the smooth sea-sand, ready to be blotted out by to-morrow's tide ! Nay, but this woman's eulogy has, in point of fact, been more securely preserved and more widely published than the victories of Rome or the art of Greece. All generations read her praises, and call her blessed. She has been greatly honored. In one point she has been made like the Lord, she has left us an example that we should follow her steps. Many are treading in her track to-day; and the world is greener for us because of the footsteps that she left imprinted on its sand.

Some monuments, such as that of Sir Walter Scott at Edinburgh, when they have obtained a high place in the judgment of educated men, are reduplicated in pictures, and spread in many specimens throughout the civilized world. The one original monument raised to Dorcas in the sacred record has in like manner been many times copied. Societies which are constituted for continuing her work frequently adopt her name: and thus she lives to-day in the world. Being dead, she yet speaketh through the manifold energies of Christian women in all the Christianized countries of the world.

This kind of charity was new in the world when Dorcas began at Lydda to make with her own hands garments for the poor of the neighborhood. The seed of that kind came from a far country, even an heavenly. It was dropped from the lips of Jesus on the furrows of some tender hearts, and it has propagated itself from generation to generation. The Lord will doubtless find some fields of it growing ripe at his second coming.

Christian love is generic; it sends out many subordinate species, all partaking of the same essential nature, and each exhibiting particular features peculiar to itself. The species which Peter found flourishing at Lydda is not unfrequent in our own day and land. Where it is genuine it is as beautiful as the violet growing under the hedge; and, like it, fills the air with fragrance. Female love, working outward through female hands in making garments to clothe the naked, is a well-known and comely form of Christian benevolence. Behold, it is very good. It is Scriptural, useful, safe. It is twice blessed—blessing those that give and those who receive.

The resources at our disposal are much greater than those which belonged to the primitive Christians. There is a greater number of loving hearts, and there is greater power in the operator's hands. Cotton, the spinning-jenny, the power-loom, the sewing-machine—who shall calculate how many times these modern discoveries have multiplied love's power of doing good wherever

there is a real living love ?   Besides all these, we have
more money in our hands, easier means of transit, and
greater facilities for combination.   The earth produces
more, and the powers of nature perform for us all the
harder portions of the labor.   One Dorcas in our city
to-day could do more with her own hands than five in
Lydda in the time of Peter.

Yet with all these advantages we have not overtaken the destitution.   In some quarters it is increasing on our hands.   Widows and orphans are in want
within sound of our Sabbath-bells.

The state of the poor around us should put us to
shame—should hush our manifold divisions and dis-
putes, and bring us into one that we might be stronger
for the Lord's work in the world.

I could point to scenes of horrid cruelty which would
make the blood stand still in your veins if you saw
them; and yet they are at our own doors.   Children
in our cities are starved and killed by slow degrees for
want of food and clothing.   Why should this be while
there are so many really benevolent hearts and so great
resources at the disposal of the community ?

There is a deeper thing than the hunger and nakedness of the children.   There is a root which bears these
bitter fruits.   It is the drunkenness of the parents.
This is the gulf which we are unable to fill.   There
it yawns, as represented by public-houses and pawn-
shops, between the warm hearts of Christians and the
starving children.   There it yawns—a bottomless pit.
You may throw into it all the wealth of the kingdom:
the mighty contribution will sink out of sight in the
quagmire, and you will be as far from the naked children as before.

Dorcas sits at home with a burning heart, for she
has seen ragged, barefooted children on the street in
the winter's cold.   She sits and sews.   Stitch, stitch,
stitch; love makes the needle go until the garment is
completed.   With light feet she trips down on the
morrow to the place where the naked child dwells.
She clothes it, and departs.   Next day she will visit
her charge and see how it fares.   The child is naked
again; the mother is drunk, and the house is cold.
The garment that Dorcas made lies on the shelf of the

pawn-shop, and the money in the till of the nearest public-house. Thus the mill goes round—the mill that grinds little children to feed the real giants, more terrible than all the pictured monsters that terrified the nursery.

This process is conducted on a great scale, crushing the little ones into premature graves. If the geologists of a future era should dig into the strata of our cemeteries, they will be amazed to find so large a proportion of the remains to be infants' bones. They will judge it contrary to nature. What can be the cause of the phenomenon? If the history of our time shall then be extant, they will learn from it what their philosophy could not tell them—that the vice of the parents slaughtered the children! Yet the nation looks on helpless!

It is certain, and easily proved, that the poverty which is true and natural, caused by providential circumstances, is small in quantity, and of a kind that is easily cured. We could relieve it and not be burdened by the effort. The exercise would be pleasant and healthful to the community. Instead of being a punishment it might be realized as the fulfilment of a promise, "The poor ye have always with you," that we might never lack an object to draw forth our charity, and so might never miss the larger blessing—the blessing which belongs to those who give. But the pauperism which springs from vice is not only so great that to relieve it becomes a burden—it is of such a kind that to relieve it is impossible.

There is need of two things: *first*, a perennial spring of charity in Christian hearts, finding or forcing a way into every home of misery in the land; and, *second*, an effort by a united people, acting through the legislature and the government, to deal effectively with the material feeders of vice, and so abate the nuisance.

There is some advance in public opinion at the present day; but, alas, great bodies move slowly, especially against the stream. In some of our colonies vigorous experiments have been made. In one of the Australian governments, for example, a law has been enacted under which, when a man or woman has been convicted of being an habitual drunkard, society has a claim for damages against those who supply the drink.

Proposals pointing to a restraint of the traffic have been earnestly advocated in our own community, and formally submitted to the legislature. I cannot predict whether this method will be successful, or that; but the attempts are most interesting to all philanthropists, as symptoms that society is awakening to a sense of danger, and beginning to cast about for remedies. It is especially cheering to the heart of Dorcas, as she toils to roll her stone up-hill, only to see it rolling down again, to observe that the commonwealth is bestirring itself to put some check on the huge machinery, driven by greed of gain, which revolves night and day, summer and winter, to manufacture a wholesale pauperism.

Meanwhile individual disciples of Christ, whilst they are permitted and even bound in their capacity as citizens to lend their influence to beneficent legislative measures, should not wait on the slow movements of a nation. They should, from love to the Lord and pity for men, put their own hand to the work wherever they can descry an opening. Dorcas enjoyed the blessed privilege of clothing the naked who were within her reach. It was her meat to do her Redeemer's will, and her appetite was abundantly gratified. It is a beautiful feature of the Christian Church at the present day, and a symptom that the Spirit has not forsaken us, that "honorable women not a few" both lay out their means and labor with their hands to feed the hungry and clothe the naked, in loving obedience to the Word of the Lord.

A Light to Lighten the Gentiles
(Acts 10)

" There was a certain man in Cæsarea called Cornelius, a centurion of the band called the Italian band," etc.

ALREADY Christ had come, the glory of his own people Israel; and now he must be set forth as a light also to the Gentiles. The second half of the promise must be fulfilled as well as the first. Shiloh has come to hold the sceptre in Judah; but to him must the gathering of the peoples also be. It is not enough that the law of the new kingdom should be established in Zion: the word of the kingdom must go forth from Jerusalem. The king hath prepared his sacrifice,—he hath bidden his guests. All things are now ready; the servants must now go out into the highways and the hedges, and compel the outcasts to come in. North, give up; south, keep not back; bring my sons from far, and my daughters from the ends of the earth.

The outflow of the gospel upon the Gentile world is a great turning-point in the history of the primitive Church.

That the Gentiles should be fellow-heirs, and of the same body, and partakers of his promise in Christ by the gospel, was not at first known to the followers of Jesus: it was part of the mystery of godliness specially revealed to the apostles after the ascension of Christ. "Other sheep I have," said the Master, "which are not of this fold: them also I must bring; and they shall hear my voice; and there shall be one flock* and one Shepherd" (John x. 16). This chapter narrates the accomplishment of the promise. Here we learn how the door was opened; or, rather, how the middle wall of partition was broken down, so that henceforth there should be for the Church neither Jew nor Greek.

Although individuals here and there had already been admitted into the fellowship of the Church, it needed yet a revelation to show the believing Jews that the way into the gospel was as open and free to the nations as to themselves. Those who had entered hitherto, entered first into the Jewish communion, and thence were introduced into the Christian Church. Now it is made evident that the Gentiles may come direct to Christ, without passing through Judaism on their way. God's own hand had hung up the separating veil to serve important purposes for a time; but now, when it has fulfilled its purpose, his own hand will rend it.

---

* "Not ONE FOLD, but ONE FLOCK; no one exclusive enclosure of an outward Church,—but one flock, all knowing the one Shepherd and known of him."—DEAN ALFORD.

Peter and Cornelius are chosen as the two points at which the two bodies shall come in contact, so that they may be joined in one.

Cornelius was a favorite name among the noblest families of Rome. He was an officer of the Italian band. The body-guard of the governor was composed of native Italians. Levies raised in the provinces were not trusted near the ruler's person. This circumstance makes it sure that Cornelius was a Gentile. He belongs to the Roman Empire, the representative at that day of the world's power.

He was a devout man. Whether he was a proselyte of the gate cannot be certainly ascertained; but, at all events, he was not further initiated into Judaism. He worshipped God, but did not conform to the Jewish ceremonial.

He worshipped God with all his house. This is a feature in family life that is always mentioned in the Scriptures with honor. Jesus is pleased when parents bring the little ones and place them in his arms. Grace not only flows down like water, so that from the head of the house it reaches the youngest; it also, by a cognate law, rises up like vapor, so that it may find its way from a godly child to a worldly father. Parents, bring your house to the Church; and bring the Church to your house.

"Thy prayers and thine alms are come up for a memorial before God." Prayers and pains were equally yoked in the life of Cornelius. Body and soul together constituted the religion of this devout Roman. It is not that the giving of alms makes the giver just with God. It is rather that the gifts accompanying the prayer serve to embody his desires. The charity was not a dead work, for it ascended to heaven; the gifts were the outgoings of an earnest but unenlightened soul groping after God.

"Now send men to Joppa and call for Simon." The Lord puts honor on the gospel in that he sends an angel from heaven to set a train in motion for conveying it to an anxious soul; but he also puts honor on the human ministry in that he does not entrust an angel with the work. The angel is employed to run an errand—to call the preacher to the spot. The matter is so great that an angel must be sent in order to get it accomplished; but the matter lies so exclusively between sinful man and his Divine Redeemer that the angel is not further employed, after he has told where a minister of the gospel may be found.

When there is great illness in a family, a loving neighbor comes in; but he does not presume to prescribe. He will run for the physician. So do angels minister to "the heirs of salvation."

This arrangement is wise and good. When Paul was constrained in faithfulness to tell certain men of Philippi that they were "enemies of the cross of Christ," he told the stern truth "weeping." He who has himself been taken by free grace out of the pit, knows how to pity those who are left. The words that win souls run thus:—"Come with us and we will do thee good." "We have found him of whom Moses in the law and the prophets did speak; is not this the Christ?" "The blood of Jesus Christ cleanseth us from all sin." This is preaching; and therefore angels cannot preach. They seem to say—"We can but desire to look into this mystery; send for one who has passed through it." Send for the man who denied his Lord, and thereafter melted under his look of pitying love. Send for Peter, who has himself been saved, and he will tell you what you must do to be saved.

We know by the answer sent what the centurion's prayer had been. The answer is an echo of the request; and the answer is to show him the way of life.

There were many strong barriers between this man and Christ. He was a Gentile, a Roman, a soldier, a centurion: each word indicates a fence within a fence to keep grace at bay: but grace burst through all, and led him captive.

Peter went to the house-top about noon to pray. The house-top was the place of retirement. Peter's closet was large and lofty. Its roof was the dome of heaven; yet it served his purpose well, for it was secluded. The closet, in the sense of our Lord's instructions on prayer, is any place where you may be shut out from earth below, and open upwards to heaven. That is the best closet which does for the spirit what the house-top did for the body,—which veils off the earth, and leaves all heaven open above the suppliant.

It is good to have associations of special communion with God connected with particular spots. The sight of these Bethels may revive sweet memories in later years. The tree, more hoary now, in the rural haunts of your youth, under whose shade, in the long summer twilight, you were wont to kneel and lift your soul to God, when the life of faith was young; the avenue along which you were wont to walk communing with a present Saviour, when the sense of his presence was new;—sweet spots! beautiful rays of light from above seem still to linger over them! This world is sweeter to a Christian than to other men. It contains for him many spots of holy ground on which he loves, even unto old age, to dwell; and even if some places call up sad memories of evil, they remind him also of his Saviour's love in blotting out all his sin.

The vision of Peter marked a great crisis of the Church. The apostles must have experienced at this time much difficulty in reconciling the Lord's command, Go ye into all the world, with their adherence to the Mosaic ordinances, which they still considered binding. On the general principle that you may discover in the answer sent to prayer what the suppliant pleaded for, we have good ground to assume that Peter, on the house-top that day, cried to the Lord, O send out thy light and thy truth, let them guide me on this very thing. The vision that followed was the opening of the gates, that the kingdom long pent-up in Israel might flow out upon the world. It is the bursting of the chrysalis, in which the life has been preserved indeed, but confined. The life that now issues forth is the same; and yet it is so much more glorious, that to observers the Church of the New Testament seems a new creature.

Saved by the Word
(Acts 11:14)

" Who shall tell thee words, whereby thou and all thy house shall be saved."

CONVINCED by the concurrence of the vision and the arrival of the ambassadors, Peter at once consented to go to Cæsarea. When he arrived, and found that Cornelius had been directed by a Divine message to send for him, he consented to preach the gospel freely to the Gentiles, and to receive them into the fellowship of faith, without imposing on them any part of the Jewish ceremonial.

When the Church at Jerusalem, which consisted of converted Jews, heard what Peter had done, they found fault. " They that were of the circumcision contended with him." Placed upon his defence, Peter narrated the whole case, and obtained from the assembled council a favorable judgment on his conduct. There is certainly no Popery here. Yet this is subsequent to the time when the Lord had said to him, " Thou art Peter," etc. Either he was pope at this time, or he never was pope. The council placed him on his defence: he accepted the position, and defended himself. He assumed no autocratic authority. He simply submitted himself to the authority of his brethren.

At the date of Peter's mission I should not venture to say that Cornelius needed to be saved; but he needed to be taught the way of salvation. There was before this time a quickening by the Spirit in his heart, but as yet he knew not the truth with his mind. Although at that moment the new life was already begun in his soul, so that if he had been called hence ere Peter arrived he would have entered the mansions of the Father's house, the Word speaks of him as still needing to be taught how he should be saved. I shall adopt the same tone, and show the necessity of conveying even to such a man the message of the gospel.

Peter must go to Cæsarea for the express purpose of telling this man how he may be saved. If his alms and prayers had been sufficient, there would have been no need of this message. They that are whole need not a physician.

This was no common publican or sinner. Before the angel promised a minister, or the promised minister came to preach, Cornelius was a "devout man, and one that feared God with all his house, which gave much alms to the people, and prayed to God alway." Here is a man who possesses all the qualifications of a saint, if a saint can grow in the soil of this earth, without a seed sent down from heaven. He was devout in spirit, exemplary in the training of his children, beneficent to the poor, and constant in his religious duties. Here is a model man. If any man could be just with God, apart from faith in Christ crucified, surely this is the man. A better specimen of humanity you can nowhere find; yet the word of God treats him as a sinner, and forthwith proceeds to tell him what he must do to be saved. There is no escape from the force of this case. It effectually shuts out all hope in the merit of a man. In presence of this word every mouth must be stopped, and all the world become guilty before God. If this man could not appear before the judgment-seat until his sins were blotted out in the blood of the Lamb, how shall we appear with our own sins or our own goodness marked to our account?

The difficulty of attaining a thorough practical conviction that if God should mark iniquity we could not stand, is greater, in some respects, where the sins are less gross. Open vices, although not more sinful, are more manifest than the rebellion that acts in the heart of a correct but carnal man. Hence the experience, renewed from age to age in history, that publicans and harlots go into the kingdom of heaven more readily than smooth and sombre Pharisees. A child or a savage realizes easily and completely that yonder mountain which lifts its head to heaven is matter; but cannot comprehend that the air which encircles and overtops the mountain is matter too. An educated person knows that air is as truly matter as the rock. It is in some such way that those who are childish in spiritual perception take in more easily the thought that vice is sin, than that the godless bent of the carnal mind is sin. It needs a keener spiritual perception to realize that this devout and charitable centurion is lost by sin, unless and until he be found in Christ.

By what means shall Cornelius be saved? By *words;* "He shall tell thee words whereby thou shalt be saved." Strange: when the loss is so deep and real, will words bring deliverance?—words—articulated air.

It was natural for Naaman, with his hardy intelligence as a practiced soldier, to toss his head in contempt at the proposal of a bath in Jordan as the cure of his disease. There is a class of scholars in our day who sneer at the proposal to cure sin by words, as Naaman sneered at the proposal to wash a leprosy away in water. They have no confidence in doctrines that come into a man's mind from without; they will rather trust to principles that spring up within the man. A salvation by words they despise. Dogma is the scorn of the unbelieving philosophy of the age.

Beware of wandering into the mist here, and so losing your way—your life. Words become life or death when God employs them to express and proclaim his will. God said, Let there be light, and there was light. Jesus cried with a loud voice, Lazarus, come forth, and he that was dead obeyed. But these were the words of God, our Maker and Redeemer. They were; and on that depended all their power. But may he not send his word into the world still? and may he not employ human lips and human ears as the channels through which it shall flow?

Even in the ordinary experience of life, men are saved or lost by words—the words of their fellows. An ocean-steamer at dead of night is rushing through the water, at the speed of a race-horse, bearing in its bosom a miscellaneous throng of men, women, and children, some asleep, some at work, some at play. Two words—*breakers ahead*—pass quietly but clearly from the watchman at the bow to the master on the gangway: two other words—*starboard hard*—ring out from the master to the man at the helm. As soon as these accents fall on the steersman's ear, he presses the rudder mightily to one side, and the ship bounds clear of the rocks, only leaping a little higher for a moment, in the surf that surrounds their roots. These words, that passed away as breath on the breeze, saved five hundred warm human beings from a cold bed that night in the bottom of the sea.

The world with its teeming freight of humanity is rushing on like that ship through the sea of time. Mankind, like the globe on which they cluster, are, as regards their own sensations, still and stationary; but in the unseen, unfelt reality, sweeping forward, like smoke on the wind. All are in motion always. A lost world will one day strike, and sink, and die. God, who is rich in mercy, did not leave the world to its fate. He sent his *Word*, and saved it.

Truth, like a spirit, is invisible until it put a body on: and words are the body in which truth incarnates itself, in order that it may be known and felt. They may be spoken by human lips, or exhibited on a printed page, or sent along a wire in throbs of electric light—it matters not what form the words may assume, as it matters not what may be the color of the ink in which the letters are written: in every form they are the body in which a spirit dwells. Evil spirits also become incarnate in a body of words. The wicked one embodies himself in words whereby men may be destroyed. The whole Word of God is the body which the Holy Spirit animates for his quickening and sanctifying work. Take heed how ye hear: the missing of a word may be the loss of a soul.

Thou and all Thy House
(Acts 11:14)

" Who shall tell thee words, whereby thou and all thy house shall be saved."

GOD'S hand in providence is always busy, bringing the saving word to bear on the lost that they may be saved. Ordinarily, the process is conducted behind the scenes, in secret; but now and then, as in the case of Moses and Cornelius, the curtain is drawn aside, and the whole machinery exposed to view, that we may learn the method of the Divine government. The centurion is dwelling quietly in his own house at Cæsarea: he is training his children and servants in the right way as far as he knew it: he is finding out every frail widow and every helpless orphan in the neighborhood, supplying the necessary food and clothing from his own stores as long as they lasted, and begging from his friends when they were done. Feeling his own need meantime, he is crying unto God for help. God in heaven hears the cry, and determines to answer it; but a complicated machinery must be set in motion ere the water of life reach this thirsting soul. The method is not in this case a whit more complicated than that which is adopted in the daily course of the Divine administration. This case is uncovered as an illustrative specimen; all the rest are of the same character, although they are concealed from view; messages from heaven are sent both to Peter and to Cornelius; and when speaker and hearer have been separately prepared, they are brought together. They meet; and at the point of contact the water of life flows from the charged into the empty vessel. The word of salvation, already through grace dwelling richly in the Lord's apostle, overflowed into the open and prepared heart of the Roman centurion. By that word the man was saved.

In the Garden of Plants at Paris, a certain rare tree grew for many years. It was a thriving, mature plant. Year by year it was covered with blossom, and year by year the blossom was shed on the ground, leaving no fruit behind. After every promise, it remained barren still. At last one season, although nothing extraordinary had been observed, after the flower came fruit. The fruit swelled apace, and in due time ripened. The tree for the first time formed and brought to maturity self-propagating fruit. They sought and found the cause. Another tree of the same species, but bearing flowers the counterpart and complement of this one, had that season for the first time blossomed in a garden at some distance. The small white dust from the flowers of that other tree, necessary to make the flowers of this tree fruitful, had been borne on the feet of bees, or wafted by the wind into their bosom, and forthwith they bore fruit. This, in the natural department, is the work of that same all-wise God who prepared the heart of Cornelius for receiving Peter's word, and brought Peter with the word to Cornelius. In both departments he is wonderful in counsel and excellent in working. The devout Roman centurion was a goodly tree, spreading its leaves and opening its blossoms to the sun year by year on the eastern shore of the Mediterranean, very hopeful, and very promising, but bare and desolate, until words, as if wafted on the wind, came from Joppa by the ministry of an apostle and fell upon the open, receptive, thirsting soul. Life sprang from that union.

You have passed ten or twenty or fifty years in this life. If you have passed over from death unto life, it is well. Hold the beginning of your confidence steadfast unto the end. But if not, think how much has been done to spare your life, and your reason; how much has been done to bring message after message to you. Be on the watch, lie open; at a time when you think not the hour may come, and the man, and the word— the word whereby you may be saved. The word may come to you at a moment when you are open for the word, as accidentally and yet as definitely determined and designed as the dust which makes the flower fruitful is brought on the feet of unconscious insects, or wafted on the bosom of the wind. But if your heart be closed and cold, when the word of life comes, you will be left in your sins. Beware lest you miss the word which is sent to quicken you.

Machinery boxed in goes round and accomplishes its work as well as if it were all exposed to view. At one extremity the raw material goes in, and at another the manufactured article comes out. This is all that the visitor sees. For once, and to instruct a stranger the master may take the covering off, and lay bare the intricate system of cylinders and wheels; but soon he shuts the door again. Under cover all the work goes on as steadily as when the observer's eye was watching it. Thus has the author of salvation, in the case of Cornelius and some others, opened up the processes of his providence, which are usually conducted in se-

cret; but to-day, and here, he as truly works, and as
wonderfully, in preparing hearts for receiving the seed
of the word, and bringing vessels charged with seed to
the right place at the right time. By the ministry, it
may be, of angels unseen, or by the ministry of flaming
fire and stormy winds unsuspected, or by the ministry
of men whom I have not yet met, the word of salvation
is coming to me. All things are now ready; be thou
ready also, O my soul.

The words which Peter brought to Cornelius were
intended and offered for the saving not of himself only,
but also of all his house. The prayer of the centurion
is not recorded. It is written that he prayed, but his
prayer is not written. We have, however, the means
of knowing what was in his prayer. As you may
thoroughly know a man's countenance by seeing it
reflected in a mirror, although at the moment a partition wall stands between him and you, so, from the
answer which a suppliant receives, you may learn what
he asked. The message sent to Cornelius in answer
to his prayer tells him how both he and his house may
be saved; therefore we know he had asked salvation for
his family as well as for himself. Wife, children, do-
mestics, and the soldier who waited upon him continually, bulked largely in the supplication of that earnest
striver into the kingdom. He prayed in secret, and
therefore we know not in the first instance what he
put into his prayer; but God rewarded him openly, and
by learning what he received, we learn what he asked.

If I am told in general terms of a mother that she
has gone to the studio of a photographic artist to obtain a portrait of herself; and if the question afterwards
arises, Did she sit alone, or did she group the children
round her feet, and hold the infant on her knee? I do not
know, for I was not there; but show me the glass which
the artist has just taken out from a vessel of liquid in a
dark room, and is holding up to the light. What figures
are these that are gradually forming upon its surface,
like hoar-frost on the window on a wintry day? In
that glass, dimly at first, like a thought springing in
the soul, but anon with greater distinctness, like articulated language on the lips, rises the outline of that
matron's form; and see, the forms of the children come

gradually in, variously grouped around her, and the infant sleeping in her lap. Ah, I know now, though I was not present at the operation, that this mother sat not alone when the sun in the heavens painted her picture in that glass.

Thus, by observing the group that cluster round Cornelius in the answer to his prayer, I learn who were crowding round his heart and rising to his lips, when he pressed his own need before the throne of grace.

We pray in secret; it is a privilege. We enter our closet and shut the door, as the Lord commanded—permitted us to do when we pray to our Father. No one knows our thoughts and words; none knows except the Hearer of prayer, who feels our longings pressing on the mercy-seat. But suppose our prayers—all their thoughts—were somehow impressed on a prepared plate, to start out in full outline, and be shown to our neighbors; what then? Then shame only to the Pharisees; but as many true wrestlings would be seen as might win a whole world to the Lord. It was this thought that was in Paul's mind when he said, "Would that ye knew what great conflict I have for you."

1. Parents and masters! God has placed the young under your charge, that you may bring them to him in prayer, and by instruction bring him to them. Nature's affections are at once soft and strong to draw them by. Are there ten in your house, yourself and nine besides, all leprous by a birth in sin? You, conscious of your disease, come to Jesus for healing, but if you come alone he will miss the rest. He is still the same, and he will certainly complain. His complaint will be, Were there not ten souls in that house; and where are the nine?

If you bring them, as Cornelius did, to the Lord in prayer, you will also like him bring them to the word and ordinances of God when an opportunity is offered. Cornelius was able to say, before Peter began to preach, We are all here before God, to hear all things that are commanded thee of God.

2. The children.—The word that is sent to the father and mother of a family, is a word that saves the children, and servants too, if they receive it. The parents who receive the word cannot save the children.

For the natural life the children must get and take sustenance for themselves. The bread that their parents eat will not preserve the children alive. So the life of parents, when it is hid with Christ in God, will not carry the children into heaven. I am the vine, ye are the branches. Every branch in me, etc.

Cling with all your strength, not to your godly father, but to your father's God.

Primitive Christianity
(Acts 11:19-21)

" Now they which were scattered abroad upon the persecution that arose about Stephen travelled as far as Phenice, and Cyprus, and Antioch, preaching the word to none but unto the Jews only. And some of them were men of Cyprus and Cyrene, which, when they were come to Antioch, spake unto the Grecians, preaching the Lord Jesus. And the hand of the Lord was with them: and a great number believed, and turned unto the Lord."

THEY speak of primitive Christianity. The word is sweet. Wearied of manifold errors and corruptions, we listen gladly to its sound. We would fain possess the thing which the word signifies. But, alas! those who are most ready to adopt the name are the most ready to abuse it. They write Primitive Christianity on their banner, and boldly set out in search of it; but they halt before they reach the object. They lose their way in the Dark Ages, and never emerge into the Scriptural light that shines beyond. It is here, in the Acts of the Apostles, that real primitive Christianity is to be found.

Three things appear at this point in the history—three things connected like links in a chain:—1. The ministry of men; 2. The hand of the Lord; 3. The fruit that followed.

1. The ministry of men. Some disciples belonging to Cyprus and Cyrene, scattered by the persecution, travelled as far as Antioch, and addressed themselves to the Gentiles of the Eastern capital, " preaching the

Lord Jesus." The missionaries are not named. They kept back their own names, and put forward that of their Lord. They have left no record of themselves on earth; but they have as their record on high a great multitude brought by their ministry to the Saviour. The persecution that culminated in the martyrdom of Stephen was intended by the Adversary to crush the infant Church; but it became the blast which spread the living seed over all the regions of the East.

Being themselves Jews, though born in foreign countries, they in the first instance preached to the Jews only; but they were soon led over the barrier, and entered a wider field. By special interposition from heaven the first opening was made, when Peter preached to Cornelius at Cæsarea. The crevice widened rapidly; and in a very short time the gospel, hitherto pent up within the limits of Israel, flowed out without impediment on the nations. True to its own nature, it refused to be confined. According to the Word of the Lord, it began indeed in Jerusalem; but true also to another part of the same Word, it speedily spread to the ends of the earth.

There is great precision in the history here. There is a Divine perspicuity in the statements, that presents a striking contrast with the crowd of dim inconsistencies that sprang up in succeeding ages. The theme of these primitive preachers was "the Lord Jesus." The Christianity of the apostolic age is distinguished by this, that it everywhere presents a personal Saviour to a disciple's faith. The wisdom of God is here. Man's Maker knows man's need. He only can devise, and provide, and apply the remedy for the ailment of humanity. Doctrines, however true and Divine, cannot arrest and control a man. They are not suited to the case. They are like spirits not embodied. They do not get hold of us; we do not get hold of them. When the soul of doctrine is incarnate in a person, we can comprehend and apprehend it. When that person is recognized to be the Lord Jesus—God with us—faith looks to him and lives.

This is primitive preaching: it is to tell the story of Jesus, and tell it until hearts of stone give way and flow down like water. Tell of our fall by sin; tell that we have departed from the living God; that a great gulf is fixed between the prodigal and his Father. We have no power to pass over it; and no will to try. He came to seek and save. The Good Shepherd came out to seek the lost sheep. The Just gave himself for the unjust. The eternal Son of God gave himself for us— wrought a righteousness for us that we might not be naked at the judgment-seat, and shed his blood to blot out our sin. He rose from the dead, and intercedes for us now at the right hand of God. He waits, our way to the Father, and our righteousness when we approach. They preached to the Greeks in Antioch the Lord Jesus, and—

2. "The hand of the Lord was with them." The instrument is all human, but the power is all Divine. We learn here with great simplicity and clearness these two things:—(1) that in conversion the hand of the Lord operates; but (2) that it operates through the ministry of men. In this work men can do nothing without God; but in this work God will do nothing without men. "How shall they hear without a preacher; and how shall they preach except they be sent?"

In 1 Cor. iii. 9 Paul explains of set purpose the union and relations of Divine and human agency in the conversion of men: "We are laborers together with God: ye are God's husbandry." Men are taken into partnership with God in the work; but the terms and conditions of the union are clearly defined. It is not an indefinite announcement that some part of the work is confided to human skill. A case is given which determines the limits of the two departments with infallible precision. The union of the Divine and human in conversion is the same as that which takes place in the cultivation of the fields. The people are the field to be cultivated; God and man in concert carry on the work. We know what man's department is in common agriculture. Besides the main, central act, the sowing of the seed, he does many things before and after it. He breaks up the ground, and makes it small; then he watches, weeds, and drains the field. The God of nature does not perform for man any of those operations which man can do for himself. For his part, he gives rain, and sun, and air. Without these human industry would not avail; but without human industry these would fail to produce fruit, Divine though they be.

Such in the spiritual field is the coöperation which took place at this point in the experience of the primitive Church. Men do all the cultivating; and when they have done all, they must wait for "the hand of the Lord" to give effect to their labor—must look up for the Spirit to be poured out as floods upon the dry ground.

3. The result was, "a great number believed, and turned to the Lord." The two acts, "believing" and turning "to the Lord," stand here in an interesting relation to each other. In some cases these two expressions may have substantially the same meaning; but here, where they occur in company, the "believing" must be the root, and the "turning" the fruit which it bears.

The root of the tree lies out of sight. The manner in which it lives and operates is in a great measure concealed. But the fruit can be both seen and tasted. By the fruits we know the tree. To believe is the secret act of the soul; to turn to the Lord, is the visible course of a disciple's life.

The fact that the first act of these disciples after they believed was a turning, shows clearly that before the gospel reached them they were walking in the way of sin and death. When through the blood of the cross a reconciliation takes place, the life-course is changed. The new creature in Christ now abandons all that he most fondly loved before. He casts away his idols, and worships the living God. The works of the flesh are abjured, and the works of the Spirit appear.

The converts were many. Like doves darkening the air by their multitude, they flocked to the name of the Lord as their refuge. In such a revival the Lord sees of the travail of his soul, and is satisfied.

It is a common and a true observation regarding that sort of gain which the Scriptures denominate "filthy lucre," that those who obtain much, instead of being satisfied, rather thirst more eagerly for more. The gain obtained in winning souls is in this single aspect like its carnal namesake, as an angel of light may be in some sense like an angel of darkness. It is true of those who win souls—both of the Head and his members—that the more of this gain they get, the more they desire to obtain.

The Grace that Barnabas Saw
(Acts 11:23)

" Who, when he came, and had seen the grace of God."

SCATTERED abroad by the persecution, the disciples of Jesus preached him in Antioch, the great Eastern capital of the empire. Here a wide field lay before the laborers. They cultivated it diligently, and soon were cheered by a harvest waving like Lebanon. Great numbers were converted, both Jews and Greeks.

This thing was not done in a corner. The rumor quickly spread. Friends and foes alike published the tidings. The world, at one of its great central marts, was turned upside down by these Galilean preachers. In such a case those who love the change and those who loathe it spread the report with equal diligence. It soon reached the ears of the believers who still remained in Jerusalem. The church there immediately despatched a messenger to the spot, with instructions to examine and report. Barnabas was chosen for this important mission. "He was a good man, and full of the Holy Ghost." He could discern between the chaff and the wheat. He was a man who might be trusted. He could observe with discrimination and report with faithfulness. It were greatly to be desired that modern Synods should adopt the same method in similar emergencies, and that they had equally judicious agents at their disposal. The plan was good, and it was well executed. Barnabas, sent by the assembled Church at Jerusalem as their commissioner, to examine and report upon the state of religion in Antioch, was the right man in the right place.

The result is briefly recorded under three heads:—

1. What he saw: "The grace of God."
2. What he felt: "He was glad."
3. What he did: "He exhorted them all."

I. What he saw. "When he came, and had seen the grace of God." What a man sees in any place depends in a great measure on what he looks for. Different persons observe different objects on the same spot. The taste of the observer goes far to determine what kind of sights he shall see. An architect visiting Antioch in those days would have seen many gorgeous edifices in the city. He would have found much to attract his attention in the commingling of Greek and Roman styles with the indigenous Oriental tastes of the people. A merchant would have examined the wares that were exposed in the market, and speculated on new openings for trade. A soldier would have scanned the fortifications, and measured their capacity to withstand a besieging force. In such a case a Christian too has an eye in his head, and a bias in his heart to turn it in a particular direction.

Barnabas had an eye to business as well as other people when he entered the Eastern metropolis. The edifice that arrested his regard was a holy temple built of "living stones." To "win souls" was the gain he coveted. From the soldier's view-point too he looked upon the city, and considered how its teeming multitudes might be made the subjects of Christ the King. Barnabas came to Antioch looking for the grace of God, and he found it in abundance there. He saw also other sights—sights that made him weep. The multitude of that heathen city was wicked, and the wicked are like the troubled sea when it cannot rest. The corruption that met his eye on every side grieved, but did not surprise him. Here and there in the desolation he observed portions of that "new earth, wherein dwelleth righteousness." These were the spots which he came to seek, and these accordingly arrested and absorbed his attention. When a navigator is sent out on a voyage of discovery, he observes wide tracts of sea; but he does not report that fact on his return. Green islands,

great or small, protruding here and there above the
level waters,—these are the objects for which he
searched during the voyage, and of which he speaks
when he comes home again. Such was the errand on
which Barnabas was sent, and such the method that
he followed. Of a sea of sin that was spread before his
eyes at Antioch we read not a word. His report refers
exclusively to the grace that rose above it. As the
coral islands of the Pacific rise and bask in the light of
heaven, flowery and fertile, while their base is surrounded by the barren, salt, angry waves of an unfathomable ocean, so the group of Christians that clustered
together as a Church in Antioch were rich in all the
graces of the Spirit, although they had sprung from a
dreary heathenism, and were surrounded by it still. He
reports not the sin of men, but the Grace of God.

Barnabas had grace in himself, otherwise he would
not have seen it in others. When the Christian doctrine first spread in the empire, certain Romish philosophers, intelligent and impartial as matters go among
men, reported to the government that a vile superstition was inundating the land. It was the truth as it is
in Jesus that was so characterized. It was the pure
gospel, as it came from the lips of the apostles, trans-
fused into the hearts and lives of believing men. Those
who called it a vile superstition did not intend to give
a false representation. The thing that was exhibited
before them was the very thing that Barnabas saw at
Antioch. It appeared before them, but they did not
perceive it. They did not see grace, because they did
not possess it.

Some persons among ourselves, not deficient in understanding and the power of observation, persever-
ingly and energetically represent earnest Christians
as a set of loathsome, selfish hypocrites. They think
that they are telling the truth, and doing good service
to God and man; but they are in the main mistaken.
Although they had entered Antioch in company with
Barnabas, these men would not have seen the grace
of God. They would have reported that they found
the majority of the population living in undisguised
vice, but that a knot of knaves might be observed in
the crowd, who wore long faces, and spoke in snivel-

ling tones, and were tenfold more detestable than other people, because they falsely professed to be holier. Grace—that is, God's favor bestowed through Christ, and accepted in faith—is a spiritual thing, and it is "spiritually discerned." It requires grace in one man to enable him to observe and own grace in another.

But this grace—this favor freely bestowed—is nothing less and nothing else than free pardon of all sin, given by God and accepted by men. He who has obtained it is forgiven through the blood of Christ, and renewed by the Spirit. He is reconciled and at peace. The quarrel between his conscience and the Divine law is settled. He is in Christ Jesus, and therefore there is to him now no condemnation. The man no longer dreads God as an offended King, but trusts and loves him as a Father. Now this grace, as it comes in the covenant from God, is an unseen thing. It is a secret in the soul. How then can it be seen by Barnabas, or by any other man? Like other things, both good and bad, it is known by its fruits. Life is invisible: and yet you know well where life is: you know life by the actions of the living. It is thus that grace in human hearts becomes known: it is known by its fruits in human life. Grace in its germ is invisible to all; but those who, like Barnabas, have tasted it themselves, can detect its presence by the fruits which it bears.

The Christians in Antioch had abandoned idols. They bore the name of Christ, although it might expose them to persecution. They lived "soberly, righteously, and godly" in the world. They were patient in tribulation, and instant in prayer. The rich gladly helped the poor, and the poor industriously helped themselves. "Faith, hope, charity, these three," beamed in their eyes and moulded their actions. There was a great exhibition in the Eastern capital at this time, and Barnabas went down to see it. It was a noble palace, built of living stones, growing together into a holy temple. He scanned it from its foundation on the Rock of Ages up to the brotherly love that effloresced richly from its loftiest pinnacles; and while he acknowledged a beneficent change in the life of those saved men, he ascribed it all to the goodness of God their Saviour.

The Gladness that Barnabas Experienced
(Acts 11:23)

" Who, when he came, and had seen the grace of God, was glad."

II. BARNABAS "was glad" when he saw the blessed effects which the gospel had already wrought in Antioch. Incidentally this throws light upon the character of the commissioner himself. Tell me what gladdens or grieves a man, and I will tell you what sort of a man he is.

The prosperity that made him glad was moral and spiritual, rather than material. Men of such an eye and such a taste are greatly needed in our modern commonwealths. We are carried away in a mighty tide of material progress; and although moral worth is gracefully owned as indispensable, there is a tendency, strong and constant, to give it only a secondary place. The vastness of a nation's wealth and power will only make its fall more terrible, if it is rotten at the root. Physical resources, even when directed by cultivated intellect, do not insure the happiness or the safety of a people. Man has been made with a side for God and a side for the world: if the side that lies toward eternity loses its life, then, however actively the side toward time may perform its functions, the whole body is paralyzed. We have railways, and telegraphs, and ships; and these, in their present measure of perfection, are new acquisitions made by our own generation; but the gospel is a more precious treasure, and our ancestors possessed it in its fulness long ago. I rejoice in the recent attainments of my country, for they are good; but I rejoice more in "the grace of God" that reigns in the hearts of my fellow-Christians, for it is better.

The grace or virtue that made Barnabas glad was possessed and exercised by others. There is not a finer feature in any man's character than the capacity and tendency to rejoice in a neighbor's prosperity. This is the mark of a true Christian, for it is a mark that belonged to the Master. Christ's command is, "Love one another, as I have loved you." Another law of the spiritual commonwealth is, "Put off the old man,—put on the new man" (Eph. iv. 22–24). When the old man is put away, his essential and characteristic affections go with him. Selfishness and envy are cast off, and a generous self-forgetting love springs up in their room. "Charity envieth not."

But the fruit in which this evangelist rejoiced not only grew in other hearts; it was planted, too, by other hands. It is easy for a minister of the gospel, if he be a true man at all, to be glad when he sees his own work prospering. It is a lawful and a pure enjoyment. The Apostle John experienced it: "I have no greater joy than to hear that my children walk in truth." It is pleasant employment for Paul or Apollos to come back to the garden which his own hands have planted or watered, and find the trees all laden with ripened fruit. But a deeper humility and a loftier faith are implied when an evangelist rejoices to see another man's garden prospering, while comparative barrenness broods over his own. Indeed, there is scarcely any weakness into which even sincere ministers of the gospel are more liable to fall than into that species of jealousy which consists in rejoicing less heartily over fruit which another hand has cultivated. In recent times a spirit of more enlarged charity has been poured upon the Church. True workers rejoice in each other's success. Of late, Christians have frequently been called to visit scenes of revival, and have learned to be glad, like Barnabas, over a more vigorous and devoted spiritual life in some hitherto heathenish Antioch, than they had ever witnessed under their own inspection in a privileged Jerusalem. The Sovereign Lord is still teaching us that converting power does not reside in an arm of flesh. To him every knee must bow; to him every tongue confess. He may, for wise purposes in his administration, employ in his work a feeble instrument, and lay the stronger for awhile aside. Some unknown, ungifted refugees may successfully found a Church in Antioch, while the greatest apostles seem to be spending their strength in vain.

Although only the gladness of this evangelist is recorded, we know well that a great grief lay beside it in his heart, as he paced the streets of Antioch. He saw the evil as well as the good. The good shone more brightly in his eyes by contrast with conterminous evil; and the evil seemed blacker because the good was beaming so near. This is a feature that adheres to all the delight of Christians in the present world. Such is our condition here that we cannot open our eyes to look on purity without perceiving impurity lying near. It is even by the dark shade of contiguous wickedness that we are able to trace the features of holiness among men. As a painter fills his background with darkness, deeper and deeper according as he desires to project his central figure more vividly into view, so, by the necessary conditions of our present state, the beauty of the new creature implanted by Divine grace in true disciples is brought more brightly out by the surrounding of sin in which it is set. The sadness that sat silently on the heart of Barnabas while he was making his inspection did not destroy, but rather enhanced his joy. The heaving sea of wickedness that stretched on all sides as far as the eye could reach, made more lovely the green islands that were projected above its surface and seemed to lie upon its breast.

The gladness of this deputy from the Church at Jerusalem was not a sentimental emotion terminating in the person who enjoyed it. It was an active, outgoing, operative passion. It was a spark that lighted up a flame within the man; and that flame quickly spread over surrounding objects. A selfish joy is an ignoble thing. The gladness that goes no further than the childish exclamation of the ancient idolaters, " Aha, I am warm ! " as they sat round their fire, is a matter that belongs to man in common with the brutes. But the joy which thrills in a Christian's heart at the sight of " grace " in the life of men, makes its higher nature known by its instant, energetic action. When a true Christian is made glad by seeing some grace, he forthwith begins to labor with all his might for more. It is a well-known law, operating both in the temporal and the spiritual spheres, that while the heart is hopeless the hands also hang down. The desponding cannot work any deliverance. Glad hope that makes a man

happy, makes him also useful. Had Barnabas seen no
good in Antioch, he would probably have done no
good there. There were many adversaries, but there
was a door of hope. With the unerring instincts of a
true disciple, when he gets encouragement, he both
gave himself to the work and enlisted others. " Then
departed Barnabas to Tarsus for to seek Saul: and
when he had found him, he brought him unto Antioch.
And it came to pass that a whole year they assembled
themselves with the Church and taught much people."

There is no enjoyment stronger or sweeter within
our reach in time than that which filled the hearts of
these evangelists at Antioch; but those who do not
share their zeal are strangers to their joy. Those who
do not keenly desire to see Christ's kingdom coming,
experience no delight when it comes. Blessed are they
that hunger and thirst after righteousness, for they shall
be filled. They who wait for the Lord, as lonely night-
watchers wait for the morning, are sure of their reward;
for to them that look for him he will appear, and his
coming will be like the morning. If I long to see the
likeness of Christ in the life of my neighbors, I shall
certainly be made glad one day. This desire is a vital
seed, which will bear its fruit of joy either in earth or
in heaven.

The man who rejoiced in the grace of God as he
saw it struggling through hard soil, beneath ungenial
skies, in the young believers of Antioch, looks on
brighter fields to-day. By this time he has asked in
astonishment, with the beloved disciple, " Who are
these that are arrayed in white clothing, and whence
came they ? " The man who has an eye to see and
a heart to love true believers, marred by many imper-
fections on the earth, shall look, ere long, upon the
saints made perfect. The eye that glistens now at
the sight of grace, will be permitted soon to gaze on
glory.

The Exhortation that Barnabas Gave
(Acts 11:23)

" And exhorted them all, that with purpose of heart they would cleave unto the Lord."

BARNABAS was happy, but not satisfied. The taste which he obtained of God's goodness to the Christians of Antioch whetted, rather than satiated his appetite. When a miser, who is already rich, suddenly obtains a great accession to his wealth, the effect of the increase is to stimulate his desire for more. The evangelist did not let the Christians of Antioch alone because he saw they were truly converted. Perhaps if he had observed nothing but a grovelling earthliness or a hollow hypocrisy in the infant Church there, he might have held his peace. His experience might have been like Ezekiel's: " Thou shalt be dumb, and shalt not be to them a reprover: for they are a rebellious house " (Ezek. iii. 26). It is comparatively easy to administer reproof to those who are willing to receive it. Hence "to him that hath shall be given, and he shall have abundance."

This is a useful and needful example. There is much fickleness even in true Christians: there is much deceitfulness even in a renewed heart. " Let him that thinketh he standeth take heed lest he fall." We should not assume, either for ourselves or others, that after conversion the time for warning and exhortation has passed.

God knows our weak points better than we ourselves. His promises of help may serve to show us where we are liable to fall. One of those rich and precious promises that were addressed to Israel through the prophets is, " I will heal their backslidings." We learn what disease is wasting us from the physician's offer to cure it. Alas, this malady is still epidemic in the Church! How difficult it is to hold fast even the attainments that we may have reached! That same

Saul whom Barnabas brought from Tarsus to be his coadjutor in Antioch, at a later date, and after he had attained a larger experience, placed on record a very full and specific warning against backsliding: "Wherefore we ought to give the more earnest heed to the things which we have heard, lest at any time we should let them slip" (Heb. ii. 1). The allusion in the original points to leakage from a vessel. In such a case the water slips gradually and secretly away, and is all absorbed in the earth. Thus some who seemed charged to the full with grace, have gradually lost the spiritual mind. How shall a wooden vessel be kept water-tight, so that the precious supply of the household may not ooze through its joints into the ground? By keeping it always full of water. It is by a similar method that grace may be preserved in the heart of a Christian. Keep the vessel full, and the vessel will not leak. Comparatively few make shipwreck of the faith through a deliberate change of opinion in the direction of infidelity. Many more are ruined, ere they are well aware, by a secret backsliding in heart and life.

He "exhorted them all;" and therein he acted wisely. If the word of truth is rightly divided, every member of the Church will get his share of reproof as well as encouragement. In the Christian brotherhood there is no privileged class. If any one thinks that his age, or attainments, or office should exempt him from listening to a warning word, that very thing shows that he needs a warning more that his neighbors.

The substance of the exhortation was that they should cleave to the Lord. Those who ministered in the Church at that time went straight to the root of the matter. There is no dallying here about sacramental grace, and the true Church, and a rightly consecrated priesthood. One thing in those days possessed the preacher's heart and burst from his lips when he addressed the assembled Christians,—"Cleave unto the Lord." In this "primitive Christianity," everything is made to depend on personal union to a personal Saviour. The exhortation in its nature refers not to the commencement, but to the continuance of faith. Those who have not yet returned, like the prod-

igal, to the Father's bosom, can neither understand
nor comply with it. Only those who have embraced
Christ can continue cleaving to him. If you bid a
man hold fast who has not yet ˜gotten hold, your
words will be unintelligible to him. It is as if you
should advise a man to lean on the air: if he try to
comply, his hands go through, and find no support.
But a dove finds that same air a sufficient support for
her body's weight. Faith is the wing that spreads,
and leans on the Omnipresent Spirit. As a bird without wings, is a human soul that has never learned to
trust in God. There is that around and underneath
us which would sustain our weight, but the unbelieving feel nothing firm, and fall helpless. The exhortation to cleave unto the Lord is appropriate to disciples who have already come to him, and tasted his
mercy.

There is mystery in this exhortation. This cleaving is an unseen thing. But it need not on that account seem strange. We meet with equal mysteries
in nature. I have seen a heavy piece of solid iron
hanging on another, not welded, not linked, not glued
to the spot; and yet it cleaved with such tenacity as
to bear not only its own weight, but mine, too, if I
chose to seize it and hang upon it. A wire charged
with an electric current is in contact with its mass,
and hence its adhesion. Cut that wire through, or
remove it by a hair's-breadth, and the piece of iron
drops dead to the ground like any other unsupported
weight. A stream of life from the Lord, in contact
with a human spirit, keeps that spirit cleaving to the
Lord so firmly that no power in earth or hell can
wrench the two asunder. From Christ the mysterious life-stream flows; through the being of a disciple
it spreads, and to the Lord it returns again. In that
circle the feeblest Christian is held safely; but if the
circle were broken, the dependent spirit would instantly drop off.

The phraseology of the evangelist designates the
"heart" as the point of contact in this cleaving. Here
the Scripture coincides with the laws of nature. All
moral attractions hold by the heart. The connecting
link is love. We love Him because he first loved us.

They who propose to keep a human being close to God in a conscientious obedience, by brandishing the terrors of the judgment in his face, misunderstand the essential principles of the case. They turn the wrong pole of the magnet to the steel, and thereby repel, instead of attracting it. You may as well expect a stone to rise from the ground spontaneously and float in the air, as expect that a human being will cleave to the Lord whom he dreads. I cannot keep close to Christ until I learn to love him, and I cannot learn to love him until I see that he offers his love to me. When he holds me by my heart, he holds me fast, and holds me for ever.

But there must be "purpose" or predetermination as well as love, in order to attain a trustworthy, permanent attachment. Random impulses will not suffice. There must be method even in the affections. It is not wise, it is not safe, to leave our highest interests at the mercy of varying mental states. Frame a plan, and execute it. Without forethought and plan and stern resolution, we do not expect to be successful in any effort. If half the skill and energy and perseverance expended in the community in the acquisition of wealth, were applied to the gain of godliness, we should soon have great treasures laid up at God's right hand.

Barnabas, commissioned by the Church, and full of the Holy Ghost, must have known what was a seasonable word for young Christians; and his exhortation to the believers in Antioch was, *Cleave to the Lord*. Bleeding heart of Christian to bleeding heart of Christ, both glued into one,—the severed branch inserted into the wounded Vine for life—for life in the Lord.

Barnabas and Saul at Antioch
(Acts 11:24-30)

" For he was a good man, and full of the Holy Ghost and of faith. and much people was added unto the Lord. Then departed Barnabas to Tarsus, for to seek Saul:" etc.

AT Jerusalem progress was checked. The blood of the martyr Stephen was indeed the seed of the Church; but the seed was scattered abroad, and the harvest sprang in other lands. The apostles seem to have considered themselves bound as yet by the Lord's command to remain at Jerusalem, but they remained there in comparative seclusion. There was no great enlargement like that which they had enjoyed after Pentecost. The ruling classes, in alliance with the mob, had succeeded in driving away or silencing most of the disciples; Christ, rejected by his own, had now turned to the Gentiles. So the French rulers, by the massacre of St. Bartholomew, cast a shower of precious seed on other lands, and brought desolation for many generations on their own.

While the apostles were waiting in comparative inactivity at Jerusalem, tidings strange and stirring reached them from a distance. At Antioch, the Eastern capital of the Empire, a great number of the Gentiles believed and turned to the Lord. Immediately the assembled brethren despatched Barnabas as their commissioner to examine the state of affairs, and act according to circumstances. When he came to Antioch he saw the grace of God there. He had the second sight, for he had the new birth, and the spiritual perception was a faculty of the new man. He rejoiced in the progress that the converts had made, and exhorted them to follow on to know the Lord. The result of his preaching was a great number of new conversions.

The expression employed here to indicate the decisive change is striking and suggestive—" Much people was added unto the Lord." It occurred before, v. 14. It represents an intimate vital union between the

Saviour and the saved, like the union between the vine and the branches.

One fact worthy of special notice emerges here :— the ministry of Barnabas on this occasion was a ministry specifically intended for the edification of believers, and yet, in point of fact, it was eminently effective for the conversion of those who were without. The preacher addressed himself to the converted, and exhorted them to cleave to the Lord; and, as a direct result, many strangers were brought nigh. The word, aimed at the living for increase of grace, strikes the spiritually dead, and awakens them to newness of life.

Those who rightly divide the word of truth, alternate between these two departments of effort. The word is addressed now to those who are within, and now to those who are without. Yet in the ministry of the Sovereign Spirit, sometimes the word meant for edification is effectual for conversion; and sometimes the word meant for converting sinners is used for the growth of grace in believers.

" Then departed Barnabas to Tarsus for to seek Saul." When the work of the Lord was at its height in Antioch, the worker went away from the city. He went away, although a great door and effectual was opened to him—went away because a great door and effectual was opened. He saw the door so wide and hopeful, that he determined to call in a colleague—a colleague on whom his eye had for some time been set, and of whom he expected great things. Taking advantage of the proximity of Tarsus, he went to that city to summon the lately converted Saul to his aid. His own net cast into the sea at Antioch was so full, that he found it necessary to beckon to his partner in another ship for help to draw it to land. So, when a miner in the gold-fields has fallen upon a piece so large that he is unable single-handed to remove it, he leaves it where it lies—leaves the precious lump buried in the ground—leaves it, though his heart is in it, because his heart is in it—and goes away in search of a friend who may help him to bear the treasure home.

I hope the two will not quarrel over the spoil when they come, for there is enough to make the fortune of both. Now there is an opportunity afforded to these winners of souls to make great gain. Not about this work and this treasure did Saul and Barnabas fall out. They agreed to share the labor and the reward: it was about another and a smaller thing that they afterwards quarrelled in a moment of unwatchfulness.

It has been an instinct of true disciples from the beginning hitherto, to concentrate all their available forces on a spot where success has already begun. The specific call for additional laborers is not strongest on behalf of places and populations that merely show great need; it is strongest on behalf of places and populations that are at once needy and promising. The call for help is ever more commanding when you are able to say, not only that there are many out of Christ, but also that not a few are coming in.

This is a beautiful feature in the character of Barnabas. Besides working faithfully himself, he has the skill to enlist others in the work. He doubtless prayed to the Lord of the harvest to send forth laborers; but to his prayers he added pains: he went out and did what he asked the Lord to do.

Of all the disciples of that day, Barnabas was best acquainted with the talents and character of Saul. He had already (ch. ix.) introduced the convert to the apostles at Jerusalem, and now he introduces him to his great work among the Gentiles. At Antioch a mighty two-leaved gate was opened to the Gentiles for the first time, and it was appropriate that the apostle of the Gentiles should there begin to exercise and to magnify his office.

The historian notes, in passing, that the disciples were called Christians first at Antioch. Then and there the disciples began to be known by the name of the Lord that bought them. Looking to the result, this circumstance is memorable. We are not distinctly informed by whom this designation was first applied. We may gather, however, with a considerable measure of certainty, that the term was employed by the Gentile Greeks to indicate the disciples of the Nazarene. The name is not assumed in this book by the Christians themselves; and the unbelieving Jews would not employ it, for in their lips it would seem to concede that Jesus was indeed the Messiah. It is more likely, therefore, that the Gentiles, hearing that name continually from the lips of believers, employed it to designate the sect.

The name is sweet, when it is true. But, alas! it has often been made contemptible in the world through the impure lives of those who bear it. To be called by his name is nothing, unless we be renewed into his likeness.

The other name, most commonly applied in Scripture to designate our Redeemer, has experienced a similar diversity of use in the history of the Church. "How sweet the name of Jesus sounds in a believer's ear!" And yet a Jesuit has become a synonym for all that is false and cunning and corrupt throughout the civilized world. What's in a name? Nothing, even though it be the highest of all names, unless the new nature be formed in him who bears it.

At this time certain prophets from Jerusalem warned the disciples at Antioch of a famine that should afflict the Empire at an early date. It came in the reign of Claudius: it was severely felt in many provinces, but most of all in Judæa.

This announcement is introduced into the narrative not for its own sake, but on account of the fruit which immediately resulted in the form of contributions made out of their abundance by the believing Gentiles in Antioch, to sustain the believing Jews at Jerusalem in the day of their distress. These gifts have the peculiar fragrance of first-fruits. A very great harvest of charity for the sake of the common Head has since been reaped; and the latest reapings have been richest. Never and nowhere have the fruits of Divine love, in the form of help to the needy, grown so great as in the wake of great wars lately waged on the far-separated continents of America and Europe. As the prospect of famine in Judæa drew out the love of Christians at Antioch, and exhibited in the love of brethren a glory to the Lord, so the great wars of recent times have generated a self-sacrificing helpfulness that has, both for its quantity and its quality, become the wonder of the world.

The power of Christ's love was made peculiarly manifest in the case of these contributions from Antioch, inasmuch as the contributors were mainly Gentiles, and the recipients Jews. What hath the Lord wrought?

The sun has gone back on the dial. Surely the partition-wall has at length been broken down, and Gentiles and Jews flow softly into one.

Here too, in the first springs of that stream which ever since has flowed to bless the world, we learn one of the rules divinely prescribed for the management of charities: Among the disciples (1) every man gave; and (2) every man gave as the result of a deliberate determination, a spontaneous act of his own will; and (3) every man gave according to his ability. There was a measure to determine the quantity of the gifts; and that measure was the degree of prosperity that God had given to each. But this measure was not mechanically applied by any external authority: it was determined in every case within the court of conscience, and by the contributor's own judgment.

The love of Christ, in giving himself the just for the unjust, supplied the power which impelled the early Christians into a life of benevolence; but while in this matter they gladly placed themselves under law to God, they refused to become the servants of men.

Herod Vexes the Church
(Acts 12:1-8)

" Now about that time Herod the king stretched forth his hands to vex certain of the church. And he killed James the brother of John with the sword," etc.

IN the beginning of chapter xi. we learned that sufferings separated those who were united; and so the truth was spread: in the end we learned that sufferings united those who were separated; and so, by contributing food to the Jewish Christians, the Gentile Christians bridged with love the dividing gulf, and permitted the body of Christ to flow into one.

When the converted Greeks at Antioch learned by prophecy that the brethren in Judæa would soon be in straits, they forthwith began to make contributions. Evidently they were cheerful givers. They would not murmur when the subscription list came round. They counted it blessed to give, and were ready. Before the calamity came, it was provided for.

The scene changes. From Antioch we are conducted back to Jerusalem again. After intimating that the door was opened among the Greeks, the historian proceeds to show that it was shut among the Jews. Indeed, it was the shutting of the door at Jerusalem that opened it at Antioch. When one channel was closed, the pent-up waters escaped by another. It was the persecution at home that drove the preachers abroad.

But now another stage of the process is exhibited. Closer and closer was the door shut at Jerusalem; wider and wider it opened toward the Greeks. By his apostles, as well as in his own personal ministry, Christ came unto his own, and his own received him not.

The king who appears here is Herod Agrippa, grandson of Herod Antipater who slew the infants of Bethlehem, and son of Herod Antipas who beheaded the Baptist. He was mild in his natural temper, but fond of popularity. He persecuted the Christians not of his own motion, but to please the Jews. Hence the rejection of Messiah lies articulately on the Jewish people and their priests. To please them, Pilate delivered Jesus to be crucified; to please them, Herod Agrippa killed James, the brother of John, with the sword.

Hitherto the lives of the faithful apostles had been preserved. Like Daniel in the lions' den, they had been kept from the power of their enemies. The Lord reigneth; and for a time he threw a shield round the chiefs of the infant Church. While the flax is only smoking, he will not permit a blast to blow on it, lest the feeble life should be quenched; but when the fire has gained some head, he allows the blast to come, that it may be fanned into a greater flame.

Keeping Judas out of view, this is the first breach in the apostolic circle. They had in some measure learned to walk by faith, and even the fall of an apostle will not crush them now. In the case of James, the Lord shows that he will not always interfere to protect his servants from their enemies; and in the case of Peter, he shows that he will interfere sometimes, lest the spirit should fail before him, and the souls that he has made. He will not suffer his people to be tempted above that they are able to bear.

The first martyrdom in the apostolic college marks for us a law of the kingdom. It illustrates the meaning of Messiah's word, " My kingdom is not of this world!" Not an inch of this world's surface will Christ maintain for himself by the sword. The kingdoms of this world will one day be all his; but they will be subdued by the sword of the Spirit. It was Antichrist that gathered mercenaries from many lands to sustain the Roman bishop's throne, and crush the liberty of the Roman people.

Observing that no Divine power was put forth either to protect James or avenge his death, this weak and unjust king ventured a step further in the same course. Finding that one murder procured him favor with the Jewish people, he determined to perpetrate another. Peter was designated as the next victim. He was arrested and imprisoned. The plan of the persecutor was to gratify the people by a public trial and public execution of the most distinguished follower of Jesus.

But the remainder of the king's wrath it pleased God in this instance to restrain. To this raging sea the word of its Maker came, " Hitherto shalt thou come, but no further."

" Peter therefore was kept in prison; but prayer was made," etc. This is a remarkable antithesis. Man proposes, but God disposes; and the prayer of faith reaches the Disposer's hand. James was suddenly seized and taken off; but in Peter's case there was time for the whole Church to unite in their prayer for his preservation. God in providence opened a door of opportunity through Herod's desire to keep all quiet till after the Passover; the Church eagerly entered that door. They "inquired" by a concert of prayer; and God in heaven was " inquired of" by them to do it for them.

Four times four soldiers were employed to guard the prisoner. The night was divided into four watches·

and four watched at one time—two chained to the prisoner, and two on guard at the prison-door.

On the morrow Herod meant to bring the victim out, for he will politically or hypocritically comply with the rule that no trial should take place on the feast-day. As soon as the service of God shall be over, we shall gratify the mob with the shedding of innocent blood! On the morrow! It seems a thin veil of one night's darkness that hangs between these wild beasts and their prey, that hangs between these suppliant disciples in John Mark's house and their great bereavement. The prayer-meeting is prolonged into the night —is prolonged to the morning. A mighty pressure is then brought to bear on the door of the kingdom—on the heart of the King. This is the violence that takes the kingdom by force. The pressure increases as the night wears on, and at last prevails. The Lord within the veil loved to feel that strain. He delights to answer such a cry.

Peter, meanwhile, was sleeping. That sleep was the triumph of faith. Peter's sleep in the prison that night was as much glory to God as his wakefulness would have been, although he had sung psalms till the rafters rang again. Peter slept in Gethsemane, with the two brothers, on the night of the Master's supreme agony. Then he slept through weakness of the flesh; now and here he sleeps through the strength of his faith. There he slept through weariness, although his Lord was enduring agony; here he sleeps in confidence, because his Lord was exalted to the throne of heaven, mindful and mighty to protect his own.

Argyle's sleep, an incident in Scottish history, commemorated by art in the Legislative Hall of Westminster, shines out as a bright particular star among the honored deeds of our ancestors in a heroic age. The deep, placid sleep of the innocent Scottish noble on the morning of his martyrdom was a better testimony to his valor than any that could have been borne on the battle-field.

Here is a precious lesson for disciples in this latter end of the world. How sweet it is to lie down every night, reconciled to God in Christ, and at peace, ready, if the Lord should so will, to awake in the eternal world!

This privilege need not be the rare attainment of a few; for it is offered as free as the air to all. "Whosoever will, let him come." "Come unto me, all ye that labor and are heavy laden, and I will give you rest."

" The apostle sleeps; a light shines in the prison,
　　An angel touched his side:
　Arise, he said; and quickly he hath risen,
　　His fettered arms untied.

" The watchmen saw no light at midnight gleaming,—
　　They heard no sound of feet:
　The gates fly open, and the saint, still dreaming,
　　Stands free upon the street.

"So, when the Christian's eyelid droops and closes
　　In Nature's parting strife,
　A friendly angel stands, where he reposes,
　　To wake him up to life.

" He gives a gentle blow, and so releases
　　The spirit from its clay;
　From sin's temptations, and from life's distresses,
　　He bids it come away.

" It rises up, and from its darksome mansion
　　It takes its silent flight,
　And feels its freedom in the large expansion
　　Of heavenly air and light.

" Behind, it hears Time's iron gates close faintly,—
　　It is now far from them;
　For it has reached the city of the saintly,
　　The New Jerusalem."

J. D. BURNS.

Antioch Occupied for Christ
(Acts 12:20-25;13:1)

"And Herod was highly displeased with them of Tyre and Sidon: but they came with one accord to him, and having made Blastus the king's chamberlain their friend, desired peace; because their country was nourished by the king's country. And upon a set day Herod, arrayed in royal apparel, sat upon his throne, and made an oration unto them," etc.

THE account of Herod's death, introduced into the narrative, accords in all main points with the statements of Josephus. He had removed his residence from Jerusalem to Cæsarea, that he might be on the sea-coast, and in closer communication with Rome. On the occasion of a grand assembly, connected with an embassy from the commercial communities of Tyre and Sidon, he entered the theatre in his robes of state. His royal robes, studded with precious stones, glittered in the sun as he moved, and the obsequious multitude shouted, ascribing Divine honors to their idol, according to the custom of Roman mobs. The judgment of God fell upon the frail mortal, and he died soon after of a most loathsome disease.

So died the persecutor; "but the word of God grew and multiplied." This precious note is inserted in the history for comfort to the Church in time of trouble. Fear not, little flock; greater is he that is for you, than all that are against you. The word, a living power, had free course through the nations when the feeble monarch who attempted to quench it lay in his grave. Thus Pharaoh and his army sank in the sea, while Israel, emancipated, praised the Lord and resumed their march.

If the princes and peoples of the earth should combine in an effort to destroy all the grain that exists—to stamp out the staff of life—they would not succeed. The seed has life in itself. Some of it, as the destroyers bore it to their bonfires, would be spilt upon the ground, and be lost to view. The lost would live and spring. From its resurrection a manifold return would be obtained; and the fields would be sown and ripen—seed-time and

harvest would follow each other, after the foolish ex-
terminators had returned to the dust. In like manner
the efforts of persecutors have proved abortive; they
have not been able to extinguish the word of life. God
has secured that there shall be seed to the sower and
bread to the eater, both in the temporal and spiritual
spheres, even unto the end of the world.

"The word grew:" the expression is general; but in
point of fact the widespread result was made up of many
individual conversions, as a river is composed of many
drops all obeying the same law. In ten thousand
separate seeds the word fell into ten thousand separate
hearts, and each heart, rent for receiving the seed, was
further rent by the seed, when it swelled and grew.
There is no wholesale spiritual growth. The wide revival consists of many persons, each of them separately
renewed in the Spirit.

Barnabas and Saul returned to Antioch. There is
great significance in the going and coming of these
messengers. These are the couriers of the Great King,
carrying his commands from province to province of his
realm. First, they carried from Antioch a contribution
to sustain the Christians of Jewish origin at Jerusalem
through the famine. That gift was well fitted as an
instrument to remove barriers, and unite Greeks and
Jews in the common faith. From Jerusalem, and from
Jews, came forth the spiritual things wherewith the
Gentiles at Antioch were enriched; they only obey a
law of the kingdom when they load the returning train
with temporal gifts for Christian Jews in Jerusalem.
Such reciprocal charities were eminently fitted to break
down the partition-walls, and blend all believers into
one.

By this time the Christian leaders were aware of
the importance of Antioch. They determined to occupy it for the work of the kingdom. Foreseeing the
expansion of missionary work both in and from the
capital, Barnabas and Saul induced John Mark to accompany them and share their labor. He was the son
of Mary, sister of Barnabas, in whose house the prayer-
meeting was held while Peter was in prison, and to
whose house Peter went when he was free. This young
man would go to Antioch probably in two capacities,

—both as an assistant to the elder missionaries, and as a witness of their work, who might afterwards give evidence in Jerusalem regarding its character.

On the return of the deputation from Jerusalem, the College of Evangelists was constituted at Antioch. Excluding John Mark as a junior and a new-comer, it consisted of five members. Besides the two missionaries already introduced to our notice, there were "Simeon that was called Niger, and Lucius of Cyrene, and Manaen which had been brought up with Herod the tetrarch." The note attached to the name of this man is full of interest. He was foster-fellow of that Herod who slew the Baptist, and set at nought the Lord on the morning of his death.

Manaen thus seems to be another Moses drawn out of the water. Brought up in the company of an ungodly and licentious prince, he was nevertheless chosen as an object of mercy, and employed as a messenger of grace. Perhaps, like Moses, he had it in his power to obtain and keep a position near the throne; but, like Moses, he esteemed the reproach of Christ greater riches than the treasures of Egypt. We have no account of his conversion; but, whatever may have been its date and its circumstances, it is certain that when he became a disciple of Christ he no longer set any value on his connection with Herod's house.

The power and sovereignty of grace are frequently displayed in choosing one from the steps of a throne, and making him a vessel to bear the name of Christ. Manaen was snatched from the side of a murderer, and numbered among the saints of the Most High. His name was blotted from the family register of the tetrarch, and written in the Lamb's book of life. Those who have been saved, as it were by fire,—who have been arrested and won in spite of the strong man's greatest efforts to keep his goods in peace, have peculiar delight in looking back over the way by which the Lord has led them. On the other hand, those who remain in Herod's house, entangled by its business and gains, should learn from this case that they are welcome to Christ. It was a true word that fell from lying lips, when the Pharisees murmured, "This man receiveth sinners." Whosoever will, let him come.

There is scarcely a congregation of believers that lacks its Manaen, highly esteemed now as a brother in the Lord, who seemed destined in his earlier years as devotee and victim to the pleasures of sin. It is a peculiar delight to the Christian brotherhood, and a peculiar glory to Divine grace, when one who has been brought up for the world, is snatched from the world, and admitted as an heir of the new kingdom. It is sweet to see the children of Christian parents born to the Lord, in their childhood, through means of a pious nurture; but it is perhaps more gladdening and inspiring to see the goings of the Lord, when he puts forth his power to wrench subjects from the god of this world, and make them princes round his own throne.

The First Foreign Mission-Cyprus
(Acts 13:2-12)

" As they ministered to the Lord, and fasted, the Holy Ghost said, Separate me Barnabas and Saul for the work whereunto I have called them. And when they had fasted and prayed, and laid their hands on them, they sent them away," etc.

" As they ministered to the Lord and fasted, the Holy Ghost said, Separate me Barnabas and Saul for the work whereunto I have called them." While they were enjoying privileges for themselves, they heard the command to carry these privileges to others. Behold the natural history of missions! Freely ye have received, freely give. They possessed the gospel, and therefore they must spread it abroad.

Two were sent out together. They remembered the act of the Lord Jesus, how he sent out the seventy in pairs, and they will follow his example. The ministry of the Spirit is sovereign here on every side. Antioch is chosen as the first sight of a Gentile Church, and consequently becomes the starting-point for the first foreign mission. The same features that commended the place to Imperial Rome as the Eastern capital, commended it to the apostles of the Lord as the head-quarters of the kingdom that is not of this world. Situated in the East, it enjoyed, by the Orontes and the Mediterranean, easy access to Greece and Rome. From this great mart the glad tidings will be borne along with the stream of commerce to the nations of Africa and Europe.

The men chosen for foreign work in accordance with the mind of the Spirit, were the mightiest men. They did not send out some persons who had turned out useless at home. The foreign field always needs, and in that age actually obtained, the ablest laborers. I suspect the chief obstacle to the success of modern missions lies here. The Church at Antioch sent the cream of the ministry abroad; if they had sent the grounds, their success would have corresponded to their effort. Here and there in our own time, when the Spirit has descended in power, some men mighty in word and deed have taken the field, and the result has been a gain corresponding to the outlay; but it is the grief and the weakness of the Church at the present day that her chiefs are for the most part occupied at home.

They sent Barnabas and Saul. Barnabas had already been tried, and found faithful. His gravity, his authority, and his benevolence seemed to point him out as leader of the expedition. But they have at hand this young man Saul—a man of vast knowledge, of fiery zeal, of great courage, and unflagging perseverance, but withal not much tried and not much known. Send him out under the direction and influence of Barnabas, that his great talents may be turned to the best account. Soon shall the whole Church know that the Lord has destined this man for the foremost place. When the pair departed it was Barnabas and Saul; when they returned it was Paul and Barnabas.

Westward the expedition moved. Europe must be won to Christ. The light of life, like the natural sun, travels from the East.

The two missionaries were solemnly ordained to their specific work, and set out on their journey. Whether by land or by the river, they first travelled to

Seleucia, the sea-port of Antioch, on the Mediterranean, and taking ship at that port, they crossed over to Cyprus, the nearest of the large islands.

Having landed at Salamis, a town on the eastern side of Cyprus, they crossed the country without much delay or much success until they reached Paphos, the residence of the Roman governor, on the western shore. This was a place notorious for its licentiousness even in that age. It was the shrine of impurity for the heathen world. There the unclean spirit had his seat. These soldiers of Jesus Christ, in their first campaign, marched right up to the capital of the enemy's kingdom.

Among Roman provinces Cyprus was small. The governor held not the highest rank. One may suppose he was disappointed when he learned that this comparatively insignificant sphere was assigned to him, and envied the better fortune of competitors who obtained Gaul and Spain. He lived, however, to thank God for the providence that cast his lot in Cyprus. He did not enjoy so large a salary as the chief of a richer province, but he obtained through the missionaries a greater treasure.

This governor was a prudent man. He was thoughtful and sober. He was probably dissatisfied with the worn-out superstitions of idolatry, and longing for something solid on which his soul might lean. It is probable he asked Pilate's question, "What is truth?" with an earnestness that Pilate never knew. Alas! when people in high places become earnest inquirers, false teachers swarm around them like flies, eager to suck sustenance from the wounds of the great. The governor had at this time in his train a certain fortune-teller, who called himself Elymas—that is, "the wise," for the root in Arabic seems to be the same as the Turkish *ulemah*, or priest. This man's own Hebrew name was Bar-jesus, "son of the Saviour." He pretended, through soothsaying art, to cure the ailment of the governor's spirit; and poor Sergius, precisely because he was ailing in spirit, had not force to throw off the incubus. The mountebank stuck to the governor, and fattened on his wealth. When the missionaries from Antioch reached the city, and opened their commission by preaching Christ, the governor sent a message to summon them to his court, that he might hear their doctrines. They willingly obeyed the summons, and presented themselves at the palace.

But the sorcerer, fearing lest his own influence should be destroyed, endeavored to prevent the governor from listening to the gospel, or to hinder him from receiving, if he had already heard it. How eagerly the modern sorceress, who sits on the seven hills, strives to hinder a meeting between human souls and Christ in his Word!

At this stage we would be apt to say, What a pity that Elymas was on the spot to interfere with the good work when the Christian missionaries obtained an opportunity of preaching to the ruling classes at the capital! Nay; He doeth all things well. As Christ said when Lazarus died, "I am glad for your sakes that I was not there;" so he might say, in the case of Sergius Paulus, "I am glad for his sake that Elymas was there with his sorceries, seeking to turn away the deputy from the faith:" for the efforts of the sorcerer to turn him away were overruled as the means of bringing him near. If Elymas with his wicked arts had not been there, it is probable that the governor would not have been converted. In his later experience, Paul became well aware that the opposition by adversaries is often an essential means of success. On one occasion, reporting a very favorable opportunity for conducting his work, he describes it by two features—a wide door, and *many adversaries*. He seems to intimate that one of these two factors alone would not have constituted the opportunity which he valued and enjoyed. Both were needed. If there had not been a fierce wind blowing against his kite, it would not have been able to rise. The experienced missionary accordingly was glad of the storm.

Who shall tell whether the sermon would not have fallen flat on sleepy ears, and whether the governor would not have yawned the preacher away to make room for some new excitement, if the opposition of Elymas had not arrested his attention, and the judgment on Elymas had not struck him with astonishment. All things wrought for good: the things that happened then and there turned to the furtherance of the gospel.

Here first the name Paul appears; and Saul is not employed again, except in narratives of his earlier experience. Here, under his new name, Paul springs to the front, and he is never found in the second rank again. Now, first, he is fully installed into office as the Apostle of the Gentiles. It is in his short, sharp rebuke of Elymas that he reads himself in.

In allusion to the meaning of the sorcerer's name, "son of the Saviour," the apostle sternly denounces him as a "child of the devil;" and through inspiration speaks the sentence which God inflicts—the sentence of temporary blindness. This judgment falling on the adversary, convinced Sergius that Paul and Barnabas were men of God, and made him reverently listen to their word. "Then the deputy, when he saw what was done, believed, being astonished at the doctrine of the Lord." What was done could not have enlightened and renewed the Roman; but it opened his mind for the reception of the word of life. Thus the Lord in providence at this day employs judgment-strokes of many different kinds to open a path for the gospel into hearts that otherwise would have remained closed. Welcome the Lord's hand, even though its stroke be painful, when it prepares the way for the Lord's word! If we had access to the great multitude who stand round the throne in white clothing, and could ask each saved saint to tell his own experience, probably nine out of every ten would answer that providence, generally feared and fretted at, came crushing forward first, and broke up a way for grace to follow.

The judgments of the Lord's hand opened a way into the heart of Sergius for the Lord's word. That word, when it entered, filled him with wonder. "He was astonished at the doctrine of the Lord." After the storm and thunder, the "still small voice" asserted its power. The story of the cross was a new thing to the Roman. It was not like the doctrine of the Greek philosophers: it was not like the doctrine of the Jewish soothsayer. These missionaries told the governor that God is love, and that he so loved the world that he gave his only Son to save the lost. They told him that God, in our nature, had given himself a sacrifice, the just for the unjust. As this doctrine fell on the governor's ears, his heart melted. Felix trembled, and returned to his sin: Sergius trembled, and cleaved to Christ. One is taken, and another left.

Poor Sergius had lived up to this time in a dark, sunless world. He was uneasy, and knew not what ailed him. He craved for light, and yet knew not where to find it. We know that he longed for something to satisfy his soul, for he kept the Jewish magician hanging about his court. He clutched a shadow; and this showed at least that he had an appetite for the substance. In his darkness he had heard of this man's pretensions, and sent for him. "Can you strike some light for us, stranger? for we are in darkness unendurable here. Give us some light for our souls, if you can, by your magical arts." To such a man, in such a mood, the doctrine of the Lord, when it was unfolded, was like the sunlight bursting through the primeval mist upon a hitherto benighted world. It was sight to the blind, and life to the dead.

The Gospel in Asia Minor
(Acts 13:13-52)

" Now when Paul and his company loosed from Paphos, they came to Perga in Pamphylia: and John departing from them returned to Jerusalem. But when they departed from Perga, they came to Antioch in Pisidia, and went into the synagogue on the sabbath day, and sat down. And after the reading of the law and the prophets the rulers of the synagogue sent unto them, saying, Ye men and brethren, if ye have any word of exhortation for the people, say on. Then Paul stood up, and beckoning with his hand said, Men of Israel, and ye that fear God, give audience," etc.

PAUL had already taken the lead in the interview with Sergius; and he keeps it, now when the missionary company take leave of Cyprus, and make for the mainland of Asia Minor.

The immediate reason why Cyprus was chosen as the field of operation when the mission first started for Antioch, was probably the connection of Barnabas with that island as the place of his birth. Perhaps the journey northward to the province of Pamphylia now was in like manner due to the predominance which Paul had attained in the councils of the company. They sailed from Paphos, on the western shore of Cyprus, to the nearest point of the neighboring continent. The landing-place was not, indeed, in Cilicia, Paul's native province, but it was in the bordering territory, and must have been familiar to him in his youth.

"Paul and his company loosed from Paphos and came to Perga in Pamphylia." The great work is begun; the messengers run to and fro; knowledge of the Lord is increased. Forth from Jerusalem the word has gone; and it will never be shut up within one nation again. The word has come to the world; the people who sat in darkness saw a great light.

These isles of Greece!—green spots that stud the bosom of the sea, and stud our memories too from childhood with romantic associations—we think of them as the early home of the arts, at a time when our country was the hunting-ground of barbarians. These isles of Greece!—we remember with youth's enthusiasm, that on the waters which surround them the battle of liberty was fought and won, when the small Greek communities broke the power of the Persian monarchy, as the country's rocky shores broke the waves of the Mediterranean.

But on the page of Scripture a more entrancing scene is displayed. The feet of the men who publish salvation tread the isles of Greece, and touch the waters that lave its shores. These heralds proclaim to the nations peace with God through the one Mediator. The barque that bore the missionaries of the cross was buoyed up on the same waters that carried those classic navies which bore back the tide of invasion from their shores: but a greater than classic fleet is here; here a greater victory is won, and a more precious liberty achieved. If the Son make you free, you shall be free indeed.

The apostle of the Gentiles is now fully under way. This is the beginning of his course; and what a course! No mere man has left his mark so deep and broad upon this world. No conqueror, ancient or modern, can be compared with this wandering Jew, either as to the magnitude or the beneficence of his influence on the character and history of the human race.

There is a tendency in our day to escape from some of the doctrines which Paul has clearly expressed and fully expounded in his epistles. These doctrines are by some persons disliked, and therefore disbelieved. In connection with this subject some indisputable facts should be carefully noted and remembered. These deep abstract doctrines which Paul taught—the doctrines of justification by faith and pardon through a sacrifice—communicated the impulse to the greatest practical life known to history. These were the impelling motives of the largest and most fruitful of human lives. It was by the proclamation and inculcation of these doctrines that the old things of human civilization were swept away and all things were made new. In them lay the power that turned the world upside down. Those who nibble at the Pauline dogmas should take along with their criticisms the fact that these dogmas have in very deed put forth more power to mould the character and destinies of humanity than any or all other doctrines put together.

As soon as the missionary group reached the mainland, Mark left them, and returned to Jerusalem. We do not exactly know his reasons; but we know that Paul thought them insufficient, and publicly blamed the act. So much did he disapprove of Mark's conduct at this time, that at a subsequent stage he refused to accept him as a companion, although that refusal implied separation from his beloved Barnabas. Possibly Mark may have been offended by the change that had silently been effected in the leadership of the expedition. When he left Antioch as the junior colleague, his uncle Barnabas was at its head; but when he left Paphos the whole group passed under the designation of "Paul and his company." Barnabas himself was superior to such jealousy; but it does not follow that the younger evangelist altogether escaped the tinge.

Leaving Perga, on the coast, the two elder missionaries penetrated to Antioch in Pisidia—a much less important city than the Antioch from which the expedition sailed—and there opened their commission as

preachers of Christ's gospel. They modestly entered
the synagogue on the Sabbath, and sat down among
the ordinary worshippers. The elders in charge conducted the usual service in the usual way, and then
sent a message inviting the strangers to address the
assembly.

Paul is the spokesman abroad, as Peter had been at
home. Having been led to the proper place, he waved
his hand as a token for silent attention, and proceeded
with his address.

Following the method of Stephen, which he doubtless
remembered well, he sought an entrance to the sanctuary
of the gospel through the vestibule of venerated Hebrew
history. When he had carried his sketch down to the
time of David, he turned aside from the narrative and
plunged into his main theme—presented David's Son to
the faith of David's subjects.

At the close of the sermon, when the bulk of the
congregation dispersed, a band of earnest inquirers,
partly Jews, but for the most part Gentiles, remained
with the missionaries—their appetites quickened, not
satisfied by what they had heard. Pleasant excitement
it must have been to these fishers for men when they
felt many grasping and drawing. Fuller explanation
was given in private to all the inquirers, and a promise
made, in answer to their eager request, that the same
doctrines would be taught in the synagogue next Sabbath-day. I think those men of Antioch who remained
after the sermon to converse with the ministers would
have many thoughts and conversations on the subject
during the week. When they came up to the house of
God next Sabbath they were sure of the blessing; for
the finding is, in the Lord's promise, made sure to those
who seek.

It is remarkable that Paul, though rejected by his
own countrymen at Jerusalem, and sent out as the
apostle of the Gentiles, yet uniformly addressed himself first to the Jews wherever he found them. He
maintained the spirit of the Lord's rule, when compliance with the letter was no longer possible,—"beginning at Jerusalem." The Jews of the dispersion par-
ticipated in the privilege: the first offer was always
made to the seed of Abraham. In each case the

gospel was presented to the heathen when it was rejected by the Jews.

When the Greek inhabitants of the city came out in mass to hear the gospel, the Jews were envious, and violently opposed the apostles. In his defence Paul quotes a promise (Isa. xl. 6; Luke ii. 32), calling it a command. It is eminently instructive to observe that when God promises light to the Gentiles, Christians understand the word as an order to themselves to spread the light in the dark places of the earth. When God proclaims that the thing shall be done, true disciples of Christ go forth to do it. They count the promise a command, and render themselves instruments of righteousness unto God. The result was, " the word of the Lord was published through all that region." They rightly understood the Scripture, " Work, for it is God that worketh in you."

Besides appealing to the civic authorities against the missionaries, the Jews, in their eagerness to obstruct the work, secretly enlisted the services of certain women, high in social position, and full of superstitious zeal, to counteract the effects of the preached word. This is an agency that has from the beginning been sought and used both for good and for evil. Women were employed by the Lord himself for certain appropriate ministries in the establishment of his kingdom. But false teachers have in all times availed themselves of the combined weakness and strength of the feminine nature for their own ends. They find in many women the religious element strong, and the faculty of judgment comparatively weak. By the weak side they enter in and take possession; when once in, they wield the strong side for their own purposes. The Romish hierarchy have always made much of female agency, and especially the agency of women in high social rank.

But as Christ himself employed their tenderness, and patience, and perseverance in his own cause, he has encouraged his disciples in all ages to go and do likewise. Let woman stand on her true foundation, the family; and forth from that citadel let her go to her daily task wherever the Lord hath need of her service: but back to the family let her ever return, as to her refuge and rest. Colonies of women, cut off from family relations and affections and duties, and bound by vows, are mischievous to themselves, and, notwithstanding superficial apparent advantages, in the long-run dangerous to the community. God made the family; man made the convent. God's work! behold, it is very good; man's is in this case a snare.

The unbelieving Jews, through secret influence and public authority combined, succeeded in driving the missionaries away from Antioch. On their part, the missionaries, with the symbolic protest of shaking the dust from their feet, made the best of their way to Iconium, filled, as they fled, "with joy and with the Holy Ghost."

It is not enough to say that they were joyful although they were persecuted; for they were joyful because they were persecuted. Suffering made them glad, because it was a distinct fulfilment of their Master's word. He warned them that these troubles would overtake them for his name's sake. Now that they have experience of cruel treatment at Antioch, they are convinced of two things,—that the Lord saw the end from the beginning, and that they are on the right way. The way was rough indeed, but its roughness was a mark by which they knew it to be right. It was a uniform experience, that wherever their word told, enemies rose up against them. Wherever they met with great success, there they met with great opposition. As soon as the door of opportunity opened, a crowd of adversaries rushed in. This was according to law. Where the heaviest blow is dealt against his kingdom, there the god of this world gathers all his forces for defence. When the ant's hill is stirred, the busy little angry creatures rush out in crowds to the rescue.

In this passage we read of two distinct and opposite fillings. The Jews were filled with envy; the apostles with joy. These were tormented before the time by an evil spirit indwelling; those enjoyed a foretaste of heaven's happiness in the Holy Spirit as a spirit of joy possessing their hearts.

Iconium, the place in which the missionaries next sought refuge and employment, was the nearest town to the east, and lying within the limits of another province. Though they had been persecuted at Antioch for preaching Christ there, the first thing they did when they reached Iconium was to preach Christ. The fire burned in their breasts, and they could not restrain it: Woe is unto me if I preach not the gospel!

They entered the synagogue as before, and preached to the congregation at the close of the usual service. A rumor regarding the extraordinary power of their preaching had preceded them, and accordingly a great miscellaneous crowd of Jews and Greeks were assembled to hear. Again the immediate result was the conversion of many, both Jews and Greeks. The high and broad partition that divided these classes was giving way. That mountain had begun to flow down at the presence of the Lord.

Once I was Stoned
(Acts 14:1-21)

" And it came to pass in Iconium, that they went both together into the synagogue of the Jews, and so spake, that a great multitude both of the Jews and also of the Greeks believed. But the unbelieving Jews stirred up the Gentiles, and made their minds evil affected against the brethren. Long time therefore abode they speaking boldly in the Lord which gave testimony unto the word of his grace, and granted signs and wonders to be done by their hands. But the multitude of the city was divided: and part held with the Jews, and part with the apostles. And when there was an assault made both of the Gentiles, and also of the Jews with their rulers, to use them despitefully, and to stone them, they were ware of it, and fled unto Lystra and Derbe, cities of Lycaonia, and unto the region that lieth round about: and there they preached the gospel," etc.

An intimation occurs here, worthy of careful regard by all who undertake any work for Christ's kingdom,— "They so spake that a great multitude believed." We are often warned that the power of the gospel does not depend on excellency of speech, or man's wisdom —that the harvest is due to the vitality of the seed on the one hand, and the sun and rain of heaven on the

other, not to the sower's skill. All this is true; and
yet it remains that, by Divine appointment, the instrument has a place, and the result is to some extent
affected by the manner in which the ministry is conducted.

It is expressly announced that the manner in which
the word was preached had something to do with the
numbers who believed in Iconium. All preaching
that is equally orthodox and faithful is not equally
successful. The preacher should publish the gospel
in "acceptable words;" and acceptable words should
be "sought out" by careful study, if they do not readily
leap to the lips. There must be labor, and skill, and
perseverance; there must be the exhibition of human
tenderness, as well as the possession of secret faith.
We should ply the work of winning as if all depended on
our own exertions; and yet cry to the Lord for power,
as if we could do nothing. When it is intimated that
the apostles so preached that a great multitude believed, great honor is put on the ministry, and great
responsibility on the minister. In particular, it does
not become any minister of Christ to fling out the challenge hard and dry to his audience,—Accept this message or reject it; if you reject it you perish, and your
blood will be upon your own heads. It may be necessary to give that challenge, but he should give it
"weeping:" if the expression of it do not rend the
speaker's heart, it is not likely to melt the hearts of
the hearers.

The native heathen did not take the initiative in persecuting the apostles; they remained passive, until they
were instigated to action by the more positive enmity
of the Jews. Instead of being intimidated by the combined opposition of Greeks and Hebrews, the preachers
of the gospel remained longer and spoke more boldly because the enmity was redoubled. They spoke boldly
" in the Lord," and so they were enabled to speak boldly
for the Lord. Their courage sprang from their faith.

There was a division among the people, and a commotion in the city. There was peace in the neighborhood before Paul and Barnabas arrived. It is probable
that some accused these preachers as the cause of the
strife. They would then remember the words of the

Lord Jesus, how he said, "I came not to send peace on the earth, but a sword." When the community is dead in sin, to throw the word of life into the stagnant mass necessarily disturbs it. Although the Redeemer is Prince of Peace, he is not satisfied with the serenity of a dead sea. He casts in a solvent whose nature it is in the first instance to arouse and separate. The peace which he values is the purity which is reached through conflict. People must take sides when the cross of Christ is preached in time, as they must take sides when the throne of Christ is set in eternity.

When the persecution reached such a height that it threatened their lives, the missionaries retired from the city, according to the law of the Lord for that case laid down—"When they persecute you in one city, flee ye into another." They took refuge in Lystra and Derbe, cities of Lycaonia, whose site is not now accurately known. "There they preached the gospel." This was the work of their life; this was their ruling passion; it was a passion, and it ruled them. They cared indeed for life, and fled when death threatened them; but they valued life, and sought to preserve it, mainly for the work that life enabled them to perform. They preserved life in order that they might preach; but they would not cease to preach in order that they might continue to live.

A cripple was healed at Lystra, and the act became the occasion of an incident characteristic of the prevailing idolatry. The imagination of the polytheistic Greeks immediately invested the missionaries with Divine attributes, and acknowledged them as human impersonations of two of their deities—Jupiter, the chief; and Mercury, his attendant minister. It is worthy of notice, in passing, that the primitive idea of making the tallest king still prevailed in that region. Barnabas, as the more commanding presence, was made to represent Jupiter; while Paul, whose spiritual supremacy they were unable to understand, was placed in the position of a subordinate.

Promptly following up their wild belief with an equally wild practice, they forthwith led garlanded oxen to the place of sacrifice at the gate, and were about to slay them as propitiatory offerings to the supposed celestial visitants, when the apostles, shocked by the blind and guilty superstition of the people, ran in among them and summarily suppressed the horrid design. The address which the missionaries delivered to the idolaters of Lystra on that occasion was in substance and form the same with Paul's more elaborate argument afterwards delivered on the Areopagus at Athens. It will be more convenient to notice the sentiments as expressed at a greater crisis and on a more prominent sphere.

Before they left Lystra, another event occurred which exhibits heathenism on its other and opposite side. Jewish emissaries from Antioch and Iconium, following the track of the missionaries like blood-hounds, so successfully incited the mob that "they stoned Paul, and drew him out of the city, supposing he had been dead." It is enough for the servant that he be as his Lord: "Hosanna!" to-day; and "Crucify him!" to-morrow. As the Jews treated Jesus, the Gentiles at Lystra treated Paul: they worshipped him in the morning as a god, and at night stoned him as unfit to take his place among men.

"Once was I stoned," wrote the apostle of the Gentiles, referring to this event. Yes, Paul; and once another thing happened, equally memorable. Once he stoned another, and once he was stoned himself. Strange revolution of the wheel! Now it is his turn to enact the martyr, praying for his murderers, and looking forward to rest. What a crowd of memories must have rushed up when he felt his spirit swooning away under the stone shower! This would seem the echo of his own dread act. Stephen's heroic death must have left its mark deep on the heart of the converted Paul. Perhaps, when he felt what he believed to be the sleep of death creeping over his senses, he expected that at his next awakening he would find himself in Stephen's company.

In all probability a young man, of whom we shall afterwards hear, stood among the mourners who assembled round Paul's lifeless body at Lystra. The young man Saul looked on approving at Jerusalem when the Christian hero Stephen died: a young man, Timothy, I believe, looked on weeping when Paul was

Stoned at Lystra; and afterwards, with unspeakable joy, saw the apostle awaking from his swoon. When Paul, after an interval of two years, visited Lystra again, he found Timothy residing there, a disciple of Christ, already well known and highly esteemed by all the brotherhood (Acts xvi. 1). At a later date he writes to him as his "own son in the faith" (1 Tim. i. 2). From these two facts, it results that Timothy was converted by the word of Paul on the occasion of his first visit to Lystra. Here then, as in many other cases, the work prospered while the workman was discouraged and persecuted. The missionary, when he left that place, thought that he had visited it in vain; yet the seed that fell from his hand there found soft soil in one young ingenuous heart, and brought forth fruit an hundred-fold. We know (2 Tim. iii. 10, 11) that Timothy was intimately acquainted with the peculiar sufferings through which Paul passed on this occasion at Lystra ; and we know also that from his childhood he had been trained in the Scriptures by the pious care of his mother and grandmother. From these circumstances we are enabled, in a good measure, to complete the history of the young man's spiritual experience. With the Scriptures, in their evangelical meaning, impressed on his mind and memory, he heard Paul preach. While the word which presented the Christ as the fulfilling of the law was still sounding in his ears, he beheld the great preacher stoned, as he thought, to death for his testimony. The word preached and the sufferings endured, conspired to complete the victory, and the youthful Timothy was won. It was not till a subsequent visit that the apostle was cheered by the knowledge of this event; but the event sprang direct from the seed that has continued prolific down to our own day—the blood of the martyrs.

From Lystra the missionaries retired still eastward through the interior of Asia Minor. At Derbe, the extreme limit of their progress in that direction, they preached the gospel with great success, for they made many disciples there. The term literally means a sufficient number—that is, a group of believers was gathered there in numbers sufficient to constitute a Church whose members might hold together and hold their own in the place after the departure of the apostles. These planters were afraid to plant one or two trees on the sea-shore, exposed to the blast; they greatly preferred, wherever it was possible, to plant a wood on the spot ere they left it, and then they expected that the wood would shelter the trees;—the community of disciples would support and cheer each other through evil days.

At Derbe they were close to a pass in the mountains, called " the Gates of Cilicia," which led, by a short and direct route eastward, to Tarsus, the home of Paul. "If he had been mindful of that country from whence he came out, he might have had opportunity to have returned" (Heb. xi. 15). But his native place had no charm that could draw him aside from his mission. He had severely condemned Mark for going home before the work was done; and he will not himself fall into the same snare. He obtained grace to turn his back upon home when the work of the Lord beckoned him abroad. He turned his face westward again, and retraced his steps to that Lystra which was to him the place of blood. Luther, when his friends advised him to consult his own safety, declared he would enter Worms although every tile of its roofs were a devil! Paul will go straight back to Lystra, where he had been stoned for preaching Christ, that he may preach Christ there again. By such men God has done great things at various periods of the past; and when he has similar work in hand, he will, I suppose, raise up similar instruments.

Through Much Tribulation
(Acts·14:22)

" Confirming the souls of the disciples, and exhorting them to continue in the faith, and that we must through much tribulation enter into the kingdom of God."

THIS noble pair of brothers turned on their own steps and travelled westward, revisiting in reverse order all the places where they had preached and founded societies of disciples. Their specific task this time was different. They set themselves on this occasion to confirm the souls of the converts, and exhort them as to their subsequent course. The Christians in those places were already born, but they needed to be nourished into strength. These are the two main points in a missionary's work. On their former visit, they occupied themselves mainly with the first; and on the latter, mainly with the second. The first necessity is, to see that they are in Christ; and the next, to see that they grow strong in the Lord.

They valued the right and orderly constitution of the Churches, and this matter accordingly was not neglected; but they gave their first attention to the work of confirming souls. What boots a well-organized Church, if it consists of dead members? The living may live without organization, but organization is nothing without life. Let us remember the apostolic order of these two things: it is first, get souls confirmed; and then, get the community constituted under a sound and scriptural government.

Corresponding with their specific object, the burden of the missionaries' preaching this time is not "Repent, and believe the gospel," but, "Continue in the faith." And for the rest, the warning word rings clearly out, "We must through much tribulation enter into the kingdom of God." Nothing strange will happen to these Asiatic believers: the preachers include themselves in this description of the Christian life. It is a law of the kingdom that they announce here. The forewarned are forearmed. Remembering this word they will not faint when persecution for Christ's sake comes.

Much tribulation! Yes; but they will pass *through* *it*. What a word is this! Thanks be to God for this blessed transitive preposition! No part of speech so sweet as this in all the lessons of the grammarian! There is trouble, but the disciples of Christ get through it Trouble changes its nature when you are assured that it cannot last long. Can you measure the difference between abiding in tribulation and going through it? No; it passeth all understanding. You never read of the unsaved passing *through* their suffering, or of the saved in Christ passing *through* their joy. In the one case, it is a passing through joy (the pleasures of sin) into tribulation; in the other, a passing through tribulation into the joy of the Lord.

The life of a disciple on earth is like a voyage on the sea. The sea is rough; the heart is sick; the land is not in sight. Helpless and miserable, the voyager lays himself down at night. He looks and feels as if he cared for nothing, and hoped for nothing. But underneath all this sadness a living hope is burning which these stormy waters cannot quench. He has confidence in the ship and the crew; he expects soon to reach the shore. And when he reaches it his sorrow is over, and even the memory of it almost blotted out. Suddenly, from the open sea, the ship has passed through the portals of the haven, and there is a great calm. He has passed through the tribulation.

Those who have watched the death-bed of Christians have seen such a storm suddenly settling into a calm. It is a great relief to weeping witnesses when the tossing ceases, and the peace begins.

It is not only that in point of fact tribulation happens to lie between Christians and their rest: it has been placed there of deliberate design by a wise and loving Father, in order that, by passing through it, they may be prepared for a rest beyond.

In some of the most delicate manufactures of this country, the web, in a rude and unsightly state, enters a vessel filled with a certain liquid, passes slowly through and emerges continuously at the opposite side. As it enters, the cloth seems all of one color, and that one dim and unattractive; as it emerges, it glitters, in a variety of brilliant hues arranged in cunning figures, like a robe of needle-work for the adornment of a queen. The liquid through which the fabric passes is composed of certain fiery, biting acids; and the reason why it is strained through such a bath is, that in the passage all the deforming and defiling things that have adhered to its surface in preceding processes may be discharged, and the figures, already secretly imprinted, may shine out in their beauty.

Thus the disciples of Christ are in this life drawn

through great tribulation, although the Lord who loves them has all power in heaven and in earth; nay, precisely because the Lord who loves them has all power in heaven and in earth, they are bathed in this sea of sorrows. It is not that this sea lies in their way, and that by a kind of geographical necessity they must go through it; rather, the Lord that bought them has provided that sea, and placed it across their path, that in its bitter waters the manifold incrustations that defile their beauty may be discharged ere they appear before the great white throne.   Already, and by the ministry of the Spirit, the various features of their Redeemer's likeness have been secretly imprinted on their hearts; but these features have been so overlaid by manifold corruptions in actual life, that the new nature can scarcely be recognized.   Hence the necessity of providing a searching medium, and making even those who are "his workmanship" pass through it for their own good.

Much tribulation: He is wise and loving who determines in each case its amount and its duration.   He does not spare the patient so as to spoil the work by leaving it half-done.   A child is ailing; and some slight but rather painful operation is required.   The mother will herself perform it.   But after she has begun, the child cries pitifully: the mother's courage fails.   She desists, lays down the instrument, takes the child in her arms, and wipes away the falling tears.   The child's crying ceases under this process, but the child's ailment is not cured.   The case must be put into the surgeon's hands.   He has both skill to know what is needed and courage to carry it through.   He will not spare for the patient's crying.   This treatment is better in the long-run for the child.

I have been informed, as I looked curiously on the web in perpetual motion passing through, that if it were allowed to remain one minute too long in the bath, the fabric itself would be destroyed.   The manufacturer, skilful and careful, has so tempered the ingredients on the one hand, and timed the passage on the other, that while the impurities are thoroughly discharged, the fabric comes out uninjured.   In wisdom and love, both infinite, the Lord has mingled the ingredients, and determined the duration of the baptism; so that, on the one hand, none of his should be lost, and, on the other, every grace of the Spirit should be brought out in its beauty upon all his own.

Thus, there is a "need be" for the great tribulation; but we shall miss more than half the meaning of the word here if we think of this necessity as applicable only to the suffering. Another thing is necessary—a better and a brighter. True, it is said of all Christ's people, that they *must* pass through much tribulation; but it is also said of them, that they *must* enter the kingdom. As certainly as he came out to seek, those whom he finds shall go in. He shall see of the travail of his soul, and shall be satisfied. The Captain of our salvation will bring many sons into glory. The "must" is spoken of the abundant entrance as well as of the narrow road. Fear not, little flock; it is your Father's good pleasure to give you the kingdom.

The Missionaries Return to Antioch
(Acts 14:23-28)

"And when they had ordained them elders in every church, and had prayed with fasting, they commended them to the Lord, on whom they believed," etc.

WHILE the apostles devoted themselves mainly to the preaching of the gospel, they did not neglect the organization of the Church. The young disciples were not left long without institutions and order. For edification and discipline and defence, each community was constituted a corporation; and in each corporation elders were ordained. It was on the second visit of the missionaries that this was done. An interval was permitted to elapse, that the fittest men might emerge; and already the rule, "Lay hands suddenly on no man," was practiced before it was prescribed.

The term translated "ordained," etymologically signifies election by a show of hands; and although, in later times, the word was employed to express the act of a bishop without election by the congregation, the original root remains as a fossil evidence of the liberty that prevailed in the primitive Church. This and many other privileges which were enjoyed in apostolic times were gradually undermined by the encroachments of ecclesiastical power in a later age.

The founders of these infant communities could not remain with the inexperienced converts. They were obliged to leave the Christians among unbelieving Gentiles and Jews, as sheep in the midst of wolves; and yet they were not overwhelmed with fear for the safety of the Churches. Faith was then young and fresh, and full of life. They commended their charge "to the Lord, on whom they believed," and proceeded on their journey. They had no' arm of flesh whereon to lean, and they seem never to have thought such a support needful.

Having traversed the province of Pisidia, they came to Perga, the place at which they had first landed when they crossed from Cyprus to the continent. For some reason not expressed, they had merely passed through that place on their first visit; and now, when they returned to it the second time, they paused and preached. This town was in communication with the sea by means of a river; but though the missionaries desired now to return by sea to Antioch in Syria, they did not sail direct from Perga—probably because the larger ships did not frequent that port. Another harbor further westward, called Attaleia, better suited their purpose. A greater traffic congregated there, and there accordingly they might more readily obtain a passage to Syria.

From this port a great army of Crusaders sailed for Antioch in the middle ages—a wretched, unfortunate rabble, who perished by thousands on the way. Alas! the gospel which Paul and Barnabas brought to these shores was greatly corrupted in the course of a thousand years. How unlike the clear, certain sound of the first preachers, was the echo which returned from West to East in the crusading times! These two men, not fighting, but suffering, came from east to west, with no weapon but the Word, mighty through God to subdue the nations; but when the West, in an evil day, proposed to make a return missionary visit to the East, they bore carnal weapons, and wasted the territories of friend and foe. They took the sword, and they perished by it. A fleet with an army sailed from the port of Attaleia.

After the lapse of another six centuries, the Western nations have again turned their faces to the East, and preached a new crusade. From America and Europe they stream eastward—soldiers of the Cross, to re-conquer Palestine from the disciples of Mohammed, and to win India and China for Christ; but they have returned to the means and methods of apostolic times. We send a few earnest believing men and women, armed with the sword of the Spirit; and they are waging a successful war against the superstitions and idolatries of Asia.

From Attaleia by sea Paul and Barnabas returned to Antioch in Syria, whence they had been sent out on their first missionary tour. That great city of the world became for a time the centre of effort for propagating the faith of Christ. From it the missionaries departed, and to it they returned when the work was done. Immediately the Christians of the city assembled to hear the report of their agents. It must have been a glad and exhilarating scene. Every eye would glisten, and every countenance beam with joy, as these pioneers of the gospel rehearsed in the assembly the great things that the Lord had done.

" To him that hath shall be given, and he shall have more abundantly." This promise was fulfilled in the experience of the Church at Antioch. They possessed grace which induced and enabled them to give to others and their gift to others came back in redoubled blessings to themselves. From them the mission went forth, and to them the missionaries returned, charged with the blessing of a world that was ready to perish. Like swallows returning to their nests, the apostles came back to Antioch. The successful laborers longed for kindred spirits, who might sympathize with them in their sorrows and their joys; but who could rejoice with them over the work accomplished, so well as those who had commissioned and sent them out for the work ? The success of its own mission was the means of quickening the Church.

The element of novelty in the report which Paul and Barnabas brought home was, that God had opened the door of faith to the Gentiles. Hitherto, although converts from beyond the pale of the Jewish nationality had been freely admitted, they had been accepted as individuals, on profession of their faith, into communion with believing Jews. But now, in Gentile cities, churches were constituted mainly of Gentile converts. The door was open, and the gospel, overleaping the boundaries of Israel, had obtained access to the world.

The Church at Antioch while Paul and Barnabas resided there, after their return from the Greek cities of Asia, seems to be no longer a lodge in the wilderness, but one of the golden streets of the New Jerusalem. There was so much of faith, and love, and joy, and that of so long continuance, that they might well begin to think they had already passed *through* the great tribulation—that the kingdom in its glory would soon appear. But a dark cloud suddenly overshadowed the bright landscape. "Certain men came down from Judæa, and taught the brethren," etc. Alas! the ailment under which we suffer to-day, afflicted the Church in that early age. Certain men with narrow superstitious notions attempted to thrust their own crotchets down the throats of their brethren. How much has the kingdom been obstructed in the world by men within the Church attempting to impose unnecessary beliefs or practices upon the consciences of their brethren? This baleful spirit manifested itself at an early date, and it has not yet been cast out. These men, acting like all other creatures after their kind, did not go to the heathen to proclaim the gospel where it was unknown; they came to those who were already Christians, and zealously proselytized in favor of their own sectarian watchword. They settled among the disciples at Antioch, and taught in a very positive form, that unless the Gentiles conformed to the Mosaic ritual, their trust in Christ could not save them. The apostles perceived at once that this question was vital. Here they must take their stand. The entrance of this leaven, they saw, would corrupt the whole body. It would introduce another gospel.

It was one thing for converted Jews to continue for some time the practice of the Mosaic ritual, with which they had been familiar from their childhood; and it was all another thing to impose that ritual on the Gentiles as if it were necessary to salvation. The question was keenly discussed for some time at Antioch, between Paul and Barnabas on the one side, and the Judaizing teachers from Jerusalem on the other; but as there was no authority competent to decide between the parties, no progress was made. In these circumstances, the whole Church resolved to lay the matter before the apostles and elders at Jerusalem. Accordingly it was arranged, with common consent, that a deputation, including Paul and Barnabas, should proceed to the Mother Church of Judæa, to state their case and maintain their interests.

In adopting this resolution they were wisely led. A right and authoritative decision on this subject was necessary, not only for the immediate peace, but also for the future prosperity, and even the ultimate existence, of the Church. To have admitted, as authoritatively binding the consciences of believers, that something additional to faith in Christ crucified was necessary to justification, would have essentially changed the nature of the gospel. It would have been to draw the pen through the glorious word, "It is finished," and to throw despairing sinners back on their own resources, as if no Redeemer had undertaken and accomplished the work. We owe much to the watchful faithfulness of these primitive missionaries in asserting for themselves and transmitting to us "the simplicity that is in Christ."

The Council at Jerusalem
(Acts 15)

" And certain men which came down from Judæa taught the brethren, and sa'd, Except ye be circumcised after the manner of Moses, ye cannot be saved," etc.

WHEN the deputies arrived at Jerusalem, the interest in the missionaries and their accomplished work among the heathen was so great, that the dispute on a point of doctrine was in the first instance thrown into the shade. Even on their way through Phenicia and Samaria every town claimed a meeting, and every church rejoiced in the glad news. In the capital, too, the desire to hear of the Lord's work predominated over all other claims; and nothing was done towards the adjudication of the appealed case, until first the disciples were all satisfied with the details of the mission in Cyprus, and throughout the cities of the Lesser Asia. When this great appetite was satisfied, then the apostles and elders made preparation for an assembly to sit in judgment on the question, whether the Mosaic rites should be imposed upon the Greek converts. The Christian Pharisees lost no time in bringing the question up, and pressing for a decision in their own favor. Whether these were the same men now returned from Antioch, or others resident in Jerusalem, who entertained the same opinions, is not made clear. " The apostles and elders came together to consider of this matter." The assembly was called to order, the case was introduced, and the debate began.

After a good deal of preliminary discussion, Peter took occasion to narrate his own experience, and to express his views. He had, at an early date, been Divinely called to carry the gospel to Gentile families residing within the territory of Judæa; and reasoning by analogy, he held strongly the view, that Paul and Barnabas were justified in admitting the Greeks on a foreign soil directly and simply into the privileges of the Church, without enjoining the observance of the law of Moses. The next step was to hear a narrative of the facts from the lips of the two missionaries. A great impression seems to have been made by the intelligence from foreign parts. "All the multitude kept silence, and gave audience to Paul and Barnabas." It is clear that besides the apostles and elders, a very great number of Christians were present when this report was submitted.

Immediately after the address of the missionaries, and while the assembly were under the solemn and tender impressions of the scene, James, the Lord's brother, who seems to have acted as a kind of president, summed up the evidence, and proposed the decision of the court. The proposal submitted by James was unanimously adopted. It unequivocally condemned the demand made by the Pharisaic Christians upon the Gentile converts. It maintained for the Church an absolute freedom from the bondage of the ceremonial law. It enjoined abstinence from certain pollutions which were common among idolaters, but prescribed no ritual as necessary to salvation. This is the charter of the Church's liberty to the present day. No man or body of men has a right to prescribe for Christians, as of authority, any observance or any form. The conscience is not subject to human law.

It is well worthy of observation in our own day, that when a schism was threatened between two portions of the Christian Church, the difficulty was overcome, and the breach prevented, by refusing to adopt a new and additional term of communion. The introduction of new dogmas as essential to salvation, necessarily rends the body of Christ. Christians must hold and profess all that their Saviour gave them, even at the risk of division; but woe to those who on any pretext disturb the brotherhood by imposing any yoke which the Master did not impose !

The Council at Jerusalem deputed Judas and Silas, two of their own number, to accompany Paul and Barnabas on their return to Antioch. These two confirmed the testimony of the missionaries, and certified the authenticity of the letter which they bore. The Christians at Antioch greatly rejoiced in the consolidation of their liberty, and the suppression of the threatened schism.

Silas, one of the deputies from Jerusalem, having become interested in the foreign work, remained at Antioch with the missionaries when his colleague returned. The work of evangelization was now prosecuted with renewed zeal in the great Syrian capital. The foundation of the Church in that city must be laid deep and broad, that it may serve as a basis for carrying the mission into Europe. But the spirit of Paul could not long submit to the conditions of a settled ministry. He longed for labor on the foreign field. His restlessness was of the Lord for the good of the world. It would have been an unspeakable loss to the Western nations if this man had grown indolent, and settled down in comfortable and honorable employment at home.

Accordingly, after a period of united effort in Antioch, Paul proposed to Barnabas that they should revisit the Churches which they had planted in Western Asia. Barnabas acquiesced heartily in the main features of his brother's plan; but a hitch occurred in the choice of a junior assistant. Barnabas preferred Mark, his own nephew; and Paul refused to concur in the choice, on the ground that Mark had prematurely deserted the mission in its time of need before. This weakness, against which the good Barnabas was not proof, has wrought much mischief both in Church and State. It has obtained a name,—nepotism,—from the very relation in which Mark stood to the senior missionary. So greatly has it interfered with every good work in the world, that those men have always been held in special honor who have been able to resist it, and have appointed the fittest men to important trusts, without respect to family connections.

But when a decisive difference of judgment occurred, although the altercation was sharp at the moment, these two men ultimately adopted a wise resolution, and permanent good sprang from incidental evil. Two well-appointed missions sprang from one, and the benefit was doubled. So the Lord over all makes the wrath of even his own servants to praise him, and the remainder of that wrath he restrains. How tender and long-suffering is our Father in heaven! Instead of punishing us for our quarrels, he often turns them to the furtherance of his own cause. He served himself of the weakness, as well as of the strength, of these two primitive missionaries.

Barnabas, with Mark as his companion, went by sea to Cyprus; Paul, with Silas as coadjutor, travelled overland westward through Syria and Cilicia, confirming the Churches.

Thus each of the two senior missionaries on that occasion visited the home of his youth; for Tarsus, the place of Paul's nativity, was the chief city of Cilicia.

Nothing is said of Paul's reception as a prophet in his own country. It is evident that he did not linger long about Tarsus. Probably he found too much curiosity among the people there regarding himself personally. He disliked and resented everything that turned the people's attention from the Christ whom he preached. He pressed accordingly westward through the province, and tarried nowhere long till he reached Derbe and Lystra, the scenes of his success and his sufferings on his former tour.

At Lystra on this occasion occurred his first interview with Timothy. This young man was already a Christian of high reputation in the neighborhood, and we know that the early religious training of the youth had been quickened into positive spiritual life by Paul's word spoken during the former journey. This must have been a glad and tender meeting. When Eunice, Timothy's mother, introduced her son to Paul, and informed him of the youth's conversion, the spirit of the laborious missionary must have been greatly refreshed. Here was evidence that his labor and his sufferings had not been in vain. At sight of Timothy, Paul would thank God and take courage. The history is fresh and full of consolation still. It contains encouragement to every sower of the good seed, down to the end of the world. Many seeds which go out of the sower's sight, take root and bear fruit unto eternal life.

The Gospel Introduced into Europe
(Acts 16:8-13)

"And they passing by Mysia came down to Troas. And a vision appeared to Paul in the night; There stood a man of Macedonia, and prayed him, saying, Come over into Macedonia, and help us," etc.

HERE the history of the Church reaches a great crisis. The missionaries of the Cross pass the narrow sea that separates Asia from Europe, and the gospel is introduced among the nations of the growing West. In the person of "the man of Macedonia," Greece and Rome invite the apostles of the Cross. Weary and empty, the warriors, artists, and philosophers of the Empire thirst for the living water. Europe on the west, as Ethiopia on the south, humbly stretches out her hands to God.

At Lystra the apostle of the Gentiles had been gladdened by the accession of Timothy to the missionary band. At that place he had suffered more than elsewhere; but there, as elsewhere, the blood of the martyrs had become the seed of the Church. From the seed of his own suffering and testimony at that place a goodly fruit had secretly sprung. By the time of his second visit the fruit was ripe, and he who sowed was permitted also to reap. In the former visit he had gone forth weeping, bearing precious seed: now when he leaves Lystra, moving westward to new fields, he bears his sheaves rejoicing. Faithful is he that promised: the missionary is sustained in his work. "His heart is lifted up in the ways of the Lord." Let all men know that the sad things which happened to the preacher at Lystra have turned out for the furtherance of the gospel.

Paul invited his son Timothy to join the mission, and Timothy consented. Having in his bag a supply of parchments containing the decrees of the council which refused to bind circumcision on the conscience of the Gentile converts, Paul was at liberty to yield to the feelings of the Jews from motives of expediency; and so he circumcised Timothy at the outset. He had contended earnestly and successfully for the liberty of Christians; but he was not the man to put all his rights in force, without regard to circumstances. He delighted to concede in tenderness to brethren that which he would not surrender to the legalists who demanded it as of right. He refused to circumcise the Greek Titus at the demand of Jewish Christians, because they demanded it on the ground that it was necessary to salvation; but Timothy, by the mother's side and by education a Jew, he readily circumcised, in order to smooth his way into the synagogues, and enlarge his opportunities of preaching Christ.

Providentially prevented from prolonging their stay and penetrating to the northern provinces of Lesser Asia, they soon arrived at Troas, the extreme western point of the continent. There Paul's spirit was stirred within him as he saw the isles of Greece in the foreground, and the continent of Europe in the distance. He longed to preach Jesus and the resurrection in Athens, the eye of Greece and the centre of European civilization.

At Troas a fourth missionary joined the group— Luke, the beloved physician. From this point the narrative proceeds in the first person plural, because from this point the historian was personally a witness of the events which he records.

By two stages they made the passage across the straits. The first day's sailing brought them to the island of Samothracia, and next day they landed on the European shore at Neapolis. Thence they journeyed inland to Philippi, the nearest city of importance. Here they opened their commission and began. The Church of Philippi is thus the metropolitan Church of Europe. The seed of the kingdom imported from the East, first fructified there, and thence spread through the neighboring regions.

Philippi was a colony. This was doubtless one of the reasons why the missionaries selected it as their first station. It brought them into contact with the peculiar institutions of the Roman Empire. Located in the provinces, it was colonized by native Italians, and enjoyed the privileges of an Italian city. Chiefly inhabited by discharged soldiers, it was a stronghold of defence on the frontiers. In that city the missionaries abode some days, apparently without meeting an opportunity of prosecuting their work. At this rate Paul will not linger long in the place. Life is short; and he must be about his Master's business. But when the Sabbath arrived an opportunity occurred. The few Jews who resided at Philippi seem not to have possessed a synagogue; but a station had been provided in a sequestered spot by the side of the river where the worshippers of God, whether native Jews or proselytes, were wont to meet for prayer.

Some women resorted to the spot: on this Sabbath, women only were there. The Roman veteran, lording it on the soil of Macedonia, would sneer at the humble group as he saw them passing to the conventicle; perhaps a philosophic Greek, himself oppressed by the military conquerors, uttered a sarcasm at the expense of the women-worshippers. No matter: those who win have the right to laugh. These women were on the winning side, and a windfall of great gain will meet them to-day at the trysting-place.

Among the worshippers was Lydia, a Gentile proselyte from Thyatira in Asia, settled in Philippi as an agent for the sale of purple, the staple manufacture of her native place. There is abundant evidence from other sources, that Thyatira was celebrated as a seat of this manufacture. Inscriptions have been recently found on the spot, which show that the guild of dyers were an important corporation in the city. Perhaps Lydia's husband had emigrated on this business, and died at Philippi; and the trade being prosperous, the widow had braced herself to the effort of conducting it, until her boys should come of age.

The ancient "Turkey-red" dyers of Thyatira sent their goods westward for sale in the Roman colonies of Greece and Macedonia, as our manufacturers send theirs to India and China. Each great factory in Asia must have accredited agents in the several marts of Europe. Probably the ship that bore the missionaries across the strait a week before, had carried some bales of purple cloth for the Roman residents of Philippi; and the heavy goods might at that time have been slowly winding up the ascent from the shore to the city. Commerce and Christianity in those days, as now, gravitated to the same centres, and flowed in the same channels.

This honorable woman prosecuted a lawful industry. She went into a far country to earn bread for herself and her children; and in that far country she found the life of her soul. Labor is honorable and healthful. Merchandise is specially honorable when it is conducted with truth and righteousness. Merchants are channels through which the precious products of the earth flow and reflow, to the places where they are needed, to minister to the necessities and the comforts of men. Blessed are those buyers and sellers who, like Lydia, find in the intervals of ordinary business the pearl of great price. When they have obtained the true riches their souls will not again cleave to the dust. When they have obtained the peace of God in Christ to keep their hearts and minds, they will not be too much oppressed by care, and not too much distracted by fluctuations in the market.

Lydia

(Acts 16:14,15)

" And a certain woman named Lydia, a seller of purple, of the city of Thyatira, which worshipped God, heard us: whose heart the Lord opened, that she attended unto the things which were spoken of Paul. And when she was baptized, and her household, she besought us, saying, If ye have judged me to be faithful to the Lord, come into my house, and abide there. And she constrained us."

ALTHOUGH Lydia attended to her business, she did not allow it to occupy her whole heart, and absorb all her time. She took advantage of the Sabbath to rest awhile from labor; and her time of rest she filled with the worship of God, and the society of the good. He who lays out one talent well, will get it redoubled soon. A shed for shelter in a sequestered spot, and a few Jewish women for fellow-worshippers, and probably a parchment containing some of the Scriptures as Sabbath lessons—these constituted the extent of her privileges. She used her little well, and more was given to her.

Paul and Silas went to the place on that Sabbathday. It was a place for prayer. Perhaps there had never been any preaching in it. The women had often met, and prayed, and parted, with none to speak to them. They would read the Scriptures, and, like the Ethiopian prince, would bend, and sigh, and weep over " the Lamb led to the slaughter;" but there was no one near who could answer their question, " Of whom speaketh the prophet this ?" They could not understand, and there was none to guide them. But they persevered. At last a distinguished preacher appeared— the greatest of all preachers, led to the spot by the same Divine Spirit who conducted Philip from a city of Samaria to the desert of Gaza. At last a sermon was preached in the praying place, and it took effect.

One design of this history is to show believers in all lands and all ages, that the Redeemer is near his people still, and orders all things for their sakes. The meeting between Paul and Lydia was arranged in heaven. When the missionaries desired to prolong their stay in Asia, and to evangelize another province there, the Spirit suffered them not; for the same reason that at a former time the Spirit had not suffered Philip to remain in Samaria, but sent him into the desert. Paul was not permitted to remain in Asia, but forwarded hastily across to Europe; for a group of women convened in a shed near the town of Philippi, gave the Lord in heaven no rest until he should send them a messenger to open the way of salvation. The Hearer of prayer could not bear that cry another week without an answer; and so the missionaries must leave all other work behind, and hasten to the spot. There some inquiring souls were thirsting like dry land for the living water; and Paul was the vessel chosen to contain it and bear it to the spot.

The Lord opened Lydia's heart so that she attended to the things that were spoken by Paul. Although no report of the sermon has been preserved, we know well what its burden would be. The missionary, not knowing whether he should have another opportunity, would preach Christ crucified. He would make plain the way of pardon through the blood of the Lamb. Now it is intimated that Lydia's heart needed opening ere she could attend to the doctrines of grace. Probably the opening was a process that had been going on for a long time. From day to day her heart longed more for God; from day to day her prayer rose more eagerly to the throne. This was the opening: she was growing ready for receiving the gospel.

I think Lydia's heart was opened in some such way as the gates of a canal-lock are opened. It is by water coming in secretly below, and gradually swelling up within, that at length the folding-doors allow themselves to be opened. As long as the water presses from above and from without, the pressure tends to shut the gates more firmly, rather than to open them. The lock keeps itself empty, and resists the offer of the water to come in. But when by secret channels the interior is nearly filled, then the resistance ceases, and the gates are thrown wide. Ah, many an empty heart resists the offer of mercy from God; the offer of that mercy rather shuts the gates more firmly! But when secretly some grace finds its way in, and more follows, and the empty space gradually fills, then the enmity disappears, and the whole soul opens out to Christ.

It was by receiving some grace within her heart, that Lydia was opened to receive more. She was made willing in the day of the Lord's power.

But the Lord has other keys at hand by which he sometimes opens closed hearts. There are diversities of operations. The resistance is sometimes gently overcome by droppings silent as the dew; and sometimes the bolts that barred an unbelieving heart are broken by terrible things in righteousness. Some sorrow may have crushed this industrious widow, and so prepared her for taking in the healing balm of the gospel. Was her son disobedient, or her foreman unfaithful; or was the current of trade changing its channel, and threatening to leave her business to break in pieces like a stranded ship? By any of these operations, or by others different from all these, the Lord may have conducted the process of opening, so that when the word of the kingdom came, it found ready entrance.

It is good to wait on the Lord, both for our own refreshing and for the quickening of those whom we love. Watch and pray. We do not know when the Bridegroom may pass. Let us and ours be ever ready to follow him in to the marriage-supper. The Bridegroom passed the place of prayer that day on the outskirts of Philippi, and Lydia, with her lamp well-trimmed, was on the alert to hear his approaching footsteps, and follow him to the feast.

Even the preaching of Paul did not save unless an opened heart attended to it and took it in. In this example of primitive preaching, it is made clear that more depends on the preparation of the hearer, than on the preacher's skill. The Master, in the parable of the Sower, has clearly shown the necessity of two conspiring things—the good seed sown, and the ground broken soft to receive it. Alas! how much precious seed falls on the beaten wayside, and bears no fruit, when hearers' hearts are trodden hard and smooth by a week of cares and pleasures, and the preaching on the Sabbath takes no effect! We have in our day, through God's good hand upon us, much good seed; oh for broken ground! The preparation of the heart is from the Lord.

Lydia and her house were admitted into the Church by baptism. Glad and grateful, she offered hospitality to the strangers, and pressed them to accept it. From them, or at least through them, she had received an immeasurable spiritual good; and it is the instinct of her new nature to take pleasure in imparting temporal things to the servants of her Lord. Here, in Lydia's opened heart, rises the spring which the Master has provided to supply the temporal wants of his minister's, in all lands and all times.

The Pythoness
(Acts 16:16-24)

" And it came to pass, as we went to prayer, a certain damsel possessed with a spirit of divination met us, which brought her masters much gain by soothsaying: the same followed Paul and us, and cried, saying, These men are the servants of the most high God, which show unto us the way of salvation," etc.

HITHERTO in the experience of the missionaries persecution had always originated with the Jews. At this place, however, they were few and destitute of influence. In these parts of the empire the Jews were themselves crushed, and so they lacked the power to crush the Christians. Here the opposition sprang directly from the Gentiles.

As they went on some subsequent occasion to the place of prayer, a slave damsel, "possessed with a spirit of divination," followed them, uttering a remarkable testimony in favor of the apostles as the servants of the Most High God. This slave was owned by a company of speculators. Great gains might be made from the oracles, half mad and apparently half inspired, which she uttered. A copartnership was formed to manage the concern. They bought the slave, and farmed out her oracles to the credulous. This was the ordinary form of the heathen oracles. A priestess either permanently possessed, or artificially thrown into a raving condition at certain times, was concealed in the shrine. From her mouth ambiguous answers issued, and skilful attendants wrote them down for the superstitious inquirers. Wicked men fabricated the imposture, and the wicked spirit availed himself of the prepared deceit. The people were both deceiving and being deceived. Such was the moral condition of the community into which the gospel of Christ was making its entrance. Such was the corruption of that earth upon which the salt was about to be spread.

The raving Pythoness followed Paul and his company, crying out in an excited and passionate voice, but emitting an unexpectedly sober and far-reaching testimony in favor of the missionaries and their work. Such a witness was borne by the possessed man to Jesus when he cried out, " I know thee who thou art, the Holy One of God." These testimonies were perhaps expressions of the victims, emitted at momentary intervals of freedom contrary to the will of the possessing spirit. Perhaps the hope of the captive somehow revived at the approach in the one case of the Master, and in the other of his servant Paul. So the captives lately held in cruel bondage by the Emperor of Abyssinia remained quiet, and seemed submissive to the tyrant, while no help was near, but changed their tone and defied him when the British army appeared at Magdala. This enthralled human spirit seemed to speak out with courage when deliverance was nigh.

When this had continued many days Paul was grieved at the interruption, and had compassion on the captive. Remembering the commission given by the Lord to his ministers, he cast the evil spirit out by the name and power of Jesus Christ. The slave was restored to her right mind. No more the wild rolling eye, and no longer the fitful, incoherent ravings which the evil spirit had palmed upon the people as superhuman inspirations. But the investment of the greedy shareholders had lost its value. We paid so many thousands to her owner for this woman, and now, though we possess the legal right to her services as a slave, all that she will bring in that capacity will not reimburse us for a tithe of our outlay. Here is a predicament. The gains are gone; Paul and Silas are the cause of all the loss. A mob is gathered; a tumult is excited; an assault is made upon the strangers. The apostles are dragged into the *forum*, and accused before the magistrates as the propagators of a faith not recognized by Roman law.

To give force to their charge, the accusers are careful to intimate that the prisoners are Jews. Already the Jews had, in a violent tumult, been expelled from Rome, and the colony will imitate the metropolis. Both the populace and the magistrates will readily receive an accusation against men of that hated and persecuted nation.

Stirred up by this great outcry, and thinking they might safely perpetrate any outrage upon Jews, who were beyond the pale of the law, the magistrates—two men who exercised authority over the colony—stripped the accused, and commanded the lictors to beat them with rods. Many stripes were inflicted before the cruel appetite of the mob was satiated. It is difficult for us to estimate the severity of this punishment. The victim was beaten on the naked flesh with thick rods by trained professional executioners. The insignia of a Roman ruler consisted of a bunch of rods tied together like a sheaf, and an axe protruding from the end of the bundle. The rods symbolized secondary, and the axe capital, punishment.

After the scourging the missionaries were cast into prison. The magistrates did not prescribe the treatment in detail, but they gave a general charge that these men should be kept with special security, and left the jailer to adopt his own methods. That officer, with an eye to his own safety, shut them in an interior cell of exceptional strength, and fixed their feet in the stocks besides.

On another occasion, when he was himself in chains, Paul exulted in the remembrance that the word of God was not bound (2 Tim. ii. 9). He meant that God's word to men might have free course through the Roman world although one of its preachers was silenced. There is another sense in which *word* may go free although the speaker's body is bound in chains. Not only the word that comes from God, but also the word that goes to God, is free though the speaker be in fetters. Christ is the way, and that way lies open up to the Father's presence when the prison-doors have shut upon a suppliant. The word which an afflicted child pours into the Father's ear was not bound that night in the prison of Philippi. The stocks had no power to grasp prayer, and hinder it from ascending heavenward. Blessed be God, nothing can block the way of prayer. It is long since the record was written, "Out of the depths have I cried unto thee:" and I suppose, when the books are opened, it will be found that most of the cries that have really reached the throne were cries that ascended from the deep. It is when you look from the bottom of a well that you descry the stars in daylight; on the surface, with the glare all round, although they are there, you cannot discern them. It is thus that faith's eye cannot pierce the heavens so well from the bright surface of prosperity as from the low, low place of some great sorrow.

We may leave Paul and Silas in the dungeon for the night. The Lord that bought them will so reveal himself to his witnesses, that the darkness shall be light about them.

Songs in the Night
(Acts 16:25)

"And at midnight Paul and Silas prayed, and sang praises unto God: and the prisoners heard them."

" PRAYING, they hymned God:" for such are the words when literally rendered. Prayer and praise in the dungeon that night were not two distinct and successive acts. They sang in concert their address to God: and, doubtless, like the psalms of David, the address included both requests for mercy and ascriptions of praise. It may, indeed, have been the psalms of David that they sang—both the prisoners had the verses by heart: they had not a book, and did not need one.

God heard their prayer, we know, for he gave it a signal answer. But there were also other listeners: "the prisoners heard them." One would like to know who these prisoners were. Like the contents of other prisons, they were probably of various characters and conditions. Some may have been the callous *habitués* of the place; and some may have been men of the highest consideration, awaiting trial for political offences. But to all the inmates alike the sound of psalms at midnight would seem strange and startling. It was probably whispered through the prison in the evening that two Jews had been brought in—severely scourged —accused of teaching some new doctrine regarding

the resurrection of the dead.   Then the tender yet joyful song of two blended voices rose on the midnight
silence of the prison.   The wakeful listened, and the
slumberers awoke.   The hymn was probably in the
Greek tongue, and the more acute ears would catch
glimpses of its meaning.

That was a night much to be remembered by the
inmates of the jail.   It is altogether probable that some
who heard that strange psalm-singing were among the
Philippian Christians to whom Paul subsequently addressed his most affectionate letter from another prison
in Rome.

"Songs in the night" are the special gift of God,
and they are well fitted to arrest attention and impress
their mark.   When there is evidence of peace with God
prevailing over the heaviest of outward troubles, it takes
effect on the conscience of an observer.   It is a great
thing to see one taken up from a miry pit, and his feet
set upon a rock and his goings established; but it is
when a new song is put into his mouth that many shall
see it and shall fear, and shall trust in the Lord (Ps.
xl.).   It is specifically joy in believing when it bursts
forth in great tribulation that takes effect on others and
wins them to the Lord.

A lamp when lighted may burn by day, but it is only
at night that it is seen by the neighborhood.   The darkness does not kindle or cause the light, but the darkness
reveals it and spreads it around.   It is thus that consistent joy in the Lord, when believers attain it in a time
of trouble, becomes an effective testimony for Christ.
Not a few owe their conversion instrumentally to the
light that streamed from a saint in the hour of his departure—to the song that rose from the pilgrim when
he was traversing the valley of the shadow of death.

Thus, though the speakers were bound that night,
the Word was free; not only the word that went upward to the throne of God, but also the echo of that
word, that pierced the gloomy partition-walls and sank
into the startled ears of weary and wretched prisoners.
It seemed a roundabout road that the Word of the gospel took to reach these motley groups of Greek and
Latin Gentiles; but the Word did not miss its way.
There was a dead-wall between the apostles and their

audience, and therefore they did not preach that night. But there was no wall between them and the Father of their spirits: praying, they hymned God in the inner prison, and the prayer sent upward fell down again on the other side of the partition, falling there on listening ears. In this circuitous method the gospel reached some needy souls.

It is thus that in modern warfare they often overcome a fortress which is too strong to be taken by direct assault. The wall frowns thick and high between the defenders and the assailants. No missile sent in a direct line can touch the protected garrison. The besiegers in such a case throw their balls high into the heavens: these fall within the inclosure, and do more execution in their fall than they could have done by direct impact on the walls. When a good soldier of Jesus Christ cannot by direct preaching of the gospel reach the ears and hearts of men to subdue and win them, he may sometimes effectively accomplish his object by prayer and praise. His arrow, going first upward, may in its descent wound some conscience and subdue some soul.

Christian families or groups, travelling in Romish or otherwise darkened districts, might in this way scatter blessings on their track. They may possibly not possess talent or find opportunity for preaching; but if, in the evening in the hotel, they should " pray and sing praises to God," some prisoners might hear and turn to the Lord.

But the same lesson admits of application on a greater scale and nearer home. Some disciples of Christ have the misfortune to dwell in an ungodly neighborhood. But alongside of the misfortune, if they are watchful, a privilege lies. If their lamp burn, the surrounding darkness will reveal and utilize its light. Satan's prisoners are within earshot of Christ's freemen. Perhaps a hard partition of prejudice shuts out the ungodly from direct instruction and reproof; but nothing can defend them from the indirect stroke which Paul and Silas dealt on their fellow-prisoners at Philippi. Let the prayer-hymn rise, soft and sweet, from the church in the house when the door is shut; and the notes sent up to heaven will drop down again into

houses where no church meets. The indirect method
is the best for reaching the rough, ungainly elements
that crowd and cluster in the centres of modern cities.
Some sprinkling of "the salt of the earth" in close
contact with the corruption, would, under God, be the
most effectual healer.

Of late years many instances have occurred of songs
being given in the night to miners imprisoned by some
catastrophe in the recesses of a coal-pit. The most
touching example I know is at once the latest and the
nearest. It occurred a few weeks since, on the waters
of the Forth estuary opposite Edinburgh. Three fishermen belonging to Newhaven went out in their boat
at night to ply their calling. A sudden squall upset
their boat. All three rose to the surface, and laid
hold of the capsized boat. Sustaining themselves thus
above water, they alternately conversed on the subject
of the preceding Sabbath's sermon, and sang hymns
which they had by heart. First one, and then another, after bidding affectionate farewell, let go through
weariness, and passed away from suffering into rest.
A pilot-boat bore down on the wreck in time to save
the strongest man, the single survivor. From his lips
came the narrative of their experience while they trod
together the valley of the shadow of death. In circumstances still more dreadful than those of Paul and
Silas at Philippi, they also obtained songs in the night.

By the use of the imperfect tense, it is clearly indicated in the history that the missionaries were hymn-
ing God, and the astonished prisoners in other cells
pricking up their ears to listen, when the crash of the
earthquake came. The psalm was cut short in the
middle of a verse and, the sense, which the listeners
strained to gather, broken off before it was completed.
The foundations of the prison were shaken, so that the
doors were thrown open, but the walls were not thrown
down. The jailer living in some wing apart, did not
hear the song, but was awakened by the earthquake.
Mark here God's mercy in its fullness and overflowing.
Those who cannot or will not hear the still small voice
of praise, will be aroused by a providential visitation.
They are not suddenly destroyed, but sharply shaken,
that they may hear and live. God is long suffering.

If he had cast us off and shut us out on our refusal of one invitation, where would most of us have been to-day? He has waited to be gracious. When we turned a deaf ear to his Word, he has made the earth shake beneath us, that we might be compelled to listen for our own life.

The Jailer
(Acts 16:26-31)

"And suddenly there was a great earthquake, so that the foundations of the prison were shaken: and immediately all the doors were opened, and every one's bands were loosed. And the keeper of the prison awaking out of his sleep, and seeing the prison doors open, he drew out his sword, and would have killed himself, supposing that the prisoners had been fled. But Paul cried with a loud voice, saying, Do thyself no harm; for we are all here," etc.

THE jailer's first thought was suicide. This was the highest point to which heathen culture could soar. It was held in high repute among the Romans. In particular, at this same town, Philippi, many illustrious examples of self-destruction had occurred. In a battle near this place, the republicans were finally defeated by the imperial army. The vanquished patriots, knowing no way of escape, died in great numbers by their own hands. It is quite possible that the proximity of these events may have raised suicide to an exceptional measure of honor in Philippi.

The keeper supposed that his prisoners must have escaped. Remembering the special charge connected with the two strangers recently committed, he believed that his life was forfeited, and determined not to await the humiliation of condemnation and punishment. Paul rushes to the rescue, eager to save life. Quickly he adopts the most direct and efficacious means. "We are all here!" he exclaimed: he has hit the nail on the head. He has removed in a moment the cause, and the intended effect falls to the ground. The safety of all the prisoners removed the jailer's fears: his hand dropped from the sword's hilt, and the horrid deed was left undone.

Relieved now, and relieved completely from his first fear, a second instantly seizes him. "He called for a light, and sprang in, and came trembling." Trembling? what makes the man tremble now, when his danger is all removed? Not a prisoner has escaped; the magistrates have not a case against him. Why is he still in terror?

This is another fear. In a moment, one great fear left him, and another, a greater, took possession of his heart. It has been suggested by some critics, that this is the first terror not yet removed,—that the displeasure of his superiors is still the cause of his apprehension,—and that his cry, "What must I do to be saved?" pointed to the punishment due to the officer who slumbered at his post. Those who take this view of the history must be under a strong doctrinal bias; for it is a view that is forced and unnatural. It is interesting, even as a critical study, to mark how manifold and complete is the evidence that his fear and his question now point to pardon and peace with God. (1.) Had the object of his fear been punishment by his superiors, he would not have fallen on his knees before Paul and Silas. They had no power to shield him. But he had now the presentiment that these men were servants of the Most High God, who could show him the way of salvation. On this supposition, his act becomes rational and consistent. (2.) The answer which they gave him shows what they understood by his question. They enjoyed the best opportunity of knowing what he meant. They saw in his terror his conviction of sin: they so understood his question, as to answer it by offering him Christ. (3.) And the man was satisfied with the answer he obtained. Assuredly, if he had feared for his head on account of the prison being open, to believe in the Lord Jesus Christ would not have protected him from the sentence of his heathen masters on the morrow.

For his first fear, the appropriate and sufficient cure was the assurance, "We are all here;" for his second, the appropriate and sufficient cure was, "Believe in the Lord Jesus Christ." These two distinct and suc-

cessive consolations show what were the two fears
which in rapid succession had occupied and oppressed
his heart. The first fear was, lest he should lose his
life for allowing the prisoners to escape; the second
fear was, lest he should be cast out of God's presence
because of his sin. Although it is not necessary that
we should be able to trace the way of the Spirit in the
rapid succession of this man's experiences, the difficulty would be much diminished if we should suppose
that the jailer was an attentive observer of events,
and was acquainted with all the circumstances that
led to the commitment of the apostles. The things
had not happened in a corner. The strange persistent
cry of the Pythoness, articulately acknowledging these
men as servants of the Most High God, and the subsequent change in her attitude and conduct, were matters
of notoriety in the city. Now, although the jailer did
not, when he received his prisoners in the evening, believe them to be the divinely inspired teachers of a
new salvation; yet, if he was aware that this character
had been ascribed to them in the raving responses of
the prophetess, the shock of the earthquake at midnight would in a moment throw a new light over the
whole scene. The startling announcement which he
had heard with incredulity, and, perhaps, with sarcas-
tic hilarity, in the sunshine of the preceding day, might
suddenly flash upon his conscience as a truth, when
the earthquake had thrown open the doors, and yet
the prisoners had not made their escape in the darkness.

These things are written for our admonition. The
word that records them is a die deeply cut, that will
receive broken hearts in succession till the end of the
world come, and mould them anew, and turn them out
new creatures in Christ. The cutting of that die at first
was a great work: it was engraven when the Son of God
was exceeding sorrowful even unto death. The drops
were eating deeply in when he cried, "If it be possible,
let this cup pass." It could not pass; it was poured
out to the dregs. That fiery out-pouring cut its way
in, and formed the matrix into which melted men might
afterwards be cast. Only one such type was ever formed.
None other than "God with us" could endure the baptism. Only one such type was made in the dying of

the Lord Jesus; but it serves for all the world, and for all time. Whosoever will, let him come. Let melted hearts flow in; and forthwith they become new.

This precious answer, "Believe in the Lord Jesus Christ, and thou shalt be saved," it is not easy to describe and define. If you were asked to explain what sunlight is, you would not know how to answer. There is nothing better known to those who see; but there is nothing more difficult to make known to those who are born blind.

Manifestly it behoved Paul on this occasion to put into his answer the whole marrow of the gospel. If it is possible to give in one mouthful the essence of all that he ever preached, he is bound to give it here and now. We are warranted in assuming that this answer contained all that is necessary to salvation, and nothing more. There is not too little: there is not too much. It is manifestly a matter of life and death; and it is at his peril if the apostle treat it otherwise. The penitent sprang in, and fell down, and cried. His cry was, "What must I do to be saved?" The missionaries are bound, as they shall answer to God, to tell the man this, and at the moment nothing else. It would have been to trifle both with the sinner and the Saviour, either to have kept back anything essential, or to have dallied with redundant prescriptions. The missionaries are equal to the crisis. They spring out as eagerly and sharply as the jailer springs in. He hungers: they give him the bread of life. He is lost: they offer him the Saviour. They give him enough; and nothing more. Believe in the Lord Jesus Christ, and thou shalt be saved.

Faith and Obedience

(Acts 16:31-40)

" And they said, Believe on the Lord Jesus Christ, and thou shalt be saved, and thy house. And they spake unto him the word of the Lord, and to all that were in his house. And he took them the same hour of the night and washed their stripes; and was baptized, he and all his, straightway. And when he had brought them into his house, he set meat before them, and rejoiced. believing in God with all his house," etc.

CAN faith save you, then, without works ? Suppose a man should "believe in the Lord Jesus Christ," and continue to exhibit a profane and impure life, will he be saved by his sound faith in spite of his wickedness ? This question does not deserve an answer. It is a foolish question: it assumes an impossibility.

Suppose one should address to an eminent physician the question, Pray, sir, tell me, is the blood necessary to life ? and he should answer, It is. Suppose the questioner then proceeds to say, But if a great artery is cut, and all the blood of the body escapes, and the man still lives and acts with undiminished vigor, do you persist in your opinion that the blood is necessary to life ? The physician will not answer. You have put a foolish question, and he treats it with contempt. Or, if he answer at all, he will say, First show me a living man with no blood in his body, and then I shall consider the causes of the phenomenon.

Such treatment he deserves who inquires, Shall I be saved if I believe in Christ, though I live in sin ? The supposition is an impossibility. To believe in Christ as that jailer believed is the death-blow to the reign of sin in your members, as the letting out of the heart's-blood puts an end to the life. People who, with a whole heart, merely talk on the subject, may suggest many objections to the doctrine; but when a man is convinced of sin by the secret power of the Spirit, and closes with Christ as his sacrifice, substitute, righteousness, and intercessor, he is at that moment and by that act placed in enmity with his own sin as fire and water are at enmity. When he is in Christ, he is a new creature.

Surely, if people would apply their minds to the subject, it should not be very difficult to comprehend that actual obedience by the man—that is, his good works—must be withdrawn from the ground of his hope, and take a place as the fruit of his faith.

Here is a water-channel that has been dry all the summer. Straws and leaves and dust have accumulated in it. To make all clean and clear again, you do not say, Let a stream of water be poured through it from the fountain-head, and let all the straws and leaves be gathered up and carried away. Let the water from the fountain-head gush into the neck of the channel, and it will sweep away the miscellaneous rubbish that encumbered the course. Thus it is in the spiritual life. It is not faith and good works together that make salvation sure. Faith, when it begins to flow, carries works in its train. Faith in Christ as your substitute, your peace with God, will make short work of the ten thousand encumbrances which blocked the channels of your heart and life. "This is the victory which overcometh the world, even your faith."

Even in the brief sketch given here of the jailer's conversion, you see beautiful bunches of fruit quickly ripening on the branch as soon as it is in the Vine. He took them the same hour of the night, and washed their stripes, and set meat before them.

The current of this man's life is reversed. He could not but see that the flesh of his prisoners was lacerated by the rods. He did not ask whether they were hungry. As the easiest way of securing his own safety, he thrust them into the inner prison, and pinioned their feet in locks of iron. He then went to bed, and slept so soundly that no psalm-singing disturbed his rest. He did not awake till the earthquake awoke him. All care in the evening was for himself; and his selfishness was cruel. Now, when the midnight scene had passed, he has no care about himself; all his attention is devoted to his prisoners. Not a thought now about the possible displeasure of the magistrates, if they should learn that he had invited these notable prisoners unguarded into his own house. In the evening he was heedless of the apostles' wounds and hunger: now he washes their wounds and gives them bread. Behold the good works that his infant faith was already bearing! These were the first duties that lay to hand. Give me the subsequeut history of that Christian, and I will show you in it other things to match them. Every creature after its kind; and the new creature is not an exception to the rule. His faith in the Lord Jesus Christ saved him; and that faith instantly reversed the volume of his life, as the rising tide of the ocean meets and flings back the river's stream.

This is a crucial case as to the power of faith in Christ to save a sinner. It is parallel with the example of the thief on the cross. The man was taken in the very act of murder. He intended to take away his own life; and according to the principles which the Lord laid down, the intention carried within it the guilt of the deed. Suppose now that Paul's cry had been one minute too late—that the uplifted arm had fallen, and that the dagger had severed a vital artery. Suppose that the wound is mortal, but that the life-blood takes an hour to ebb away. It is not conceivable that the preacher would in that case have made any change in his terms. The word would still have been, "Believe in the Lord Jesus Christ, and thou shalt be saved." Thus an offer of free pardon would have been made to the murderer while the blood of his victim was still flowing warm. The murderer might within the hour have believed, and at the end of it have entered into rest. There is glory to God in the freeness and fulness of his mercy.

"By terrible things in righteousness wilt thou answer us, O God of our salvation" (Ps. lxv. 5). The earthquake was the answer to the prayer which Paul and Silas, lying on their backs, hymned upward to God in heaven. But although the earthquake could open the doors of the prison, it could not break the bonds in which the jailer's soul was held. In that sense God was not in the earthquake. After the earthquake came a still small voice from the lips of the imprisoned missionary; and God was in the voice—God our Saviour. Before the power of that voice the heathen's heart gave way, and flowed down like water.

When a man begins to care for his own soul, he instantly cares also for those who are dear to him. Knowing this law of human nature, Paul provides, in the same breath, comfort in regard to himself and in regard to his house. On the same terms the jailer's family will be received; and accordingly the word of the gospel was spoken to him and to all that were in his house. It is good when every family is a small Church, and every Church a large family.

The magistrates of the city, having been hurried into the arrest by the daring attitude of the mob, determined next morning to desert the diet and discharge the prisoners. Accordingly, an officer was sent to the prison, with an order for their release. The jailer joyfully proceeded to execute the order of his superiors ; but Paul saw meet to stand on his rights, and declined the offer. It is now pretty generally acknowledged that Paul did not enjoy the privileges of a Roman citizen in virtue of his birth in the free city of Tarsus. Although the city was free, its freedom did not confer the dignity of Roman citizenship on all its population. It is more probable that the honor was conferred on some of the apostles' ancestors for services rendered to the State. It was the custom of Roman governors so to reward loyal services in the provinces. Alarmed at the claim of Paul, the magistrates acceded at once to his demand. They came in person to the prison, and gave the prisoners a public and honorable acquittal.

This was not a display of pride or of vengeance. The apostles did not court suffering. Rather, for their work's sake, they desired to avoid it. They saved their lives at one time by flight, and at another time by invoking the protection of imperial law against the excesses of particular magistrates. There is no fanatical rashness in their conduct. Their conduct is guided by wisdom and courage and common sense.

"My Kingdom is Not of this World"

(Acts 17:1-9)

"Now when they had passed through Amphipolis and Apollonia, they came to Thessalonica, where was a synagogue of the Jews: and Paul, as his manner was, went in unto them, and three Sabbath days reasoned with them out of the Scriptures, opening and alleging, that Christ must needs have suffered, and risen again from the dead; and that this Jesus, whom I preach unto you, is Christ," etc.

ANOTHER missionary journey begins here. Leaving Timothy and Luke in charge of the infant Church at Philippi, Paul and Silas pursued their journey towards the south-west—towards Athens, the eye of Greece. I think the good soldier of Jesus Christ already felt the swelling of a sanctified ambition to meet Athenian philosophers on their own chosen field. He may, for aught I know, have allowed a secret consciousness of power to lead him in that direction. It is the instinct of a warrior to seek a worthy foe. If this motive wrought in his mind, it is probable that his pride was soon crushed; for he does not seem to have obtained so much success at Athens as elsewhere. His epistles to the Christians of Corinth, Thessalonica, and Philippi attest the extent and solidity of his work in these places; but although he enjoyed an opportunity of debating with Stoics and Epicureans, and of declaiming in Mars' Hill, no epistle to the Athenians remains to edify the Church. It would appear that the soil in which human speculation grew rank was not well fitted to receive and nourish the living seed of the Word.

Here the narrative drops the first person and assumes the third; this is the only intimation of the fact that at this point Luke, the historian, parted company with the missionaries. The first person indicating the presence of the narrator, is not resumed until we reach chapter xx.

They passed through Amphipolis and Apollonia, two successive stages on the Roman road that extended from the Bosphorus to Rome, and came to Thessalonica at a distance of about one hundred miles from Philippi. It appears that the Jews possessed no synagogue at the intermediate stations, and therefore the missionaries made no halt till they reached the more important city of Thessalonica. There Paul, "as his manner was," entered the synagogue, and opened his commission first to the seed of Abraham.

Three Sabbath-days he reasoned with them out of the Scriptures. It is clear from the result that the audience on these occasions was not limited to Jews. The apostles found by experience that by preaching to the Jews they found the readiest access to the Gentiles. The Greeks in great numbers, both male and female, came into the synagogue and listened to these distinguished strangers. The preacher based his discourse on the Scriptures. His method is described by the terms "opening and alleging"—that is "opening out and laying down."

The Old Testament he treated as a nut. He broke the shell, opened out the kernel, and presented it as food to the hungry. The Jews were like little children who had a fruit-tree in their garden, their father's legacy. The children had gathered the nuts as they grew and laid them up with reverence in a storehouse; but they knew not how to break open the shell, and so reach the kernel for food. Paul acts the part of elder brother to these little ones. He skilfully pierces the crust and extracts the fruit, and divides it among them. The passage, for example, that Philip found the Ethiopian reading on the road, or the passover lamb, or the second Psalm, he opened, and from it brought Christ.

This able reasoner laid down a major and a minor; for in Greece he is mindful of his syllogism. (On his way from Philippi he had passed Stagirus, the birthplace of Aristotle.)

Major premise: The Christ expected by the Jews must suffer and die and rise again.

Minor premise: This Jesus whom I preach unto you suffered and died and rose again.

Conclusion: Therefore the Jesus whom I preach unto you is the Christ.

But it is not logic for its own sake; it is logic grasped and used as an instrument to commend Christ to sin-

ners. Whatever method he may adopt (and in that
he will become all things to all men) he will know no
other subject than Jesus Christ and him crucified. They
speak of successors of the apostles; their best successors are those who walk in their steps.

The result is, that some Jews believed, and a great
multitude of Greek proselytes and not a few chief women. While a remnant of the chosen seed is gathered
everywhere, the kingdom is in the main gliding over
to the Gentiles. Another feature of the success is,
that almost everywhere the higher and more educated
classes are attracted. In the great Greek city of Thessalonica many ladies of the highest social standing
were arrested and converted. This doubtless gave the
gospel a home in the place after the missionaries were
obliged to leave it.

"But the Jews which believed not," etc. Again a
conflict. Woe is me that I should everywhere be a
man of strife. There is much to make the missionary
weary, and induce him to fling up his commission in
disgust. But these men were forewarned, and so forearmed. They knew that, like their Master, they came
not to give peace on the earth. Wherever the two
kingdoms came in contact, there was conflict. No
cross, no crown.

The army that assails the mission here is an allied
host. It consists of two different but confederated
elements—of the Jews who believed not, and of certain
lewd fellows of the baser sort. These two do not look
with kindly eye on each other, but they unite to oppose a common enemy. This is not a new experience.
Herod and Pilate become friends when Christ must be
crucified. Pharisee and Sadducee, at daggers drawn
on ordinary occasions, combine to compass the death,
first of the Master, and then of his servants.

The unbelieving Jews allied themselves to the mob
of the market-place, in order to silence the testimony of
the apostles. In different ages and countries tyrants
of the ruling class have had recourse to the rabble whenever they have found it necessary to stifle the reprover's
voice. The seething caldron of a large city always
casts up a quantity of such scum. A multitude swarm
about the streets, lacking not only character but even

clothes. Persecutors have frequently found a use for these off-scourings. Christians should have their eyes on the same class for another purpose. They might be turned to a better account. If they were won and sanctified, they might swell the ranks of the white-robed when Christ comes to be glorified in his saints.

It was by these same instruments that the Jewish rulers in Jerusalem compassed the death of Christ. They engaged the mob to create a tumult, and thereby intimidated the governor. Crucify him! crucify him! from a surging excited multitude was a formidable cry for a governor with a troublesome province on his hand and a small garrison at his disposal. "If they have persecuted me, they will also persecute you;" and the persecution of the servants follows the type of that which the Master endured.

It is a remarkable cry that was raised before the magistrates of Thessalonica—"These that have turned the world upside down have come hither also." The rumor of the great effect produced by the preaching of the gospel in other places must have reached the city. After making allowance for the tendency to exaggeration in such circumstances, we find enough remaining to show that the wave of success already accompanying these two witnesses threatened to shake the foundations of society, and overturn the old established religions of Europe.

Another cry—"These all do contrary to the decrees of Cæsar, saying that there is another king, one Jesus" —is identical with that which was employed against Christ himself. These degenerate Jews did not comprehend their own Scriptures—did not understand the kingdom which the prophets proclaimed. The Son of David reigns, but reigns over an unseen kingdom. His own word is, "The kingdom of God is within you." His reign, having a different sphere and character, may have free scope; it will never come into collision with lawful human governments. The Lord's own words, "My kingdom is not of this world," remain a perennial rebuke to all persecuting governments on the one hand, and all political ecclesiastical organizations on the other.

Magnetism and gravity act at the same place and

the same time, but do not come into collision with each other. Each of these powers pervades all the earth's surface; each is supreme everywhere for its own objects; the one does not stand in the other's way. There is not less of gravity on any given spot because magnetism has free scope there. If one of these were subordinated to the other, the system of the world would be destroyed. This might help us to conceive of Christ's spiritual authority reigning with absolute sway over spirits, and yet not interfering with any legitimate function of civil government.

This question is assuming greater breadth and prominence in our day. It is rising not only in this country, but all over Europe. It is abroad in Italy and Germany. That which was the turning-point at the crucifixion of Christ comes up again for solution, and men must work its solution out. They overpowered it in Pilate's judgment-hall. But they made a mistake when they buried that small, and to their vision scarcely perceptible atom; to bury it was not to get rid of it for ever, for it is a living seed, and so it rises again.

Churchmen must learn to obey Christ without encroaching on the divinely appointed supremacy of civil government in its own domain; and civil rulers must learn to leave the kingdom of Christ in the world absolutely free.

Berean Nobility
(Acts 17:10,11)

" And the brethren immediately sent away Paul and Silas by night unto Berea: who coming thither went into the synagogue of the Jews. These were more noble than those in Thessalonica, in that they received the word with all readiness of mind, and searched the Scriptures daily, whether those things were so."

JASON and his companions were admitted to bail. The tumult for the time subsided. The brethren sent Paul and Silas away by night to Berea; for they were free to act on their Master's rule, "When they persecute you in one city, flee ye unto another."

That night-journey demands a passing notice. They started at night in order to escape the rage of the persecutors; but they could not reach Berea in one day's march, for the distance was about sixty miles. The road led at first westward, through a great plain, and then ascended the mountain. Berea lies on the eastern slope of the Olympian range. It is still a town of 20,000 inhabitants, and contains some remains of Greek and Roman buildings. Behold the two missionaries, with their guide, toiling along by night, eager to reach another station, where they might work and win before the wave of persecution should overtake them.

It is instructive to compare the occupation of this night with that of the last night of which the history is recorded—the night in prison at Philippi. Then they sang praise and prayer. They were enclosed within prison-walls, and fastened to the ground. What could they do? All was bound except their lips, and with these they sang. But this night, when they had escaped from the persecutors in Thessalonica, they did not sit down and sing. There, worship was work; here, work was worship. Generally the history tells what was done in the day-time; but in these cases the events of the night are mentioned because these events concerned the King. In the first of these nights, the men, finding work impossible, worshipped; and that act of worship turned out a successful work, for numbers were thereby won to Christ, and a footing for the gospel obtained in a heathen city. In the second night, when they could neither sleep nor work, the missionaries marched; and the march became the means of life from the dead to many in Berea, for by that sudden night-march the preachers got the start of their enemies, and had laid the foundations of a permanent edifice, before the Jews of Thessalonica could discover the direction of their flight and take measures for opposing them.

In Berea, they immediately addressed themselves to the Jews in their synagogue. "These were more noble than those in Thessalonica, in that they received the word with all readiness of mind, and searched the Scriptures daily whether those things were so."

There is a heraldry, it seems, in the kingdom of God as well as in the kingdoms of this world. Our King's throne, too, is encircled by a high-born nobility. In the Scriptures you will find the record of their deeds and the patent of their rank. The disciples of Christ are taught neither to vilify nor extol a temporal nobility. Christianity is not revolutionist. It is so deeply occupied with an inner revolution for eternity, that it cannot bestow any attention on the political revolutions of time. As it will not spend its strength in setting these thrones up, neither will it turn aside to pull them down. It leaves them precisely where it found them, and passes on in pursuit of its own aim.

If we could obtain a view of this earth from a great height in the heavens, the mountains would not appear very high, the valleys would not appear very deep. The inequalities on the earth's surface, which from our present view-point seem great, would disappear, and all would be reduced to a level. Precisely the same law rules in the spiritual sphere. When any one attains spiritually a great elevation, the differences of social condition, which bulk largely in other men's eyes, almost altogether disappear. To one who looks on the community as from the throne of God, the artificial distinctions which prevail in society seem to be blotted out: in his view, all are low until grace raise them up.

But distinctions there are, notwithstanding—distinctions between one man and another—real, deep, permanent. Some are slaves when seen from the higher view-point, and some are free; some are dead in sins, and some have been raised to newness of life; some are rich in grace, while others are wretched and poor and miserable and blind and naked; some are high-born, and some low.

These were more noble—high-born. Two things go to constitute nobility in its temporal form: first, the sovereign's choice in its origin; and second, the actual birthright of each individual noble in successive generations. The spring of all lies in the good pleasure of the king. The same feature is found in the nobility of the heavenly kingdom. Abraham was one of the multitude "beyond the flood"—on the east of the Euphrates. He was of plebeian blood and training. His tribe served idols in the rich plain of the Tigris, and lived without God in the world. He was sovereignly chosen and called. He received the patent of his nobility in the specific promise of the King eternal; and large possessions were bestowed upon him for the support of his dignity. To him, many generations afterwards, kings and nobles proudly traced their pedigree.

At a later period of the empire, when the King's Son was sojourning in this province, he called others —certain common plebeian men—and conferred on them the patent of nobility. Some fishermen were at that time raised from the ranks. In Rome they call Peter a prince: the title is not amiss, although they apply it falsely. About the same time some tax-collectors were admitted into the princely rank; and after the King's Son had returned to the seat of government, a noted rebel was first taken captive, and thereafter made a noble at his conqueror's court—an ambassador to the nations in the service of his reconciled King.

Further, each noble of this kingdom is himself born to his title and estate. Nicodemus, though a son of Abraham by his first birth, must himself be born again ere he could enjoy the privileges of a peer.

But there is one broad distinction, which should be carefully observed, between the kingdoms of this world and the kingdom of Christ, in regard to the manner in which peers are made—in regard to what constitutes nobility. In the kingdoms of this world there are two distinct methods; and of the whole body of the peerage, some are admitted in one way, some in the other —none in both. Some are called from other classes by the free election of the sovereign, and some are born into their dignities. In the kingdom of Christ, every noble unites in himself both these rights. He is chosen from without into the circle of the princes; and he is also born into the family. It requires both the earthly things to represent the heavenly. One represents the election by the sovereignty of God, and the other represents the actual change which in the regeneration passes upon the heart and life of the man.

These two represent salvation respectively on its upper and its under side, as the Parable of the Good Shepherd and the Parable of the Prodigal represent it.

The upper side of the seal contains the legend, "The Lord knoweth them that are his;" and the under side, "Let every one that nameth the name of Christ depart from iniquity."

Two characteristic features of the Berean nobility are recorded, in order that we in the end of the world may be able to distinguish between the genuine and the spurious; "They received the word with all readiness of mind, and searched the Scriptures daily whether these things were so." These qualities are distinct from each other, and yet are so bound together as to constitute a pair. The one is a tender, childlike receptiveness for revealed truth; the other is a manly independence of judgment. Their hearts drank in readily the water of life; but their understandings sifted the doctrines that were preached, and tried them by the law and the testimony.

1. Their hearts were receptive. In this matter the Jews of Berea were favorably distinguished from those of Thessalonica. Those who, like Saul before his conversion, had a knowledge of the law, and a full stock of variegated merits, did not so readily open to receive the gospel. They were like a field that is soaked and soured with stagnant water: when a shower falls on such a field it trickles off again. It is the dry land that drinks in the rain.

The distinction is similar to that which the parable makes between the good ground and the hard beaten wayside. The seed that fell on both places was the same. It was the quality of softness in one that rendered it receptive, and the quality of hardness in the other which caused it to reject the seed. Here lay the cause of the difference disclosed in harvest. As more depends on the condition of the soil than on the skill of the sower, so more depends on a receptive spirit in the hearers than on the peculiar ability of the preacher. There is a remarkable analogy, too, between the immediate cause of receptiveness in the cultivated ground on the one hand, and the immediate cause of the receptiveness of a human heart on the other. A broken, a contrite heart is the ordinary expression for a humble disposition of soul, crushed by a sense of sin, and thirsting for the living water. It is where the ground is broken small that the seed finds its way into the soil and the grain is gathered in harvest; in like manner it is in those who have been bruised by conviction of sin, and as it were melted by the mercy of God, that the offer of the gospel goes home, and the fruits of righteousness ripen apace.

2. The second characteristic of Berean nobility is the exercise of private judgment. They searched the Scriptures daily, whether these things were so. This short, simple intimation puts to shame the sophistry with which Rome has for ages striven to conceal the Word of God from the people. Charity is popular in our day, and "great is the company of them" that preach it; but we must see well to it lest we make a fatal mistake as to what is charity. Charity is not an equal regard for truth and falsehood,—for light and darkness. Charity is love; but how can you really love your brother if you do not loathe and denounce that which destroys him ? You cannot love your brother, and fondle the serpent which is stinging him to the second death. The political sentiment which in the name of charity supports the Papacy is a delusion. It is a dream from which political men will be awakened by some rude shock. It is a spurious liberalism that under any pretext pets and feeds the greatest enslaver of mankind. It is noble, says the Spirit of God, for private men to search the Scriptures daily in order to determine thereby the truth or falsehood of any doctrine that may be proposed for their acceptance: for this noble act the Romish hierarchy has everywhere persecuted even unto death.

The term rendered "searched" in the text indicates that they pored over the page; and after having read a sentence, returned to traverse the lines again, in order that the track of the sense might be more deeply graven on their minds. They avoided the two extremes of easy credulity and hard unbelief. Some stand rigid against the truth and yield not at all; others bend easily before every doctrine that is plausibly presented, but bend as the willow bends to the breeze, taking every position but keeping none.

It is a general law of human nature that what comes lightly, goes lightly. What we gain by a hard struggle, we retain with a firmer grasp, whether it be our fortune or our faith. Those men who have obtained great wealth without any trouble or toil of their own, often scatter it, and die in poverty. It is seldom that the man who gains a fortune by gigantic labor wastes the wealth he has won. In like manner, give me the Christian who has fought his way to his Christianity. If it is through fire and water that he has reached the wealthy place, he will not lightly leave his rich inheritance.

Some a Hundredfold
(Acts 17:12)

" Therefore many of them believed; also of honorable women which were Greeks, and of men, not a few."

THEY believed. The word is little; the thing is great —is life from the dead. By this one step they passed from a state of condemnation to a state of peace with God. They escaped from a house built on the sand before it fell, and took refuge in the house that was built upon the rock. The moment before they were without Christ, and therefore without hope in the world: the moment after they were in Christ, and heirs of eternal life. The step they took that day separated them conclusively from all the wicked, and allied them for ever with the true and pure. Their life is hid now with Christ in God: none shall ever be able to pluck them from their Redeemer's hand.

If any should ask, How could interests so vast turn on a point so small? How could the act of a moment, —the secret quiver of the soul's affection in transferring itself to the Saviour,—how could this mental act become the turning-point between woe and weal for eternity? All decisive turnings are made on points. It is on sharp points that great magnitudes can best be turned. He was born: he died. These are small points; and how vast the issues that move on them! People speak vaguely about the poles of the globe: these poles are mathematical points; yet how huge is the mass that spins round upon them from age to age!

Many believed. A swelling of spiritual life sometimes comes over a city or a country, as the tidal wave comes over the ocean,—lifted and led, in both cases, by a distant power in the heavens. Therefore many believed: the effects are distinctly traced to their immediate cause. The minds of the listeners inclined and opened to the word of life, and what they received lovingly they examined diligently. The symptoms that preceded and portended the revival were, A bent of mind toward the preached word, and a daily reverent searching of the Scriptures. When we see the same symptoms in any place, we may confidently expect a similar enlargement.

Interesting and instructive is the specific enumeration of classes that were on that occasion won to the Lord, "both of Greek women of good station and of men not a few." Four distinct characteristics of the persons who were converted at that time in Berea have been counted worthy of a place in the record, and should therefore be counted worthy of our special study.

I. Greeks were converted. There is no respect of persons with God; all are in his sight equally lost in sin, and all are alike precious when redeemed. Expressly in Christ's kingdom there is neither Jew nor Greek. Yet circumstances may be such that the conversion of a Greek gives more joy to an apostle's heart, and does more for the spread of the kingdom, than the conversion of a Jew. As a rule, the first converts in every city had hitherto been of the seed of Israel. But Paul and his companions, although they began their work in the synagogue, were aware that their mission was to the world; they rejoiced accordingly with a peculiar delight over the first-fruits of the Gentiles. These Greeks who believed in Berea were in themselves precisely as precious as the same number of Jews, and no more; but over and above the worth of individual souls, their conversion opened a door by which the gospel might enter a new and spacious field. This, to the weary laborers, was like the breaking forth of waters. The barrier at one spot had given way, and a gap was formed in the dyke by which the tide might enter and inundate the land. To the apostles those successes were sweetest which seemed earnests and promises of more.

2. Both men and women. God made them in marvellous wisdom for each other; together they have gone away from him; it is a gladsome sight when they return in company.

It is sad when the sexes are separated by that partition which divides the kingdom of God from the world lying in wickedness—separated so that while the one stands safe within the narrow gate, the other is still groping blindfold against the blank wall on its outer side. The separation takes place on both sides. There is not favor to one and frown to another. As there is neither Jew nor Greek, so there is neither male nor female, for partiality to either, in the kingdom of Christ. Sometimes the husband or brother truly seeks and finds the kingdom of God and his righteousness, while the wife or sister seems content to abide by the stuff of this world as the soul's portion. The cares of this life frequently become the specific means whereby the spiritual life is overlaid and smothered in the mothers and daughters of a house. On the other hand, sometimes the women of a family are devoted to Christ, while the men are too philosophic or too self-indulgent to be troubled with spiritual anxieties.

Husbands and wives, brothers and sisters, sons and mothers, come all, and come in company to Christ. Be heirs together of the grace of life—helps-meet in the rugged path—brothers and sisters in the whole family of God—entrants together into the joy of the Lord.

3. People of high standing, respectable people, were converted. And is there any peculiar ground for gladness there? Are the upper ten thousand more precious in God's sight than the myriads who occupy a lower place? No; this word comes from heaven, and does not shape itself by the fashion of the world. But though poor and rich are equally precious, there are times and circumstances in which conversion in high places is more noted and more noteworthy than conversion in a low place. If for nothing else, the early disciples valued it as men value certain gems, on ac-

count of its rarity. The common people heard the Master gladly, but the rulers held aloof and boasted that they were not tinged with any trust in Jesus of Nazareth. On that very account there was great joy in the circle of the disciples when a magnate joined their band. Even the Lord longed to have some of them, and looked fondly on the young rich man who came running and kneeling and calling him Master.

Another reason why people of high station are warmly welcomed into the company of Christians is, that their influence is greater; and so, when their talents are consecrated to the Lord, a larger gain accrues to the kingdom. If you looked from aloft upon a dry and parched land, you would be glad to see a well rising even on its lowest place; but you would be gladder if you saw a spring leaping from the ground on its loftiest ridges, for, from its position, it could be employed to irrigate a larger portion of the land.

Great temptations beset the wealthy and noble; the cords that bind them to the world are very strong; a louder song of praise, therefore, bursts from the lips of the free when one of these is liberated. It is more glory to the Lord, and greater gain to his cause in the world.

4. Many were converted. The emphatic phrase is, "Not a few." There is a strange appetite for more in a Christian's heart. It continually cries "Give, give." That cry is never silenced, that appetite never satiated, till the whole world is won. This feature of a Christian's new nature is inherited from Christ. He opened his mouth wide for the food which he loved. When many came and followed him, he continued to invite the rest as eagerly. When his ministry was nearly finished he wept in agony over Jerusalem, because few of its teeming multitude would accept pardon and eternal life at his hand.

There is a species of liberality in vogue at present which denounces indiscriminately all proselytism. It is quite true, we confess, that much impure zeal has been exhibited in the name of Christ. Woe to those, whatever name they assume, who compass sea and land to make a proselyte, and, when they have got him, steep him deeper in the same uncharitable fanaticism that gives energy to their own efforts. There is an evil proselytism, even as there is a spirit of darkness who assumes the robes of an angel of light. Every case must be judged on its own merits: it is irrational to denounce all proselytizing indiscriminately. There will, and should, and must be a proselytizing spirit in every true Christian. What do men mean by condemning it in the lump? Jesus Christ was a proselytizer, and all are like him whom he has inoculated with his love.

Paul's Arrival at Athens
(Acts 17:14-16)

"And then immediately the brethren sent away Paul to go as it were to the sea: but Silas and Timotheus abode there still. And they that conducted Paul brought him unto Athens: and receiving a commandment unto Silas and Timotheus for to come to him with all speed, they departed. Now while Paul waited for them at Athens, his spirit was stirred in him, when he saw the city wholly given to idolatry."

BEREA seems a very paradise for these missionary men. There was eager attention to the gospel; there were many conversions, and as yet there was no sign of any persecution springing up. But the persecution that did not spring on the spot was imported from a distance. "When the Jews of Thessalonica had knowledge that the word of God was preached of Paul at Berea, they came thither also and stirred up the people." The place was soon made too hot for Paul. As being manifestly the chief, he was more obnoxious than his two younger associates; for when it was found necessary to hurry him off from the place to preserve his life, Timothy and Silas ventured to remain behind to carry on the work which had been so hopefully begun.

The brethren sent away Paul, to go as it were, to the sea. It has been generally thought that stratagem was employed here; that they started in the direction of the sea-coast, to lead the persecutors on a false

scent, and afterwards took the road to Athens. But
it is more probable that the transaction was simpler.
As there is no mention of any place on the way between Berea and Athens, there is some ground to
infer that the journey was not made by land; that
they embarked at Dium, near the base of Olympus,
and landed at the Piræus. In the circumstances it is
probable that the route and the destination were not
determined until they were far on the way. When
they left Berea there was no time to consider their
course. The thing that pressed was to get Paul away
from a place of danger; out of Berea with all haste
for the missionary's life, and when we are a safe distance we shall consider where we shall go next.

Paul seems on this occasion to have been passive
in the hands of his friends. They who lived in the
country knew best both the danger that threatened
and the means of escape. They will manage the
whole business. The journey to Athens was no plan
of his. "They that conducted him brought him to
Athens." Arrived at this celebrated city, Paul seems
to have taken the measure of it at the first glance.
Before his conductors had left him to return to their
home, he had made up his mind and determined the
plan of the campaign. In view of Athens, Berea diminished in importance as a mission-field. He had
left Timothy and Silas there; but as soon as he saw
Athens, he sent a message back with the returning
escort, requesting his associates to join him without
delay.

Those two laborers were digging a well on the
spot where he left them—digging a well, and getting
water—the water of life, to refresh a parched neighborhood; but he hesitates not to call them away from
their work; for the well that they were digging was
in the lowly plain, and though they obtained sweet
water there, that water could not flow far for the
benefit of others. Here, however, and now, Paul had
discovered a spot on an exceeding high mountain,
where a well might be hopefully pierced, and if they
should obtain water there, it would, in virtue of the
height of its site, flow far and wide over the nations.
Accordingly this master-workman recalls his hands

from the successful but less important mission in Berea, that they might strike home for the Lord in the very heart and head of the civilized world.

The plan was that Paul should wait at Athens till his associates arrived, and that then they should begin the work in company. It is not easy for a solitary missionary to begin alone in the high places of the earth to bear a testimony for God. Poor Jonah was so overwhelmed by the prospect of standing unsupported in Nineveh to denounce God's judgments against the people's sin, that he rebelled and ran away that he might escape the hard and scathing ordeal. As Jonah at Nineveh, crying out, Yet forty days, and Nineveh shall be destroyed—as Jonah at Nineveh was Paul at Athens, proclaiming Jesus and the resurrection. It is too much for one man alone to dare and do. He will wait in silence the arrival of his friends, and then, shoulder to shoulder, three stronger than one, they will stand, and stand up for the Lord, and stand fast against the adversary. Bid them come both and come quickly, said the eager, impetuous apostle to his escort, as they turned to retrace their steps toward Berea; "and receiving a commandment unto Silas and Timotheus, for to come to him with all speed, they departed."

Away went the escort out of his sight, and Paul began his part of the programme—that is, to wait. He will wait at Athens till Timothy and Silas should arrive. But ah! this is not a man of the waiting kind. He had undertaken more than he could perform. The spirit of the prophet was not subject to the prophet. Paul was not a good waiter, and Athens was not the place for Paul to wait idle in. It was hard to begin alone his testimony for Jesus in that Greek capital, and therefore he laid the plan of obtaining associates; but it was harder to look on in silence where Satan had his seat, and therefore he broke through the plan that he had laid. He burst through all bonds and began. "Now while Paul waited for them at Athens, his spirit was stirred in him, when he saw the city wholly given to idolatry. Therefore disputed he," etc.

He saw the city given over to idolatry and felt a stirring, a thrilling through his soul, like the vibrations of a harp when the wind breathes on its strings. Not only were these two connected in point of time; they were connected as cause and effect. The sight which he saw without, caused the emotion that he experienced within. The idolatry of the city kindled this mission-ary's soul into a paroxysm of holy zeal which could not be restrained.

Two things are observable and memorable in con-nection with what Paul saw in Athens—two things very needful and very profitable to supply us with fixed foundation principles of action in these latter days.

First, this great and true man—this real philosopher, who both feared God and regarded man, was arrested and transfixed by the idols of Athens, so that he noticed not or regarded little the many other sights which the city contained. This intellectual capital of Greece present-ed in those days many attractions to men of cultivated taste; and Paul's taste was cultivated. It was not that he valued marble statues less, but living men more. He was not blind to the beauties of Greek architecture, or deaf to the music of the Greek tongue; but he felt the expulsive power of a deeper affection, that occupied his heart, and drove its rivals from the field. Ah! he is not the weak but the strong man who regards immor-tal souls as transcendently more important than fine arts. This man is not carried away by vanities, but governed by sound reason. Accordingly, he scarcely observes the curiosities that strangers went to see in Athens; he was taken up with that which obtruded itself on the traveller's eye at the corner of every street—idols, idols everywhere; and living men boasting them-selves to be God's offspring, bowing down before images of wood and stone, graven by art and man's device.

Another thing observable in the missionary's view is, that he considered the idolatry of the Athenians to be a grave and grievous thing. This is not one of those frivolous travellers who think idolatrous rites very pict-uresque, and very becoming, and very harmless. We have fallen upon an age when shallow men, in order to prove themselves deep, count it needful to laud the interesting and innocent religious ceremonies of the heathen on their native soil, and to deprecate Christian missionaries as intruders, who make the people worse. A sort of crusade is at the present time waged against

Christian missions by a section of the students of philosophy and nature. It cannot deal heavy blows, or continue long to deal any blows at all; for it is false in its facts, and unphilosophically presumptuous in its pretensions.

But, meantime, observe how this great and strong man regarded the matter. Idolatry was in his sight the height of all abomination. It was dishonor done to the living God, and degradation to intelligent human souls. It was, moreover, the fruitful parent of all vice. The law of God is a living and eternal thing. The law, like Christ, is not divided so that a man can take a part, and neglect the rest. The second table hangs dependent on the first. When the soul is debauched by the worship of a false god, the body is abandoned to every species of corruption (Rom. i.).

A City Given to Idolatry
(Acts 17:16)

"Now while Paul waited for them at Athens, his spirit was stirred in him, when he saw the city wholly given to idolatry."

THE city was wholly given to idolatry—full of idols. There is historical confirmation of the description from many sources. In the public opinion of those days Athens was considered to be supereminently a city of idols. Art had attained a higher state of perfection there than elsewhere. Their architecture and sculpture were not equalled in that day—have perhaps not been equalled in our day. This pre-eminence in art in connection with the exquisite taste which was a general characteristic of the people, greatly increased the public zeal in the worship of idols. When fine art, of the highest order of excellence, is consecrated to a false and sensual worship, it exerts a great power for evil. Modern Rome is in this respect like ancient Athens. The idolatry of the Papacy is fostered by the

fine arts, especially music and painting. Art has been
the sword-arm of Rome for modern conquests. And it
is among the classes whose education lies more in æs-
thetics than in thought that her converts have most
frequently been made in our own times. For, as
in ancient Athens, the imagination is captivated by
voluptuous art; and when the spirit is thus enslaved,
it may be led over into the coarsest idolatry! This
intoxication of the soul is not unlike the intoxication of
the body, whether you look to its soft, gradual approaches—or to the giddy, swimming pleasure to
which the captive abandons himself—or to the abject
degradation to which the intoxicated submits when he
is given over to the mysterious witchcraft.

What emotion did the sight of Athenian idolatry
excite in the missionary's breast! His spirit was stirred
in him. A fire was kindled that would have consumed
the man if it had been pent up. Allowed to get vent,
it blazed forth, and precipitated him with all his force
alone against the world.

It is worthy of notice here, however, that it is not
every human spirit that is kindled into a godly zeal by
the sight of a neighbor's sins or sorrows. This same
Saul was not always so tenderly susceptible. His heart
had once lain still without a flutter within his iron bosom,
when the blood of the martyr Stephen was shed, and
the clothes of the murderers lay at his feet. The martyr's eyes were raised to heaven in his sight, and a light
from God's countenance made his face to shine like an
angel's before the time; the martyr's last prayer was
uttered, and its gentle accents fell on the persecutor's
ear—" Lord, lay not this sin to their charge;" but Saul
of Tarsus felt no pity thrilling in his cold heart—no
shudder of remorse trembling in his callous soul. Hard
and dull and blunt as the nether millstone his spirit remained under the most melting sights and sounds that
can fall on human sense.

A great change had passed on Paul between the
time when he saw unmoved Christ's first witness die,
and the time when the sight of Athenian idolatry lighted
a flame of godly jealousy in his breast, and threw him
headlong on the god of this world, at the spot where
he was covered with all his panoply. Now Paul was

himself redeemed, and it grieved him to see a brother lying under condemnation. Now he was himself delivered from the power of Satan, and he could not bear to see silly birds going blindfold into the fowler's snare. This is the rule: it is when we have ourselves been brought out of darkness that rivers of water will run down our eyes because men keep not God's law. It is at Christ's love to us that our hearts take fire for other men.

Although the state of society is greatly advanced in our land and day, yet sights may be seen amongst us that should fire the heart of the observer as much as the idolatry of Athens fired the heart of Paul. A light and frivolous spirit is abroad—altogether Athenian—which seems to be rendering the generation incapable of earnest moral purpose, or self-sacrifice for noble ends. There is an impatience of the sober, the real, and the true, with a corresponding chase after the new, the exciting, the fictitious. We have indeed some use for the men who lived great lives and died great deaths for God and man on our own soil in a former age; for we gather scraps of their weakness from history wherewith to adorn our tales; but true appreciation of their excellence does not seem to lie within reach of those who assume to lead opinion in these days.

Some may be disposed to congratulate themselves that although the Athenian lightness be rife, yet the Athenian idolatry that grieved Paul does not venture to rear its head in Christendom. Even this comfort does not rightly belong to us. Without taking into account the Romish image-worship, which, in this country at least, is mainly confined to churches, and is not often obtruded before the public, idolatry in another form is rampant; for " covetousness is idolatry." The old Greeks, like the modern Asiatics, worshipped with bended knee the idols that were made of gold: we worship in our hearts the gold of which their idols were made. The various vices that ravage our cities, if not in themselves more hideous than those that greeted the apostle's eye in Athens, are fitted to stir into greater keenness the compassion of an observer, because they display their vileness in presence of a brighter and holier light than that of Greek philosophy. Considering our privileges and attainments, I suspect there is more to make an apostle shudder in Edinburgh and London than there was in Athens and Rome. Oh, it is pitiful, that near a whole cityful of comfortable christianized inhabitants, so many wretches in human form should be permitted to torment and destroy themselves and one another by open, organized, wholesale vice and crime.

For dealing effectually with the plague-spots of the land and the plague-stricken of the people, we have already means and machinery in abundance. What is wanted is a great fire of love in human hearts to set the apparatus in motion. We have good meaning, but little might. We have principle already; it is passion that we want,—passion such as burned in the heart of Paul when he looked on the idolatry of Athens.

The Philosophers
(Acts 17:17,18)

"Therefore disputed he in the synagogue with the Jews, and with the devout persons, and in the market daily with them that met with him. Then certain philosophers of the Epicureans, and of the Stoics, encountered him. And some said, What will this babbler say? other some, He seemeth to be a setter forth of strange gods: because he preached unto them Jesus, and the resurrection."

ALTHOUGH it was the idolatry of the Greeks that stirred Paul's spirit, and launched him single-handed on the work, he kept his old rule of giving the first offer of the gospel to the Jews. Even here he began in the synagogue; but, as might have been expected, the mission to the heathen soon sprang to the foreground, and occupied his energies.

In the market-place he discoursed daily to all who were willing to listen. The method indicated by the term "disputed" was universal among the Greeks. It consisted of question and reply. It was both more lively in itself, and better fitted to elicit truth than any of our modern methods. At Tarsus, Paul was trained to such disputations in his youth; and doubtless he felt himself at home in the Agora of Athens. The "vessel" was chosen because of its capacity; or rather, capacity was providentially imparted to the vessel, because such an instrument was needed in the service of the King.

Two of the leading sects into which Greek philosophy after the time of Socrates had broken up, immediately appear upon the field—the Epicureans and the Stoics. These two systems were reciprocally antagonistic. In their nature and mutual relations they resembled somewhat the Sadducees and the Pharisees among the Jews. Paul was a Pharisee before he was a Christian, and if he had lived in Athens would certainly have attached himself to the Stoics.

Both sects dealt with the same questions: with man, his duty, his destiny, his relation to the universe and to God.

Epicurus bought a garden in the city, and taught his disciples there. His main principle was, that the chief good of man is enjoyment. It is due, however, to the founders of the sect to say that they measured enjoyment by a high standard. They repudiated sensual pleasures. It was in the later period of the Roman Empire that this philosophy developed into unbridled licentiousness. But even in Paul's time its maxims tended to degrade humanity. The apostle alludes with horror to its fundamental maxim, "Let us eat and drink, for to-morrow we die." They made special efforts to free themselves from the fear of death. Listen, O ye disciples of Epicurus! a preacher stands in the Agora to-day who really can impart to you this secret. He will tell you of One who can "deliver them who through fear of death were all their lifetime subject to bondage." *

---

* Thoughtful heathens of that time were much exercised about the shadow which the prospect of death casts over the path of the living. They wove many curious and acute reasonings together, by way of covering; but, alas! these threads, though exhibiting great ingenuity, possessed no power. Cicero—"Tusculan Questions," Book I.—puts the matter thus:—All men are either alive or dead. Those who are alive are free from death, and those who are dead are free from it; therefore all are free, and none should fear. He points out, with laborious hair-splitting, that no man has anything to do

The Stoics, so called because their founder, Zeno, taught in a porch (Stoa), were in many respects the opposite of the Epicureans. They taught that man's chief end is to be virtuous. But, alas! they had no certain knowledge of what virtue is; and they possessed no power to lead a human spirit in the right path, even although it had been known.

When the representatives of these two philosophical sects encountered the learned Jew in the market-place of Athens, they would soon discover that he was not a novice in their own arts. The Stoic system, especially, must have been familiar to Paul in his youth at Tarsus. It is remarkable that from the time of Zeno to the time of Paul, a period of about three hundred years, almost all the leading Stoics were Asiatic Greeks; and three of these, each of them a leader in his day, were of the same province—Cilicia—and two even of the same city—Tarsus—in which the apostle was educated. Discussions between Epicurean and Stoic, in the schools of Tarsus when Paul was young, must have held the same place which the dispute between Romanists and the Reformation holds with us. There was the same interval, the same separation into sects, and the same antipathy.

Both sections, however, soon turned against Paul, as Sadducee and Pharisee, at a later period, combined at Jerusalem for his destruction. All parties were especially scandalized by his doctrine of "Jesus and the resurrection." These philosophers could not bear to be told of a crucified Redeemer. They would not receive the fact on which the salvation of the world depends —that Jesus died for our sins, and rose again for our justification.

Paul was as eager to win these Greek philosophers as he had been to win those low, ruffian fortune-tellers who haunted the precincts of the temple at Ephesus. He had learned from the Master to have no respect of persons. He looked on the learned and unlearned as all alike lost, unless and until Christ were formed in

with death. It cannot come to the living, for when it comes, he is no longer living, but dead; and it cannot come to the dead, for he is already past it. How poor are these speculations of philosophy, in presence of the gospel of Christ!

them. These were noble specimens of humanity, but they were fallen. They were dead in sin, and they could not bring themselves to life again.

Conceive of a race of intelligent beings springing up and attaining maturity in an hour: suppose that hour to be the beginning of the night; they are Ephemera; their life-course lasts only twenty-four hours. The first half of their existence is night. They exercise their faculties on all the nocturnal phenomena of nature. This night, we shall suppose, has been varied. At first there was darkness; afterwards the stars appeared, and later still the moon. The world, they thought, was now glorious: their privileges were complete. Expectation, imagination, could no further go. At length the day dawns in the east, and the sun rises in his strength. But these ephemeral creatures do not relish the light of day. Their faculties have developed under the feeble lights of the night; their senses have accommodated themselves to their circumstances. They are content with what they possess, and busy themselves in weaving thick curtains to keep out the sunlight.

Such were the Athenian philosophers when the gospel reached them in the preaching of Paul. They had light of a kind. Their light, such as it was, reached them as a reflection from that Sun which they had never seen. But so accustomed were they to the darkness, and so contented with it, that when the Sun appeared they shut their eyes against his healing beams.

The discussions which sprang up in the market-place between Paul and the philosophers soon attracted a crowd. The Greeks were sharp enough to perceive that there was something deeper in the discourse of the stranger than the daily gossip of the streets. By common consent it was agreed that these matters were too grave to be dealt with in the noise and jostling of the market. All felt instinctively that there must be an adjournment. The cry, "To the Areopagus!" was raised; and the whole mass—preacher, philosophers, and people—moved together from the low, level market-place up to the venerable rock. The ascent, abrupt on one side, was an easy gradient on the other. The rock rose to a height of about sixty feet above the plateau that lay between it and the much more elevated Acropolis. It was levelled on the top, and seats for the magistrates were cut in the rock. The temple of Theseus, the most ancient, and still the best preserved of their shrines, was close by. The Acropolis, crowned with the Temple of Minerva, the patroness of the city, overhung the spot, as the Castle rock of Edinburgh overhangs the plateau on which Heriot's Hospital stands.

In this open-air court all the great trials of religion and politics had been conducted. Grand associations were connected with the spot. In this case it was not the trial of a criminal. No charge was preferred against Paul. It was an adjournment to this place of grave and solemn traditions, that, under the presidency of the magistrates and in presence of the people, the sublime themes concerning man and his relation to God, broached by the Jewish stranger, might be reasoned out. Here met the wisdom of this world and the foolishness of preaching. Here the Cross of Christ came into contact with the best that human reason had been able to discover. Here, as elsewhere, the preached gospel will be a dividing word. The cross raised on the Areopagus will be like the cross erected by Pilate's soldiers on Calvary in this—that on one side of it there will be a scorner, and on the other side a sinner saved by faith. From the one side you hear the sneer, "If thou be Christ, save thyself and us;" from the other the prayer, "Lord, remember me when thou comest into thy kingdom." In Athens, as in Jerusalem, it is "on either side one, and Jesus in the midst."

All Things to all Men
(Acts 17:22-31)

" Then Paul stood in the midst of Mars' hill, and said, Ye men of Athens, I perceive that in all things ye are too superstitious. For as I passed by, and beheld your devotions, I found an altar with this inscription, To the unknown God. Whom therefore ye ignorantly worship, him declare I unto you," etc.

PAUL'S address on the Areopagus is, even in a merely literary and archæological point of view, one of the most beautiful gems that have descended from ancient to modern times. In itself, and in its adaptation to circumstances, it exhibits great literary power and consummate skill. It is a fine example of the preacher's own rule—that is, of becoming all things to all men that he might gain some. He grasps firmly at the same moment both his own aim as a missionary of Christ, and the peculiar character of his audience. His speech is a noble effort to win for the gospel the most cultivated and refined people of that age. It is a grand crisis; and this Jew is equal to it. The apostle of Jesus Christ is at length face to face with human civilization in its highest form, and his aim is to overturn it—to place it on a new foundation and animate it with a new spirit. He stands up, waves his hand, and begins. "Athenians, everything I behold gives evidence that you are very devotional." The words of the English version—"too superstitious"—are not happily chosen. It is quite true that in Paul's view their worship was superstition, and in his mind the word he employed attributed to them a reverence for demons. But the word was ambiguous, and to his audience it might convey the idea of religiosity without suggesting anything offensive. They will discover as he proceeds what he thinks of their religious rites; but, in the first instance, he conveys to their minds only the idea that he considered them very religious. He speaks the truth according to his own judgment; but he carefully avoids such harshness at the outset as might have bereft him of his coveted opportunity. He will not offend the audience in the first sentence.

This missionary is a philosopher as well as a Christian. He will preach Christianity, not philosophy; but he will employ philosophy as an instrument in his work. According to the symbolic phraseology of the Apocalypse, the earth will help the woman. In the intense devotion of the Athenians Paul recognized a power which might yet be turned to good account. This appetite for the spiritual proclaims man to be the child of God, although in a state of disease it seeks impure food. This appetite may yet be fed with the bread of life. He knew that the "demon-dread" with which his audience were affected was a dark superstition; but he did not openly or offensively, in the first instance, say so. He will lead them by a gentler and, as he hopes, a surer method to the truth. He conciliates their favor by acknowledging their religiousness; and then endeavors to turn the wandering stream of their piety into the right channel.

Paul paced the streets of Athens like other strangers. He looked eagerly on every object of interest. He observed men as well as things; actions as well as scenes. He took mental note of all that he saw, and classified the facts in his memory for subsequent use. This is a most precious faculty. Any person can see the objects; not every person can arrange his observations in order, and lay them where they will be available in time of need.

Of the various objects which had attracted his attention on the streets, one now started to his memory, and leaped to his lips. "As I passed by, and beheld your devotions, I found an altar with this inscription, To the unknown God." Some pilgrims were bringing a votive offering and laying it on an altar as the apostle passed. He will turn aside and study them. He sees the inscription—"To the unknown God." The sad words are written not with a pencil in a note-book, but with a pen of iron on his memory. He weeps in secret over the blindness of the heathen. He possesses a light which will chase away that darkness. He longs to make God known in the Mediator.

These idolaters seem to have advanced one step beyond their own idolatry. They felt, and sadly owned, that with their thirty thousand deities, and their city full of temples, they had not yet discovered the truth. There remained something which they could not reach, and without which they could not be happy. After this unknown One they grope blindfold. They stretch out their arms into night, and on closing them embrace only the damp air.

The astronomers Leverrier and Adams, in separate countries at the same time, observing certain motions among the spheres which could not be accounted for by any known cause, concluded that there must be a body not yet discovered, somewhere in the regions of space in which the disturbances were observed. Seeking in the direction thus indicated, they found the far distant and hitherto unknown world. So Greek philosophy was able, from the appetites and vacancies of the human mind, which all the idols could not satisfy, to determine that there must be some God hitherto from them concealed, to whom these appetites pointed, and without whom they could not be satisfied. Their skill could discover in a general way their need, but they could not by their searching find the missing Portion for a human soul. This messenger who now speaks to them can supply the lack. Through Christ he can make known to them the Father. "Whom therefore ye ignorantly worship, him declare I unto you." Paul was willing to take their confessed sense of want as inquiry after the living God, and offered to lead them by the gospel into his presence.

Incidentally, while preaching to the philosophers, the apostle declares the unity of the human race. Of one blood are all nations. The blood is the life. He conceives of it as a river flowing from one fountain, and branching out into many channels. The stream has, in point of fact, been continuous, like waters that fail not. The blood that flows in the veins of this generation has descended in an uninterrupted stream from the primeval man. This stream is one; it had not several distinct fountains.

The Greeks were a fine race of men; and they knew it. In regard to physical symmetry, they thought of themselves as the Pharisees thought of their spiritual attainments. They trusted in themselves that they were intellectually and physically beautiful, and despised others. Mankind were divided in their conception into two great sections—Greeks and Barbarians. They would not admit a community of race with other peoples; but alas! in order to isolate and so distinguish themselves, the highest fiction they could invent was that they had sprung from the soil of Greece!

This old heathen fable is curiously cognate with the latest speculations which a sect of secular philosophers are at this day zealously propagating. The old fiction assumed a poetical form—the living men, full-bodied and perfect, sprang from the mother earth; the modern myth, as becomes its date, is dressed up in a complete suit of scientific garments. But it is the same in its substance; for it represents that men, body and soul as you now behold them, came, through an infinite succession of steps indeed, but still came, without an intelligent cause, from dead matter—that is, that they sprang from the ground. Thus human reason, when left to itself in matters that relate to God and the soul, spins round in a giddy circle, and thinks it is making progress.

After glancing at God's providential reign over the world, the preacher comes more closely home to his heathen audience, and out of their own lips convicts them of not acting up to the light they possessed. By the mouth of their own poets they professed themselves to be the offspring of God, and yet they worshipped wood and stone—the work of their own hands. It is worthy of remark here that Aratus, the poet whom Paul quotes, was a native of Tarsus. Paul must have been acquainted with his writings in the schools of his native place. An almost identical phrase occurs also in the hymn to Jupiter by Cleanthes, a distinguished disciple of Zeno, the founder of the Stoic sect. Perhaps the preacher glanced toward the colossal statue of Minerva, the patron saint of the city, fixed on the top of the temple that crowned the Acropolis, the pride of Athens and the work of her greatest artist, while he uttered the withering words, "Forasmuch then as we are the offspring of God, we ought not to think that the Godhead is like unto gold, or silver, or stone, graven by art and man's device."

The times of this ignorance God looked over—that is, he waited for his own set time, and then sent the Word forth from Jerusalem to the nations. In that Word he commands all men everywhere to repent. God in the gospel not only permits and invites, he commands men to repent and believe and live. This is his commandment—to Greeks and to Britons—in the first century and the nineteenth—his *commandment* is, " That we should believe on the name of his Son Jesus Christ, whom he hath sent."

Some Fell on the Wayside, Some on Good Ground
(Acts 17:32-34)

" And when they heard of the resurrection of the dead, some mocked; and others said, We will hear thee again of this matter. So Paul departed from among them. Howbeit certain men clave unto him, and believed: among the which was Dionysius the Areopagite, and a woman named Damaris, and others with them."

ON the Areopagus, as elsewhere, Paul would have more fully opened the gospel of Christ if the proud audience had been willing to hear him. But when he reached his favorite theme, the resurrection of Christ, they lost patience, and raised an uproar. They rudely shut the preacher's mouth, and so shut the door of mercy against themselves. It is instructive to observe wherein the offence of the cross specifically lay in those times and for those people; it lay in the resurrection of Christ, which implied also his death as an atonement for sin. The Athenians could bear the cutting remarks of the stranger on their own ignorance, as confessed in the memorable altar-inscription; they could bear the exposure of their own inconsistency in acknowledging God their Father, and yet paying homage to a marble statue; they could bear the announcement of a great assize in which the whole world must stand before a human judge, Divinely appointed to distribute rewards and punishments; but when Paul proceeded to declare the central fact on which the hope of men must hang—the atoning death and the glorious resurrection of the man Christ Jesus—their philosophy and politeness could not bear them further—they broke out into scornful interruptions, and the speaker's voice was drowned in the tumult. This is the offence of the cross to-day. How significant in this aspect are the words of the Lord: "Blessed is he who shall not be offended in me."

Paul departed from among them doubtless with a heavy heart. It seemed to him at that moment that his labor was lost. Not long after, however, he learned that some of the good seed had fallen into broken ground. Even on the hard soil of the Areopagus, where he had scattered his seed weeping, he gathered sheaves with joy.

That congregation of Greeks was divided into three distinct parts. The descriptions are given with great distinctness. Paul rightly divided that day the Word of truth, and the Word divided the hearers into distinct and well-defined groups: into mockers, hesitators, and cleaving believers. Examine them one by one.

1. The *mockers*. When the preacher spoke of the resurrection of the dead, a portion of the audience loudly jeered him. Paul told the story of the cross: how the Son of God took our nature, and in it suffered death for our sin; that through Divine power he rose from the dead and ascended into heaven; and that all who accept him as their Saviour, will rise to reign with him for ever. It was at this point that a portion of these volatile Athenians began to make sport of the preacher. These, whether socially higher or lower, were in spirit the hardest and coldest of the company. They were fast and free livers. Probably they belonged to the sect of Epicureans. They enjoyed life, and kept the thought of death away. They made no apology to the distinguished stranger; they did not take the trouble of making a hypocritical promise to consider the subject and call again. Nor were they content with simply neglecting the message. They made sport of the preacher and his theme in presence of the assembly. They went away laughing at the truth of God and the God of truth.

If our voice could reach the modern representatives

of these jolly Greeks, we should affectionately and solemnly suggest to them that if God is, their laugh will not make him cease to be; that their destiny is long, but their views at present short: that they have not made sure that when we are dead we are done; that it is a fearful thing for a scoffer to fall into the hands of the living God. What if the very intellect that enables you to entertain the question whether there be a God, be conclusive evidence that there is a God who gave it? What if this "No God," a judgment pronounced by an intelligent self-conscious spirit, be itself evidence that God is? If God had not been, there could have existed no creature capable of entertaining the question whether there be a God.

2. The *hesitators*. "Others said, We will hear thee again of this matter." They listened respectfully to the public address; and when the hubbub caused by the scorners had subsided, they approached the speaker and politely excused themselves for not complying with his invitation. These men were between two opposites, and perhaps found themselves in a strait. On the one side, in a group that clustered round the preacher, they might observe gushing tears and other symptoms of broken hearts; and on the other side, they might see the smile of scorn curling on the lips of scoffers as they descended the steps into the *forum* again. Perhaps these men were really perplexed, and meant to reconsider the subject. Convinced in their consciences that the testimony of the apostle had all the air of truth, they did not dare to scoff; but wedded to their own ease and pleasure, they were not willing to take up the cross and follow Christ. Accordingly they adopted an intermediate course. They made a respectful apology to the preacher and went away. Counting the time of closing with Christ an evil day, they put it as far off as they could. They did not venture to say Never; but they went the length of saying, Not now.

This intermediate class is very numerous in our own age. They are a very large flock; and in their present condition it is not the Father's good pleasure to give them the kingdom. They do not erase the gospel from their creeds; but they will not permit it to reign in their hearts and mould their lives. They are willing to possess a religion; but not willing that religion should possess them. They will wear it as a very becoming ornament; but they will not flee to hide in it as their life. They will keep near the door which it opens, that they may run into it at any moment when their case becomes desperate; but they will not press through it now, lest some right arm should be torn off in the passage, and the presence of Christ within should cast a damp over their vain pleasures. They would fain hope that Christ will stand ready to open the door of heaven for them on that day; but they are not willing to open the door of their hearts for him this day. They slumber while the Bridegroom passes; alas! it is to be feared the Bridegroom will refuse to open when at length they begin to knock and cry.

We have reached deep waters at last, after passing the noisy foam and the deceitful shallows. After passing in review the scorners and the procrastinators, we have come to—

3. The *believers.* "Howbeit, certain men clave unto him and believed." First of all, it is instructive to observe the relations in which the Athenian believers stood to Paul the minister on the one hand, and to Christ the Redeemer on the other. They clave—they were glued to the preacher. As iron under the influence of the magnetic current cleaves to the magnet, their hearts held to the man who made the Saviour known. To the stranger Jew who told of Jesus crucified and risen, those Greek citizens, including one at least of the ruling class, fondly, firmly clung as to their life. Strange; and that too at the moment when their quick-witted countrymen were making merry with the outlandish opinions and speech of the foreigner. A principle more secret and more strong than magnetism had been generated in their hearts by this preacher's word. By an irresistible law of the new nature they were drawn to the man who made known the Saviour of sinners. But, tender though their love was to Paul, through whom the word came, it did not terminate on him. They cleaved to him and believed; that is, while this man's lips were the channel through which the word of life reached them, the ultimate longing of their hearts—their ultimate grasp—reached and rested on

Christ crucified, whom Paul preached. They cleaved to Paul, but they believed in Christ.

No wonder that these newly converted Greeks cleaved to the skirts of Paul. He was already a strong man. He had reached full stature, and was more vigorous in faith and hope than others, because his graces had all been greatly tried. They were little children, and the world a treacherous sea; it was natural that they should cling to their spiritual father, as if for their life.

An artist has painted a marine scene at the crisis of a heart-stirring event, and the group is constituted thus: From the rigging of a distressed ship on a wild sea a stout rope hangs over the side. In the lower extremity of that rope a solitary seaman, evidently a volunteer in the business, his strong limbs and stronger heart going into it with all their might, a solitary seaman hangs. To the seaman clings a mother, and to the mother, seen dimly through the drifting spray, clings an infant. The cry, " They're saved," rings out that moment from the eager spectators who watch the crisis from the deck. The seaman was the child's saviour that day; yet the seaman touched not the child; the child touched not the seaman. The mother was sustained by that hero's strength, and the child hung upon the mother. It is in some such way as this that Christ was the Saviour of those Greeks, although they grasped Paul, as if they were glued to his person. The apostle served at the moment as a link between them and the Lord: " ministered by us."

We know that this minister was faithful. He was zealous for the honor of his Lord and the safety of his brethren. If he had seen that those Greeks were making him their idol, he would have skaken off their grasp with livelier loathing than that with which he shook the venomous reptile from his hand into the fire at Malta. If he had seen that they were superstitiously looking to him for help, he would have rebuked them as he rebuked others with that terrible demand, "Was Paul crucified for you?"

There is a world of meaning in this cleaving—this glueing of themselves to their instructor. The danger is great, the time is short, the struggle is hard. Christianity is not a pleasant dream; it is a real warfare. The corresponding expression in Peter's exhortation throws light on the eager cleaving of our text. " The righteous," he intimates, " are scarcely saved." It is a close run, a hair-breadth escape, like the escape of Lot from Sodom when the angels laid hold of him and dragged him away from doom. It is the salvation of one who strips off not only his wealth and his pleasures and his ornaments to escape through the narrow gate as poor as he was born, but of one who strips himself off—the old man with his deeds—and enters life as he was born again—the new creature only. I think I see groups of sinners saved, assembling immediately within the gate, telling each other of their dangers and escapes, every heart beating with the recent tumult, but every eye beaming with unspeakable delight. Through fire and water they have been brought; but now they are in a wealthy place.

Let none be surprised when they see the anguished earnestness of awakened souls. Be surprised and suspicious rather when the matter is taken coolly.

The first sensations of this cleaving are beyond measure sweet to a missionary at home or abroad. He has toiled in the ministry for a series of years, wearied, and almost wearied out, by a dreary alternation of Paul's first two Athenian experiences—the scoff of the mockers, and the heartless, soulless apology of the worldling as he turns his back. When he is at the point of giving over in despair, he is startled by an unwonted, almost unexpected sensation. Surely the line that he has held dangling loose over that dreary sea for so many nights was tightened a little. It is even so. The line is tight and heavy. His heart leaps for joy. The missionary feels living souls cleaving to his own, that he may help them to Christ their life. This cleaving to the servant is a symptom of believing in the Lord.

Although Christ alone is the Saviour, the ministry of man holds an important place. How tender are these relations in time! How happy in eternity!

The World by Wisdom Knew Not God
(Acts 18:1-9)

"After these things Paul departed from Athens, and came to Corinth;"
etc.

"AFTER these things Paul departed from Athens."
Alas! he had seen little fruit in that city. "The
world by wisdom knew not God."

The apostle seems to have been interrupted by an
outburst of contempt, as soon as he reached his main
subject,—Jesus and the resurrection. They listened
respectfully as long as he contended with the Epicureans and the Stoics: they were interested by his discourse on natural religion; perhaps they admired his
dialectic against idolatry: but as soon as he began to
preach Jesus, they raised a shout of derision and drowned
the preacher's voice.

"They walked according to the course of this world,
the spirit that now worketh in the children of disobedi-
ence." The spirit that ruled them permitted them to
hear Paul's philosophy, but raised a tumult to prevent
them from listening to Paul's gospel. The strong man
armed kept his goods in peace, as long as the preliminary argument lasted; but at the approach of this testimony to Jesus, he dreaded lest a stronger than he
should burst in; accordingly he quickly shut the gates.

It is a melancholy reflection that the gospel in great
measure failed in Athens. There is no epistle of Paul
to the Athenians, while no less than two letters of his
to each of the two great mercantile cities, Thessalonica
and Corinth, have come down to us. Athens in the
midst sat alone as a queen, representing the philosophy
and the art of Greece. There the kingdom of Christ
could not obtain a footing. But Thessalonica on the
one side, and Corinth on the other, became the scenes
of great missionary success, the sites of early and flourishing Christian Churches.

The wealth and luxury, and even profligacy of Corinth, did not in point of fact present so hard a wayside

for the seed as the earthly wisdom of Athens. Not only licentious Corinth, but barbarous Melita, and warrior Rome, afforded to the living word a better seed-bed than the schools of contending philosophies.

Some have connected this lack of success with the special method adopted by the apostle among the Athenians. They have said, his experience discourages every effort to accommodate the presentation of the gospel to the tastes and attainments of the audience. In short, they imagine that Paul made a blunder in attempting to adapt his discourse to the mental habits of the philosophers; and that the result shows he should have delivered his message in the same form at Athens as at Philippi. But this is a mistaken view. The preaching comparatively failed at Athens, not because of the preacher's method, but in spite of it. The message was rejected although Paul did much to commend it to the cultivated Greeks; how much more if he had neglected all art and effort in his approaches! This sower went forth to sow, and sowed very skilfully: but the seed did not grow, because the ground on which it fell was dry and hard.

Every minister of the Word should do his utmost to become all things to all men, that he may gain some: but when he has delivered his message, and the message has been neglected, let not men deceive themselves with the reflection that the cause of their carelessness was the unskilfulness of the preacher.

I do not excuse negligence in the preacher. I ask no leniency of judgment in his favor. He is inexcusable if he do not put all his force and skill into his work, for it is an errand of life and death on which he is sent: but I earnestly warn all who hear the gospel that no charge against the preacher's methods, however well founded, will relieve from condemnation those who are not in Christ.

He came to Corinth, about forty-five miles distant. The province of Achaia then, like the modern kingdom of Greece, consisted of the Morea and a portion of the mainland on the north. There were two Roman provinces—Macedonia on the north, with Thessalonica as the capital; and Achaia on the south, with Corinth as its capital. The city occupied an advantageous position on the neck of the peninsula, with shipping on either side. At several periods attempts had been made to cut a canal across; but they had never been successful. It was often in time of war fortified by a wall. Corinth had been destroyed by a Roman army; but Julius Cæsar restored it; and at the time of Paul's visit it had again become a great city. It enjoyed an extensive commerce.

Here Paul attached himself to a worthy Jewish couple, Aquila and Priscilla, who were tent-makers, and who subsequently at various places gave effective aid to the ministers of the gospel. In their company and in their workshop he labored with his hands, earning his daily bread, and preaching as he obtained opportunities in the city. A workshop is not a bad place for preaching in. If the heart of one workman is filled with the love of Christ, all the hands will hear of it. Every Sabbath-day the synagogue was open, and Paul plied his opportunity there. He seems in the first instance to have associated almost exclusively with the Jews in Corinth, perhaps because of the bitter disappointment he met at the hands of the Greeks in Athens.

After Silas and Timothy rejoined him, Paul launched out more boldly in his mission at Corinth. But again a storm of persecution arose. The Jews as usual were the bitterest enemies of the gospel. In the midst of his discouragement, however, a great consolation was conferred upon him in the conversion of Crispus, the chief ruler of the synagogue, and all his house. Writing afterwards to the Church at Corinth, Paul said that with the temptations that had been allowed to come, the Lord had also opened a way of escape. He spoke from his own experience. Very heavy trials overtook him in that city; but God who sent them did not leave him to sink. He made a way of escape; and that way was a Divine revelation. "The Lord spake to Paul by a vision." Left to his own sagacity and vigor, the treatment he met at Corinth, coming immediately after his experience at Athens, might have been too much for the missionary. At Athens he addressed himself to the Gentiles, but his efforts failed; in Corinth he returned to the synagogue, but the Jews opposed themselves and blasphemed. "Then spake the Lord:" man's extremity is God's opportunity. When all seemed shut around this witness, a door of escape was opened. Help came precisely when it was needed. When Pharaoh is already pressing on the rear of the camp, the Red Sea divides in front, and the people pass over, the people whom the Lord has redeemed. When Timothy and Silas prove too feeble as comforters, the Master himself sustains his fainting servant in the everlasting arms. "Lo, I am with you always." It is ever so in the experience of disciples: when I am weak, then am I strong.

The Missionary and the Governor
(Acts 18:9-17)

" Then spake the Lord to Paul in the night by a vision, Be not afraid, but speak, and hold not thy peace: for I am with thee, and no man shall set on thee to hurt thee: for I have much people in this city. And he continued there a year and six months, teaching the word of God among them," etc.

WE may learn much of Paul's inner character by observing what the Master promised him for encouragement in his difficulties at Corinth. The Lord knew the r. issionary's heart—where its weakness lay, and what would avail to give him support. Now, by marking what the omniscient Physician precribes, we gain an infallible diagnosis of the patient's ailments. Two distinct grounds of comfort are supplied; therefore, we may conclude, two distinct fears oppressed the missionary's heart. The twin comforts are assurance of personal safety, and the promise of many souls as his hire; the twin fears accordingly were, lest the violence of the persecutors should crush him, and lest his labor in the ministry of the Word should be in vain. The one fear shows Paul's weakness, and the other shows his strength. In fear of danger and love of life, Paul was like other men, and needed the assurance of Divine protection; but the motive of his ministry was to save men, for he who knows his heart is able to assume, that the hope of winning souls will make him brave every danger in the prosecution of his work.

"Speak; for I have much people in the city." Despondency was freezing the stream of motive, and the machinery of the missionary's life was about to stand still: hope of success, given by the word of his Master, melted the ice, and the work went on. This demonstrates that Paul preached in order to win souls.

An interesting and comforting view of Divine sovereignty is opened up here, a view that tends to reconcile all differences of opinion among the disciples of Christ, and induce them to accept meekly all that the Scripture reveals, waiting for the solution of mysteries till the books are opened. The Lord intimates to Paul, "I have much people in this city," at a time when these persons were Jews or heathen. It was in purpose and prescience as yet that he had them as his people, and not in accomplished fact. Now, whether we be able to understand that doctrine in its depth or not, the Lord, who revealed it, knows his own meaning. Observe what he considers is its tendency, and to what purpose he applied it. He gives no countenance to the dilemma, suggested sometimes in sadness and sometimes in scorn: " I am either chosen, or I am not: if I am chosen, I shall be saved, and so need not exert myself; and if I am not chosen, I cannot be saved, whatever exertion I may make." Whatever the doctrine of election, as revealed in Scripture, may mean, it does not mean that. Oh, the Divine simplicity of the Word of God ! "Speak; for I have much people in this city." This prescience, instead of suppressing effort, is given as the encouragement to exertion. And Paul understood his Lord. The intimation that a multitude of the Corinthians would certainly be saved, spurred him on to instant and persevering labor in the gospel, that thereby he might save some. Let the doctrine be understood as the Lord then gave it, and as his servant then received it, and instead of placing a millstone on the shoulders of a missionary, it will take a millstone off.

"People " here is the exact equivalent of the term employed throughout the Old Testament to designate

Israel the chosen nation. This people is now no longer Abraham's seed according to the flesh; it is a community gathered from all kindreds and tongues, knit into a new brotherhood by faith in Christ. As the Lord had warned Paul at Jerusalem that the Jews would reject the gospel, he warns him at Corinth that the Greeks would receive it. The promise is transferred from a particular family to believers of every land.

The apostle "was not disobedient to the heavenly vision;" he continued there a year and six months, which, with his views of life and work, must have seemed to him a lengthened sojourn.

It was because his hands were full and his gains great that he remained so long in one place. I do not venture to say that we should exactly, in this matter, follow the apostle's example; but I do venture to say that we should not exactly reverse it. If a minister should occupy one place for a lifetime, precisely because he was altogether unsuccessful, it would be a melancholy reversal of apostolic practice. The Church would be stronger in our day if the rule were, that those laborers who fail to "get gain" in one city, should quickly move on to another.

In this history there is no account in detail of Paul's labors in Corinth. We know, however, from hints given elsewhere (1 Cor. i. 2, 26–28; vi. 9–11), that he materially changed his method. In particular, he ceased to frame his address so as to suit the habits of the Greek philosophers, and simply told the story of the cross. This change might be due to a combination of two causes; he might think that his comparative failure at Athens did not encourage him to persevere in the plan he adopted there and he might also find that busy merchants of Corinth required a simpler and more direct treatment than the literary circles of Athens.

While Gallio represented the Roman Emperor as Governor of Achaia, the Jewish inhabitants of the city concocted a criminal accusation against Paul, and followed it up with tumultuous demonstrations. It was precisely thus that the Jews of Jerusalem dealt with Paul's Master under the government of Pilate. By the combined action of fanatical Jews and a heathen ruler, the Lord was put to death; how shall Paul, in similar circumstances, escape a similar issue ? How shall the promise, " No man shall set on thee to hurt thee," be fulfilled now ?

If Gallio should vacillate and yield like Pilate, the missionary's life might indeed be spared for the time, for he could again exercise his privilege as a Roman citizen: he might have appealed to Cæsar. But this would have put a stop to his preaching in Corinth, and how then could the " much people " be won to Christ ? The time was not yet. The Lord hath need of this missionary for a while in Greece and Asia before he is sent to Rome.

How then was the promise of preservation fulfilled to Paul ? Through the personal character of the proconsul Gallio. Some clear notes of this man's history and disposition have been handed down to us. He received this name through adoption into the family of one Gallio, a rhetorician. His brother was Seneca the philosopher. He was a man of singular gentleness and amiability. His brother writes of him in terms of the most admiring affection. His health was feeble: he left Corinth sick, declaring that his illness was due to the climate of that region. His brother Seneca soon after fell a martyr to Nero's cruelty; and there is a tradition that Gallio himself ultimately shared the same fate.

The Jews had obtained from the government a legal license and protection for their religion; and they hoped that on their complaint the preaching of Paul would be suppressed by the magistrate. They stated their case before the proconsul's tribunal; but when Paul, in turn, was about to speak in his own defence, the judge intimated to him that no reply was necessary. He would not enter into the case on its merits. He would dismiss it without argument as incompetent. If it had been any matter of civil right, he would have tried the case, and pronounced judgment; but as it related only to different views of the Jewish religion, he declined to interfere. It did not lie within his jurisdiction.

Gallio seems to have seen pretty clearly the distinction which puzzles many legal and legislative heads in our day between things civil and things sacred— between that which touches a citizen in person and property, and that which lies between a man's conscience and God. His refusal immediately afterwards to interfere when the Jews beat the ruler of their own synagogue in his presence, I rather think is not really inconsistent with this view; for it is altogether probable that the beating was only a formal affair, intended not to punish Sosthenes, who was their own rabbi, but to draw the governor out of his neutrality by a sort of trick.

How great the difference between Pilate and Gallio! And how great issues, in the purposes of God, depended on that difference! Pilate was a cold-blooded, selfish man; he was consequently a weathercock when the storm arose and beat upon him from opposite directions in quick succession. But he settled down at last on the point to which he was driven by the popular breeze, and a selfish regard for his own interests. Gallio, on the contrary, was a man at once just and gentle and unselfish. He was proof alike against the legal pleas and the insurrectionary violence of the Jews. He saw through them, and despised them. He would not suppress Paul's free speech to please his fanatical adversaries. He did what he believed right, without considering what it might cost him.

If Gallio, instead of Pilate, had been proconsul in Judæa when the priests conspired to put Jesus to death, what would have been the result? But we need not speculate. I have put the question in order to intimate that it should not get an answer. Christ, our Passover, was sacrificed for us. He offered himself: and all things conspired to fulfil his great design. If it had been his will to avoid the cross and leave mankind to perish, he could have placed a Gallio on Pilate's judgment-seat.

Paul and Apollos
(Acts 18:18-28)

"And Paul after this tarried there yet a good while, and then took his leave of the brethren, and sailed thence into Syria, and with him Priscilla and Aquila; having shorn his head in Cenchrea: for he had a vow," etc.

UNDER cover of this providential deliverance the missionaries were enabled to prosecute their work until a Church was organized in Corinth. Then Paul took leave of the brethren,—perhaps of Timothy and Silas, as well as of the native converts. His work in Europe for that time was accomplished. Four Churches had been founded. He had completed a square in the Roman provinces of Macedonia and Greece. There stands the "Quadrilateral,"—Philippi, Thessalonica, Berea, and Corinth,—erected on the soil of Europe, and manned by soldiers of Jesus Christ, who will hold it for him against all assaults. The true Heir of the world is infeoffed now in possession of its brightest continent. Here already in germ dwell the ruling race. Here the plenipotentiary of the Great King has planted the royal standard, and although there may be many recedings and advancings, as in a prolonged battle, it may be assumed that the Lord will find that signal still floating when he comes again.

Paul "took leave" of his friends at Corinth. Though a strong man, he was also a tender one. Tears fell on the shore at Cenchrea that day, as afterwards at Miletus. Although this apostle seemed to be a man of iron when endurance for the sake of the gospel was required, he manifested an almost feminine softness in his intercourse with those who loved him. No letter that I am acquainted with, either ancient or modern, contains such a list of special and distinguishing love-messages as the Epistle to the Romans. The Jewish-Christian couple with whom he lodged and labored in Corinth accompanied him in his journey. Besides their desire to continue longer in the company of their instructor, they may have found that their trade could be more advantageously prosecuted in Asia, the seat of the manufacture.

I do not think that much importance should be attached to the fact, incidentally mentioned here, that he had his head shorn in Cenchrea, before embarking, on account of a vow. Paul's idea of liberty under the gospel did not go the length of forbidding liberty. He bore witness that those who made any of these observances their righteousness before God, shut themselves out from Christ: but when any one was justified through faith in the Redeemer, Paul and his fellow-apostles allowed the convert unlimited liberty to observe or not observe the Jewish ceremonial. It is pleasant to suppose that Paul himself would rejoice to practice occasionally some of these rites, now that he knew their typical meaning. He had often toiled through them when they were to him a dead letter: I could conceive that it might be a refreshment to him to observe some of the old ordinances after they had become to him spirit and life through faith in Jesus.

We have much to learn yet in the matter of the liberty which the Gospel brings. We have an inveterate tendency to lay bonds on ourselves and our neighbors, where Christ meant that we should be free. The tightness of this binding confines and weakens the life. The principle of the rule laid down regarding the second marriage of a widow might be extended so as to reach many other cases; "She is at liberty; only in the Lord."

"He came to Ephesus." Corinth and Ephesus were the great commercial centres of Greece and Asia, the New York and Liverpool of those times and regions. Cicero made the passage by sea in fifteen days, but he considered the voyage a long one: thirteen days were occupied in the return.

On his arrival at the city Paul separated from his fellow-travellers, and instantly began his work, in the usual way, by reasoning with the Jews in the synagogue. His ministry at Ephesus on this occasion, however, was very brief. Determined, for some reason not explained, to be at Jerusalem during the approaching feast, probably Pentecost, he resisted the entreaties of his friends, and took ship for Cæsarea.

He reached Jerusalem according to his plan, but the record is silent as to his occupation and experiences there. Did he call the Christians together, and " rehearse " all that the Lord had done by him among the Gentiles ? Did he make a pilgrimage to Calvary ? Did he stand and weep on the spot where Stephen died ? We do not know: not one word of information is given on these subjects. Probably no result bearing on the kingdom sprang from that visit to Jerusalem; and the Spirit, not ministering to our curiosity, passes it over in silence. To Antioch again the attention of the reader is directed, for that great capital had now become the point of departure and return for the missionaries of the cross.

Paul did not retrace his steps to Antioch in order to remain there. After getting and giving refreshment through intercourse with the Church for a time, he set out on another missionary tour. Nor did he on this occasion take a new route. He traversed Asia Minor westward on the track of his own former journey. He revisited the Churches that he had formerly planted. To cherish and instruct and edify young and feeble believers is recognized as worthy occupation for an apostle, even although the work of bringing in the heathen should be for a time postponed on account of it. The little ones of the family are dear to the Master and therefore dear to all his servants.

Incidentally we learn (1 Cor. xvi. 1) that on this journey he requested contributions for the poor Christians in Jerusalem. This is at least one fruit of his brief visit to that city. Like his Lord, he went about doing good.

Here the history leaves Paul for awhile, and introduces some things that happened at Ephesus in his absence. Apollos, a Jew of Alexandria, intellectually trained in the celebrated schools of his native city, learned and accepted the gospel through a true but defective ministry. This man came to Ephesus, and began to preach with great acceptance and power. He only knew the testimony borne to Christ by John the Baptist: but he pressed the truth, as far as he knew it, with great eloquence and great zeal. Priscilla and Aquila heard him, and discerned his spirit. At a glance they saw three things: 1st, that he was a true disciple of Christ; 2nd, that he had great power as a reasoner and orator; and, 3rd, that he was defective in his knowledge of the gospel. Here was an opportunity for the tent-makers. They could not teach in the synagogue; but they could instil their knowledge privately into the mind of Apollos. They could not preach; but they could make a preacher.

Here we discover the reason why the Lord in his providence, when this pair were expelled from Rome, guided their steps to Corinth, where they learned the gospel from Paul; and then induced them to go with Paul to Ephesus, and remain in that city after their great instructor left it. The same Divine care that brought Philip and the Ethiopian prince together in the desert, brought the tent-makers and Apollos together in the city of Ephesus. He was a capacious vessel: and they possessed that word of the Lord with which the vessel must be charged. As soon as they met, they imparted, and he received, what was lacking to make him an able minister of Jesus Christ. This meeting which took place on earth was arranged in heaven. It is not in man that walketh to direct his steps; He who directs them hath done all things well. "Whoso is wise and will observe these things, even he shall understand the loving kindness of the Lord." When disciples of Christ, coming from different directions, meet and hold intercourse, let them watch and pray. They may expect to give or to get: perhaps they may both give and get reciprocally.

After profiting by his intercourse with Aquila and Priscilla, Apollos crossed over into the province of Achaia, and was of great use to the infant Churches there. Paul had planted; but he was not able to remain long beside his work. The plants in the scorching of that season were ready to die: Apollos arrived opportunely to water them. Paul planted the Church in Corinth; Apollos watered it; and God gave the increase.

Convincing and Persuading
(Acts 19:8)

" And he went into the synagogue, and spake boldly for the space of three months, disputing and persuading the things concerning the kingdom of God."

WHILE Apollos was ministering in Corinth, Paul, in fulfilment of his promise, returned to Ephesus. He had hastened eastward to Palestine, landed at Cæsarea, hurried up to Jerusalem, and saluted the brethren there. Thence he travelled quickly northward to Antioch. From Antioch he started on his third missionary circle. Passing through Asia Minor, doing a little everywhere, but remaining long nowhere, he again came to Ephesus, the principal city of the whole region, on the western coast. It was the entrepot between Greece and Asia.

The missionaries of the earliest age always found their way to the great cities. It was a wise method. The cities were the pulsing hearts of their several provinces; and principles deposited there soon spread by natural arteries to all parts of the land. The missionaries skilfully seized the chief centres of influence and power.

On his arrival at Ephesus, he found a little company of disciples in the heart of the great heathen city. All the Christianity of the place gravitated toward Paul. Like draws to like. The apostle in Ephesus was like a magnetic bar thrust into a great heap of rubbish: forthwith all the filings of real steel that existed in the miscellaneous mass were found adhering to its sides. The attraction and cohesion of kindred spirits is a beautiful and beneficent law of the new kingdom.

We discover in this far-off region some direct results of the Baptist's preaching in the wilderness of Judæa. Some of those who heard that preacher must have emigrated before the death of Christ and the descent of the Spirit at Pentecost. They had beheld, at John's invitation, the Lamb of God, and believed to the saving of their souls; but they had not obtained the fuller knowledge of the gospel which came after the resurrection to the chosen witnesses. To these men, and in answer to their prayers for greater light, the apostle of the Gentiles was sent, as a vessel, bearing the name of Christ more fully revealed. As Philip was sent to the desert of Gaza with the water of life to the thirsting Ethiop, Paul was sent on the same errand to those twelve men and their companions who panted for the living water in the desert-place of a huge idolatrous city. The Lord knoweth them that are his, and how to find them out. He will never leave them, nor forsake them.

He entered the synagogue as usual, and "spake boldly for the space of three months." In this Book much is made of boldness. The early disciples felt their need of it, longed for it, prayed for it, and obtained it. Courage displayed by the preacher implies a cruel persecution by the enemies of the cross. Strange that when a message from heaven is about to be proclaimed, great courage should be requisite in the herald who bears it. The message is peace and pardon. Surely a servant of the government may risk himself in the very heart of a convict prison alone, if he is the bearer of a royal pardon for all the inmates. In such a case, it would not be necessary to look out for a man of rare courage, who might dare to carry the proclamation to the convicts. Give him but the message of free pardon, and he may go in unarmed with all safety, like Daniel in the den of lions.

When Christ himself came to the world—the great convict prison of the universe—came the ambassador from God, bringing peace, they said, This is the heir; come, let us kill him. He came unto his own, and his own received him not; and the servant is not greater than his Lord.

Do preachers of the gospel need courage still? Not in the same sense and of the same kind. They are not put in prison for faithfulness in declaring the whole counsel of God. But as long as the carnal mind is enmity against God, there must be opposition to the gospel from some quarter. You might as well expect to escape from the law of gravitation when you travel to China, as expect that, when so many centuries have run their course, courage is no longer necessary to a preacher of the cross. The Jews opposed the gospel at an earlier stage. They opposed the publication of the doctrine: we allow the doctrine to pass freely from the preacher's lips, but do not permit the kingdom to come in power over our hearts and lives. If we should denounce as boldly that form of opposition to Christ which is rife amongst ourselves, as the apostles denounced that which prevailed in their day, perhaps we should taste some of their experience.

In those days the testing-point lay higher up; in our days it lies lower down. Then the real struggle occurred at the profession; now it occurs at the practice. The cross then was to own themselves the disciples of Christ; it was this step that cost: the cross with us is not there; it is easy for us to own his name; the difficulty lies in so following him that our lives shall be a continual reproof. Their temptation was to fall into the track of the first son whom the father ordered to work in his vineyard—to say, "I will not." Our temptation is to copy the answer of the second, "I go, sir;" and then to spend the day in seeking our own pleasures. The stress for them lay in the promise; the stress for us lies in the performance. If modern ministers were as bold in demanding performance, as the apostles were in demanding profession, perhaps their course would not flow so smoothly.

The theme of the preacher was "the kingdom of God." The preaching of these men was a new thing in the world. They were not contented with a niche in the temple for another idol, a day in the calendar for an additional saint. They demanded the overthrow of all idols, and the establishment of another throne in their stead. They proposed a King who should be absolute and sole.

The things that Paul preached did, no doubt, concern the kingdom in its final glory; but this kingdom in heaven afar, he uniformly presented as the legitimate and certain issue of a kingdom now established in believing hearts. First, the kingdom of heaven in you; and next, you in the kingdom of heaven. Let Christ reign in you now, and you will reign with him in that day.

If I leave him standing at the door knocking throughout the day of grace, he will leave me standing at the
door knocking when the day of grace is done.

Mark the manner of the apostolic preaching: "disputing and persuading." The first makes the matter
clear to the intellect, and the second makes it powerful on the will. The first enables you to know the
true, and the second induces you to do the right.
These are the two elements of which all right preaching consists. The proportions may vary indefinitely
with circumstances; but every sermon should contain,
in some measure, both constituents.

On the one hand, a discourse should not be merely
exposition of doctrine; it ought to persuade as well as
unfold. The preacher may not meet the hearers again,
until he is called to give an account. He ought to beseech them to be reconciled unto God. On the other
hand, mere exhortation will not suffice. God, who
has given us understanding, expects us to exercise it
in the highest of all concerns. He who would persuade
his brethren to serve the Lord, should endeavor to
convince them that it is a reasonable service.

Disputing means reasoning; but this does not imply
that religion is founded on reason. Reason is the builder,
not the foundation. Reason constructs religion, not
on itself, but on the Scriptures. There is a good deal
of pretence on this subject at the present day. Those
who affect to be philosophers, freely insinuate that
religious people put reason aside when they approach
the spiritual sphere, and proceed upon faith instead.
This is a false issue. Reason and faith are not antagonistic, so that, in accepting the one you discard the
other. Reason is no more discarded from religion than
from philosophy. In former times human reason occupied too exalted a place in philosophy. It was
made the foundation; and the structure, consequently,
crumbled and fell. Bacon introduced a radical reform.
He removed reason from its usurped position as a foundation, and gave it the place of operator. For basis he
substituted ascertained facts; on these, as a foundation,
reason was permitted to rear her fabric, and a goodly
palace meets our view to-day as the result of this new
method. By the Reformation a parallel process was

established in the sphere of religion. As the facts of the material or mental creation constitute the basis on which reason builds a philosophy, so the doctrines and facts of revelation constitute the basis on which reason builds a theology. On both spheres reason is the builder, not the basis.

In regard to the place of reason in the domain of religion, two opposite extremes exist. Positivism makes reason everything; Popery makes it nothing. The one will make it master; the other will not permit it even to serve. The Protestant principle stands midway between these extremes. It permits and demands the free exercise of human reason, but limits it in this domain to what is revealed in the Word: precisely as the Baconian philosophy permits and demands the exercise of human reason in the sphere of philosophy, but limits it to the observed facts and laws of nature.

After expounding the truth, the preacher *persuades* his auditors to comply with it. Exposition is necessary but not sufficient; without it you must fail, but even with it you may fail. Though the understanding be convinced, the will may remain perverse. A man may be convinced that God is lovely, and yet not love God. You may own that Christ is offered to you, and yet not accept Christ. You may know truth, and yet follow lies. This is a fact in history; it cannot reasonably be denied, and should not be carelessly overlooked. It is a startling and solemnizing discovery. Paul was greatly moved when he found " a law in his members" warring against the law of God which was in his mind. His understanding was carried; but his heart still resisted. In his own experience he found out the power which was able to control the will and mould the life. The love of Christ constrained him, when all other motives failed. This power, accordingly, he was always ready to apply when he found reasoning to be impotent. He will beseech his Roman correspondents to yield themselves a living sacrifice, holy and acceptable to God; but he beseeches them " by the mercies of God." He depends on this weight to overcome the inertia of the carnal mind, and set heart and life in motion like a running stream in the service of God and man.

The two great constituents of the Christian ministry are to convince and persuade; to enlighten the understanding, and to win souls.

The Strong Man Cast Out by the Stronger
(Acts 19:9-17)

*" But when divers were hardened, and believed not, but spake evil
of that way before the multitude, he departed from them, and separated
the disciples, disputing daily in the school of one Tyrannus. And this
continued by the space of two years; so that all they which dwelt in Asia
heard the word of the Lord Jesus, both Jews and Greeks. And God
wrought special miracles by the hands of Paul:" etc.*

JESUS, preached by Paul in Ephesus, did not bring
peace to its people. In the first instance there was
a sword. "Divers were hardened and believed not."
These Jews spoke evil of "the way." Christ announced himself as the way, and the only way, to the
Father; but when he came to his own, they received
him not. They would have none of him. The servant
retired from those who rejected his Master. He obtained accommodation in the school of one Tyrannus,
and taught there for two years. It is not certain
whether Tyrannus was a Jew or Greek. In either
case his academy was independent of the synagogue,
and thus he was enabled to shelter the preacher of the
cross.

All that dwelt in Asia heard the gospel. The people from the surrounding country and the adjacent
towns took an opportunity of hearing the new doctrines when they came to the capital on business.
This method prevailed in the times of the Reformation. The country people, after having sold their
produce in the market-square, crept into the neighboring church and heard the Scriptures expounded.
Then they returned to their homes with both gains—
one in their hearts, and the other in their pockets.

Thus the Word had free course, and was glorified throughout the neighboring provinces.

Besides the preaching of the Word, special miracles were wrought in Ephesus. The passage is somewhat obscure. There may have been some testimony given to Paul's word in that heathen city, on account of the magicians who plied their craft there, similar to the signs wrought by Aaron in presence of the Egyptian wonder-workers. In any case, this was not the ordinary experience of Paul. It was peculiar and extraordinary. An exceptional testimony is vouchsafed to him once in exceptional circumstances, and it is wide as the world apart from the degrading and tricky traffic in spurious relics, which has become a permanent institution of the Papacy.

As the Egyptian magicians in some form imitated the signs wrought by Moses, the soothsayers of Ephesus—in this case disreputable Jews—attempted to work wonders in imitation of Paul by pronouncing the name of Jesus. There is much material for thought in the answer given by the possessed maniac to these sorcerers: "Jesus I know, and Paul I know; but who are ye?" It is the same in kind with the response of the Pythoness at Philippi. It is a remarkable declaration. It is not only out of the mouth of babes and sucklings that the Lord can draw forth his own praise: he can make the wicked praise him, as well as the weak. Such a testimony was borne by an unclean spirit to the Lord himself: " I know thee, who thou art, the Holy One of God."

An application of this Scripture is possible to our own day and our own circumstances. The evil spirit seems to possess, and energize, and weild at will, certain classes and sections of the people. They seem like the man who cut himself and wore no clothes, and dwelt among the tombs. They are a torment to themselves, and a terror to their neighbors. They might have clothes, and food, and home; but they wildly cast all these away, and live like the beasts.

The evil spirits of the present time, like those of Paul's day, are subject only to one power. They do not give way before reading and writing. New houses and good wages will not drive them out. Even the prison and the gibbet fail to scare them. A goodly number of the legion have in our sight been cast out; but the work is done by the name of Jesus. Many of them are even now sitting at his feet, clothed and in their right mind. There is no healing for these wounds of the body politic except in the gospel of Christ, borne to the hearts and homes of the outcasts by the self-sacrificing love of them that believe.

None other than He who made the world at first can make it new again. "Jesus I know:" this witness is true, even though the evil spirit utter it. Yes, prince of this world, thou knowest him to be the Holy One of God. Thou hast felt him crushing thy head each time that a slave of sin has been ransomed and renewed. Thou, strong man, holding a human soul captive, bound in the thongs of its own lusts, hast felt the power of the Stranger, wrenching one by one a multitude of victims from thy grasp. Thou knowest, too, this Jesus in his mercy to men; for often, when thou hast set a snare for a believer's feet and made him stumble, and when there was a shout in the camp of the adversary as if one of Christ's saved were lost again, thou hast been compelled to relax thy hold and yield up the backslider to the Lord that bought him at the first, and has healed again his backsliding.

Nor is it only Jesus the Saviour whom the evil spirits know and acknowledge; they know in the same way the ministers whom he employs. "Jesus I know, and Paul I know." Christ has personally ascended; it is by his servants, as his instruments, now that he reaches down to the lost and saves them. The powers of darkness know all who yield themselves instruments of righteousness unto God. In this respect the servants share the Master's lot: "If they have persecuted me, they will also persecute you."

The first Atlantic cable was broken and lost. It sank to the bottom where the sea was several miles deep. Though bouys were left at the spot, they drifted away. Who shall now find the spot in that pathless ocean where the precious line is lying; and who shall bring it up, although the place were known?

They find the spot, not by marks on the sea, but by the lights that are fixed in heaven. Hovering over it, they drop their grappling-irons, and pay out line till they strike the ground. They feel in that dark abyss —feel for the lost. By the instrument sent down they grasp the broken cable and haul it up. They bring the dead to life, and through it thought throbs again in pulses of unseen fire from shore to shore.

That lost line seems like a human soul in its sin. This creature that God has made for himself, and qualified to receive and transmit his own Divine will, has fallen, has fallen. The prey seems secure in the jaws of the pit. But down in that abyss an instrument of salvation touches the lost. The powers of darkness who thought their victim secure, learned to know both the Living One on high who planned redemption, and the instrument which he employed in his work. "Jesus I know, and Paul I know."

Lend me your imagination for a moment, that by aid of it I may go yet one step further on the line of this analogy. Suppose that broken, lost line a conscious intelligence, cut off from all communion with his kind in that dark abyss despairing. It is dark; there is none who can reach him to save. Lost, for ever. Now imagine that this despairing creature feels some instrument touching him from above—touching him with intelligence, power, and love—touching him with intent to save. Suppose he feels himself grasped, and drawn up —up, and ever up, through the dark waters. At length light begins to dawn overhead, and increases as he rises, like the morning. At length he emerges into the light of heaven, is restored to life, and enters the society of his kind again.

Such is the lost estate of the sinful; and such the redemption that Jesus brings.

The Two Dimensions - Breadth and Depth
(Acts 19:20)

" So mightily grew the word of God and prevailed."—ACTS XIX. 20.

CHRISTIANITY was new in those days. The dew of its youth was on it; the experience of its disciples accordingly was fresh and tender. If their knowledge was less extensive than ours, their life was perhaps more vigorous, and their love more warm. The faith of those ancient believers excelled in directness and simplicity; when it had less of human attainment, it had more of Divine power.

It is better to have a faith which you cannot explain, than to be able to explain a faith which you do not enjoy. Here is a philosopher who understands thoroughly the circulation of the blood, but whose blood, through lack of vital vigor in the heart, is almost standing stagnant in his veins; and there is a little child, whose blood bounds through his body like a mountain stream at every pulse, but who does not know that the blood is circulating in his veins. The philosopher would fain change places with the child. Give me at all hazards the spiritual life, and let me add a scientific theology if I can. It is better to believe in Christ to the saving of the soul, although you could not demonstrate the nature and origin of saving faith, than to possess the power of analyzing faith so as to resolve it into its elements, while you do not yourself believe to the saving of your soul.

Faith in those days seems to have been simple, and direct, and strong, like life in childhood. Such was the experience of the Ethiopian treasurer. He thirsted for the redemption of Christ, as dry land thirsts for rain from heaven; on his thirsting soul the water of life was poured from the Scriptures through Philip's ministry; the thirsty traveller drank the living water, and went on his way rejoicing.

The instrument which these primitive preachers

wielded was "the Word of God." They had no confidence in the enticing words of man's wisdom. In
simple faith they set forth Him who is the Word of
life, and looked to the spirit for the quickening power.
This method was successful. Great results immediately appeared.

The terms employed to express these results are
worthy of special attention. The Word "grew and
prevailed." The work of these missionaries, like that
of the husbandman, has two dimensions—breadth and
depth. One measurement indicates the superficial extent of the field, and another the perpendicular depth
fo the furrow. The gospel, through the preaching of
those ministers, reached a great multitude, and it
penetrated the joints and marrow of each. The Word
is said to "grow" when it spreads widely in the world,
and to "prevail" when it makes all things new in the
heart and life of a believer.

The Word of the Lord *grew*. The mustard-seed
dropped into the ground, became a spreading tree.
In the hands of Paul and his associates, it soon overshadowed the philosophy of Greece, and the arms of
Rome.

For a long period during the Middle Ages the Word
of the Lord did not in this sense grow. A very general corruption overlaid and choked the Word in
Europe, and the power of Mahomet quenched its light
in vast regions of the East. After the Reformation,
the Word, brought up from its grave again, lived and
grew afresh. In our own day, it displays all the energy
of its youth. Its way has been better prepared in recent times, and accordingly it has reached many regions
which the feet of the apostles never trod. The Lord
reigneth. He has remembered Zion, and is healing
her breaches. He is building up the walls of his own
Jerusalem; children are playing again on her long-
desolate streets. A good time has come, and a better time is coming. Those who have lived during the
earlier half of the present century have seen great
things, and those who live out the latter half will see
greater.

The word of the Lord *prevailed*. It put forth a
power which penetrated every obstacle, and bore its

message home. A thing which is in its own nature beneficent may be widely diffused, and yet fail to confer a benefit for lack of power to penetrate. Sunlight in summer floods the polar regions in continuous day, and yet no grass grows green—no harvest field grows yellow—under its beautiful beams. The light *grows* there into an immense diffusion, but does not *prevail* to melt the ice and fructify the soil. Times have passed over our own beloved country in which the gospel was like the light of a polar summer—shining everywhere, but melting nowhere. And the same phenomenon may be observed at present in some districts of Europe that are distinguished as Protestant. Men may be proud of Christianity, and yet ashamed of Christ. Our lot has fallen in more pleasant places; we have obtained a better heritage. God has in mercy granted to his Church a little reviving. Besides the growth of the Word in its diffusion over the land and among the nations, there has been a prevailing of the Word in the conviction and the conversion of sinners.

May the kingdom come not in word only, but also in power. We have precious seed, and there are many sowers; it remains that we give heed to the ancient prophet's specific exhortation: "Break up your fallow ground, and sow not among thorns."

"So mightily grew the Word of God and prevailed." The form of the expression directs us to the preceding verses for an enumeration of the effects actually produced at that time by the preaching of the Word.

1. "Fear fell on them all." Both in the nature of the case, and in the experience of the Church, this result is first in order. The sense of need is an essential preparation for the reception of the remedy. The immediate means of producing fear are various. The earthquake that shook the prison first alarmed the jailer; the crowing of the cock was the spark that fell on Peter's heart and set it on fire. At one time it may be some external danger, and at another a still, small inner voice; but in all cases of conversion at first or reviving afterwards, a fear springs in the conscience, and constrains the convicted to flee for refuge to the hope set before him. That fear is blessed, which, like the approach of the wolf, compels the wandering sheep

to return to the fold. When heads that heretofore were held high in pride begin to droop on sobbing breasts; when groanings which cannot be articulately uttered begin to rend the frame, as the thaw of spring rends the ice which spanned the river; when the pent-up agony of the inner man gathers itself up at last into the cry, What must I do to be saved?—the fear is blessed, not for its own sake as a result, but for what it promises as a symptom.

2. "The name of the Lord Jesus was magnified." This is a sure mark of a genuine and thorough spiritual progress. It is dangerous when a religious movement brings men's names into great prominence. It is true that those who preach with much success must endure a large measure of publicity. The city that is set on a hill cannot be hid. But neither the successful preacher nor his friends for him should court this distinction. Human hearts are in their own nature all too liable to spontaneous combustion; no wise man will do anything to fan the flame either in his own or his neighbor's breast. The preacher who on this occasion proclaimed the gospel with success, has taught us by his own example to handle roughly this tendency to idolatrous adulation. "I am of Paul," said one large, very evangelical section of Christians in a certain Church; but this minister was not pleased to see his own name placarded in too large letters on the walls. I think I see him breaking forth like a tempest upon those too zealous admirers. Extending his frame, and raising his arm, and knitting his brow, the fire flashing from his eyes as he spoke, he hurled at the obsequious partisans the piercing challenge,—"*Was Paul crucified for you?*"

Convicts and converts should enter their closets and shut the doors, and forgetting the preachers of the Word, occupy themselves with the Christ whom they preached. When the stars grow bright, it is a proof that the sun is down; while the sun is shining, the stars, though still in their places, cannot be seen. Let Jesus be magnified and all instruments will be lost in his light.

3. "Many that believed came, and showed their deeds," etc. I assume that this confession of sin to

men was the external accompaniment of confession in secret to the Lord. Confession of sin to one another is a suitable body; but if be not animated by the living soul of confession to God, it is nothing but a carcass.

They who believed, confessed. They did not confess until they believed. You do not throw away one portion until you begin to get hold of a better. The prodigal, I suppose, kept his rags closely round his person as long as they constituted his only covering; it is when he gets the fair robe from his father's hand that he casts the filthy garments passionately away. You will never show your own deeds and count them vile either before God or man, until you begin to see the way of pardon.

When Christ forgives a soul, he gets that soul's secrets; when he gets a soul's secrets, he forgives that soul's sins.

4. "They who used curious arts, brought their books and burned them." The converts on this occasion were of the baser sort. The apostle had disturbed a nest of fortune-tellers and sorcerers that were burrowing under the shadow of Diana's temple, and preying on the dissipated multitudes of Ephesus. Where the carcass is, there will the eagles be gathered together. To the poor the gospel is preached. The Master received sinners; his servants followed his steps. The most damaged specimens of humanity will serve the Lord's purpose when they have been renewed into his own likeness. Manufacturers of paper do not reject the raw material because it is torn and filthy. These sorcerers who plied their disreputable trade in the precincts of a heathen temple, will be beautiful when they are new creatures in Christ.

How quickly the tree, when it is made good, brings forth its pleasant fruit! They gave up their trade and their stock in trade as soon as in the light of life they saw it to be sinful. Their right arm they resolutely cut off as soon as they perceive that it injures themselves and dishonors the Lord. Would that all the Pharisees of the modern Church should, in this respect, follow the footsteps of these publicans and sinners as they entered the kingdom of heaven.

The Uproar in Ephesus
(Acts 19:21-41)

" After these things were ended, Paul purposed in the spirit, when he had passed through Macedonia and Achaia, to go to Jerusalem, saying, After I have been there, I must also see Rome. So he sent into Macedonia two of them that ministered unto him, Timotheus and Erastus; but he himself stayed in Asia for a season. And the same time there arose no small stir about that way," etc.

THE sphere of the Christian Church is rapidly enlarging; and the ideas of the great missionary are enlarging along with it. Ephesus is now a station in the middle of his field. He proposes to make a journey eastward to Jerusalem, and afterwards to visit Rome. "I must also see Rome:" yes, Paul, this is a necessity in the plan of Providence; but thou knowest not yet in what capacity thou shalt travel to the capital. What thou knowest not now, thou shalt know hereafter. Sufficient unto the day is the evil thereof. If we could see as far before us, as by memory we can see behind, our courage would fail, and we should faint by the way. He who leads us, sees his own way: it is better for us to be led blindfold.

At this time a great commotion occurred in Ephesus, which the historian has minutely related. There arose no small stir about *the way*,—that is, about the gospel which Paul had preached. The *emeute* did not spring directly from the fanaticism of the idolaters; it had a baser origin. Certain artificers of the city had been accustomed to carry on a profitable trade in the manufacture of small models in silver, both of the temple and the image of the goddess. These men perceived that the general acceptance of Paul's doctrine would inevitably drain the sources of their trade. To save their own profits, therefore, they endeavored to crush or banish the foreign preachers by a popular tumult.

The temple of Diana at Ephesus held a high place among heathen shrines. It had a romantic history.

It was built on artificial foundations in a marsh below the city, as a security against earthquakes. The sumptuous edifice was destroyed by fire in 356 B. C. A fanatic named Hesostratus confessed that he set it on fire in order to make his own name immortal. It was destroyed the same night in which Alexander the Great was born. It was restored in still greater splendor; the dimensions of the new temple were 425 feet by 220. It had 127 columns, 60 feet in height. This second edifice was standing in all its glory at the date of Paul's visit.

It was consecrated to Diana, one of the twelve greater deities of the Greeks. She was worshipped as a huntress, and also as the moon. The month of May was sacred to her, and was called Diana's month. It is abundantly obvious that a great portion of Romish Mariolatry was borrowed in a dark age from the worship of Diana. The appellation Queen of Heaven, and the designation of May as Mary's month, are evidently old pagan rites, repainted and regilded for modern use.

A mob of interested artificers, instigated and headed by Demetrius the silversmith, attempted to suppress by violence the liberty of the gospel in Ephesus. The oration of this demagogue is in outline preserved. It is an interesting antique. Its arguments are skilfully constructed. They are well fitted to gain the object which the speaker had in view. Not relying on one ground, he cunningly groups two or three reasons together in order to enlist a greater number on his side. The craftsmen are reminded that the prevalence of the gospel means loss of employment, and starvation for themselves and their families: the zealous idolaters are told that the temple of the great goddess will be despised: and the patriotic citizens are warned that with the decadence of the temple, the supremacy which Ephesus enjoyed among the neighboring provinces will certainly disappear. The prosperity of the city depended on the popularity of the Diana-worship. The religious capital of Asia will dwindle into insignificance if Paul's doctrine prevail.

This inflammatory address was successful. The meeting was stirred into rage. Indications appear in the narrative that the preachers were gaining ad-

herents among the cultivated classes. The town-clerk
and some of the Asiarchs were, if not positively believers in Paul's doctrine, at least favorable to free
discussion.

After the speech of Demetrius, the multitude rushed
tumultuously into the theatre. Ancient theatres were
entirely different in structure from the edifices known
by the same name in modern times and more north-
erly latitudes. They were immense structures shaped
like the hull of a ship, without roof, having a level
space of oval shape at the bottom for the performers,
and seats in tiers for the spectators.

Paul's impulse was to go into the theatre, and speak
in his own defence. His friends, however, by a friendly
constraint prevented him from risking his life in that
excited mob.

A certain Jew, named Alexander, was put forward
by his countrymen to address the crowd. Probably
he was selected as spokesman in order to show the
Greek population that, among Paul's own countrymen
there were many who did not take his part. But whatever may have been the policy of the leaders in select-
ing this man, it signally failed. The people would not
listen; they hooted him down.

This was the commencement of a violent uproar.
For two hours the living contents of the vast amphi-
theatre heaved like the sea in a storm, shouting in
chorus, "Great is Diana of the Ephesians." This extraordinary commotion was at length quelled by the
presence and authority of the town-clerk, a magistrate
who, by right of office, was accustomed to read all
public documents in the assemblies of the people.
Yielding to habit, the assembly settled down into
quietude when this great officer presented himself.
His address was sensible and moderate. He gently
flattered the populace. Having soothed them into a
calmer spirit, he skilfully insinuated some cogent arguments against their riotous proceedings. A plain
hint of possible penal consequences for this outrage on
the liberty of peaceable inhabitants finally brought the
rioters to reason, and the assembly was quietly dismissed.

Some incidental statements and allusions in the

speech of the town-clerk are worthy of attention here. A prevailing tradition that the rude little wooden image preserved in a particular shrine of the temple, had originally fallen down from Jupiter (or the sky, for the same word has both meanings), he skilfully assumes as an acknowledged fact; although it is very doubtful whether this trained official had faith in it. It is a general rule in all forms of idolatry, that those idols are most reverenced that are covered with the rust of antiquity, and encircled with miraculous legends. This seems inconsistent with the apology usually given by Romish controversialists for the veneration of images. They are accustomed to represent that the devotees do not worship the image before which they kneel; but employ it as a help to raise their conceptions to the being whom the image represents. If that were true, the best executed likeness would be most effective in aiding the spirit of devotion. But practically this is not the case. The most ungainly and repulsive representations which enjoy a reputation for sanctity, are frequented in preference to the most perfect results of the sculptor's art. The worshipper is moved by a conception that there is something sacred in the image itself. This is the nature and the fruit of all idolatry. If we disregard the letter of the law, we shall inevitably transgress its spirit: " Thou shalt not bow down thyself to them."

" These men," continues the town-clerk, "are neither robbers of churches, nor blasphemers of your goddess." It would appear from this that Paul had proceeded at Ephesus with the same caution which he had displayed at Athens. He effectually undermined all idolatry by preaching Christ; but he did not fly in the face of what his audience considered sacred. His argument was always grave and considerate. He would not needlessly trample on the prejudices of the heathen.

We obtain here a glimpse of the regular method in which the law was administered in the Roman Empire. The town-clerk was able to say in the public assembly that the Courts of Justice were open, and that every citizen who had a grievance was at liberty to bring his case in a regular way before the judge. The Roman power allowed a large measure of spontaneous action to the municipalities of conquered provinces in the regulation of internal affairs; but they would not tolerate tumults that endangered the public peace. Thus the apostles were again delivered by the legitimate action of a regular government. The powers that be are ordained of God. The shields of the earth are his; and he knows how to throw now one and now another around his servants to preserve their lives for subsequent usefulness. He sits King on all these floods; and will make the tumults of the people turn out for the furtherance of the gospel.

A Communion Sabbath at Troas
(Acts 20:1-12)

"And after the uproar was ceased, Paul called unto him the disciples, and embraced them, and departed for to go into Macedonia. And when he had gone over those parts, and had given them much exhortation, he came into Greece," etc.

"DISCRETION is the better part of valor." Although that proverb is often tauntingly employed in a sinister sense, it contains and conveys a precious practical truth. Valor is often crippled and deprived of its result for want of its "better part." A man who has courage without prudence is apt to throw away his life.

Paul was as remarkable for his caution as for his courage. When duty calls and a grand object may be gained, he will not count his life dear unto himself; but he will count his life very dear both to the Lord and the Church if he can preserve it from needless danger, and so retain it for future use. This is the distinction between a hero and a fanatic. A true hero will preserve his life as far as he can with honor, and will never give it away cheap.

Ordinary opposition from Jews or Gentiles the apostle scarcely regrets. He would rather have waters stirred by such a breeze than waters stagnant, for his great operation as a fisher of men. Accordingly we

learn that " the many adversaries " are reckoned among
the grounds of encouragement to continue his work in
this city. But when such a serious tumult occurs as
that which has just been quelled by the address of the
town-clerk, he considers that he will better serve the
great cause by bending to the blast than by braving it.
He will not, by mere bravado, make the place too hot
for the Christians afterwards. It will be expedient to
retire in the mean time, and allow the troubled sea to
subside.

Besides, his work was done in Ephesus. He had
spent eighteen months almost constantly there. The
seed of the Word had taken root. The tumult was
the evidence and the measure of his success. New
work awaits him in another place. This missionary
must arise and run his race.

He determines to revisit Macedonia, but first there
must be a farewell meeting with the Christians of
Ephesus. " He called the disciples." How the meeting was summoned we do not know, but we know from
all history that amazing powers of intercommunication
exist among a persecuted people. Sufferers are inventive in the matter of signalling to their friends. It has
often puzzled tyrants to comprehend how their victims
obtain information. It appears sometimes as if the
ground were a network of telegraphs, transmitting from
the dungeon the groans of the prisoners. By some
word that passed surely and quickly through the circle
of disciples, all the faithful in the city were convened.
There is no report of Paul's parting address, but it is
certain he would not omit so good an opportunity of
exhorting that infant Church in the heart of a heathen
metropolis. Some burning words would drop from his
lips as he embraced them, one by one, and commended
them to the grace of God. These tender partings are
profitable though painful. They drive home some precious lessons that were lying on the surface and liable
to be rubbed off.

On leaving Ephesus it was his design to go to Macedonia, but there was a long delay ere he reached it.
The history here is a very meagre outline. Materials
exist in the Epistles for filling up the blank, but it will
not be expedient here to gather up the scattered

threads. Let it suffice to mention merely the successive stages without writing down the various references.

From Ephesus he went to Troas, on the western coast of Asia Minor. He meant to remain and establish a Church there; for when he was at that place before, he was hastening over in answer to the call from Macedonia, and could not begin any mission work. Titus had been despatched to Corinth, bearer of the epistle to the Church of that city, and Paul expected his messenger to meet him at Troas with news from the congregation at Corinth. He longed to learn how the letter had been received, and what effects it had produced. We may assume that while he tarried at Troas he watched eagerly every ship that arrived, to learn if Titus were on board. Months passed, and no appearance of Titus. Hope deferred made the heart sick. He had no rest, because the care of the Corinthian Church, with its contentions and schisms, lay like a millstone on his heart. But though sorrowful, he was not idle. He preached in Troas. He found an open door; he planted a Church.

At length, unable to wait longer, he crossed the sea to Macedonia without having obtained news from Corinth. Among the converts at Philippi he was at home again. While he was enjoying there the society of his friends, Titus at last joined him, bringing good news from Corinth. His letter had been received with greater favor than he expected. The divisions were healed, and prosperity restored. The converts acknowledged the great apostle's authority, and submitted themselves to his reproof. This good news from a far country was as cold waters to his thirsty soul. "When we were come into Macedonia our flesh had no rest, but we were troubled on every side; without were fightings, within were fears. Nevertheless God, that comforteth them that are cast down, comforted us by the coming of Titus; and not by his coming only, but by the consolation wherewith he was comforted in you, when he told us your earnest desire, your mourning, your fervent mind toward me ; so that I rejoiced the more " (2 Cor. vii. 5–7).

At last Paul, leaving Macedonia, came himself into Greece. Although it is the country only that is mentioned, it was doubtless chiefly at Corinth that he spent his time. He remained about three months. When his work was accomplished there, he desired to go by sea from Corinth to the East; but having discovered a plot laid by the Jews to assassinate him, he changed his plan, and travelled northward once more into Macedonia.

Seven men, whose names and nations are recorded, accompanied Paul on the journey as delegates from the Christians of various provinces, to present the contributions of the West to the impoverished disciples in Judæa. This deputation was appointed, not merely as bearers of the gift, but mainly to express to the Church in Jerusalem the sympathy of Gentile believers, if so be the two constituents of the Church might be run into one by offices of love, and all jealousies between Jews and Greeks be nipped in the bud. We know that Paul experienced a great desire to be at Jerusalem by the Pentecost, which occurred seven weeks after his departure from Macedonia. He was bringing with him, in these seven delegates, the first-fruits of the Gentiles, a pledge aud foretaste of an abundant harvest. At one Pentecost the Word as a seed had gone forth from Jerusalem, and at another Pentecost the fruit that sprang from that seed shall be brought back. The sower who had gone forth weeping, bearing precious seed, will return rejoicing, bringing his sheaves with him.

The seven delegates crossed the sea to Troas, while Paul and Luke remained for a time at Philippi, probably induced by urgent entreaties of the Christians that he should minister to them at the approaching passover. The ship in which Paul and Luke at last took passage must have been detained by rough weather or other causes to us unknown, as the voyage occupied five days. Having rejoined their comrades at Troas, they remained there another week. There is here a clear trace of Sabbath observance, and that on the first day of the week. They landed on a Monday, the second day of the week, and left on a Monday. The disciples in Troas assembled for public worship and the communion on the first day of the week. Paul preached the evening sermon, and proceeded on his journey next day. Although he was hastening eastward, he must remain in Troas no less than seven days, because, through the disappointing length of the voyage, he did not arrive till the Lord's-day was past. This consecration of the first day was neither Jewish nor pagan; it was distinctively Christian. It is interesting to meet with the institution of the Christian Sabbath very clearly marked in that early age. From that day to this all Christians have agreed to make the day of the Lord's resurrection a day of rest from common labor —a space cleared for communion between the members and their exalted Head.

The case of the young man who, having fallen asleep, fell from a great height, seems to be introduced into the narrative mainly for the purpose of showing the mighty power of God in his restoration. But it reveals incidentally an interesting fact, that the evening sermon on that communion Sabbath was prolonged till midnight. After the assembly was dismissed the preacher needed and obtained refreshing food, and held protracted conversations with inquirers. In this occupation the night was spent, and the earnest groups were surprised by the break of day. Paul and his companions resumed their journey with the daylight, without having retired to rest at all.

This incident does not prove that the preaching of the gospel in the public assembly should ordinarily be prolonged far into the night; but it proves that, on great occasions, when the people are in earnest, and especially if the preacher is about to leave the country with little prospect of returning, if the preaching be prolonged far into the night, nothing harmful or unreasonable has been done. For such an object a night's rest might well be given away.

In modern fashionable society, great companies of young and old not unfrequently protract their amusements till the unwelcome sunlight expose too faithfully their faded finery; and yet some of these very persons would be the first to cry out in most virtuous displeasure against late religious meetings in a reviving time. It is not difficult to thread our way through these labyrinths. The right way may be found and followed. The rule is plain, written clearly by the finger of God on earth and sky: the day for useful labor, and the silent night for rest. But great cardinal points occur here and there in the life of men which invite and justify occasional exceptions. To hear the word of life from the lips of an inspired apostle when you do not expect to hear his voice again, is one of these points; and to watch by the sick-bed of a brother, who needs your help, is another. But so clear is the law assigning the night for rest, that a great solid ground is required to sustain an exception. Such a ground occurred at Troas when Paul preached. Blessed, busy night for the Christians of that place: they would be more refreshed by it than by the sweetest slumbers.

Paul's Address to the Elders of Ephesus
(Acts 20:13-30)

" And we went before to ship, and sailed unto Assos, there intending to take in Paul: for so had he appointed, minding himself to go afoot. And when he met with us at Assos, we took him in, and came to Mitylene," etc.

IN sailing from Troas to Assos a ship must go round a projecting tongue of land, and a passenger may cross the neck of the peninsula and reach the port on its southern side before the ship has made the circuit. Paul alone preferred the short land journey; all the rest sailed round the headland. The details of the voyage, though interesting in many aspects, are not necessary for our purpose: we pass them accordingly, and meet the party at Miletus, the harbor at which they would disembark, if they meant to go to Ephesus. Paul had made up his mind not to visit Ephesus at this time, not because he loved it less, but because he loved it more. He can afford to go on shore at Miletus, for that place had not power to detain him, when he was bent on another object; but knowing himself and his friends, he has a presentiment that if he go up to the city to visit them, farewell to his prospect of being in Jerusalem at Pentecost. Because his love of the disciples at Ephesus was very great, therefore on this occasion he did not venture to intrust himself among them. Having landed at Miletus, he sent a message to the elders, requesting them to meet him on the sea-shore. The distance was about thirty miles. These same men who are here called elders are addressed (ver. 28) as bishops.* And so it is placed beyond controversy that at that early date a number of grave and good men, named indifferently elders or bishops, were conjoined, in the oversight of the disciples resident in one city.

The address which Paul delivered to the Ephesian elders at Miletus is recorded at considerable length. It is a precious and pregnant document. It is a rich legacy to the Church in all ages and all lands. It does not accord with our plan, however, to expound and apply this discourse with a fulness proportionate to its intrinsic worth. Precisely because of its exceeding richness, we must leave the greater part of it untouched; for even a moderately full exposition of this chapter would occupy all the space that can be allotted to this series. A few detached expository and practical notes on some of its leading topics must for the present suffice.

After some very tender allusions to Jerusalem, and the uncertainty of the reception that awaited him there, he proceeds (v. 25) to deal very solemnly and faithfully with the bishops of Ephesus regarding the edification of themselves and their flock. Personal affections are freely employed whenever they can be of use. He would hardly be justified in wounding their loving hearts by express allusion to the fact that this was the

---

* Controversial matters are in these expositions sedulously avoided, but this point is not now properly a matter of controversy. The most learned and eminent critics of the episcopal communion acknowledge frankly that the term translated "overseers," should have been rendered bishops, as it is in all other places where it occurs.

It may be satisfactory to some of our readers to see the late Dean Alford's note on this subject. "So early did interested and disingenuous interpretations begin to cloud the light which Scripture might have thrown on ecclesiastical questions. The English version has hardly dealt fairly in this case with the sacred text in rendering επιδκοπους (v. 28) *overseers*, whereas it ought there, as in all other places, to have been 'bishops,' that the fact of elders having been originally and apostolically synonymous might be apparent to the ordinary English reader, which now it is not."—*Alford on Acts* xx. 28.

last interview, if the grief could not be made conducive
to his great aim. But he desires to print a great resolution deep on their hearts, and thinks it needful to
get these hearts first of all melted. He softens the
material by the flame of a great brotherly love, and
then applies his prepared seal. Sometimes the departure of a faithful minister from an affectionate flock has
produced a greater amount of good than his sojourn
among them. Those who slumbered while the mill
was going, may be awakened by the silence when the
mill is stopped.

He takes them to witness that, in his comparatively
lengthened ministry at Ephesus, he had so fully declared the gospel, that he remained " pure from the
blood of all men." The form of expression is striking
and memorable. It is borrowed from the crime of
murder, and the method by which guilt is ordinarily
brought home to the criminal. In many cases conviction depends on blood being found on the clothes of
the murderer. Hence in almost all cases of violence
we hear of desperate efforts being made by the terrified
evil-doer to efface the stain. These efforts, and the
testimony connected with them, bulk largely in criminal trials.

This is the conception that leaps into the apostle's
mind. He cannot hope that all who have heard the
gospel from his lips in the city are now in Christ. He
fears that some of them may be still under condemnation. If they die in their sins, how unspeakable the
loss—the loss of a soul ! He shudders at the thought:
and in order to quicken their diligence when they should
return to their labor, he endeavors to impart some of
his own anxiety to the elders. He in effect invites
them to look to their hands and garments to make sure
that there is no blood on them.

The double application of his warning, "Take heed,"
presents very vividly some great lessons. The logic
and the theology of the sentence are equally good.
The first care of the spiritual shepherd is for himself;
the next for the flock. In some parts they paint garden walls black, that they may absorb more of the
sun's heat and so impart more warmth to the fruit-
trees that lean on them. Those who in any sphere

care for souls, stand in the position of the garden wall. The more that the teacher absorbs for himself of Christ's love, the more benefit will others obtain from him. It is not the wall which glitters most in the sunshine that does most for the trees that are trained against it. It is the wall which is least seen that takes in most heat for itself; and the wall that has most heat in itself gives out most for the benefit of the trees. So it is not the preacher who flashes out into the greatest flame himself that imparts most benefit to inquirers who sit at his feet. Those who drink in most of the Master's spirit are most useful in the world. Those who first take heed to themselves will be most effective in caring for the spiritual weal of those who look up to them.

The Church of God, considered as a flock, has been purchased by his own blood. The term purchased points to a possession obtained by a price. Israel in the typical dispensation were acquired as the Lord's portion at the Exodus by the blood of a lamb; but the true Israel of the New Testament by his own blood. The price paid for them enhances their value. The greater the sum that any possession costs, the greater care is bestowed upon it. How can the under shepherd lightly esteem the flock, which the Chief Shepherd bought with his blood ! This is the strongest motive which Paul could think of to draw forth the assiduity and faithfulness of pastors.

As an additional ground by which to enforce his injunctions to earnestness, he intimates that after his " departure " grievous wolves will enter the fold. The word departure is ambiguous. It may mean simply the speaker's departure from Asia on his voyage to Jerusalem, or it may mean his departure from this life. I think Paul employed the term precisely because it was ambiguous. He secretly thought of the ravages which would be committed among the Ephesian Christians after his own death; but he expressed it softly, that they might in the first instance think of his leaving them for that time. But the word would return with new power to their memory, when the news reached Ephesus of the apostle's martyrdom.

In such cases this great missionary always felt himself in a strait betwixt two. In prospect of heresies and immoralities rending and defiling the Churches, he desired to abide in the flesh, that he might help the feeble; but for himself the prospect of departure was sweet, for it would bring him straight to Christ.

The "grievous wolves" here point not to persecution from without, but corruption within. The conception must be framed in consonance with the parallel,—wolves in sheep's clothing. They enter in; and when they are in they destroy. They are admitted as friends; and by being inside have more power to do mischief.

These warnings are not of private interpretation. They are written for our admonition in this end of the world. The flock in our day is exposed to the same dangers. The presence of false teachers within the fold of a Protestant Church is the gravest fact of the day for all intelligent and true-hearted disciples of Christ. Prayers and pains must go together. We must cry mightily unto God, and strive mightily with men. "The Lamb shall overcome them; for he is King of kings, and Lord of lords: and they that are with him are called, and chosen, and faithful" (Rev. xvii. 14).

The Larger Blessing and the Less
(Acts 20:35)

" I have showed you all things, how that so laboring ye ought to support the weak, and to remember the words of the Lord Jesus, how he said, It is more blessed to give than to receive."

THIS "word of the Lord Jesus," like the great apostle who has reported it, is one "born out of due time." It found no place in the evangelic histories: it lay silent in loving hearts, or flowed in whispers from loving lips when the disciples met after their Master had departed, until, spoken by Paul on the sea-shore to the weeping elders of Ephesus it was recorded by Luke, his companion, for the use of the Church in all coming time. In another aspect this word is like the man who quoted it at Miletus;—if it, among the words of Christ, like Paul among his apostles, was late in coming, it is, like him, not a whit behind the chief of them in preciousness and power, now that it has come.

Luke reports the speech of Paul, and Paul's speech holds in its bosom a priceless fragment of the Redeemer's word. It is as when a seaman in a shipwreck has seized in his strong arms a servant of the family as she was sinking; and when she is raised, the spectators discover that she holds the infant son of the family living in her arms.

Here then we have a word of Christ rescued from sinking into oblivion—a word of Christ with a word of Paul wrapped round it; the jewel and its setting—the kernel and its shell are both here.

"It is more blessed to give than to receive:" these words were indeed employed by Paul as a practical maxim to stimulate and direct the Christians at Ephesus in their charitable contributions; but if you limit your view to that specific application, you will miss the deepest of their meaning. An untaught barbarian, or an undeveloped child, sees in the stars some small twinkling lights set in the blue canopy higher than the clouds that flit across its face; but you know more of their grandeur and of their Maker's might when you look upon them as central suns, with subject systems of their own, while they also act as lights to the darkened hemisphere of our earth. As the difference between the intrinsic greatness of the fixed stars, and their incidental usefulness to this world at night, is the difference between these words in their origin as the declared experience of God our Saviour, and these words in their application as a stimulant to liberality in Christian contributions. We must consider these words in the depth of their Divine fountain, and not confine our view to the particular stream that happens to flow from them here. Before we speak of the object to which the maxim is here applied, we must reverently look to the source whence it was taken.

When our Redeemer said, "It is more blessed to give than to receive," *he expressed his own experience.* This word of Christ is beyond conception precious, especially to "the meek and poor afflicted ones" among his disciples. When, conscious of our own unworthiness, and especially of our backsliding, we tremble even before a throne of grace, it is sweet to learn that the Giver of pardon takes pleasure in giving. He who loves a cheerful giver, is a cheerful Giver. A penitent may encourage his soul to come near in confidence, not only with the argument which the spectators addressed to the blind man at Jericho, "Be of good comfort, rise; he calleth thee," but with the much stronger reason,—the cure of the disease will impart greater joy to the Physician than to the patient. This word of Christ, rightly accepted, is enough to drive away all the dread of fearful souls, as wind drives smoke away.

Forms of amazing elegance and beauty may be thrown off in millions by the hands of common workmen; but the one type whence all the specimens have derived their shape grew slowly, like the germs of life in the secret of a greater soul. So, off the experience of Emanuel in his work of Redemption, from its beginning in the eternal purpose till its finishing in the fulness of time, was this maxim taken, which Paul found useful to stimulate the liberality of the Ephesians,— which we find useful to stimulate liberality amongst ourselves to-day. The love wherewith Christ loved us is the mould on which the practical rule was cast. Unless he had lived in the world, the world would never have possessed such a rule for the regulation of its course. This principle is not of the earth. It bears the mark of another origin. It at once reveals the character of its author, and gives shape to the aspirations of his followers. It is a print of his footsteps, marked by the Spirit in the word, to direct the way of his people through all time.

This feature belongs indeed to the lessons of every true teacher who undertakes to mould into better forms the spirit and conduct of his neighbors. All apostles who have left a beneficent mark on the world have first practised what they afterwards preached. In this respect the Apostle and High Priest of our profession was made like unto his brethren. He lived this lesson first, and taught it then.

He tasted the blessedness of giving, and thereafter told his disciples how sweet it is.

The redemption which Christ accomplished, and the gospel reveals, is a system of giving and receiving. It consists of these two, and of these two only. The whole transaction between the Saviour and the saved is comprehended in giving and getting. He gives; they get. This is the sum of the whole matter. Christ gives all, and gets nothing; Christians get all, and give nothing.

The Lord Jesus speaks from experience when he explains how pleasant it is to give. He is entitled to speak on that point with authority. On that subject he speaks what he knows. He has had much to do with giving, first and last. If there is sweetness in the act, he must have enjoyed that pleasure to the full.

He gave himself for us: this is a gift unspeakable. We have no line wherewith we may measure its greatness. It is as when a little child looks down into the blue heavens mirrored in a still lake; the child exclaims, "These skies are deep, deep!" But how deep he cannot conceive, far less adequately express. Inconceivable to men and angels,—infinite is the gift which our Redeemer bestowed when he offered himself to take sin away. The Giver of Himself knows what giving is, and is entitled to speak with authority on the amount of blessedness involved in the act.

Nor has the giving ceased, now that he is exalted. He continues to dispense his bounties. When he ascended after his ministry on earth was done, it was for the express purpose of giving. He gives the Spirit: he gives pardon and peace day by day to "him that cometh." He gives grace in this life, and glory in the next. On this part, it is all giving; his bounties are waters that fail not. And he is "not weary in well-doing." When he was hungry and faint at the well of Samaria, it was not the water from the woman's vessel or bread from the baskets carried by the twelve that refreshed him. "I have meat to eat," he said, "that ye know not of." And his meat was *giving*—giving to a needy sinner the gift of eternal life.

This glimpse into the heart of our Redeemer is a salve that reaches to the deepest of all sores. Brother, when you begin really to know yourself, it is not easy to hope that it will be well with you in the great day. When you measure the deceit and corruption of your own heart, you know that it will require a great deal of giving on the part of Christ to make you right. Perhaps you could hope more easily if your debt were smaller. You are afraid to expect that it will be all freely forgiven, because it is so great. When you have looked a while into your own heart to see its emptiness and measure how much you need to receive, turn round and look a while unto Jesus to learn how much he possesses, how much he bestows, and how much delight he takes in bestowing. There is joy in the presence of the angels of God over one sinner that repenteth; and the joy is expressly said to be like the joy that filled the shepherd's heart when he got his wanderer home again. The joy therefore is the joy of the Lord, which surrounding angels see gleaming in his face, when he feels that virtue has gone out of him to save a sinner. Every time that from the depths of sin and misery on this world another draft is made upon his love, another throb of joy rebounds in the Redeemer's breast.

Humble and contrite hearts, that sigh and cry for the light of God's countenance, should drink in great consolation from these words of the Lord Jesus. If giving were a pain to him, he would have long ago ceased to give. If he gave grudgingly, he would not give at all; for there is no constraint laid on him, except the compulsion of his own unmerited love. When our Lord with his disciples made the journey from Judæa to Galilee, it is written that "he must needs go through Samaria." There was indeed a geographical necessity on the surface, for Samaria lay right across their path; but there was a deeper necessity—a necessity compelling the Lord to make that journey at that time; it was his hunger for the meat that his fellow-travellers knew not of, which then consumed him—the appetite for giving mercy and newness of life to a chief sinner in Sychar. He must go that way, for there lay the savory food that his soul desired.

In his goings forth from eternity, he must go by this world. All these glorious worlds that are scattered over the infinite belong to him: but it is not necessary that he should dwell in any of them and take part of the nature of their inhabitants. These were not needing anything: these remained as God had made them—all very good. He would have enjoyed no *giving* there, and a sojourn there would not have been blessed to him.

For this joy that was set before him—for this greater blessedness—the blessedness of giving, he came and companied with the empty and the lost.

Let us bear these words of the Lord Jesus on our hearts when we pray. To be assured that he counts it blessedness to give, should greatly encourage us in asking.

The words do not say and do not mean that it is unpleasant to receive. When the receiver is needy, and the gift good, and the giver generous, it is blessed to receive. Tell it, ye who have come to the Lord—wretched and miserable, and blind and naked, and have received from him pardon and peace and eternal life,—tell it to his glory. Is it not a blessed experience to receive ? Hark ! they tell it who already stand round the throne in white clothing,—Thou hast redeemed us and washed us from our sins in thy blood. Sing unto the Lord, for he hath triumphed gloriously. These jubilant hosts who have passed in safety through the Red Sea are not givers; they are only receivers. They are rejoicing with a joy that is unspeakable and full of glory; but it is the joy of receiving that swells in their hearts and thrills through their frames. When the Lord intimated that the blessedness of giving is the greater, he did not intimate that the blessedness of receiving was small. He proclaims in one sentence the twofold truth, that the joy of his people in obtaining salvation is great, and his own in bestowing it is greater.

There is an amazing affluence in the works of God, both in the covenant of his mercy and the creation of his hand. " And God made two great lights; the greater light to rule the day, and the lesser light to rule the night: the stars also " (Gen. i. 16). After the chief lights were provided, he needed some smaller sparks to supplement the moon's rays in the work of diminishing the darkness of night on this world. For this purpose, he employed a multitude of glorious orbs, many of them mightier far than the sun and all its system.

It is thus in the covenant. God needs a motive to urge his people during their probation here to greater liberality in their charity; and for that purpose reveals the experience of his Son in the work of redemption. He needed a lamp for our feet at a rough step on the journey; and lo, in order to obtain it, he draws aside the vail, rends the heavens, and displays to view the love and joy that burn in the bosom of God our Saviour! No wonder that the ravished pilgrim forgets for a time the step on earth thus illumined, and gazes on the glory that sheds down the needed light.

In a subordinate sense, the Lord's people also give to him, and he receives from them. He loves this receiving. Evidence that he delighted in the self-consecration of his disciples crops out everywhere in the evangelic histories. In the case of the woman who poured out the precious contents of the alabaster box to anoint his body for the burial, he gives unmistakable indications that he was much pleased with the lavish offering. In the case of the ten lepers, too, he does not conceal that he rejoiced in the thanksgiving of the grateful one, and missed the acknowledgments of the selfish majority.

It was kind in him to let us know that he values our gifts, although we render to him only what we have received. It would have thrown a discouraging damp over every grateful aspiration, if he had left us to suppose that, not needing our offerings to supply any lack, he was indifferent to all the loving gifts that loving hearts and hands might lay at his feet. Sometimes a little child is permitted to present a flower to the sovereign on occasion of a public procession. The sovereign takes real pleasure in the offering and the offerer: the sovereign's condescension is a mighty encouragement to the child. It is in some such way that disciples, who have attained to some measure of the little child's spirit, are encouraged to present their thank-offerings, by knowing that he loves to receive them.

And now that he has gone beyond our reach, it is his own express will that we should consider the poor as receivers for him. We have no Saviour present to the senses on whose head we might pour our precious ointment now; but the poor we have always at hand; and the Master's command is that we should turn the ointment into cash, and with the proceeds help our needy brother.

The High Priest Insulting Paul
(Acts 23:1,2)

" And Paul, earnestly beholding the council, said, Men and brethren, I have lived in all good conscience before God until this day. And the high priest Ananias commanded them that stood by him to smite him on the mouth."

" AFTER we were gotten from them" (ch. xxi. 1) means after we had torn ourselves away. It was a tender meeting, and a painful parting. They all wept sore. They sorrowed to see the missionary going away, and sorrowed most to hear him saying that they should see his face no more.

Two thoughts, constituting a pair, suggest themselves here: (1) Christians suffer as much as others from the necessary partings that occur in life, or rather they suffer more, for their faith increases their susceptibility. The affections run deeper and wax stronger in a nature that has been mellowed by faith. But (2) Christians who live up to their privileges enjoy consolations correspondingly great. If their partings are painful, their hopes of meeting again are sure. The pain of temporary separation is overbalanced by the expectation of being soon and always together with the Lord. The loving hope absorbs the sadness as the fire licked up the water in the trench round Elijah's altar, and a balance of blessedness remains.

The course of the voyage is noted briefly but clearly. First, the ship made a straight course to Coos, a small

island, twenty-three miles long, divided from the mainland by a narrow channel. The ground is fertile and
the traffic large. Next day they made the large island
of Rhodes. Passing with a fair wind through the channel which divides it from the continent, they brought
up in the harbor of Patara, the shipping port of the city
Xanthus on the mainland.

From Patara the ship's course no longer lay along
the coast. She stands out to sea in a south-easterly
direction, leaving Cyprus on the left, and steering for
Tyre on the Syrian coast. At Tyre the ship discharges
her cargo. As there must be a detention of several
days here, the missionary will take advantage of it, and
prosecute his own business. He goes ashore, and soon
finds the Christians who reside in the port. Tyre is
one of the most ancient and most celebrated of cities.
It was a great sea-port in Ezekiel's time; and the course
of events seems to point to it, or to some spot near it,
as a great entrepôt between Europe and India in the
twentieth century.

Paul found the disciples that were in Tyre. Some
were found in every city throughout those regions; and
by the law that "like draws to like," they soon found
themselves congregated in one company to hear the
Apostle of the Gentiles. Here accordingly the traveller remained a week, as in Troas, preaching no doubt,
to a great assembly on the Lord's-day. That Sabbath
would remain marked in the memory of Tyrian believers, even unto old age, as a well springing in the desert.

Although the brethren warned Paul, through the
spirit of prophecy, of the dangers that awaited him in
Jerusalem, he would not desist from his purpose of visiting it. He had repeatedly consented to retire from
danger when his life would have been exposed without
adequate cause; but he would not allow himself to be
diverted from his course when he had a great object in
view by any kind or degree of personal danger. Here
accordingly occurs another tender separation. The
whole assembly, including women and children, accompanied the missionary to the ship. They knelt together
on the shore and prayed. There was a temple consecrated to the worship of God—its floor the sea-sand,
its canopy the vault of heaven, its organ-peal the roar-

ing of the waves as they broke upon the beach! There, though marked by no material cross, and circumscribed by no man-marked line—there is a spot of holy ground. How dreadful is that spot on the sea-shore near Tyre —how dreadful and yet how gladsome! It is the gate of heaven, through which the ardent spirits of those ancient Christians, led by the lips of Paul, went in to the throne of grace—by which the Lord who heard them came forth to be with them unseen, as fulfilment of his promise. Such holy places on the surface of this earth have all the disciples of the Lord,—the sacredness, however, adhering not to the ground, but to the memory of those who have met their Lord there.

Claudius Lysias, the Roman tribune commanding the garrison of Jerusalem, and in the absence of the governor responsible for the peace of the city, found it necessary to take Paul up by force from the excited populace, and shut him for safety in the castle of Antonia. Uncertain still as to the nature of the charges which were so violently preferred against the eminent missionary, he gave orders that he should be examined by scourging; but as the men were binding his hands, Paul quietly asked the superintending centurion whether it were lawful to scourge a man that was a Roman and uncondemned. Again he appeals with success to imperial law for the preservation of his own life.

Next day, in order to get the matter cleared, Lysias summoned a meeting of the Jewish great council, and requested them to examine the prisoner. When the sanhedrim was duly constituted in a hall attached to the Temple, Lysias conducted Paul from the castle and placed him at their bar. The tribune, no doubt, after all that he had seen, took the precaution of stationing a military guard near enough to prevent any attempt against the prisoner's life.

As we enter here the last section of the history, it may be useful to pause and observe the difference in character and design between it and all the preceding portions. At this point the scope of the history becomes narrower. It is now the track of Paul alone. All other actors disappear from the scene, except in as far as they were mixed up with his experience. Nor is it only that the history concerns itself henceforth with the course of this single missionary; for even with regard to him the character of the narrative undergoes a change. Although he maintains his character as a witness for Christ to the last, the history is no longer a record of missionary journeys to found churches, and to revisit them for comfort and consolidation. The main line now is a memorial of Divine Providence, preserving the missionary's life until he should be in a position to preach the gospel in Rome as he had already preached it in Jerusalem. Precious in God's sight is the death of his saints, and precious also in his sight is their life. He will lay all the powers of nature and all the kingdoms of the earth under requisition to protect a life that he needs as an instrument in his work of righteousness until his work be done. Paul must witness for Christ at the centre of the world's power; this is fixed as the end, and the means are all provided. The remaining portion of the book is the record of these provisions.

Henceforth our theme therefore must be the arrangements of Providence for the spread and establishment of the kingdom of grace. Our business now is, to see God's hand working rather than to hear his word instructing; but to the open and watchful ear, the still small voice of the gospel will ever and anon break forth in the intervals of the earthquake and the thunder. He that hath an ear may still hear, in the concluding portion of Paul's history, "what the Spirit saith unto the Churches."

The history of apostolic missions is finished; but before the parchment is rolled up, the line of one life is carried a few stages farther forward into the centuries, by way of specimen, that we may see how the Lord fulfilled his promise, "Lo, I am with you always, even to the end of the world." We learn here how the Lord reigneth; how he sits King upon the floods; how he stills the waves and the tumults of the people; how he makes effectual his own command, Touch not mine anointed, and do my prophets no harm. When we see the waves rising, we cry, like Peter, in despair, as if all were lost. In this portion of the history the Lord addresses us with mingled reproof and encouragement— "O thou of little faith, wherefore didst thou doubt?"

The sanhedrim had assembled; Paul was led in. As soon as he entered it is intimated that he eyed the assembly—"earnestly beholding the council." There is much power in a human eye. If there be courage in the heart, it finds expressive outlet by the eye. Cowards cannot stand erect under a brave man's look. Lions, it is said, wince under a man's steadfast gaze more than under the lash which he inflicts. The eye is both a channel of emotion and an instrument of power. In this case a good conscience and a strong faith added power to the look with which the solitary missionary met the gaze of the assembly, and made the priestly judges cower under the eye of the panel at their bar. Paul did not wait till a question should be put or a charge preferred. He is not, properly speaking, on his trial before the sanhedrim. He is sent by the Roman authorities to the native Jewish council, in order to obtain a skilled and competent investigation of his case. The court are charged, not to try a criminal, but to investigate facts for the guidance of the governor. Such seems to have been Paul's own view of the situation, for he is himself the first to speak. With a salutation entirely friendly but by no means cringing he began to lay before the council a narrative of the steps that led to the present complications.

I think Paul had an intelligent object in view when he addressed the members of the council respectfully but manfully as "brother men." He is by this time such an one as Paul the aged. He saw on these benches many who had been his fellow-students, and some, no doubt, who had been both his juniors and his inferiors when they sat together at Gamaliel's feet. He had done nothing to forfeit his position as their colleague and equal. He had honored the law in confessing Christ its fulfilment. He will not, by word or deed, relinquish his position. "My brothers," says the intrepid preacher, as he opens his address. In one aspect the salutation is kind; in another, it carefully maintains his dignity and his rights. He humbles himself before God, but he will not humiliate himself before men.

As soon as Paul had uttered the first sentence of

his speech, the high priest Ananias interrupted him by abruptly giving an order to the officers of the court to smite him on the mouth. This is a very remarkable statement. It reveals a condition of extreme corruption and degradation in Jewish society. Their chief magistrate, on his seat of authority, surrounded by his council, perpetrates an act of ruffian rudeness fit only for the lowest haunts. In rejecting the Messiah the Jewish hierarchy have sunk into a low moral tone. They seem to have been given over to a reprobate mind.

We obtain here a glimpse of a general law. When a chief sinner accepts Christ in simple faith, there is an immediate and great elevation of the moral sense in the converted man. In more than one aspect he becomes a new creature. But the converse also holds good. When Christ is brought near to any mind, and his claim touches the conscience, and the man, self-pleasing, ultimately rejects the offered Christ, the last state of such a rejecter is worse than the first. Those who waste privileges and quench convictions seem to sink lower than those who have never enjoyed them. Beware of stifling convictions—of crucifying Christ.

Paul Answering the High Priest
(Acts 23:3-11)

" Then said Paul unto him, God shall smite thee, thou whited wall: for sittest thou to judge me after the law, and commandest me to be smitten contrary to the law ? And they that stood by said, Revilest thou God's high priest ? Then said Paul, I wist not, brethren, that he was the high priest: for it is written, Thou shalt not speak evil of the ruler of thy people," etc.—ACTS XXIII. 3-11.

"GOD shall smite thee, thou whited wall." This bold rejoinder of Paul presents an interesting study. In itself, and apart from circumstances, the pungency of the apostle's reproof needs no other justification than that which he gave on the spot: "for sittest thou to judge me after the law, and commandest me to be smitten contrary to the law ? " Luther was wont to launch such thunderbolts against his princely and priestly oppressors. Great and earnest men in all ages have been wont to rise above their circumstances and bring unjust judges suddenly to the bar.

Ananias seems to have been struck dumb. He loses his breath, and sits silent. They that stood by—some officials of his court or aspirants for his favor—took speech in hand to shield their astonished patron. These apologists were fain to fling his official dignity over the ermined culprit whom they could not in any other way defend. Not a word did they dare to utter in excuse or extenuation of his conduct. His act is tacitly abandoned, and they take refuge in the office which he holds.

A high-minded and honorable government is a boon above all price to a nation. Judges that are impartial and just are a good gift of God in his providence. We in this country may well thank God for the Reformation, for with it comes and with it goes the liberty of the people.

It is with the apostle's reply to the defence offered by the high priest's satellites that the real difficulty for us begins. When they reproached him with reviling the high priest, he excused himself by saying, " I wist not that he was the high priest." If he had not excused himself we should not have thought he needed an excuse; but the excuse he gives suggests a real though not a very serious difficulty. It requires explanation, but it is clearly susceptible of explanation.

It is not easy to determine conclusively which of many possible explanations is the best, but any one of several is sufficient. For example: 1. Ananias, in those violent times, may have been an intruder and usurper. 2. Some other member may have presided at that diet, and Ananias may not have been distinguishable by position or dress from the rest. 3. It is conceivable that Paul meant to say that this brutal act could not have been perpetrated by " God's high priest," and to assume before the council that such a miscreant could not be the chief of the sacred college. Or, 4. As has been lately suggested, Paul may have been shortsighted—not able, especially if the light was unfavorable, to distinguish faces across a spacious hall. This is countenanced by the attitude which the apostle assumed when he first entered the court, "earnestly beholding the council"—fixing his gaze scrutinizingly and with straining upon the assembly. Thus he may positively not have known that the rude, illegal order proceeded from the president of the council.

I mention these as possible solutions, and could mention others; but these are enough to show that Paul's words can easily be accounted for, although we do not possess the means of certainly determining which of several explanations actually constituted at the time the ground of his remark.

On the whole, I don't think that there is urgent need for apologies here. If Paul was angry, he had cause. He resented with spirit a brutal assault, and made the mitred miscreant feel that his robes and phylacteries could not protect him from the withering stroke of a just man's rebuke. On the whole, the missionary contrived, in this perplexing incident, to make clear for us a great and important distinction between the office and the man who disgraced it. He respects the priestly office, but the criminal priest he denounces sharply.

By this time Paul had seen enough to convince him that no good could result from this inquiry, and his acute intellect readily perceived the means of cutting it short. He saw that the two parties of which the council was composed, although united against him, were, on vital matters, at daggers drawn against each other as Pharisees and Sadducees. Accordingly he seized the opportunity of professing, in a loud voice, his adherence to the distinguishing doctrines of the Pharisees. This was really and notoriously true. In becoming a Christian he had not abandoned or even modified those doctrines of the Pharisees which distinguished them from the Sadducees. The doctrine of the resurrection, dear to him before, had become tenfold dearer since he knew that the Lord had risen. This profession of his faith produced immediately the expected effect. It set the two parties together by the ears. Through the avenue made by the division

Paul escaped from their hands. In the tumult the Roman tribune, fearing mischief, came with a guard, and carried Paul into the castle.

"The night following the Lord stood by him." The wearied missionary, saved from the rage of his countrymen only by the walls of a Roman fortress and the swords of a Roman garrison, lies down to sleep. The Everlasting Arms are underneath him, and he has no fear. No plague can come nigh his dwelling. The shields of the earth belong unto God, and the strongest of them—the imperial Roman power —is now interposed between him and those who sought his life. Think what must have been his prayer that night! His heart longed after Israel, although they thirsted for his blood.

I think the soldier on guard that night at the door of Paul's apartment must have reported in the morning that there were two persons in the room, as the listeners reported regarding John Welsh in the old church of Ayr. The sentry would probably hear through the key-hole an earnest reasoning and entreaty going on—" I will not let thee go except thou bless me "—as when two are engaged in close debate. Paul cried to God that night certainly; for God came at his servant's call. The answer comes as an echo of the prayer. The Lord stood by him and said, " Be of good cheer." The answer given reveals the request that had been secretly made. Be of good cheer, Paul: the answer proves that Paul's cheer had been poor when he lay down. What may have been the weight that lay so heavy on his heart? His life was not in immediate danger. He was under the protection of Roman law, in this case administered by a fair and thoughtful man. It was not fear for his own life that marred his cheerfulness. Still following our rule of discovering the ailment from the cure applied, we find the consolation offered was a specific promise that he should be permitted to bear witness for Christ at Rome. Here then we discover the cause of the apostle's sadness: he had begun to fear that he would yet be disappointed in the great aim of his life—to preach the gospel in Rome. His desire in that direction had now grown into a passion. Jerusalem, to which he hastened through all obstacles in his last journey, has now finally rejected him and his message. The Jews in persecuting the missionary rejected Christ. Paul was led to accept this decision, and henceforth he bends all his energy towards Rome. He is the apostle of the Gentiles, and the chief desire of his heart now is to make known Christ in the metropolis of the world.

Compassed with His Favor as with a Shield
(Acts 23:12-35)

"And when it was day, certain of the Jews banded together, and bound themselves under a curse, saying that they would neither eat nor drink till they had killed Paul," etc.

THE conspiracy formed to assassinate Paul and the means by which it was defeated are narrated with considerable minuteness. The history is perhaps given the more fully that it contains and exhibits a decisive example of the actual union and harmony between the prescient purpose of God and the responsibility of men for duty in their own sphere. It was determined that Paul's life should be saved from these dangers, and that determination was made known to him. He knew for certain that these schemers could not take his life; he knew for certain that the power of God was pledged effectually to frustrate their designs; yet with this knowledge Paul laid his plans anxiously and skilfully, and executed them with secresy and energy, for the preservation of his own life, precisely as if he had thought that all depended on his own skill and promptitude. This shows conclusively that in Paul's mind a belief in the decrees of God did not conflict with the obligation to diligent duty on the part of men. He framed and conducted a counterplot to defeat the conspiracy of the Jewish priesthood with as much zeal and care as if he had not obtained previous assurance of his safety. This simple history is most precious as an inspired commentary on some difficult doctrines. It does not indeed make the doctrines easy of comprehension; it does not relieve them of mystery to our minds; but it is fitted to accomplish very great practical good in two distinct yet related aspects. It is fitted first of all to show us that no view of the Divine purposes can be right that in any measure tends to slacken human zeal and energy; and, in the second place, it ought to make men very guarded, who, either from the Christian or non-Christian view-point, are disposed to attribute to the adherents of so-called Calvinistic doctrines consequences which Paul and Calvin would have repudiated. Scriptural views of the Divine prescience and sovereignty, by whatever name they may be called, stimulate and do not sopite the watchfulness and energy of disciples. To be assured that it is God that worketh in them, is the best of all motives to induce intelligent Christians to work out their own salvation with fear and trembling (Phil. ii. 12, 13).

The Jewish leaders easily found a band of desperadoes, who for fitting consideration should act the part of assassins. The rule of a superstitious and corrupt priesthood will produce an abundant crop of such instruments in any age and in any land. In connection with this plot an incidental glimpse is afforded of the apostle's family circle. A married sister, probably a Christian, and having her residence in Asia Minor, or in some region remote from Jerusalem, deputes her adult son to perform a service which she could not personally render to her brother—to wait upon him, and render him assistance it his struggle with the priest party in Judæa. This young man discovers the plot and reveals it to his uncle. Paul, enjoining secresy on the informer, loses no time in getting him introduced to the Roman commander. The result is that the prisoner is sent under a strong guard to Cæsarea, on the coast, and the conspiracy is completely frustrated.

The letter addressed by the tribune commanding in Jerusalem to his superior, Felix the governor, is preserved entire. It is a most interesting ancient document. It is in complete accord with the forms and the spirit of the time. Lysias simply and briefly recites the facts of the case, and leaves it in the hands of his chief.

Paul is now in the hands of a thoroughly bad man; but the Roman laws are around him, and these suffice to protect him, in the mean time, alike from the foul treachery of the Jews, and the mean avarice of Felix. The law will not permit him to be tried, far less to be condemned, until he and his accusers are brought face to face before a regular tribunal. Paul is placed under arrest indeed; but it is for the protection of his life, rather than for the restraint of his liberty. Herod's judgment-hall, the place of his confinement, is not precisely the cell in which they would immure a criminal. In that hall, with a Roman sentinel pacing up and down its corridors night and day, the missionary will be in safe keeping, until the preliminaries for his trial can be arranged. Signal, meantime, unseen by human eye, is displayed to ministering angels, that this man must be preserved unharmed, for the word of the Lord is pledged that he shall preach yet in Rome. Lie down, Paul, and rest a while: give some repose to thy weary limbs and anxious heart. Thy course is almost run: but a little while and thou shalt enter into rest. A few more tossings on the sea of time, and thou shalt be sentinelled, not by Roman legionaries, but by ministering spirits who attend upon the heirs of salvation. One city more to be visited, one ruler of this world more to be confronted, one trial more to be endured before a human judgment-seat, and then thou shalt be permitted to depart and to be with Christ, which is far better.

But such faith and such hope belong not exclusively to a great apostle, or to the supreme crisis of an eventful life. These may become the every-day attainments of common-place people. A disciple who has never stood before kings, who has never been a bone of contention between rival factions, whose life has been spent in a private sphere, and whose name has never been heard of half-a-mile from home, may participate in the grand inheritance which Paul enjoyed. " My peace I give unto you: not as the world giveth, give I unto you." The simplest and the humblest who is found in Christ may lie down and awake with God, day by day through life, until after falling asleep for the last time here, he awake in the presence of his Lord.

The air—the atmosphere which surrounds this globe —is a limited quantity. Its measurements are known. It can be weighed even in our balances, and fathomed by our laws; yet that body touches at the same moment all living. It enfolds all vegetable and animal life in one comprehensive embrace, and touches, presses gently on every flower of the field and every face of man. It supplies the breath of life to all, not only those who stand on a mountain-top and consciously inhale the blessing, but also, and equally, those who sleep in the gallery of a mine, and know not the value of the omnipresent boon. We can understand this fact of nature: we can realize and appreciate its truth and value. Might we not by faith as clearly realize that the love of God, unlike the atmosphere, his creature, infinite, compasses about always all his children, great and small, of every language, in every clime, clasping them round continuously, and supplying them with life !

The same atmosphere, God's creature, that was suffused round the head of Paul, when he slept in Herod's judgment-hall at Cæsarea, surrounds our heads to-day, supplying us with the breath of life: the same Divine love, Christians, that sustained Paul's faith and refreshed his spirit, when he was afflicted, persecuted, and forsaken, compasses us about to-day, for life in the Lord, a life eternal. Rejoice in the Lord always. Oh thou of little faith, wherefore didst thou doubt.

The Parties at the Bar
(Acts 24:1-23)

" And after five days Ananias the high priest descended with the elders, and with a certain orator named Tertullus, who informed the governor against Paul. And when he was called forth, Tertullus began to accuse him, saying, Seeing that by thee we enjoy great quietness, and that very worthy deeds are done unto this nation by thy providence," etc.

THE comfort given to the missionary in his extremity consists in an assurance, not that his troubles should cease, but that his witness-bearing should continue. The Lord knew what grieved his servant's heart; and in order to gladden it, announced, Thou shalt bear witness of me at Rome. This was the promise, and it must be fulfilled. Many and various agents will be pressed into the service in order to accomplish it. The bloodthirsty enmity of the Jewish priesthood, and the impartial dignity of Roman law; the plot of assassins, and the sharp-sighted love of kindred; the avarice of a profligate governor, and the discipline of the imperial legions,—all conspired, like the several parts of a machine in motion, to preserve the missionary's life and transplant him to the metropolis of the world.

At Cæsarea the distinguished prisoner was kept, for protection as much as for restraint, until his accusers should arrive. In five days the persecutors were on the spot, and the case was called. The high priest in person, with several of his confederates, represented the Sanhedrim. The priests did not venture to conduct their own case. Already they had found Paul too much for them in debate. They knew by experience that he quickly detected the weak point in an adversary's argument, and had no mercy on sacerdotal impertinence. Wise in their generation, the Jewish conclave hired a Roman advocate to conduct the prosecution. These men, after studying law in the capital, were wont to practise in the provinces. They were acquainted with legal forms, and with the judicial precedents: provincial litigants found it their interest to employ them.

It is by no means certain that the advocate used the Latin tongue; for examples occur in which the Greek was employed even in Rome.

It was a rule with rhetoricians to compliment the presiding judge at the outset; and this part of his function Tertullus greatly overdid. He was able to point with truth to the suppression of certain bands of robbers as a boon conferred on the country; but history proves that the governor's own cruel and lawless acts oppressed the people more than all the robbers he had rooted out. The glimpse which this book gives of Felix perfectly accords with the character he bears in contemporary history. He was a licentious, rapacious, cruel, and unjust man.

After the advocate's exordium comes the indictment against the prisoner. Its terms are suspiciously general. No specific act is libelled, but a vague scolding accusation preferred against Paul as a pest and a disturber. Nothing strange has happened to this servant of Christ. The Master had warned his disciples that they should be accounted and called "offscourings;" but, at the same time, he pronounced them to be "the salt of the earth." The high priest and his colleagues appeared personally and assented to the statements of their advocate. When the case of the prosecutors was closed, the governor beckoned to Paul that he was at liberty to reply. The gravity and order of a Roman tribunal contrast strongly with the lawless insolence of the high priest in his court at Jerusalem.

Paul, too, like his adversary Tertullus, begins with a word of compliment to the presiding magistrate; but he utters no falsehood and no exaggeration. He only mentions an obvious fact, that the governor had long experience of the country. As to the substance of his address, it consists of two parts: those things in the accusation that were criminal were not true; and those that were true were not criminal. The crimes falsely charged he denied, and challenged his accusers to the proof: the portions of the indictment that were true he confessed, and contended that they violated no law.

Even in an oration, whose direct object was the

demonstration of his own innocence and the preservation of his own life, Paul contrives incidentally to indulge his ruling passion—that is, to commend the gospel of Christ: he carefully points out that the belief of the gospel is not the rejection of the Mosaic system, but its natural result. He testifies to thoughtful Jews that the right understanding of Moses leads to the reception of Jesus as the Christ. In the matter of the resurrection, too, which was the immediate occasion of the tumult in the council at Jerusalem, his faith coincided with that of the Pharisees who were prosecuting him.

Besides allusions to controverted doctrines, he introduces a most interesting and instructive reference to personal, practical holiness of life; "Herein do I exercise myself, to have always a conscience void of offence toward God and toward men." This is a precious morsel; especially when we consider the position in which it stands, and the circumstances in which it was given. In great ecclesiastical and doctrinal contentions, such as those in which Paul was then engaged or those which agitate the Church in our own day, zeal in public debate too often overrides and crushes private, personal godliness and purity of conscience. It is reproving and instructive to observe that the Apostle of the Gentiles, at the very moment when he was compelled to contend alone against a nation leagued to destroy him, devoted himself habitually and with all his might to the growth of grace in his own soul, and the practice of righteousness in all his conduct. Clear in his logic as well as ardent in his affections, he rightly divides the word of truth on this subject for our instruction in the end of the world. Morality with Paul, as with Moses, diverges into two main channels,—the first containing our duty to God, and the second our duty to man. He strove to have these two commandments written, not with ink, but on the fleshy tables of his heart. Let the conscience be clean, whether it point upward to God, or outward to men. The two great commandments in this preacher's life were, "Thou shalt love the Lord thy God, and thy neighbor as thyself."

Nor did this great saint find compliance easy. Obedience to that law "exceeding broad" did not come to him by chance, without plan and effort. He speaks of it in the terms which belong to the drill of a soldier. It is a commonplace in military economy, that a soldier cannot be made in a day. Raw recruits, however perfect may be their arms and their uniform, are useless when they meet an enemy. Wherein really consists the strength of an army in the day of battle? In the previous *exercise* of the individual combatants. This conception Paul adopts and applies to his own life as a witness for Christ and a warfare against sin. For the motive to fight, and the will to make sacrifice on the side of holiness, he depends altogether on the redemption of Christ. He is bought with a price, and is therefore not his own; his life and all his faculties are at the disposal of the Lord that bought him; but for the skill and power to fight successfully on the side he has chosen he depends on a careful and constant exercise. The success of the Christian army in their holy war depends on the drill, day by day, of individual warriors.

And if the Apostle of the Gentiles, a man great in the faith, found it necessary to maintain constantly a military watchfulness and practice, how presumptuous in any of us to count on keeping the course, and acquiring the crown, by an indolent wish to be safe, without a constant watchfulness, an energetic effort, and a more than military sternness in laying aside every weight, and the sin that doth most easily beset us. Soldiers are never done with exercise: although they have served honorably for a quarter of a century, they must still submit to drill. If the soldiers of Jesus Christ were as wise in their generation and as painstaking, more victories would be won, and more captives made. The kingdom of Christ would " come " in greater power, both in the hearts of individual disciples and over the nations of the earth.

Paul and Felix
(Acts 24:24,25)

" And after certain days, when Felix came with his wife Drusilla, which was a Jewess, he sent for Paul, and heard him concerning the faith in Christ. And as he reasoned of righteousness, temperance, and judgment to come, Felix trembled, and answered, Go thy way for this time; when I have a convenient season, I will call for thee."

THERE are in the Scriptures certain grand outstanding portions, which seem to bulk more largely and shine more brightly than the rest. In the Old Testament the twenty-third Psalm and the fifty-third chapter of Isaiah: in the Gospels the interviews with Nicodemus and the Samaritan woman, the parables of the sower, the shepherd, and the prodigal: in the Acts, the gospel preached to the Ethiopian by Philip, and to the jailer by Paul; the gospel preached to Felix here and rejected;—these are specimens of words that grave themselves more deeply on the memory of Bible students, and come up more frequently for use. Nor is it either unlike the ways of God or incongruous with the nature of the case that some points should excel in beauty and power where all is Divine. On the earth's surface, some mountains rear their heads into the sky far above the valleys and the " little hills " that bound them, and some stars are superior to others in breadth and brightness. To recognize practically such pre-eminence does not disparage the body of revelation any more than the earth that bears the mountains, or the skies that hold forth the stars.

To a thirsting soul these notable portions are like wells by the wayside. The traveller drank from them in succession the first time he trod the path, perhaps fifty years ago; but if he is living still, and still on pilgrimage, with the same hot sand beneath his feet, the same hot sun above his head, he will drink from each well-remembered spring as he passes it, with as much delight as on the first day he discovered its refreshing water. He will not turn away his head with the complaint, I have known these wells so long and tasted of them so often that I am wearied of them now. Therefore, spring, O wells, as long as there is a desert, and drink, O Pilgrims, as long as you are thirsty; for the princes of the people digged them,—David and Isaiah, and Peter and John, and Matthew and Luke: and drink, reader, if thou art a wayfarer on the same path—drink at this spring in the desert yet once more as you pass.

The governor, indolent, vicious, self-pleasing, postponed decision in Paul's case, and after the trial relapsed into his pleasures. But the pleasures, long continued and not much varied, palled on the taste of the voluptuary To relieve their languor, he and his wife Drusilla determined one day to hear a sermon from the distinguished preacher who happened to be their prisoner. Accordingly, a message is conveyed to Paul that the governor and his party desired to hear him concerning the faith in Jesus. This message sent to the prison is all the heavens different from the cry formerly raised in the prison, "What must I do to be saved?" But Paul counts the occasion good, and determines to occupy his opportunity. Man proposes, but God disposes. What Felix begins in sport may end in earnest. The imprisoned apostle will endeavor to strike a blow for the kingdom of Christ in the high places of the earth.

The auditors on this occasion, although they occupied a high place in society, were both "of the baser sort." They were stained especially with cruel injustice towards others and gross impurity in their own persons. These specific vices, well known to the preacher, determined no doubt the form of his discourse. When he speaks to a large miscellaneous audience whose characters he does not know, he must draw his bow at a venture, and hope it will hit some enemy of the King; but when, as in this case, he sees clearly his object, he will take deliberate aim. Accordingly, in making justice and personal purity the chief themes of his address, Paul was coolly covering his man. He preached to the times, and the place, and the people. Taking his stand generally on the eternal law of God, he selected the two specific aspects of it that cut directly into the consciences of his auditors. He will employ the law as a fire of coals piled on the hard ore of the governor's heart, if so be he may make it flow down: if he sees it melting, he will quickly receive it into the mould of the gospel for pardon and newness of life.

It is a mistake to suppose that the discourse, so briefly reported here, consists of three consecutive heads. Its logic is better than such an arrangement supposes. The sermon consisted of two heads and an application. The two heads, Righteousness and Temperance, are meant to hedge in the governor, so that his conscience cannot escape either on the right hand or on the left; and the application—the judgment to come—is sent forward like a flood of fire between these two walls to secure conviction, and utterly to slay the old man in the heart of that chief sinner. The division by the same apostle, in Tit. ii. 12, "Soberly, righteously, and godly," is in substance the same, although the two main branches are given in the reverse order. With perfect clearness and precision Paul divides the law into two parts; *first*, its aspect outwards as bearing on other people; *second*, its aspect inwards as bearing on ourselves. Towards other men, it demands *justness;* within ourselves, it demands *purity*. These are indicated by the terms "righteousness" and "temperance" in the reported discourse.

Righteousness needs no explanation. It means what it says—rightness, justness, in thought, word, and deed towards all—towards God and towards man. Temperance, the other English word, needs to be defined. It is not employed here in the modern and narrow sense of mere freedom from all excess in the use of intoxicants. It means that, and more. Its classical and New Testament signification is much wider than that which it ordinarily bears now in our own language. It means freedom from all that defiles; it demands personal purity on all sides. In this case, although it did not exclude what we ordinarily mean by intemperance, most certainly the licentiousness of the hearers was much more prominently before the preacher's mind, and much more specifically designated by his word.

We know how Paul would bring home the word

on both sides. He would keep nothing back. He strikes with a will. He thrusts the sword up to the hilt. He has no compassion; for he knows that compassion in this place is unfaithfulness to a fellow-sinner's soul. Felix is compelled to listen; and, what is much more, Felix is compelled to listen with secret application of the dreadful word to himself. As the preacher advanced from point to point, the conscience of the governor, as the voice of God in his breast, murmured, Thou art the man. On the one side he is unrighteous; on the other he is impure; and when the judgment to come was pressed forward, he felt as if an angel with a flaming sword were approaching to destroy him, while he had no power to escape.

Felix is like a man chained to the ground in the middle of the Mount Cenis tunnel. Above, below, and on either side he is shut in. Without a figure, the barriers on all sides are nothing else and nothing less than the everlasting hills. While he is chained to the spot in that dark avenue, he looks along the gloomy telescope tube; and lo, in the distance, a red fiery spark, like a fixed star! It is like an eye, all-seeing and angry, glaring on him from afar. But as he gazes on it, he perceives that it is growing larger; and oh, horror! it is advancing. It is coming with express speed. It is the fiery engine rushing on— rushing over him!

Felix trembled; and well he might. He has reached that point in spiritual experience on which the Philippian jailer stood, when "he called for a light and sprang in trembling." But, alas! he does not seek relief from the terror of conviction where the official in Philippi sought and found it. Instead of "What must I do to be saved?" it is, "Go thy way for this time." Two men may be led by nearly the same path into those soul pangs which accompany conviction of sin; and yet the two men may follow opposite courses in life, and meet opposite rewards in eternity. It is not how you fall into the pains of conviction that fixes your state, but how you get out of them. Not how you were wounded, but how you are healed, is the turning-point of the loss or saving of the soul. Instead of seeking healing in accepting Christ his Sa-

viour, Felix sought ease by stifling the preacher's voice
—quenching the Spirit who spoke in the preacher.

But here a question occurs. As far as the report of
the sermon goes, there is no mention of Christ, and no
offer of pardon through his blood. Felix received on
this occasion no such blessed word as that which was
addressed to the jailer, "Believe on the Lord Jesus
Christ and thou shalt be saved." This difference is
real, and it is remarkable. The reason of it when discovered throws a flood of light on Paul's method as a
preacher of Christ. He seems to have preached the
law, and nothing more, to Felix and Drusilla; but he
would have preached the gospel too, if they had permitted him. He began with the law in order to work conviction of sin, ready to apply the healing balm the moment that the conscience was touched. The sermon
as far as it went was intended to inflict a wound; and the
foolish hearer, when he felt the pain, interrupted the
speaker, and lost his opportunity. Felix wanted to
play at preaching; but Paul meant earnest work. Felix
intended to amuse himself during a leisure hour; Paul
tried to save a soul from death. Thus these two were
at cross purposes. But we are sure from the whole
character and life of the apostle that he would have
offered free pardon in Christ to the chief sinner who
sat before him, if he had not been abruptly silenced
ere his work was done.

Convictions Resisted Bear No Good Fruit
(Acts 24:26,27)

*"He hoped also that money should have been given him of Paul,
that he might loose him: wherefore he sent for him the oftener, and
communed with him. But after two years Porcius Festus came into
Felix' room: and Felix, willing to show the Jews a pleasure, left Paul
bound."*

THE seed was good and the sower skilful, yet no fruit
followed.

For one thing, the hearer of the Word on that occasion did not seek spiritual benefit, and that is at least in part the reason why he did not obtain it. A plan and a purpose are necessary on the part of the hearer, as well as on that of the preacher. The promise is, " Seek, and ye shall find." Those who omit the condition, have no right to expect the result.

Further, bad company in this case contributed to the failure. Felix and Drusilla, were both steeped in wickedness. It is more difficult for Felix to yield and admit conviction in presence of his profligate companion. If he had shown symptoms of repenting, this bold bad woman was ready with her fiercest look and her most contemptuous sneer. Oh that the poor man had been alone, or had been surrounded by companions who would have encouraged him to turn and live ! Many promising impressions have been nipped in the bud by the scoff of worldly companions.

When convictions spring up as in this case, taking the shape of terror in prospect of the judgment-seat, there must and will be a rapid movement, either backward or forward. It is as if fire were falling on the spot where you stand, and you must instantly escape from it. You will go either nearer to the God whom you fear, or further away from him. If you get a glimpse of his love in Christ, you will bound forward in order to hide from all fears in his Divine compassion; but if you get no such view of his mercy, the terror of the Lord will drive you into vanities or vice, as a cover from the light of his countenance. For such a case the Word of Christ was spoken and written—" Come unto me, all ye that labor and are heavy laden, and I will give you rest."

The subterfuge of Felix—" When I have a convenient season, I will call for thee "—was natural in the circumstances, but false and shallow. He made a promise which he did not mean to fulfil. If Paul has rightly presented the reckoning, now is the most, the only convenient time for getting it settled. Now is the day of salvation; the gospel does not know tomorrow. Let any one who in modern times is inclined to follow this ancient example of procrastination, think for a moment why he desires delay. Is it that you may enjoy the pleasures of sin a little longer ?

But the case will not bear reasoning. It is false from the foundation. You, the guilty and condemned, are invited, besought, to accept instant and full pardon and peace with God free through the Redeemer; and you beg to be excused—you plead for a little delay, as if you had been summoned to the scaffold. The pleading for delay is as much as to tell God to his face that the pardon and peace which he offers you count a calamity, and if you must endure them sometime, you would fain put the evil day afar off. True repentance does not covet—it dreads delay.

It is dangerous to stifle convictions thus. The conscience cannot be so treated with impunity. When it is not listened to, it loses its sensitiveness and vitality. It will not give its testimony so clearly the next time. When a bar of iron is made red-hot and plunged into water, and that process is several times repeated, it becomes hard and brittle; it may be easily broken now, but cannot be bent. In some such way the conscience is seared by stifling convictions of sin.

The facts that immediately follow the dismissal of the preacher bear directly and decisively on a question of universal and cardinal interest in religious affairs,— the question whether a religion of terror produces any permanent good moral effect. Superficial inquirers, who examine the gospel from a point of view outside of its boundaries, cling to the conviction that it is dangerous to withdraw the fear of punishment. They think this fear is necessary to keep men from transgression. This is a mistake; but neither human instinct nor human philosophy possesses the means of correcting it. It cannot be corrected except by the experience of a more excellent way. The old question, " Do we make void the law through faith ? " cannot be answered except from the Christian view-point —" God forbid: yea, we establish the law."

The Popery of the Middle Ages maintained a religion of terror. The priests kept the line in their own hands, and by means of confession and purgatory imagined they had the hook in Leviathan's jaws. But Leviathan could not be bridled in by such childish machinery. Sin in humanity, like a sea-monster in its element, was too strong for these green withes.

The evil spirit in man said, "Jesus I know, and Paul I know, but who are you?"

God's method of binding souls to obedience is similar to his method of keeping the planets in their orbits —that is, by flinging them out free. You see no chain keeping back these shining worlds to prevent them from bursting away from their centre. They are held in the grasp of an invisible principle, which we call the law of gravitation; and it is by the invisible bond of love—love to the Lord who bought them—that ransomed men are constrained to live soberly and righteously and godly. "Neither do I condemn you: go and sin no more;" such is the method by which Jesus bound a chief sinner to obedience. He trusts that his free gift of pardon will generate a love in the sinner's breast, which will constrain him, like gravitation, to keep the law.

Let us see whether the terror of Felix in the prospect of judgment produced any good effect on his morals. Two specimens of the man's life are with great simplicity subjoined, and from these we learn that his fright had not made him a better man. In ver. 26, we learn that the governor, who never found a more convenient season for hearing the Word, summoned Paul the prisoner often into his presence for another purpose. He expected a bribe, and meanly condescended to give the innocent prisoner many a hint that a man like him need not languish in confinement, while his numerous and ardent admirers had plenty of money in their hands. Next, in ver. 27, we learn that, at the end of two years, when Felix was recalled from the province, instead of setting Paul at liberty as a man against whom no crime had been proved, he handed him over to his successor, still a prisoner, because he saw that the act would be popular with the fanatic Jewish mob. Considering the position of Felix as governor and judge, no fouler deed could possibly be recorded against him. Such is the fruit borne by an evil tree after it has been deeply cut by the axe, but not cut through and made good by the engrafting of another. Such is the fruit that the convictions of a wicked man bear when they have been arrested and not permitted to grow into conversion. Such is the result of terror where there is not faith.

One would like to know the history of that centurion who had charge of the missionary during those two years at Cæsarea, and also of the soldiers of his company who acted by turns as the apostle's sentinel. The veil has not been lifted up. The result of intercourse with Paul day by day for so long a period will not be known till the day declare it; but I think when it is declared, it will be a glory to the Lord and a crown of joy to his servant. Not a few in the ranks of the Roman army were converted during the life-time of the apostle. Even in Cæsar's household at Rome there were disciples of Jesus, sending their greetings to fellow-disciples in other lands. There is much probability that the Word of life would win the officer who had charge of Paul at Cæsarea. Ward and warder have both gone long ago to their account; and from the analogy of other cases, it is lawful to indulge the fond hope that these two men, who often promenaded together the coast of the Mediterranean, or gazed from the battlements of Herod's judgment-hall on the sun setting in the western sea, gaze together now with clearer eyesight on greater wonders, before the great white throne.

The New Governor
(Acts 25)

"Now when Festus was come into the province, after three days he ascended from Cæsarea to Jerusalem. Then the high priest and the chief of the Jews informed him against Paul, and besought him, and desired favor against him, that he would send for him to Jerusalem, laying wait in the way to kill him," etc.

THERE was a change of government. Felix was recalled, and Festus succeeded him as procurator of Judæa. The new governor coming from Italy by sea, landed at Cæsarea, remained at that port three days, and then went up to Jerusalem. Doubtless he desired to inform himself regarding the state of parties among the Jews in the interior that he might be able more intelligently to administer the government at Cæsarea.

We may find an analogous case on a much larger scale in our own administration of India. The new governor arrives at Calcutta, a city of recent origin, built by the dominating power on navigable waters, as the seat of authority. But he will do well, soon after his arrival, to make a progress into the interior—to visit Benares, Delhi, Lahore—the great capitals of the native races, or the seats of their religious worship. It is there that he may best learn the disposition of the natives, and the condition of the country, thus qualifying himself to conduct the machinery of government. A very necessary precaution, as we know to our cost: greased cartridges may kindle a rebellion.

In this spirit Festus visited Jerusalem almost immediately after his arrival in the country, that he might take the measure of men and of parties in the Jewish capital; and so be prepared to adopt such measures as should be most likely to calm the boding discontent of a subjugated nation. As soon as the governor appeared in Jerusalem, the high priest and his party approached him with the view of securing his ear against Paul. How eagerly they hunt him down! It appears as if these men could not sleep soundly on God's earth as long as the missionary of the cross lived on it. He was cherishing the bud of Judaism into its natural fruit; but to develop the germ into the full gospel would cast off these usurpers who sat there in Moses' seat: Paul had no mercy either on their greed or their superstitions; therefore they were bent on his ruin. This process has repeated itself down through the dark ages. Persecutions have seeded themselves from that generation to this, as surely as thistles—and as mischievously.

The priest party endeavored to induce the governor to summon Paul to Jerusalem to be tried. They had their own reason for this: they meant to revive the scheme of assassination. Festus, however, was firm: Let the prisoner remain at Cæsarea; I shall shortly take up my residence there; let his accusers come thither to conduct the prosecution against him in the ordinary form. It was of the Lord that Festus, though unaware, apparently, of their designs, refused to comply with them. Probably his reasons for refusing were very prosaic and commonplace. He was a stranger; he did not feel at home amongst the Jewish dignitaries in their sacred city. The permanent officers of the government who in such cases must be his councillors were resident in Cæsarea. His legal advisers were there. No; he will not summon the prisoner to Jerusalem, and begin his judicial career in such adverse circumstances; he will rather go down to the seat of government. With all his officers around him, he will more firmly plant the first steps of his course in the administration of the country. When the Supreme has a purpose to be accomplished, he has instruments at hand, whether the elements of nature, or the thoughts that spring secretly in human hearts.

By arrangement, no doubt, between the prosecutors and the judge, Paul's case was called on the very day after the governor had returned to Cæsarea. He gave his first attention to the case which the Jewish authorities first pressed upon his attention. The court was constituted, and the pleadings on both sides heard; but the trial instituted with so much formality came to nothing. Instead of pronouncing judgment on the evidence, Festus suddenly demanded of the prisoner, whether he would consent to go up to Jerusalem, and there be tried in his presence.

This may have been an honest proposal, founded on real reasons; for Festus may have discovered gradually as the pleadings went on that the case in its own nature belonged to the ecclesiastical court of the Sanhedrim, and that he, as a Roman, was not competent to pronounce in it an intelligent judgment. The request, "Wilt thou go up to Jerusalem and there be judged of these things before me ?" may mean that the Jewish Sanhedrim should try the cause under the superintendence and in presence of the governor. But there is also too good reason to believe that the enemies of Paul had, in the interval, obtained access to the governor, and gained him over. At all events, at Cæsarea he himself proposed the very measure which at Jerusalem he rejected.

This was the turning-point; and the crisis could no

longer be averted. While Paul was a man of strong faith, he was also a man of strong reason. He was cool and clear; he measured men, and framed his own plans with consummate political skill. Finding now that he had no other shield between his life and the assassin's dagger, Paul launched at length the bolt he he had long kept concealed,—" I appeal unto Cæsar."

During the period of the republic, an appeal lay to the people, or the tribunes their representatives; but now all these rights were vested in the emperor. Ordinary provincials were entirely in the power of the governor, but those who possessed the privilege of Roman citizens enjoyed the right of appeal. In Oriental romance you often meet with a traveller who possesses a mysterious talisman, which he always carries about, capable of preserving his life in the last extremity. The owner of the charm abstains from using it in ordinary dangers; and it is only when all other hope fails that at last he brings it forth. The right of appeal to the emperor was Paul's talisman; it was employed only in the last resort. But it was effectual. It represented the Roman empire; it wielded the power paramount of the world. Neither Festus on the one had, nor the Jewish rulers on the other, dared to touch a hair of the prisoner's head while he lay under the shelter of imperial law.

There is a grand burst of indignation accompanying the appeal. This man does well to be angry; he spares neither his judge nor his accusers. " To the Jews have I done no wrong, as thou very well knowest." In consenting, contrary to his own first judgment, to remove the diet to Jerusalem, Festus had in effect agreed to deliver the victim into the murderers' hands; and so now it behoved Paul to protect himself from the Roman procurator, as well as from the Jewish priests. By the constitution of the empire, a provincial judge might, on his own responsibility, refuse the privilege of appeal to notorious criminals, although their names were inscribed on the roll of citizens; but it was plain enough on all sides that Paul was no criminal—no reckless disturber of the peace. He was evidently a man of purity and power. If the governor, yielding to the importunity of the Jews, venture to override this citizen's rights, the act reported at Rome will rebound with damaging effect on his own head. The legal assessors of the governor, on being consulted (ver. 12), advised that it would not be safe to ignore the privileges of the appellant. Thus man proposes; but God disposes. All things were ordered so as to bear the apostle of the Gentiles to the metropolis of the Gentile world.

The decision of the court is pronounced: "Hast thou appealed unto Cæsar? Unto Cæsar shalt thou go." Paul, for his part, must have heard the words with profound emotion; but the prevailing element was joy. At length, according to his own long-cherished desire, and the Saviour's gracious promise, he has the assured prospect of reaching Rome. He will get a free passage at the emperor's expense, while he travels on the business of the heavenly King.

Not long after this event, Herod Agrippa—son of that Herod who beheaded the Baptist—who by favor of the emperor ruled over a portion of Syria with the title of king, came to Cæsarea, on a visit of ceremony to the new governor. Precisely in the same manner the various dependent sovereigns, who are still permitted to retain authority in various portions of our Indian empire, assemble to pay their respects to the viceroy appointed by the queen. He politely acknowledges their dignities in presence of the natives; but they understand well enough that they hold their crowns at the disposal of the power which he represents.

Although by birth an Idumean, and educated at Rome, Agrippa was a Jew by adoption. On this visit he was accompanied by Bernice, in what capacity the Scripture does not say; but it is abundantly testified by contemporary history that vices were involved in their relations which ought not even to be named amongst Christians. The bad fame of this woman for unblushing effrontery in the practice of complicated and shameful vice, was proverbial in those regions and times.

Another scene ensues, in some respects similar to that of Paul and Felix; and yet, both in its subjects and results, exhibiting several features in marked contrast with its predecessor. But in the essential features these two episodes hang like companion pictures on the wall. Agrippa, like Felix, sought, not the pardon of sin, but the gratification of curiosity; and he fared accordingly. "Blessed are they that hunger." But this man was not blessed; he died, not for want of food, but for want of hunger. This is a disease that wastes the world still.

The Gospel Fulfills the Law
(Acts 26:1-16)

" Then Agrippa said unto Paul, Thou art permitted to speak for thyself. Then Paul stretched forth the hand, and answered for himself:" etc.

PAUL'S address before Festus and Agrippa is recorded with considerable fulness. It is in form, as well as substance, an apology for Christianity, adapted to the audience and the times.

In determining his ground, he adheres closely to his former line of defence. He does not demand the sanction of imperial law for the introduction of a new religion; he takes his stand on the fact that the Jewish religion is a lawful worship, and argues that the gospel, being a legitimate development of Judaism, is already sanctioned. His language is not, Tolerate the religion which I proclaim; but, My religion is already tolerated by the laws of the state.

The first premise of his argument, the Jewish religion is tolerated in the empire, was not disputed; the second, I am of the Jewish religion, is the point on which the great apologist on this occasion puts forth his strength. This, although debated in a Roman court, was a question between Jews and Christians. The Jews accused the Christians of having apostatized from the tolerated faith; it was Paul's business, therefore, to refute this accusation—to prove that in accepting Christ he did not renounce Moses, and so make good his claim to the protection,of the government under existing laws.

Thus, the form which the question that day assumed, makes the apostle's reasoning on it very precious to the Church in all ages. Circumstances led him to show that the gospel sprang necessarily from the law, as the stalks and ears of harvest from the seed of spring.

Starting from the notorious fact, that in his youth he was himself a Jew, he proves, by a narrative of the case, that he had never changed; that his progress, instead of being an apostasy, had been the development and glory of all the Old Testament revelation.

In this aspect, the progress of revelation is somewhat like the progress of a plant that grows from seed. The first stage is in appearance very different from the second. The leaves subsequently unfolded are not a mere repetition of their predecessors. Suppose a person altogether unacquainted with the processes of vegetation has obtained some seed, which he believes to be precious, from a foreign land. He sows it in his garden, and watches its springing and growth. After having seen its first leaves spread out, he is called from home. The plants are left under the charge of a skilful and faithful servant, and the owner does not see them again for a month. On his return he visits the garden to mark the progress of his valued foreign plants. He finds them growing indeed on the same spot, but entirely changed. These are not my plants! he exclaims. I left them with leaves smooth and almost circular; these leaves are downy, corrugated, and sharply indented on all sides. He thinks the gardener has removed the original germs, and substituted others of a different kind in their place. The mistake is due to the ignorance of the proprietor; the servant has been faithful to his charge. The owner ignorantly mistakes a natural development for a dishonest change.

The Sanhedrim represents the prejudiced householder, and Paul stands for the faithful steward. The gospel which Paul preached was not indeed a mere reproduction of the Mosaic institutes; it was the growth of that germ into foliage, flowers, and fruit. All the sacrifices are promises. The Sanhedrim, in their blind zeal, would grasp these promise-buds, and hold them tight, and never permit them to open; Paul would leave these precious buds free under the sun and air of heaven, and watch to see whereunto they would grow.

Paul held fast the hope of the promise. It was not a new or strange doctrine that he proclaimed. It was the promise made to the fathers. He was aware, while he spoke, that his doctrine involved the resurrection of the dead. The resurrection of the dead in general, and the resurrection of Christ in particular, are bound up together. To deny the possibility of a resurrection, involves the rejection of Christ; for, if the dead rise not, then is Christ not risen. There is reason to believe that the Herodian family, of whom Agrippa was, at that time, the head, had imbibed Sadducean views. As the king enjoyed, by favor of the Roman emperor, the right of nominating the high priest, the Sadducees, under this ancient specimen of lay patronage, would probably obtain most of the chief preferments. Paul plainly assumes that Agrippa was a Sadducee, and endeavors to change the king's dark belief. " Why should it be thought a thing incredible with you, that God should raise the dead?" The actual resurrection of Jesus, when accepted, demolishes the foundation-stone of the Sadducean system.

Once more, on a great public arena, the apostle narrates his own conversion. He relies mightily on this as an instrument in his ministry. In order to provide a fulcrum for his lever, he carefully notes, at the outset, that he too was once against Jesus of Nazareth. And here the grand natural character of Saul emerges in striking outlines. What he thought to be his duty, that he resolutely performed. He thought the disciples of Jesus were a sect of deceivers, and therefore he determined to hunt them down. This is the essence of persecution in every age. It is a conviction lodged in a strong but unenlightened mind, that those who refuse compliance with the authorized orthodoxy should be put to death. It is that grim sense of duty, combined with a perverted religious belief, that has done all the killing of the saints. While Paul was an unbeliever, he thought it right to put the disciples of Christ to death, and he acted on his conviction; but when he became himself a disciple, he changed not only his side, but his method. After he became a Christian, he believed that the unbelieving Jews erred fatally in their faith; but we never hear a whisper of any desire on his part to put them in prison, or to take away their lives. Christ made him free, and when he was delivered from condemnation, his law was love. This experience has been repeated in more recent times. As long as the superstition of Rome was predominant in Europe, it put heretics to death; when the Reformation triumphed, argument came in place of the stake. It is remarkable how directly contrary are the maxims of Rome to the precepts of the gospel. See (Titus iii. 10) a specific instruction to Christians how they ought to treat those who maintain erroneous doctrine; " A man that is an heretic after the first and second admonition reject." Paul says, exclude him from your communion; Rome says, burn him at a stake.

We obtain an incidental hint here regarding the methods of torture adopted by ancient Jewish inquisitors—" I compelled them to blaspheme." It is not said that Christians under that cruel compulsion actually blasphemed the holy name whereby they were called. The persecutor endeavored to force them to a denial of the Lord, but he did not succeed. The heathen magistrates during the first three centuries adopted precisely the same plan, with the same result. The martyrs suffered, but would not sin.

Knowing the True and Doing the Right
(Acts 26:18)

" To open their eyes, and to turn them from darkness to light, and from the power of Satan unto God, that they may receive forgiveness of sins, and inheritance among them which are sanctified by faith that is in me."

SOME additional " words of the Lord Jesus," addressed to the stricken persecutor near the gate of Damascus, have been preserved for us in the defence before Agrippa. The design of the Lord in calling this man is clearly and minutely specified,—" To open their eyes, and to turn them from darkness to light, and from the power of Satan unto God, that they may receive forgiveness of sins, and inheritance among them which are sanctified by faith that is in me."

Limiting our view, in the first instance, to the description here given of the saving change wrought in the man at his conversion, we find that it consists of two parts,—the enlightenment of the mind, and the renewing of the life. These two parts may be separately expressed, but they cannot separately exist. They may be expounded as successive topics; but they must be gained together as parallel attainments. You do not first get your eyes opened, and thereafter your heart and life turned round; neither do you practically turn first, and intelligently observe afterwards. The opening helps you to turn, but the turning also helps you to open. In the Christian life true understanding and right action go together, as the right and left side of a living man. The regeneration is made up of truth and righteousness. Like the rays of light and rays of heat which proceed in company from the sun, they may be distinguished by philosophical analysis, but can never be separated in fact. The more that I actually turn from the power of Satan, the more do I intelligently perceive and appreciate God's truth; and the more that I know of God's truth in my mind, the more do I turn from wickedness in my life. An artist may first paint a man's body, expressing the form and action of every limb, and thereafter attach the head; or he may portray first the countenance, with the expression of every feature complete, and thereafter represent the body. But there is a great difference between the methods of nature and of art. The man was not made as he was painted. From the dim deep of non-existence, the being emerges, minute, but not mutilated. Head and body are small and shadowy at first, but head and body are both there, and both grow together unto perfection. So grows also the new man. It is not first the body of right life brought to perfection, and thereafter the spiritual understanding attained; nor is the spiritual understanding first attained, and thereafter the body of a right conduct added. Both, and both together, emerge in embryo, under the great Creator's hand, and both grow together, up to the stature of a perfect man in Christ,—a man who knows God's will, and therefore does it; does it, and therefore knows it. Having once stated the necessary connection and reciprocal influence of these two, we may now consider them separately in succession.

To open their eyes, although a figurative expression here, scarcely requires any exposition. It is that aspect of the Spirit's regenerating work which concerns the knowing of saving truth. It is the work of regeneration as it affects the understanding: it is that unction of the Holy One which enables the renewed to know all things that God has revealed for his own glory and men's good. The practical turning, on the other hand, being perhaps more difficult of comprehension, is here more fully expressed. There is only one turning; but you turn *from* two things, and *toward* two things. At least two expressions are employed to indicate what you turn from, and as many to indicate what you turn to,—

From Darkness and the power of Satan;
To Light and God.

The things on this side seem two; and the things on that side seem two: yet on either side there is substantially only one. *God* and *Light* do not here represent separate and different objects; for God is Light: *Darkness* and the *power of Satan* do not here represent separate and different objects; for the power of Satan is Darkness.

According to the word of Christ the Master, the foremost part of the servant's work is to turn men from darkness and the power of Satan. When the Saviour's word goes forth upon the world, it finds all standing with the face to darkness and the back to light, therefore the foundation of all true preaching is, *Turn:* "Turn ye, turn ye, why will ye die?" was the key-note of Old Testament preaching; and, "Repent, for the kingdom of heaven is at hand," was the harbinger of the gospel in the fulness of time.

Observe how and where we obtain the information that we are all at first in sin and under condemnation: it is not announced by an angry Judge; we gather it from the breathings of a compassionate Redeemer. It is a Friend who tells us the terrible truth that we are lost in our own sin; we should, therefore, all the more willingly take it in, and take it home. He who tells us knows all the case. He knows what is in man to deserve the sentence; and what is in God to inflict it. "Hear ye Him."

Suppose a captive in an inner prison, with many successive circles of strong walls around him; and suppose further that he has never been led or carried through these outer gates, but has been born and reared within the fastness. If he is led out at last into liberty, he will discover the number of the retaining walls, and the thickness of each. The discovery will be pleasant, although it is the discovery of the strength of his prison, when his escape first reveals the depth of his bondage.

Thus the man whom the Son of God makes free discovers the strength of his prison-house. It is in going out of it that you learn how deep and dark it is.

In the spiritual darkness Satan's power is put forth: that power seeks the darkness, and the darkness favors that power. The two work to each other's hands.

When you turn from the darkness, it is to the light: when you wrench yourselves out of the tempter's power, it is to come to God. Perhaps some are thinking about this grand decisive change. They are afraid of remaining in the darkness; but, alas! they are also afraid to come to the light: they are afraid of being longer in the power of Satan; but there is one thing of which they are still more afraid, and that is to come near to God.

The prodigal was for a long time unhappy after his money was all spent; when the pleasures of sin ,were exhausted, he endured its miseries many a day, because he dreaded more to be seen at home a beggar, and to meet an angry father's face, than to endure hunger, and filth, and nakedness in a foreign land. Perhaps some of our readers are in the condition of the prodigal during that interval between the time when he fell into beggary, and the time when he fell on his father's neck. You are not easy where you are. The darkness is now dreadful; but the light, with all your sins upon you, is more dreadful still. Satan's chain is heavy; but you would rather bear it than go right into the hands of the living God. Blessed are those prodigals who are brought the length of the grand decisive turning, " I will arise and go to my father ! "

To the filthy in his filthiness, the prospect of being exposed in the light is dreadful: to the rebellious who has broken his father's heart, the prospect of meeting his father is more formidable than all the miseries of his condition. But when he turns, all is changed; when he is clothed in the fairest robe, he need not shrink from the light of his father's dwelling, or the glance of a brother's eye; when he lies on the Father's bosom, deep in the Father's unfathomable love, he will no longer think it dreadful to come to his Father.

The second portion of this verse describes the privileges obtained in conversion. These are pardon and the inheritance. The gift, like the work, is twofold; it removes from a believer what he deserves, and bestows upon him the deserts of his Redeemer. The birthright of condemnation is taken away, and the birthright of sons is conferred. Christ has taken your portion, and you obtain his. The text teaches substitution in both its parts.

The pardon and the inheritance go together. Those who are not forgiven have no inheritance among the sanctified; and those who have no inheritance among the sanctified are not forgiven. No human being is forgiven and then left outcast; no human being is admitted to the inheritance unforgiven. None with his sins standing to his own account is admitted among the children; none of the children have their sins standing to their own account. Both, or neither. Christ is not divided. Hereafter a heaven awaits the holy; here the holy ripen for heaven.

Soberness
(Acts 26:25)

"But he said, I am not mad, most noble Festus; but speak forth the words of truth and soberness."

LONG, long ago, a native Egyptian, whose cottage stood near one of the slave settlements, might have observed a family of the captive Hebrew race bringing a lamb to the house one night, and after mysteriously sprinkling the door-posts with its blood, assembling to eat it in a strange and inexplicable fashion, with their loins girt, and sandals on their feet, and each holding a staff in his hand, as if the poor bond brickmakers had any liberty to plan or execute a journey. The people are mad, thinks the Egyptian, as he quietly eyes from his own door their eccentric and unintelligible movements. Not so thought he at next morning's dawn, as he bent over the bed on which his first-born lay a corpse, and heard in the distance the marching music of the emancipated Hebrews as they gathered to the rendezvous. No: those poor Hebrews were not mad when they sacrificed and ate their first passover: and he who thought them mad at night, observes and owns their wisdom in the morning.

The valley of the lower Jordan was a rich plain, studded with thriving cities, when Lot looked down upon it from the brow of the neighboring hill, and

chose it for his home. A lucky man was he. All his
expectations were fulfilled. Soon he became a chief
citizen of the chief city. His sons were rising men;
and his daughters were introduced into the best society.
His house was one of the most substantial in the city,
and his agricultural wealth enabled him to maintain it
on a scale of princely hospitality. One day three angels came to this prosperous man, on an errand from
their Master. They advised him to abandon all, and
flee with his family to the mountains. As he lingered,
not absolutely refusing obedience, but unable to make
up his mind to the costly sacrifice, they laid hold of
his hand and hurried him away. Are not the angels
mad to tear a prosperous and respectable man so rudely
from so warm a berth; and is not he mad himself for
consenting to go? When Lot paused, panting for
breath, half way up the hill-side, and saw the smoke
covering the doomed cities as with the pall of death,
he well knew that the words which warned him away
to a refuge in the rock were words of truth and
soberness.

In a high latitude on the southern ocean, far from
the track of the world's commerce, a noble ship, well
found and well manned, is spreading her sails to the
breeze and bounding lightly through the waves, her
rough exploring work completed, and her head turned
homeward at last. All suddenly the whole ship's company congregate astern; some hasty words are spoken;
the nearest boats are lowered; with only a bit of bread
for their next meal, and not a scrap of clothing except
what they wore, they hurry over the ship's sides, stow
themselves away in the boats, and cut adrift on an un-
frequented sea. The men are mad, are they not? No;
for a smouldering fire deep in the ship's hold beyond
their reach, has wormed its way to the magazine, and
it is but a reckoning of minutes to the time when the
ship will be blown into a thousand fragments. The
men are wise men. "Skin for skin; yea, all that a
man hath will he give for his life." They have given
away all that they had for their life; and they have
made a good bargain. Had you been there, you would
have applauded their counsel, and joined in their act.

A few years ago, in the United States of America,

a young woman of taste and genius burst into sudden and great celebrity as a brilliant writer in the periodical literature of the day. After a youth of constant and oppressive struggle she found herself at length an object of admiration and envy throughout her native land. The world was all before her; the ball was at her foot. Fanny Forester's troubles were over, and her fortune made. She has reached the throne at last, and may now sit as a queen in the highest circles of American society.

The fashionable world had no sooner recognized and accepted their favorite, than rumors began to spread, muffled at first, but anon breaking out in clear tones and distinct articulation, that their chosen heroine had consented to become the wife of Judson, now far advanced in life, and to plunge with him into the darkest heart of heathendom, there to burn her life-lamp down to the socket learning a barbarous language, taming a cruel race, and contending with a pestilential climate, —all that she might make known the love of Jesus to an uncivilized and idolatrous nation. To Burmah she went; did and bore her Saviour's will there till life could hold out no longer; and then came home to die. "The woman is mad," rang from end to end of America, echoing and re-echoing through the marts of trade and the salons of fashion,—"the woman is mad." Herself caught the word and the thought, and like the liberated Hebrews in the wilderness, consecrated what she had borrowed from the Egyptians to the service of the Lord. She wrote and published an essay on "The Madness of the Missionary Enterprise," in which she effectively turned the money-making and pleasure-loving world of her own people upside down. The missionary cleared herself and her cause, leaving the imputation of madness lying on the other side.

As long as there are persons in the world who seek first the kingdom of God and his righteousness, and other persons living close at hand who seek that kingdom in the second place, and in subordination to the claims of gain or fashion, there must necessarily be a strongly marked opposition of sentiment between the two classes. They cannot both be right. Wherever convictions are keenly felt, and the consequent conduct is distinctly outlined, both parties will observe the difference, and each will frame his own judgment regarding it. Where the principles and conduct of two persons are opposite in regard to the chief aim of life, each must necessarily think his neighbor in the wrong. If two are sleeping in one bed, and if one arise at midnight and flee to the fields from a conviction that the house is tottering to its fall, while the other though wide awake lies still in bed, the one who remains at ease within the house thinks his companion a fool for his pains. And he must think so. If he did not think so, he could not lie still another moment. For him only two alternatives are possible; either he must think that the man who fled is a fool, or he must arise and flee too with all his might. As long as he lies there he cannot afford to admit a belief of his neighbor's wisdom, for to admit that neighbor's wisdom is to convict himself of suicidal madness. Accordingly, he holds fast by his creed that the other man is a fool; and the moment that creed fails him, he arises and flees too for his life.

Poor Festus could not think—could not speak otherwise to Paul,—unless, like the jailer of Philippi, he had on the instant become a Christian, and made profession of his faith. The subject was obviously the greatest; the case had been clearly stated; this story of a Divine Saviour, the just giving himself for the unjust, is either true or false. If it is true, Paul is right; but if Paul is right, Festus is wrong. Not being prepared to confess this, and yield to its consequences, he took the only other alternative that remained. Festus, knowing well that on this point,—the turning-point of an immortal for all eternity,—where two hold opposite opinions, there must be madness somewhere, determined to throw the imputation from himself. Festus said, "Thou art mad, Paul." Paul replied, "I am not mad, Festus;" and the two men parted, perhaps never to meet again on earth.

What then? Is it another case in which two men entertain different opinions, and in which each may safely hold his own? Alas! it cannot be. One of the two is mad, and in his madness throws himself away. Paul is sober; Festus is the fool.

To make perishing treasures the true centre to which

the soul gravitates, and round which the life revolves, while the things that pertain to eternity are left to follow as they may in a secondary place, is abnormal and mischievous. The wrench is as fatal as would be the revolution in the material universe, if the sun, by external violence, were compelled to move round the earth, or the earth to move round the moon. In the practical question which every one must once in his life decide for himself,—the question whether he shall be his own master, or accept with all his heart and soul the gospel of salvation by Jesus Christ,—there are only two sides. One side is right and safe; the other side is wrong and ruinous. "O send out thy light and thy truth; let them lead me."

The Upper Classes
(Acts 26:25)

"Most noble Festus."

SIXTY years since, a certain attached domestic, presuming on the privilege that was frequently in those days tacitly accorded to his class, roundly reproved his master, a great Scottish proprietor, for the sin of profane swearing. Although no record remains of the argument, it is evident that John had taken a leaf out of the great Apostle's book, and besides speaking of righteousness and temperance, had given a broad hint about the "judgment to come;" for the laird, feeling that he had not a leg to stand on, cut the matter short by the remark, "It has pleased Providence to place our family in a superior position in this world, and I trust he will do the same in the next." This is a real case; but it is an extreme, and perhaps we may add, at least in our own day, a rare one. On the other side there are, not here and there one, but everywhere many, who wear coronets and pray. In this respect the lines of our generation have fallen in a pleasant place. For present privilege we should "thank God," and for future prospects "take courage." But between the two extremes of evil and good, of gross stolid earthliness; and humble, intelligent, strong faith, in the upper ten thousand of British society, how many diversities in constitutional character and external circumstances! How wide is the field, how difficult the culture, and how vast the product, if it were made fruitful over all its breadth!

It was an outstanding feature of Paul's character to appreciate correctly another man's difficulties, and to sympathize tenderly with those whose position magnified the offence of the cross. There is strength, no doubt, in this preacher, but there is sensibility too. He cannot be weak; but neither is it in him to be rude. "Most noble Festus," said he. Oh, I love the great missionary for that word. I think I hear his voice thrilling as he utters it. Right well he knew that, other things being equal, it was harder for the Roman governor than for a meaner man to obey the gospel, and cast in his lot with the Christians. He will not flatter the august stranger; he will not suggest that the elevated and refined may have a private door opened to admit them into heaven, and so escape the humiliation of going in by the same gate with the vulgar throng. This missionary is faithful, but he is never harsh. He makes allowance for every one's temptations, and becomes all things to all men, that he may gain some. In the polite respectful address of the Christian apostle to the Roman magistrate lies a principle that is permanent, precious, practical. Let us endeavor to understand and apply it.

We speak of the aristocracy here in no narrow or technical sense. The subject concerns the whole human race, and bears directly on their eternal destiny. We speak at present of the uppermost strata of human society, whether birth, wealth, energy, intellect, or learning may have been the more immediate cause of their elevation. We speak of those who stand highest among men, without pausing to inquire what has raised them. Now, while it is true of all this upper class, that they need the salvation of Christ, and get the offer of it on precisely the same terms as those who stand on a lower platform, it is also true that, over and above the temptations common to all men, some temptations peculiar to themselves stand in the way of the highest, increasing the difficulty of accepting the gospel. They are the wisest missionaries, and the best successors of the apostles, who own this peculiarity, and make allowance for it in their methods.

One of our Lord's sayings, in reference to the species of aristocracy which is constituted by wealth, may throw light across our whole theme: "Then said Jesus unto his disciples, Verily I say unto you, That a rich man shall hardly enter into the kingdom of heaven. And again I say unto you, It is easier for a camel to go through the eye of a needle, than for a rich man to enter into the kingdom of God" (Matt. xix. 23, 24). Of this wonderful word it is generally one side, and that the harsher, that men take to themselves, or present to their neighbors. Would that we could enter into the tender spirit of the Lord Jesus when he uttered this pungent warning! Assuming that the needle's eye represents the low narrow door through the wall of a fortified city by the side of the principal gate, for use by night or in time of war when the great entrance must be shut,—you have here a passage from danger into safety, not impracticable in its own nature, but impracticable in point of fact to a camel, because of its own huge bulk. The foe is pursuing, the fortress is near, a gate stands open, but this low door-way through the wall cannot be enlarged, and if the fugitive who seeks an entrance carry a high head by nature, how shall he be saved? Thus the elevation of the highest class makes their entrance into Christ's kingdom more difficult. Of this difficulty Jesus speaks with tenderness. Let all his servants in this matter follow his steps. "Most noble Festus," said the preacher, observing that the habitual dignity of the Roman and the official hauteur of the governor were holding high the head of a poor sinful creature, and hindering him from bowing before the Cross of Christ;—Most noble Festus, respectfully and politely said that fervent, eloquent Jew, doing what in him lay to gratify the great man's feelings, and so get the lost man saved.

From the style of the Apostle's address at this

critical moment, two lessons flow; or rather in it one lesson shines, sending out its light-beams in two opposite directions, and teaching wisdom to two opposite classes of men.

For ardent Christians of every rank, and especially Christians of humble station and moderate attainments, there lies a lesson here. If you are true disciples, none will dispute the patent of your nobility. If you are born again, you are high-born, how low soever your place may be in the registers of earth. But that is not the point in hand at present. Beware of presuming upon your place and your privilege. Be conscious of your defects, and meek in your deportment. Be all things to all men, that you may gain some. In particular, beware of throwing a stumbling-block in the way of the noble, the rich, or the refined, by any species of rudeness. Take care lest you mistake vulgarity for faithfulness, and your own ignorance for the simplicity that is in Christ. You have been reconciled unto God through the death of his Son; you have joy and peace in believing: well; there are some men near you who have not yet submitted to the gospel. They stand high, some on wealth, some on birth, some on intellect: in these matters they stand higher than ever you stood. That elevation makes it harder for them to bow down and go in by the strait gate. Had you stood on an equal height, perhaps you would not have been within the gate to-day. Be tender, careful, watchful, prayerful, regarding them. What if they should turn away from Christ because of some rude incrustations of character that they saw in you, and mistook for veritable features of the gospel which you profess! Think of their peculiar difficulties; do not make them greater; take some of them out of the way if you can. He that winneth souls is wise; ay, and he must be wise that would win souls.

For the "most noble" of every class there lies a lesson here. We frankly own that there are nobles among men. We address the chiefs of our tribe as Paul addressed the Roman governor of Judæa, and in good faith we give to each the title of respect which is his due. Sirs, you cherish a high sense of honor, and hold in abomination every mean sneaking thing wherever it may appear; you have by education and habit cultivated a refined taste, and everything rude grates upon your nerves, like rusty iron rubbing on your flesh. You have exercised your understanding, and cannot pay any deference to mere assertion, when it is backed by no proof. These attributes you possess and exercise. We appreciate their worth, and extend to you our cordial sympathy in regard to them. Well, and what follows? Great and good though these attainments be, what is a man profited if he gain them all, and a whole world besides, if he lose his own soul? These are very good, but "one thing is needful;" and it is by sitting like Mary at the feet of Jesus that any man can attain that needful thing. Strive to enter by the strait gate into the kingdom, for your attainments, though in themselves good, may be so worn that they shall greatly increase the difficulty of the process.

Finally, beware of allowing the rudeness and other defects of those who are or seem to be Christians, to scare you away from Christ. It may be true that some are hypocrites altogether, and some who are really Christians retain many repulsive faults; but oh, my most noble brother, it will be no consolation to you if you are not forgiven, renewed, and saved, that you are able to convict professing Christians of many faults. You are not asked to believe in Christians, but to believe in Christ.

The Voyage
(Acts 27:1-25)

"And when it was determined that we should sail into Italy, they delivered Paul and certain other prisoners unto one named Julius, a centurion of Augustus' band," etc.

PAUL'S voyage to Rome is recorded with great minuteness, and with great accuracy. At first we are somewhat surprised to find so large a portion of the

book occupied by the details of a voyage and a shipwreck; but on closer examination, we discover an adequate cause. This journey marks the crisis of the
Jewish people. They had resisted all offers, and finally rejected Christ. Now God had given them over;
and the departure of Paul from Jerusalem to Rome
was the transference of the kingdom to the Gentiles.

At last "it was determined that we should sail unto Italy." Away from the shore of Palestine this "chosen vessel" must go at last, to bear the name of Christ
to the central seat of the Roman power. His earlier
journeys into Asia Minor and Greece were preliminary
and fragmentary; this voyage from Cæsarea is the
great hinging-point of the world's history. Therein
the kingdom of God passed away from the nation of
Israel and took possession of the world. This journey
of the apostle constitutes the link of communion between the East and the West. By this line ran the secret
fire of the Divine life from Israel to the Gentiles. No
voyage in all the course of time has been charged with
so great results for humankind. The Word has now
in its fulness gone forth from Jerusalem; and in that
Word shall all the kindreds of the earth be blessed.

Paul, with certain other prisoners under the charge
of a Roman centurion named Julius, was put on board
a ship of Adramyttium, bound northward along the
Phenician coast, and afterwards along the southern
shore of Asia Minor. Julius distinguished Paul from
the other prisoners, and accorded him as much liberty
as was consistent with his safe custody; induced to this
kindness, no doubt, by learning that Agrippa had in
open court pronounced him an innocent man.

Sidon, their first port of call, was the great harbor
of the Canaanites. It lay within the territory prophet-
ically assigned to Israel, but it was never actually in
their possession. At this time, however, the standard
of the Lord's kingdom was planted on its soil. The
apostle was permitted to go ashore to refresh himself
in the company of his friends who resided there.
Wherever there is a disciple of Christ, there a missionary has a friend and a home. This is the result after
which Freemasonry aspires; but the faith in Christ
would gain the end better without the aid of such a

dubious ally. Freemasonry seems a fungus that has grown on Christianity at a time when the mighty stem was not in good health. It is an abnormal growth that damages the vigor of the tree.

From Sidon, on the Syrian coast, you may, in favorable circumstances, sail in a straight line to Myra in Asia Minor, keeping Cyprus on the right, and avoiding the circuituous angle round the shore; but the wind being from the west, the mariners of that day were not able to tack against it, and were obliged to creep along the coast northward till they reached the bay at the mouth of the Orontes, the river of Antioch, and then westward along the Asiatic coast to Myra.

This harbor was probably the destiny of the ship. The prisoners were here transferred to another vessel, belonging to Alexandria, and laden with grain for Rome. As the wind continued westerly, they crept slowly for many days along the coast, until they gained sight of Cnidus, a large city on the mainland, on the extremity of a long narrow peninsula, where the coastline turns northward to the Dardanelles. Here, accordingly, it was necessary to leave the shore and stand out to sea. The wind compelled them to keep a south-westerly course, till they reached the eastern extremity of the island of Crete. Passing the point of Salmone, they found themselves in smoother water, and wore westward on the southern side of the island as far as a place called the Fair Havens. There seems to have been no town at that harbor, but Lasea was not far off. At this anchorage the ship lay a long time waiting for fairer winds; but as it was now the end of September, and the navigation of the Mediterranean was considered dangerous at that season, Paul counselled the parties in charge of the ship to winter there. The master of the ship, however, in concert with the centurion, determined to set sail again, and endeavor to make Phenice, another harbor of Crete, further westward, and affording better shelter.

When the wind veered to the south, thinking they had gained their object, they left Fair Havens, and again crept westward along the coast. But ere they had been long at sea, the weather suddenly changed, and a hurricane, named Euroclydon, struck the ship as she was sailing easily with her boat in tow at her stern.

The storm must have blown from the north-east; for when they allowed the ship to run before the gale, she was carried to the island of Clauda, which lies in the sea twenty miles south-west of the spot where the tempest caught them. Creeping under the lee shore of that island, they found themselves for a time under shelter of land, and in comparatively smooth water. Here, accordingly, they took the opportunity of trimming the ship. Some very necessary things were now done which could not have been done in the gale. The boat had been in tow when the storm came on, and it was impossible to take it on board while the sea was running high: now, with some difficulty, they hauled it on board. They then "used helps, undergirding the ship." The hull was not so well constructed in those days as now. Nor was the strain so well distributed as in modern ships; for they used only one mast, and the huge sail suspended on it threw all the strain on one spot. Fearing lest the timbers should part, they brought ropes over the bow and under the keel, making the ends fast on deck by twisting, as logs of wood are fastened together on a cart. Though it seems to us a feeble and clumsy expedient, it might in certain circumstances avert a shipwreck by keeping the planks from springing, and so preventing a fatal leak.

It may be proved, by stretching a ruler on the indicated line in a map of the Mediterranean, that if the ship had continued to run before the wind, she would have been driven into Syrtis, a bay of quicksand on the African coast, greatly dreaded by ancient seamen. In dread of this catastrophe they hauled down their great sail, probably hoisting a small storm-sail in its stead, and lay to, as close to the wind as the ship would lie. It can be shown that this position would give her a drift motion precisely in the direction of Malta, the place on which she ultimately struck.

The storm increased; there was danger now lest the ship should founder in deep water. The crew therefore threw cargo overboard in order to lighten her. Subsequently, even the tackling of the ship was thrown out in the extremity of their fear and their eagerness to keep afloat. As the storm raged with unabated violence, and no observation could be obtained on account of the continued darkness, the officers and seamen abandoned themselves to despair. Man's extremity became God's opportunity. The Lord encouraged his servant Paul, and Paul became a rallying-point to the helpless multitude. When the sight of all utterly failed, the faith of one bore them through.

From the answer given by the Lord (verse 24), we can clearly gather what his servant had asked. "Fear not," said the Lord to Paul: Paul therefore had been fearful. His faith did not exempt him from the weakness of human nature. "Not for that we would be unclothed:" the watery grave that yawned beneath the creaking ship made the man's flesh creep, although his soul was upheld by a hope that runs through all these troubled waters, and fastens on the Anchor within the veil.

We learn further that he desired to live longer; for manifestly the intimation that his life would be prolonged was meant to comfort him.

Again, we gather that he must have pleaded for the lives of all the ship's company, without respect of persons. The answer, given to set his mind at rest, bears that the Lord had given him all that sailed with him. It is better for all in the ship that they have a Paul on board, hastening to execute God's commission on the earth, than to have a Jonah fleeing from his work and hiding from his Master.

Finally, the main reason why Paul so earnestly desired the prolongation of his own life, was that he might accomplish his life's great purpose—that he might preach Christ in the highest places of the heathen world. "Fear not, Paul; thou must be brought before Cæsar." This "must" points to the purpose of the Omnipotent. It was God's will that this messenger should publish the gospel in Rome; and his purpose shall stand. The tumults of the people had already been stilled; and now the waves of the sea must hear and obey the same Divine command. Neither tumult will be permitted to swallow up the "chosen vessel," until it has discharged its precious burden on the appointed spot.

In the Storm
(Acts 27:24-37)

" Saying, Fear not, Paul; thou must be brought before Cæsar: and, lo, God hath given thee all them that sail with thee. Wherefore, sirs, be of good cheer: for I believe God, that it shall be even as it was told me," etc.

" HOWBEIT we must be cast upon a certain island" (verse 26). What island ? There are two of the same name, Malta, and Meleda in the Gulf of Venice. The question long in debate may be considered settled now. It must be Malta. It seems now strange that not a few inquirers, both in earlier and more modern times, pronounced in favor of Meleda. Their reasons were founded on mistakes which have now been explained. For example, the term Adria was supposed to show that the island must have been in the Adriatic Gulf, which stretches northward to Venice; but it is certain that that part of the Mediterranean which lies between Crete and Malta was in ancient times called the Adriatic Sea; and the mistake has arisen from confounding this with the Adriatic Gulf. The term "barbarian," too, applied to the inhabitants of Malta, was supposed to be inappropriate to that island, inasmuch as under the rule of the Romans the people at that date had attained some considerable measure of civilization; but it was the custom in those times to apply the term "barbarian" indiscriminately to all except those who employed the Greek or Latin tongue.

The terms translated "driven up and down in Adria" simply mean "driven through Adria." Drifting in the direction that the wind would carry them, at the rate of a mile and a half an hour—the rate at which it is known a ship under such circumstances would go—they must strike on the north-east corner of Malta between the thirteenth and fourteenth day after leaving Clauda. Thus accurately has the narrative been given.

About midnight, while no object was visible, the

shipmen, judging from signs with which all mariners are familiar, deemed that they drew near some land. We may assume that the seamen heard the sound of breakers on the shore; but these breakers could not have been ahead. With a gale blowing towards the land, if the rocks had been right in the ship's course, she must have been so near the rocks before the sound could be heard, that she must have struck before it was possible to bring her up. On consulting the map, we find that a ship drifting in a straight line from Clauda would pass near a projecting headland, and after passing it enter a bay, still called St. Paul's Bay; and in crossing the bay, after hearing the breakers on the promontory, there would be time to bring up the ship by her anchors before she reached the land on the other side. It is known that during a north-easter, the sea beats furiously on this headland.

On hearing the sound which indicated land, they sounded, and found the depth twenty fathoms. This is precisely the depth opposite the point; and the soundings forward in the middle of the bay gave fifteen fathoms. Fearing, from the diminishing depth of their soundings, lest they should fall among rocks, "they cast four anchors out of the stern, and wished for the day." Many foolish things have been urged against this method, and against the authenticity of the narrative. It can be demonstrated that what the sailors did was right in the circumstances, although it was a deviation from the ordinary routine. They must have been so near the rocks, that if they had brought the ship up by the bow, she might have struck in the act of coming round. In the Crimean war, when the ship *Lord Raglan* was placed in similar circumstances, and all hope of saving her was abandoned, the captain run her ashore, bow on, and was much commended for his judgment.

By this time the plan of the seamen was matured. They meant to run the ship aground. They had made up their minds that she must become a wreck, and all their energies were directed towards the saving of human life. But for this object everything depended on getting the ship beached on a shelving band, and not running her on rocks. Now if her bow is to the shore when the daylight comes, they will be able to see where there is an opening, and by the use of sail and rudder, to turn her a little to the right or left, so as to strike on a favorable spot. On the other hand, if the morning should find them anchored by the bow, close to a weather-shore, with a gale blowing from the sea, as soon as they should lift the anchor she would strike, long before they could take measures for turning her about.

It is objected that a ship's anchors are always kept lying near the bow; but as this ship had at least four, none of them would be very large, and there were several hundreds of able-bodied men on board. The anchors could have been carried aft in a few moments. But even this suggestion is not necessary; for in a painting found at Herculaneum, a galley is represented with the anchor-cables running out from holes in the stern.

While they waited in this position for the dawn, they were exposed to two dangers, known to the seamen, but of which the landsmen on board would not be aware. On one hand, the anchors might drag;—in point of fact they held fast, but this could not be known till experience proved it. It is worthy of note that in the English sailing directions you learn that the ground in St. Paul's Bay is so good that " while the cables hold there is no danger, as the anchors will never start." But, on the other hand, the ship might founder at anchor. The risk of this was greater now than when she was drifting.

Fearing lest the ship should founder or strike before morning, the sailors basely and selfishly formed a plan to save their own lives and leave the passengers to their fate. They intended to make their own way to shore in the boat; but as they were in a minority, they found it necessary to dissemble, and effect their purpose by stealth. They found a very plausible veil under which to cover their design. The ship, made fast by the stern and the sea washing over her, labors dangerously. The movement may gnaw the cables asunder; if she were anchored also by the bow she would ride more at ease. But it is obvious that this can be accomplished only by carrying an anchor forward a cable's-length in a boat, and dropping it there. Thus the skilled seamen obtained a colorable pretext for lowering the boat and getting into it themselves. This done, they meant to desert the wreck and make for the shore.

Of all the landsmen on board, only one had penetration to divine the scheme. Paul had gone through a good deal of maritime experience; and as he had skill to perceive the plot, he possessed the coolness and presence of mind necessary to crush it. Not a word of objuration to the faithless seamen; only a quick whisper in the centurion's ear, and the thing was done. In a moment the soldiers clustered round the boat, cut with their swords the slings in which it hung, and allowed it to drop into the sea. Thus the skilled seamen were compelled to make common cause with the passengers to save their own lives. Thus the safety of all was secured: for if the sailors had left the ship, the soldiers could not have executed the manœuvre necessary to beach her in a place of safety at the dawn.

It may, perhaps, be useful to interpose here a note on the relation between the Divine decree and the free agency of men. Already Paul had announced, on the authority of a Divine revelation, that the lives of all on board would certainly be saved; yet he now says: "Except these abide in the ship, ye cannot be saved." Some very learned persons have gravely pointed to these circumstances as a refutation of the doctrines regarding the purposes of God—commonly called "Calvinistic." But Calvin was not such a fool as to believe that the Divine prescience precluded human freedom. There is a difficulty, but it is not greater than might have been expected to occur at the point where man's finite understanding touches the purposes of the Infinite. The difficulty, moreover, is not less for those who oppose Calvin's view than for those who espouse it. In this case, for example, it was clearly declared to be the purpose of God that all these lives should be saved in the shipwreck. Now, was that declaration true at the moment it was made, or not true? If you say it was not true, you dishonor the Scripture; if it was true, then the means necessary to accomplish the promise must be taken.

There is no liberty to omit them. The men acted freely, swayed by ordinary natural motives; but God acted sovereignly, employing the free-will as well as the power and skill of men to fulfil his purpose. There is no contradiction between the sovereignty of God and the liberty of man. There is a deep here which no human intellect can fathom; and it is easy, both on the one side and on the other, to shut up an opponent into a corner. But a more excellent way is to reverence the Divine omniscience, and humbly address ourselves to all revealed duty, counting that what they know not now, all the redeemed of the Lord shall know hereafter.

All Saved

(Acts 27:33-44;28:1-10)

" And while the day was coming on, Paul besought them all to take meat, saying, This day is the fourteenth day that ye have tarried and continued fasting, having taken nothing. Wherefore I pray you to take some meat: for this is for your health: for there shall not an hair fall from the head of any of you," etc.

WE have seen how Paul comprehended the design of the sailors and defeated it. His experience in former shipwrecks had not been thrown away upon him; and although these earlier dangers are not recorded, as not being, like this one, a great crisis for the kingdom, the lessons which they taught come in with effect precisely where they are needed. A word from Paul to the centurion, and a word from the centurion to his men, and in a moment two or three short broadswords flashed from their scabbards, the ropes by which the boat was suspended were snapped asunder, and the boat fell with a splash into the sea. It would drift away unseen among the rocks, and be dashed to pieces. The sailors, having now no means of going ashore, were obliged to abide by the ship; and by their skill in the morning all were saved.

As day began to break, when they could see each other, but could not discern the land, at Paul's suggestion food was distributed, and the men were cheered by the hope of deliverance. At that meal, with a miscellaneous multitude numbering two hundred and seventy-six, consisting of Christians, Jews, and heathens of various name and nation, the voice of the apostle was lifted up above the noise of winds and waves, giving cheerful thanks to God for his goodness. The ascendancy of the Christian missionary at that anxious hour was an honor to the gospel which he preached, and would probably contribute to commend his message to many who witnessed it. The example of one courageous man was infectious: "Then were they all of good cheer, and they also took some meat."

At this crisis the seamen further lightened the ship by throwing cargo overboard; not only to prevent her from sinking, but to diminish her draught, and so enable her to run higher on the beach. When the day dawned, the sailors keenly scanned the unknown shore, and discovering a small opening in the girdle of rocks, with a shelving and probably a sandy beach, they determined if possible to run the ship aground there.

Three operations, successively narrated but simultaneously performed, combined and conspired to the success of the plan. 1. They cut off the anchors, for there was not time to heave them up. 2. They loosed the rudder bands. The steering apparatus of an ancient ship was not like our modern helm. It consisted of two large, long, loose oars, both at the stern, one on either side of the keel. The ship's bulwarks were perforated on the two quarters for these two great projecting paddles. Now, whenever these oars were out of use, they were raised out of the water, and lashed with ropes to the ship's sides. It was necessary, the moment that the anchor cables were cut, to let down the rudders in order to direct the course of the ship. 3. They hoisted a foresail to give the ship more way, and so enable them to steer into the creek. In all this the presence of experienced seamen was necessary. The soldiers could not have handled the ship in this fashion; and, if the sailors had escaped during the night, the ship would have been wrecked on the breakers.

The scheme was successfully accomplished. The place where two seas met was probably the narrow channel between the mainland and a small island that lies in the bay close in-shore. Mr. Smith found the shore to consist of mud, fading away into clay. Striking there, the ship's bow was immediately wedged into the solid, while the hinder part, still floating, was broken off by the violence of the waves.

In accordance with the cruel and reckless habits of war, the soldiers proposed a wholesale slaughter of the prisoners, lest any of them should escape; and even the centurion Julius, although he succeeded in diverting them from their purpose, did not base his request on grounds of humanity and justice. The measure was exceptional in order to preserve the life of Paul. We are left to understand that if the apostle had not been there, an object of interest and gratitude to the whole company, no serious opposition would have been made to the cruel precaution of the soldiers. Such is heathenism, and such is war.

After the skilful manner in which the ship was beached, the escape of all on board was easy and natural. As soon as they reached the land, they learned from the natives that the name of the island was Melita—beyond all reasonable doubt the Malta which has occupied a prominent place in medieval and modern history, and remains at this day politically one of the most important possessions of the British crown.

The natives, styled barbarians, as speaking a language not understood by either Greeks or Romans, exerted themselves to alleviate the sufferings of the passengers and crew. The people would be familiar with merchant ships passing and repassing between Italy and Egypt. As the rain was falling in torrents after the hurricane had spent itself, a fire was kindled on the spot. As the shipwrecked men gathered round the fire, cold and wet in the gray dawn of that wintry morning, each, as he saw opportunity, cast in some sticks to feed the flame. Paul himself, ever thoughtful and active in things small or great, gathered also a handful of fuel and threw it on the fire. Forthwith a viper glided out and fastened on his naked hand. Evidently the reptile had been coiled up among the branches as they lay on the ground; and naturally it made its way out as soon as it felt the heat. The barbarians entertained some notions of natural religion, which were in the main sound, although in practice wrongly applied. They had an idea that sin will find the sinner out, although there may be apparent impunity for a time. They thought the bite of the viper was fatal, and that the death of a man who was saved from shipwreck was a notable example of sure though tardy justice in the administration of the world. They imagined that in this case the punishment proved the guilt.

Paul shook off the viper, and experienced no harm. In this and many other similar cases there is not specific information whether the immunity was due to natural or supernatural causes. But on either supposition alike, Paul's life was preserved by the care of our Father in heaven. The natives now changed their minds and gravitated to the opposite extreme. Him whom they had considered a murderer overtaken by vengeance, they will now revere as a deity. Such is the genius of heathenism. When it comes to any strait, such as a swollen Jordan, it cries, Where is Elijah my God; but true faith, in extremities, calls confidingly on the " Lord God of Elijah."

I suppose Paul shrunk with loathing and horror from the reptile, when he saw and felt it creeping on his naked hand. I think he did not cast it coolly and gently away: he would shake the loathsome creature passionately from his flesh, lest it should plant its poison in his blood. Oh for such a loathing of sin in our members, and such rapid energy in casting it away! If there were such grace in our hearts as would shrink spiritually from the old serpent as quickly and strongly as the natural instincts shrink from the material sting, we should tread the path of life in safety, compassed with the Divine favor as with a shield.

The Meeting
(Acts 28:11-15)

"And after three months we departed in a ship of Alexandria which had wintered in the isle, whose sign was Castor and Pollux," etc.

THE governor of the island resided near the spot. Valetta, the best harbor, and the only town in modern times, is near St. Paul's Bay. The island was subject to the Romans, but little attention was paid to it. From the fact that the governor's father was living, and in a private position, it is evident that the chieftainship was not hereditary. The cure performed afforded the missionary a lever for the prosecution of his work. It gave authority to his word among the people.

After a delay of three months—that is, when the winter was past; and the spring approaching—the party put to sea again in a ship of Alexandria that had wintered in the island. Castor and Pollux, a pair of brothers that hold a prominent place in Greek mythology, and were recognized as the tutelary deities of seafaring men, constituted the figure-head of the ship, and by their name she was known. The fact that this vessel, trading between Alexandria and Puteoli, on the western coast of Italy, passed the winter in Melita, is clear proof that it was not Meleda in the Gulf of Venice; for that island is very far out of the route. Moreover, this ship, in her voyage from Melita to Puteoli, while the weather was fair, and nothing occurred to carry her out of her course, called at Syracuse by the way. This was perfectly natural and easy for a ship that sailed from Malta, but enormously out of a ship's course from Meleda. These circumstances, added to the positive evidence already given, remove all reasonable doubt as to the locality of the shipwreck.

Syracuse was in those times the great seaport of

Sicily. It was by far the most renowned of those cities that were founded by Greek emigrants on the western coasts of Europe. It occupied an important position in the dreadful struggles between the several republics of Greece, and also in the internecine quarrel between Rome and Carthage. Perhaps no ancient city is so conspicuous in history for the sieges that it has undergone. There is a tradition that the Church at Syracuse was founded by Paul in person; and it is probable that Julius on this occasion permitted him to go ashore and preach.

From Syracuse the *Castor and Pollux* fetched a compass, and came to Rhegium. This place is on the Italian shore, in the straits which separate Sicily from the continent. It was about the same place that Garibaldi landed with his volunteers after he had subjugated Sicily. In many respects this was the most remarkable revolution of modern times. That extraordinary man, with a handful of followers, drove the Neapolitan monarch from his throne and kingdom, delivering a fair country from the double tyranny of priest and king, and introducing Italy into the community of nations.

It is intimated that in order to make Rhegium "they fetched a compass." This may mean, either that the wind blew from the west, and they were obliged to run out to sea eastward for a time, in order to catch the breeze; or that the wind was more directly contrary, and it was necessary to beat up against it. After a halt there of a single day the wind became fair, and they reached Puteoli on the following day, having run a distance of one hundred and eighty miles. On the northern side of the great bay of Naples, and not far from each other, lay Puteoli, the great mercantile seaport of Rome, and Baiæ, the favorite watering-place of her luxurious citizens.

As soon as he landed, Paul found "brothers." The family is multiplying and spreading through the empire. The fire of this Christian life is going, like the lightning, against the wind: although the sect is everywhere spoken against and persecuted, yet the sect is increasing, like the breaking forth of waters. The seven days' delay at Puteoli is a Christian and not a Roman measurement. It points on the one hand to the weekly Sabbath, and on the other to the confirmed ascendancy of Paul over all the arrangements of the journey. Julius seems by this time to have fallen into the habit of shaping his course by the advice of his prisoner.

"So we went to Rome," along the much celebrated and frequented Appian Way, from the seaport to the capital. The brothers at Puteoli must have sent express to Rome to advise their fellow-disciples of Paul's arrival, and a deputation had started from the city to meet and welcome the distinguished visitor. For the Christians at Rome, the arrival of Paul was a great event. He had been longing for them, and they for him. At last the great object of his life was almost within his grasp; and they—what a thrill of joyful expectancy must have run through their circle when the news first reached them that the *Castor and Pollux* of Alexandria, last from Malta, had actually arrived with the apostle of the Gentiles on board! Then circular messages went round: all must meet this evening, perhaps in the house of Aquila. At the meeting many eager inquiries would pass—those who had never seen the great missionary would again demand of those who had seen him what his appearance was, and wherein his power seemed to lie.

They must send a large deputation forward to meet him. They will stretch out their arms far to embrace the approaching ambassador of their heavenly King. They will give him a royal welcome. All who are able-bodied will go; none are willing to be left behind. Some seem to have started who were hardly fit for the journey; for they halted at Three Taverns, a distance of seventeen miles from the city, while those who were more vigorous pushed on as far as Appii Forum, a distance of twenty-seven miles. The apostle and his company are meantime pursuing their journey northward along the Appian Way. For the last nineteen miles a canal ran alongside the highway, partly for the drainage of the marshes, and partly for the purposes of navigation. Appii Forum was the terminus of the canal on the north, and nearest the city. It was a rough place, swarming with low tavern-keepers and bargemen. At that spot the front rank of the deputation from Rome met Paul and his companions. At that place, rude, and even disreputable among the towns of Italy, the two ends of the coil were joined, and Jerusalem brought into connection with Rome. Then and there the spirit of the kingdom passed out of Jerusalem and entered into Rome. Henceforth the gospel, withdrawn from the Jews, has its seat in the heart of the Gentile world.

The body of Christ, crucified at Jerusalem, was laid in the grave, dead. Christ himself rose from the grave and ascended into heaven. No longer was he sent exclusively to Israel. His resurrection was life to the world. The apostolate, sent out after the Lord's ascension, was the resurrection for the Gentiles. Now Christ has come to the world's great head, and Paul is the vessel chosen and used to bear him thither.

As Peter and John started in company, with equal love, to see the place where the Lord lay, that they might be witnesses of his resurrection, but separated on the road, the younger and nimbler runner coming first to the empty grave; so, in Italy that day, those who set out together to witness the kingdom of God risen from its ruin in Jerusalem, and approaching Rome in the power of a new life, separated into two bands. One portion outran the other, and first reached the meeting-place. But the feebler, who remained behind, met the apostle too, and received the Christ whom he bore. Not only so, but those who remained at home in the city obtained in due time a full portion of the spoil. According to the desires of your loving heart it will be given to you, not according to the strength of your muscles and the fleetness of your feet. Seek, and ye shall find. In the matters of the kingdom a man is accepted, not according to what he hath not, but according to what he hath.

Gratitude and Fortitude
(Acts 28:15,16)

" And from thence, when the brethren heard of us, they came to meet us as far as Appii Forum, and the Three Taverns: whom when Paul saw, he thanked God, and took courage. And when we came to Rome, the centurion delivered the prisoners to the captain of the guard: but Paul was suffered to dwell by himself with a soldier that kept him."

A SPECIAL note is taken of the effect produced by the meeting on Paul's own mind.   When he saw the brethren, " he thanked God, and took courage."   This is a pregnant example for us: this short sentence is full of practical wisdom.   This faith that Paul possessed is better than the mysterious stone that turns whatever it touches into gold.   From the point of the present he looks backward and forward.   All the past of his life he seems to count only a preparation; his work lies still before him.   It is a beautiful character that is displayed here in two great hemispheres: for the past it is devout gratitude; for the future, filial confidence.

For the past, "he thanked God."   The long vista of memory was bright with blessings.   God's mercies had been "waters that fail not," a continual stream.   No summer drought had ever dried it; no winter cold had ever frozen it.   Hitherto the Lord hath helped us.

Yet the path of life was not all smooth for this man, either before or behind.   He had been exposed to great danger and severe suffering; but he had been carried through.   He will sing of mercy and judgment.   A man's cheerfulness and contentment depend not so much on the measure of prosperity, as on the condition of mind that he has attained.   Some people never see the time and occasion for cheerful thanksgiving; and some never see the time when praise is out of place. One man can never see the end of his troubles, and therefore he is always grumbling; another man can never number up all his mercies, and therefore he is always ready with a song.   " In everything, by prayer and supplication with thanksgiving, let your requests be made known unto God."

It is worthy of remark here, that while the storm was at its height and no relief yet in view, Paul found opportunity to give thanks aloud in behalf of all the ship's company for a morsel of food. When he could not stand upright on deck on account of the rolling of the wreck, he grasped the mast in one hand to keep himself from falling, and lifted the other up to heaven in token of exultant gratitude to God for daily bread. And here, when the prospect is somewhat brighter, on the dry land, and in presence of his brethren, he gave way again to the ruling passion,—Praise the Lord for his goodness, for his wonderful works to the children of men. It is evident that his heart was habitually full, and therefore overflowed on every emerging opportunity. It is not the fulness of the basket, but the fulness of the heart, that makes the grateful man.

For the future, "he took courage." Mark well what this true, bold man "took" at Appii Forum by the sight of fellow disciples: it was not comfort, but courage. He was made glad, not by an expectation that henceforth he should have no battle to fight, but by a resolution to fight and win. The distinction between these two states of mind is practically of great importance. In some of their aspects they are like each other; and therefore there is greater risk of taking the spurious for the genuine. The element of cheerfulness is common to both. The one is selfishly cheerful, in the prospect of ignoble ease; the other is patriotically cheerful, in the prospect of successful labor. Comfort does not look forward at all, but says, Aha, I am warm; makes a soft nest, and lies down to sleep: Despondency looks forward, indeed, but sees a lion on the path, and lies down to weep: Courage looks forward, and sees the lion too, but believes him vincible, and girds itself for the combat. Courage, in the person of Luther, would go forward to bear testimony for Christ, although every tile on the roofs of Worms were a devil. This is the true Christian spirit,—the spirit of Paul and of Luther. Comfort seeks ease by declining the combat; Courage expects progress through victory. This, under the name of

Virtue, is precisely the quality which Peter exhorts good soldiers of Jesus Christ to add to their faith. In ancient times, and in human affairs, it ranked highest, and was understood to include within itself all the virtues. In the kingdom of God also it is set in a high place, and valued at a great price.

The Christian course is compared to a warfare, and to a merchandise. Both soldiers and merchants fondly cherish the hope of retiring. In the toils of war and of traffic, the prospect of rest becomes a sort of pole-star dimly shining on the low, far-off horizon. But it seldom becomes anything more than a shadow. It is as beautiful as the rainbow, and as hard to grasp. In old age it is ordinarily as far off as ever. Men have supported themselves in a life-long labor by the hope of a rich and honorable retreat; and the retreat, when they reached it, has proved more insupportable than the labor. From the Christian's warfare there is no release in this world; he must die in harness. Nor does he count this condition hard. He knows that earnest effort contributes more to happiness and health than useless rest. Paul knew, indeed, of an honorable retirement; but it lay beyond the grave. " A rest remaineth for the people of God." Christians do not rest *in* their labors; but one day they shall rest *from* them. Their works too shall follow them;—activity, effort, result, will continue in a better world,—but all the weariness will be left behind.

It is better to have courage to face difficulties, than to have no difficulties to face: the one is a leaping, sparkling river; the other is a stagnant pool.

At present there is much need of courage. The enemy cometh in like a flood. It is a motley host. Vice in the masses at the bottom of the scale: vice in the flutterers floating on the top. From the press printed sheets fall like snow-flakes,—some covertly endeavoring to undermine all faith, and some pandering to mere vulgar vice. Pleasure and worldliness invade the Christian circle, and deluge it; and at such a time, not a few are found wasting the energy that should be devoted to the help of the Lord against the mighty in contending for pin-points or chasing shadows !

Rome was at that time an immense city. It con

tained a population of two millions, of whom one half
were slaves. A few thousands of an aristocracy mo-
nopolized the wealth and power; the remainder of the
freemen were very poor. Multitudes of them had no
shelter at night but the streets, and porticoes of temples. They counted themselves above labor. Their
lot was pride and poverty. Such seems the uniform
effect of slavery. It makes the condition of citizens
who do not own property most wretched. The presence of slavery renders labor a disgrace; and when the
poor do not toil, they become a burden to themselves
and the community.

When the prisoners were handed over to the captain of the guard—at the time a man named Burrus—
he immediately conceded to Paul an exceptional measure of liberty. This was no doubt due in part to the
favorable report sent by Felix, and in part to the fervent friendship of the centurion Julius, who had conducted the prisoner from Cæsarea to Rome. As much
freedom was allowed to Paul as was consistent with
the stern military code of the empire. Instead of being confined with a crowd of evil-doers in the pretorian barracks, he was permitted to go where he pleased
in the custody of a soldier. Night and day, however,
he was chained by the arm to his keeper. It is amazing that Paul speaks so cheerfully about his condition
in Rome. The single circumstance that he was not
prevented from preaching Christ seems to have out-
weighed in his esteem all the restraints otherwise
imposed upon his liberty. In this one liberty he ex-
ults, and seems almost to forget that he is a prisoner.

During these two years, the guard was often shifted.
Night and morning the military machine moved round,
and the man who had fulfilled his term of duty was relieved by a fresh guard. But while the guards came
and went, the prisoner remained the same. There
would, doubtless, be degrees of evil. Some soldiers
who took their turn would be ruder, some more gentle;
but bad was the best, when this man, refined at first
by all the culture of the day, and purified afterwards
by having Christ formed in him at the regeneration,
was compelled to have a chance soldier of the pretorian
guards chained to his body night and day for two years.

It was a grievous bondage! but the prisoner did not complain. He had learned to count these troubles light by balancing them in the scale against an exceeding great weight of glory; he had learned to look on the troubles as of but a moment's duration by contrasting them with an everlasting rest. Paul has not yet forgotten that iron chain, or those rude Roman men to whom it bound him. The sufferings have already, in eighteen hundred years of heaven, repaid themselves many times over, in the enhancement of his joy which the memory of them supplies. Softer chains now bind him to better company. Nothing shall separate him from the love of God, which is in Christ Jesus our Lord.

Paul in Rome
(Acts 28:17-22)

" And it came to pass, that after three days Paul called the chief of the Jews together: and when they were come together, he said unto them, Men and brethren, though I have committed nothing against the people, or customs of our fathers, yet was I delivered prisoner from Jerusalem into the hands of the Romans," etc.

THERE were strong emotions on both sides when Paul and the Roman Christians met at Appii Forum. The faith and fervor manifested on his part sprang from another meeting that had happened long before, as the fruit springs from seed. Many years before this event, Paul the young was approaching a great Eastern city with a commission of high import, his heart earnest to fulfil it, as Paul the aged now approached the great capital of the West. Then, too, as on this occasion, the dangling of chains might be heard as the procession marched. Then, and there, however, Saul, the chief commissioner, did not wear them; they were borne in his train, and employed at his pleasure. Here, the chains are hanging on his own arms. Then, as now, he was met before he reached the city. Met him then, not Christians, but Christ. Not to embrace as brothers those two met; they met as foes meet on the battle-field. Christ was revealed from heaven the King of Glory, and the apostle of the high priest fell to the ground. The stony heart of the Pharisaic persecutor melted, and took on a new moulding. He became a new creature. The old man was put off, and the new put on.

That meeting with Christ on the way to Damascus was the root of this meeting with Christians on the way to Rome. From the sorrow of the first meeting sprang the joy of the second. Meetings with Christians will be cold and superficial, if we have not so met with Christ. We shall get little cheering from the light of a brother's countenance, if we have not previously been melted and remoulded by the Light of Life. When Christ is yours, all things are yours; and the fervent love of fellow disciples is an item in the vast inventory.

There must have been a liberal collection made among the disciples in Rome for the supply of the apostle's wants; for we learn that he dwelt two whole years in his own hired house. The rent of a house in the capital large enough to receive for conference all the leading Jews in Rome must have amounted to a considerable sum. Those who contributed to pay it would consider it a missionary contribution, and enter it in their books as "lent to the Lord."

There must have been a quick, spontaneous liberality in those days among the disciples of Jesus; and Paul, though he lived in poverty, had large resources at command for the work of the kingdom. Witness the sale of property at Jerusalem in the beginning of the gospel. It must have been a broad, deep, rapid stream of holy beneficence that flowed through the city, when it had power enough to float two such heavy hulks of hypocrisy as Ananias and Sapphira. Witness too, at a later date, the expectations of the keen-scented mercenary, Felix, who conferred frequently with Paul the prisoner, in the hope of getting a bribe for setting him free. Felix was well aware of two things: first, that Paul his prisoner had not a penny; but second, that by raising his finger, the missionary could draw on the purses of many substantial citizens for any object which he might have at heart.

It is worthy of remark that Paul at Rome, when near the end of his course, still maintained faithfully his original rule of addressing himself first to the Jews. Let his believing brethren wait awhile; they can afford to bide their time. On their way to the city, it is probable that he made his arrangements in concert with the deputation. He would explain to them his principle and his practice,—first to the seed of Israel. If he had gone first to the Christians, the Jews might have taken offence. He will be all things yet to these men, that he may gain some of them.

When the leading Jews were assembled to hear his explanation, his discourse, as usual, was personal and apologetic. He endeavors at the outset to remove prepossessions which might hinder the reception of his message. First of all, he zealously claims kindred with them. By his appeal to the emperor against the Sanhedrim, they might have been led to suppose that he was dragging the sacred authorities of the chosen nation before the tribunal of a heathen power. With eagerness he clears himself of that charge, and makes it plain that his appeal was taken simply to save his life, when his enemies had plotted to take it away.

The name of Christ borne by the chosen vessel has now been brought to Rome. It has passed from Jerusalem through Judæa and Samaria; and now it had reached those seven hills, which, politically, were the loftiest pinnacle of the earth, and from which it might be carried by the natural channels to the whole circle of subject nations. Wonderful were the ways of God in reaching this result. The imperial legions must furnish an escort, and the imperial exchequer must pay the passage. Even to the stormy waves of the Mediterranean the word of the Lord had come in power;—Touch not my prophet, and do mine anointed no harm. Destroy not this frail vessel, for it bears a blessing to the western world.

Those who publish maps to illustrate the propagation of the gospel in early times, mark Paul's route by a red line. In that line there are many bendings and backward turns. It is drawn zig-zag, as lightning from the cloud is represented; but with all its turns, it ever turns aright,—westward ever, to bear the gospel to the nations of the future. In a similar way the course of the electric wire from continent to continent across the ocean is sometimes designated on the map. If the course of the line lately laid between France and America were so represented on the chart, it would be like the line that marks Paul's voyage. There was a halt in mid-ocean: the cable suddenly became dumb, and could not tell the cause of its own silence. Communication with the shore ceased for several days; and when it was resumed we learned the cause of the interruption. A gale sprang up; the operators feared lest in the heavy sea the cable should part. They cut and buoyed it. Then they trimmed the ship to ride out the storm. When the storm was over, they sought and found the buoy; caught the cable, spliced it, and went on as before. Suppose for a moment that the populations of the American continent had all previously been entirely destitute of the gospel, and that this submerged conductor was the only channel by which they could hope to receive it: in that case a thrilling interest would attach to the incident,—to the storm and the severance of the wire, and the skill of the operators in healing the breach. The spot was the Malta of the modern mission voyage.

The line that the ship of Adramyttium made on the eastern waters of the Mediterranean, and that which the *Castor and Pollux* made from Malta to Puteoli, faded away a few yards behind the keels; but a line unseen was paid out in that voyage through which throbbed life from the dead to the western world. How much depended on the voyage of one mortal man across those wintry waters. The Lord had need of him, and therefore the Euroclydon could not swallow him up.

Closing Glimpses
(Acts 28:23-31)

"And when they had appointed him a day, there came many to him into his lodging; to whom he expounded and testified the kingdom of God, persuading them concerning Jesus, both out of the law of Moses, and out of the Prophets, from morning till evening," etc.

AT a preliminary meeting of the Jewish chiefs, three days after his arrival, Paul anxiously explained that he brought no accusation against his country or his people. They seem to have been much impressed by his statement, and especially by his declaration, "for the hope of Israel I am bound with these chains." This makes him one with themselves; instead of plotting against them, this man suffers on their side. They desire to hear a fuller explanation of his position; especially how he reconciles his continued hold of "the hope of Israel," with his attachment to the sect which is everywhere spoken against. By mutual consent another day is fixed; and at the appointed time the same parties return with many others in their company.

A whole day was spent in the discussion. The conference would probably, for the most part, assume the form of conversation. Questions would be asked and answered; objections stated and removed. The Scriptures of the Old Testament constituted the acknowledged authority for the disputants on both sides alike. The venerated parchments lay on the table, and were from time to time spread out to correct and verify a quotation. The substance of all that Paul said at the prolonged conference is reported in one verse: "He expounded and testified the kingdom of God, persuading them concerning Jesus, both out of the law of Moses, and out of the prophets, from morning till evening." This is a remarkable epitome. It contains the whole case in a very small compass. It is somewhat like the condensed report of Philip's sermon to the Ethiopian prince, "beginning from that same Scripture, he preached unto him Jesus."

By comparing Scripture with Scripture, Paul expounded to these inquirers that the kingdom of the future, predicted by the prophets, is not limited to one nation, but co-extensive with the world; that if it be limited for a time, it is limited like a seed, only until the set time come for its indefinite multiplication and expansion. He showed them that the King, though universal Lord, yet suffers and dies,—gives his life a ransom;—that his kingdom is not of this world; that he is King of thoughts, not of armies; that he wins by love—by enduring. He showed them that in Jesus of Nazareth all the conditions of the expected Messiah were fulfilled: he employed the law to shut them up unto the gospel.

Some were won. The laborer obtained souls for his hire after that long day's work. At night, and immediately before the company separated, Paul addressed a very solemn warning from the Prophecy of Isaiah to the unbelieving portion of the audience. He felt that this was the crisis of their fate, and yearned for their salvation. Throwing upon themselves the responsibility of rejecting Christ promised in their own Scriptures, and now pressed on their acceptance, he proclaimed that moving of the door which permitted the light to flow on the Gentiles, and at the same time left the Jews shut up in the darkness which they had chosen. After they had left the conference, it is intimated that these Jews "had great reasoning among themselves." We may be permitted to hope that another section of these grave and sad children of Abraham, as the result of that reasoning, were shut up unto the faith.

This last testimony uttered by the apostle throws light on the structure and design of the Book of the Acts. The history is designed to exhibit the transition of the kingdom from Israel as a nation to the whole human family. When this transference has been completed, the historian's work is done. Here, accordingly, the record abruptly closes. The final note, as in other melodies, is the key-note: Christ rejected by Israel, to whom he came, is offered to the Gentiles. Henceforth all distinctions are levelled except one: the distinction between those who believe, and those who believe not, in the only begotten Son of God. There is now no condemnation to them that are in Christ Jesus, whether they be Jews or Greeks, bond or free. The kingdom consists of all, out of every nation and kindred and tongue, who have washed their robes, and made them white in the blood of the Lamb. One man is not rejected because he is a descendant of Canaan, and another is not accepted because he is of the seed of Abraham according to the flesh; but whosoever shall call on the name of the Lord, the same shall be saved.

After these events Paul dwelt two years in his own hired house, receiving all comers, and preaching the gospel in all its fulness to every class, and with complete impunity. The foundations of the Church at Rome were during these two years laid deep and broad. Alas! huge piles of wood, hay, stubble, have been reared upon the true foundation there throughout the long usurpation of the Papacy. There must be much fierce burning ere all that rubbish be consumed, and the primitive Church come forth in apostolic purity and power. Let one read the Epistle to the Romans and the latest encyclical of the present Pontiff at the same sitting, and he will experience the sensation of passing from the green grass and blue sky and bright sunshine of a summer day among the mountains, into a dark cavern where the air cannot get in, and the smoke cannot get out. If a Roman citizen of this nineteenth century, who loyally accepts the Pope and his infallibility, should be led to read the Book of the Acts, and Paul's Epistle to the Church of his forefathers, he would necessarily think these two books of sacred Scripture spurious, for they say nothing of the Virgin Mary or the saints, nothing of images and relics, nothing of penance and purgatory.

While Paul was a prisoner at Rome, Nero was emperor there. Not only was he a cruel and unjust ruler, but his very name has become a proverb for vice in all its vilest forms and extremest measures. The whole power of the civilized world was wielded by that incarnation of wickedness. Yet although this monster shed the blood of both his own wife and his own mother, it was not in his power to pervert all

the acts of his administration. Even he, when under the influence of good counsellors, sometimes pronounced and executed right decisions. Some restraint
was providentially laid upon the tyrant. Contemporary history gives no account of Paul's trial. On the
first occasion he seems to have been acquitted. He
who had delivered David from the lion and the bear,
was able to deliver him out of the hand of the Philis-
tine; he who had delivered the missionary from the
hands of Felix and Festus, could deliver him from
Nero's cruelty, and shield his life until his work was
done.

From the later Epistles some incidents of the apostle's subsequent history may be gathered. These,
when woven together, seem to intimate that, after
having been tried and acquitted at Rome, he visited
Ephesus, and thence returned to the capital; that he
travelled to the east yet again, and on his return
penetrated into Spain; and that at last he was arrested at Rome, and put to death about the end of
Nero's reign.

His residence at the capital seems to have been
the most active and useful period of Paul's life, although it did not fall within the scope of the historian
to comprehend it in his narrative. Many of his best
friends were for longer or shorter periods at his side
—Luke, his fellow-traveller, for example; and Timothy, his son in the faith.

Two men, who were for a time his coadjutors in
Rome, stand contrasted with each other so as to read
a very searching lesson for disciples in all times. Demas and Mark are both recognized as fellow-workers
(Phil. 24; Col. iv. 14). These two men might almost
have sat for the picture of the sons whom the father
commanded to work in his vineyard. The one said,
I go, sir, and went not; the other said, I will not,
but afterwards repented and went. The sad apostle's
later testimony regarding Demas is, "He hath forsaken me, having loved this present world" (2 Tim.
iv. 10). Whereas, although Mark at an early date
had incurred his displeasure for preferring his own
ease to the necessity of the work, a glad reconciliation was subsequently effected; and the aged mission-

ary, when almost within sight of his crown, and at the very time when he had occasion to record the defection of Demas, sent to Timothy the message;— "Take Mark, and bring him with thee: for he is profitable to me for the ministry" (2 Tim. iv. 11).

The case of the slave Onesimus, which occurred at Rome during this period, can be restored from fragmentary notices, and is full of instruction. This man had been owned by Philemon, a citizen of Colosse. He robbed his master and ran away. The outlaw found his way to Rome, like most of his kind; for in the crowded dens of the capital the best cover could be found by those who endeavored to elude the pursuit of law. The hordes of the wretched and the criminal who at that time, we cannot say resided, but existed homeless, in the great city, cannot well be described or conceived. Modern experience, bad though it be, affords no parallel, at least in Christianized countries.

The general prevalence of slavery dislocates and corrupts society to an extent of which we in our favored circumstances have no adequate conception. Onesimus, plunged into this mass of misery and crime, was lost as a microscopic atom of iron is lost among a heap of dust; but as such an atom so lost may be found by plunging a magnet into the same heap, so was Onesimus rescued. He heard Paul preaching Christ, and was won. How the missionary and the outlaw came in contact, we cannot tell. Perhaps the missionary found his way sometimes into those quarters of the city where the baser sort do congregate. Perhaps the man, intelligent though outcast, became weary of the vile society into which his misfortunes and his faults had cast him and he may have ventured under cloud of night, trembling lest the officers should track his steps, to the place where Paul was expected to preach. But in some manner, to us unknown, He who procured a meeting between Philip and the Ethiopian in the desert, procured a meeting between the apostle of the Gentiles and the runaway slave in the metropolis of the world. The poor shivering outcast heard of the Man that "receiveth sinners"—heard and believed, and lived.

Paul found in this man, when he was made new, a special aptitude for missionary work, and determined to employ him. But Onesimus is not yet free to begin. He is willing to lay himself now on the altar as a living sacrifice; but he must pause—he must leave his gift before the altar, and go first and be reconciled to his brother Philemon. Under Paul's instructions he returned to his former master and gave himself up, confident all the while that Philemon, himself ransomed by the same Lord that had redeemed his slave, would not any more exact his legal rights. The episode of Onesimus and Philemon, with its combined godliness and manliness, its devotion to God and noble charity between man and man, shines amid the atheism and vice of heathen Rome like a lightning flash in the noon of night. Again, a new commandment I give unto you, that ye love one another.